AMERICAN INSTITUTE OF ARCHITECTS   HOUSTON

Houston
Architectural Guide

Text by Stephen Fox

Photographs by Gerald Moorhead, AIA

Foreword by Peter C. Papademetriou, AIA

Edited by Nancy Hadley

Designed by Herring Design

D1607190

Generous assistance from
The Anchorage Foundation of Texas and
The Houston Architecture Foundation

Published by
The American Institute of Architects/Houston Chapter
and Herring Press, Houston

Second Printing Underwriters
The second printing of this book was partially underwritten by:

Gerald D. Hines
3D/International
C/A Architects, Inc.
Hall/Merriman Architects, Inc.
Mitchell Energy and Development
Gerald Moorhead
T. Redyard Wilson

Published in 1990 by The American Institute of Architects/Houston Chapter and
Herring Press, Houston. No part of the contents of this book may be reproduced
without written permission of the publisher. Second printing 1991.

Text by Stephen Fox
Photography by Gerald Moorhead, AIA
Foreword by Peter C. Papademetriou, AIA
Edited by Nancy Hadley
Design and production by Herring Design
Cover photograph by Gerald Moorhead, AIA
Cover photo composite by Gilbert Retouching
Printed in Singapore

Library of Congress Number 90-080316
ISBN 0-917001-08-7

The American Institute of Architects/Houston
Frank S. Kelly, FAIA, President
John W. Focke, FAIA, Past President
William O. Neuhaus III, AIA, President Elect
Frank Douglas, FAIA, Second Vice President
Ken Harry, AIA, Secretary
Thomas H. Stovall, AIA, Treasurer
Robert A. Brooks, AIA, TSA Director
D. Kirk Hamilton, AIA, Director
Kathy Heard, AIA, Director
Josiah Reynolds Baker, AIA, Director
Martha Murphree, Executive Director

Guidebook Committee
Allen G. Weymouth, AIA, Chair
Karol Kreymer, AIA
Barry Moore, FAIA
Gerald Moorhead, AIA
Martha Murphree, Executive Director

The Houston Architecture Foundation
Ray B. Bailey, FAIA, President

The Anchorage Foundation of Texas
Anne S. Bohnn, President

Published by
American Institute of Architects
Houston Chapter
20 Greenway Plaza, Suite 246
Houston, Texas 77046
(713) 622-2081

Co-Published and Distributed by
Herring Press, Inc.
Attn: Jerry Herring
1216 Hawthorne
Houston, Texas 77006
(713) 526-1250

Table of Contents

How To Use
This Guide

This guidebook is a catalogue of the architecturally significant buildings and places of Houston. It contains 850 entries, almost all illustrated with photographic images. These are organized sequentially within geographic areas, each designated by a letter. If one wishes, all the listings in a particular section can be seen in a single tour. With the exception of the downtown tours and those of such specialized areas as university campuses, these tours are organized as driving tours.

Each geographic section is prefaced by a map, with the listed buildings and sites identified by numerals. These numerals correspond to the numerical listing of descriptive entries and images within the tour texts. In a few exceptional instances, buildings not visible from a public thoroughfare are listed as a matter of record. This is because they constitute major architectural sites. Most of the sites listed are not open to the public. Listing in this guidebook should not be construed as an invitation to trespass.

Individual entries are identified by street address or street location, the original name of a building (and the present name, if it is different from the original name), the date of completion, and the name of the architect or designer. In instances where one building is the result of multiple architectural interventions, the identifying data reflect this. Where more than one architectural firm is involved, use of the term "and" (e.g. Johnson/Burgee Architects *and* S. I. Morris Associates) indicates the type of professional relationship known as a joint venture, where firms share equally in the responsibility for a building's design. Use of the term "with" (e.g. Skidmore, Owings & Merrill *with* Wilson, Morris, Crain & Anderson) indicates that the second firm functioned as associate architect for the first firm, with the first firm having primary responsibility for the design. In instances where firm names have changed, listings reflect the firm name at the time a particular building was completed.

A number of criteria were involved in selecting the buildings catalogued in this guidebook. The highest criterion was excellence of design. This was followed by buildings representing works by important architects of the present and past, both from and outside of Houston, buildings that represent different geographic areas in or around Houston, buildings representing architecture from different chronological periods within Houston's history, and buildings representing typologies characteristic of Houston. It is to be regretted that not all buildings and sites conforming to these criteria could be included because of limitations on the size of the guidebook. Among the many deserving buildings that could not be illustrated, some are mentioned within entries to which they are related geographically.

This guidebook looks at Houston and its buildings with a critical eye, especially the newest buildings and civic improvements. Criticism is not intended so much to distinguish "good" buildings from "bad" buildings as to identify certain issues that figure in the design of individual structures and in the process of building in the city. The opinions expressed are not those of the American Institute of Architects, Houston Chapter.

Efforts have been made to ensure the accuracy of listings in this guidebook. Experience, alas, tends to demonstrate the unlikelihood that perfection has been achieved. Readers who are aware of inaccuracies are encouraged to report these to the American Institute of Architects, Houston Chapter office.

Please enjoy this introduction to Houston and its architecture.

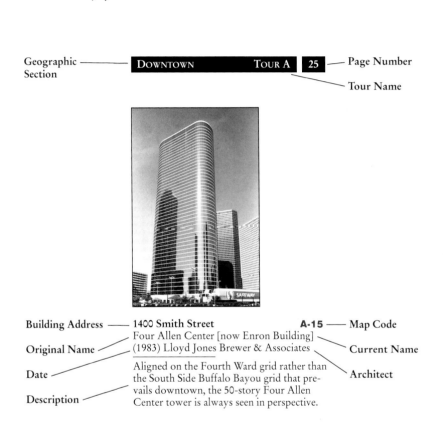

Geographic Section ——— DOWNTOWN   TOUR A   25 ——— Page Number
                                                    —— Tour Name

Building Address ——— 1400 Smith Street   A-15 ——— Map Code
Original Name ——— Four Allen Center [now Enron Building]
                    (1983) Lloyd Jones Brewer & Associates ——— Current Name
Date ———   Aligned on the Fourth Ward grid rather than   —— Architect
                    the South Side Buffalo Bayou grid that pre-
                    vails downtown, the 50-story Four Allen
Description ———   Center tower is always seen in perspective.

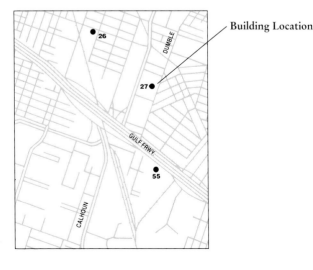

Building Location

Foreword

Nearly half a generation has elapsed since the last annual convention of the American Institute of Architects was held in Houston in 1972. As then, the event has occasioned a guide to the city's architecture, although this present edition reflects an evolution and a perspective that is very different from *Houston, An Architectural Guide*, the first guide to architecture in Houston and the first publication of any sort by the AIA, Houston Chapter. It was my privilege to conceive, write and design that effort, and it is a particular honor and pleasure to have been asked to contribute this brief commentary.

For two decades, Houston has been my home and the 1971-1972 project was an unexpected educational experience which set a subsequent course for personal research and writing, including an advocacy of regional character through my affiliations with *Progressive Architecture, Texas Architect* and the international press. This was based on a belief that only through understanding the past can one gain the perspective to make thoughtful choices in the present that will lead to a meaningful future. The past 18 years have seen a variety of developments which grew out of that awareness. Among these events has been the scholarship of this book's author Stephen Fox, then my student, a research assistant for the first guide, and now a widely recognized expert on Texas architecture, in the broader context of his discerning historical perspective and commentary.

Both the public's interest and the profession's response to issues of the built environment have evolved during this period. In 1972, the major architects were those who had been the younger generation in 1949, the year of the first AIA Convention held at Houston.

In turn, the closing decade of the twentieth century finds a new generation of architects who have taken leadership since the early 1970s. Their Houston is one in which they must respond to very different circumstances.

What fascinated us 18 years ago was the residual existence of an earlier Houston, that of the pre-War 1930s and 1940s. I vividly recall discovering, near Sugar Land, a metal-enamel neon billboard for Grand Prize Beer; here was an industrial artifact from the early days of roadside culture, not to say memories of such famous Houston characters as Howard Hughes and Glenn McCarthy. By looking at physical artifacts, we became urban archaeologists and cultural geographers. The

Houston of 1972 presented extreme juxtapositions of a past within our own memory and a future which was many times larger and potentially overwhelming. The patterns of growth had been initiated through the car culture which began in the 1920s but took on a very different character following World War II, one whose features were essentially the prototypes for the kinds of urbanism we saw. Yet, the Houston of the early 1970s was undefined and unclear in terms of its ultimate nature as an urban place. In addition to this romantic nostalgia for the 1940s there was the frightening excitement of the sheer extent of uneven rawness, jarring contrasts and spatial emptiness of a new city evolving. Suburban sprawl of the 1950s could be found next to points of extreme density or concentration emerging in the 1970s. These features of the urban landscape eluded clear or simple theoretical definition.

Houston was becoming an urbanism that simultaneously included what were perceived to be mutually exclusive, if not ideologically incompatible, images: both Frank Lloyd Wright's Broadacre City and Le Corbusier's Radiant City seemed to fit. I sought to look at analogies to describe what was happening, and my first serious critique twenty years ago, entitled "The Pope and the Judge", compared the Rome of Pope Sixtus to the Houston of Judge Roy Hofheinz; Vatican City to the Astrodomain. The similarities I described attempted to suggest, by analogy, the usefulness of a historical perspective. If anything was clear, it was that we had a special context that in an intense way embodied the essential patterns of emerging American cities, and that it would be critical to examine any preconceptions if there was to be any hope for a professional response.

RESPONDING TO EXPLOSIVE GROWTH

The past two decades have yielded three attributes which begin to be useful in describing Houston: palimpsest, pluralism, and polynucleation. What appeared to be so new were, in fact, historically derived patterns, which extended back to the city's origins; much like the ancient parchments that were reused for new writings, the old is erased or written over but it still shows through and one reads both old and new simultaneously. A perceived lack of clarity and order, in other words, will begin to come into focus once one understands historical circumstances. The radial plan of Houston's traffic arterials and freeways is virtually that of the original wagon routes to Market Square. Society is complex, and individual values diverse; since the 1970s, the rich growth of an Asian population has embellished Houston's pluralistic social mosaic, in addition to the articulation of other cultural groups. "Newcomers" historically have seemed to be the dominant

inant social group. The points of intense physical urban development have created a decentralized skyline, and these places have in turn taken on their own identity, serving both the immediate areas around them and the city and region as a whole. This polynucleated network of high density buffered by areas of low density has become the armature for the decentralized places which comprise Houston.

Sometime during the late 1970s the phrase "Houstonization" was coined. Both pejorative and normative, it simply reflected the reality of very obvious trends. The phenomenon is not exclusively limited to the Southwest, or the Sunbelt as it was called at the time, but is very much in evidence today in places such as the western suburbs of Chicago and New York's Long Island. Ironically, much as one finds high-rise towers in the fields of Illinois, transformations of suburban models have also occurred in traditional centers; the shopping mall or "Galleria" as it is often called, may be found in Boston, Chicago or New York. The Park in Houston Center has been one answer to the question of how shopping might happen in Houston's downtown, a sort of closing of the circle from suburbia-becomes-dense to density-becomes-suburban-like.

CAPITALIZING ON A PAUSE IN DEVELOPMENT

Growth has been the single constant in Houston since the 1850s. Yet, first the Energy Crisis of the mid-1970s and then the severe downturns of the 1980s significantly affected the city's perception of itself. Hard times may provide the opportunity to evaluate basic issues of the quality of urban life; perhaps quality may begin to replace quantity as a measure, more reflective of a commitment to the long haul. The only time when Houston drew back and actually cut down its incorporated limits was more than a century ago, after the Panic of 1873. A pattern of spread and extension, particularly dramatic after the 1950s, allowed urban problems to remain unresolved in a physical sense. It has been said during the 1970s when we were astonished, shocked and energized by such phenomena as the Westheimer Strip that the good part about it was that it wouldn't physically last. Perhaps the trash from the urban environment will be replaced, and depth of quality supplant the extent of its quantity.

A degree of incrementalism and a greater sensitivity to context and the provision of amenities for the use of urban places could become new aspects shaping the physical environment. Both public and private sectors, independently and together, are introducing greater diversity. Hermann Park, finally recognized as the true urban park it is, has had modest improvements. The Wortham Center is a major home for cultural activities, and completion of the first phase of the adjacent

Sesquicentennial Park, whose design was the subject of a national competition, in relation to other improvements to Buffalo Bayou provide for the possibility of extending connections from downtown to Allen Parkway. The Brown Convention Center represents the "big bang" theory of redefining a district, but its gradual linkage to historic development along Main Street may effectively revitalize downtown's East End, long a landscape of abandoned buildings and parking lots. The Museum of Fine Arts, Houston anticipates significant expansion; in 1972, the Brown Pavilion was barely under construction. Since then the Glassell School and Cullen Sculpture Garden have given definition to an arts district, and Montrose Boulevard has emerged as a lively pedestrian precinct. The Menil Collection and its adjacent neighborhood were carefully assembled and represent a new and more sensitive attitude toward intervention by a major cultural institution. The idea of infill as a strategy is particularly meaningful, continuing a tradition begun in the 1950s with the first elements of the University of St. Thomas and in the late 1960s with the Rothko Chapel. Rice University had its demonstrations of contextual response during the 1980s: the School of Architecture (Anderson Hall) became an international example through its low-key adaptation of formal themes on both an urban design and stylistic level, and Herring Hall extended the ideas of interpretation and elaboration. This book discusses numerous other examples, many of them by a new generation of young designers who were college or high school students in 1972. If the economic context is one of diminished resources, then the times have shown that more thoughtful possibilities can be created when "value" becomes a word with more than economic dimensions.

But any concept of value contains the element of relativism, the relation of the circumstantial to the whole. The case of the Rice campus is, compared to Houston as a whole, an anomaly in all ways: an environment with a clear social idea embodied in principles of architectural form, both in terms of a syntax of physical objects and open spaces they form, as well as a grammar of representation relating one building to another. Today's scene reflects the complexity and diversity of a range of taste cultures, further working against any comprehensive consensus. Stephen Fox discusses the dominant role of individualism in Houston's development. I would suggest that this American frontier ethic has been aggravated by the circumstances of the twentieth century. Not the least of these are the complex economic and technological forces that have emerged in the past half century. As much as they have affected urban development and conditioned the form of its buildings, they have remained uncomprehended, with no theoretical discourse adequate to describe, analyze or predict their impact. The natural scientist and philosopher A.E. Parr observed of sociology that it was the product of the very age it sought to examine; by analogy, he suggested that our emerging urban values had little with which to compare. This is the core of the issue of relativism in relation to values, and the critical element is that of cultural memory.

BUILDING AWARENESS OF HOUSTON'S PAST

Our realization in 1972 was that the immediate urban past of the late 1940s and 1950s was being written over by the boom of the 1970s. The perspective chosen for that little white square guidebook was to put its moment of incredible change into a context. With the creation of the Houston Metropolitan Research Center as a part of the Special Collections of the Houston Public Library, a case was made for incorporation of both architectural and planning materials; the discovery and donation of the papers of Houston architect A.C. Finn was the opportune catalyst. Subsequent support through the efforts of the Historic Resources Committee of the AIA, Houston Chapter and The Junior League of Houston have added to the HMRC collections, and *The Houston Review* quarterly brings events back from the past. Additionally, the data survey of the 1972 guide was prepared in a form compatible with the Historic American Buildings Survey, all of which (including the original artwork) became a part of the HMRC Archives. From an idea of Drexel Turner, and a challenge by then Rice Dean David Crane, the Rice Design Alliance was formed as a vehicle to educate the public and the profession on issues of the built environment. Several subsequent guides have elaborated other themes; Douglas Milburn's interpretations (which con- tinued during his tenure as the editor of *Houston City*), a downtown guide from the AIA, the RDA's tours, and a series of interesting programs by the Houston Public Library in the late 1970s articulated special places (my surveys of Spanish Colonial traditions and signs in the Houston landscape, and Milburn's survey of graveyards, all with photography by Paul Hester). Howard Barnstone's monograph on John F. Staub pre- sented a meaningful portrait of an architect and a social order. Drexel Turner's monumental six-volume *Houston Architectural Survey* of 1980-81 for the Texas Historical Commission and the City of Houston provided a critical resource of then-extant structures for the period up to 1940, without which this book would not have been as possible.

Ironically, the inclusion of extant structures as the basis for this guide, and the chronological limits of the *Survey* have let a few very important structures fall between the cracks. Among these is the Shamrock Hotel, opened in 1949 and demolished in

1987. It was perhaps not architecturally as significant as it was culturally and locationally representative of a unique era. In this regard, it joins a list of many other structures, buildings and otherwise, which embodied particular aspects of the city's evolution. The amnesiac nature of Houston's image of itself, always in search of a future, belies a complex, eccentric and revealing past, which in many ways was given physical presence in built form. There is much work to be done, including further publication and illumination of these episodes. Such a mnemonic history does not serve as a nostalgia for events and circumstances long lost, but rather acts as a gauge against which to measure the quality of our present moment and our aspirations for the future. To this end, the present work represents a critical contribution.

Peter C. Papademetriou, AIA
January 1990

Introduction

Houston is apt to strike visitors as a city of extremes, an impression to which its torrid climate, flat terrain, great distances, and lack of apparent order contribute. As June Arnold caused a character in her novel, *Baby Houston*, to exclaim when trying to describe the city: "Houston is a mess." It is and it always has been. That is its scandal and its charm. Houston is a city that appears chaotic yet is easy to inhabit, that is expansive, welcoming, and unpredictably violent, that preserves the accessibility of a small town even though it has become the fourth largest city in the United States. Visitors are appalled by the tawdriness of Houston yet entranced by its flashing skylines and the profusion and luxuriance of its live oak trees. Exaggerated contrasts, inexorable humidity, and the Texan penchant for overstatement imbue Houston with a larger-than-life intensity that can be overwhelming. But it is exciting too. For the 20th century has been a time in the city's history when energy and dynamism were not only the source of its industrial wealth and an attribute of its incessant mobility, but constituent elements of its civic psyche.

Because rapidity of growth and change, entailing the constant influx of new residents, is a historic phenomenon in Houston, the city undergoes continuous change in its understanding of itself. Before any one group of newcomers can be acculturated, they have been succeeded by an even larger group of new arrivals. Native Houstonians find that the city of their childhood is not the city of their adolescence, young adulthood, maturity, or old age, but a city that evolves and changes fluidly, transforming familiar landscapes, and the collective rituals associated with them, into memories of vanished places.

Major economic interests, eager to attract newcomers, especially large business enterprises, have historically maintained Houston as an open city. Consequently there exists no old guard charged with perpetuating the proprietary myths of an established elite and excluding, or at least appropriately indoctrinating, newcomers. Important elements within Houston's business elite have historically been attuned to leading movements transpiring elsewhere and willing to introduce them locally. Therefore, among the cultural choices that confront cities of the hinterland, Houston has consistently opted for the colonial, as opposed to the provincial, alternative. Rather than closing in on itself, it is perpetually eager to select from among what metropolitan centers of culture have to offer. Consequently, Houston architecture has not only reflected current trends, but, since the turn of the century, has been influenced by the direct intervention of those responsible for such trends. This accounts for the prominence of architecture in 20th-century Houston. It also explains a certain persistent shallowness, since what already exists is continuously neglected and devalued. Houston forgets itself: amnesia is an essential local cultural attribute.

When Houston does reflect upon itself, it has tended to see only a few extravagant images (Peter Papademetriou cites the conjunction of cowboy and astronaut) that celebrate the individual rather than the collective and idealize rather than analyze. The myth of the primacy of the individual is a significant part of what might be described as Houston's working understanding of itself. Although the corporate organization of business enterprise—of cotton, railroading, and timber in the 19th century, of oil, minerals, and petrochemicals in the 20th—has sustained Houston's economy, it has not noticeably altered this understanding, which derives from the era of the city's founding, that of Jacksonian liberal capitalism. Thomas H. Kreneck has analyzed Sam Houston, the adventurer, military leader, and statesman for whom the city was named, in terms of what he describes as a "Jacksonian frontier personality":

> "Houston, amid the perceived equality of condition in the American setting, was filled with restlessness and an insatiable enterprising nature. He was Tocqueville's archetype—an aggressive capitalist dealing in western lands who sought land not to settle and cultivate so much as to settle, improve, divide, and sell. Concurrent in Houston's nature was the desire to preserve order. He wanted no commotion that would imperil his property or position."
> Thomas H. Krenek, "Sam Houston and the Jacksonian Frontier Personality," *The Houston Review*, 8(no. 3, 1986), p. 131

The desire for a fixed, dependable order that guarantees the possibility of voluntary, individual change but exacts no demands and initiates no action illuminates the Houstonian conception of the proper role of public authority, as well as its blind faith in the conviction that individual initiative is superior to collective wisdom. Thus, Houston's habitual rejection of public planning (four times between 1929 and 1962 efforts to establish a zoning code, the legal basis of city planning in the United States, have been defeated; Houston is the only major city in the U. S. without a zoning code) but its enthusiastic endorsement of privately-initiated land-use controls (the restrictive covenant). The invisible hand of economic determinism is viewed as a natural agent of change within this scheme of things, while public controls are considered an arbitrary, artificial imposition of coercive restraint. In place of any collectively articulated, shared vision of the public good, business values tend to dominate, delimiting the range of alternatives in all circumstances.

It is Houston's lack of any vision of itself as an operational whole (rather than a collage of its glimmering high points), so tellingly apparent to visitors, that accounts for the lack of public concern about its messy appearance. This *does* stimulate citizen initiative: most of Houston's planned public spaces—Hermann Square downtown, Main Boulevard, the Buffalo Bayou Parkway, many of the major parks—came about as the result of a few individuals' prodding the city government into action, often with substantial donations of property or cash. But efforts of this kind are hard pressed even to gain a public hearing for such issues as the deterioration of vast sectors of northeast and southeast Houston (much of this of post-World War II vintage), looming ecological crises, and the price exacted to sustain Houston's pattern of discontinuous, low-density suburban sprawl. Heritage conservation has yet to register as a critical issue. Historically, Houston has ignored such problems unless a crisis threatened its ability to attract and nurture business. The growth cycle itself diffuses any sense of urgency by distracting attention and resources away from centers of trouble to the expanding periphery. There the condition of newness functions like a fountain of youth, perpetually flowing with the waters of eternal beginning. Given the constant influx of new population, Houston's profound lack of self-knowledge, the paucity of a collective sense of local identity grounded in the fabric of the city, and the emphasis on individual achievement and satisfaction to the exclusion of public good, the absence of a shared vision of how the city ought to be follows logically. The ability of this particular collective unconscious to continue operating as it has, even through severe economic reverses during the 1980s that might have triggered a reevaluation of habitual conduct, suggests that Houstonians are quite comfortable with this state of affairs. Openness, energy, and optimism, Houston's most attractive characteristics, militate against critical self-examination. This is why the mess of Houston remains the source of its scandal and its charm. As John Kaliski has warned, if Houston is to maintain its leading place among American cities in the 21st century, it must redirect these characteristics toward self-inquiry and critical renewal, working toward and taking responsibility for the whole.

Phillip Lopate has described the complexity of Houston as yielding an inner richness, unsuspected from the perspective of the freeway, unilluminated in the refracted light of mirror-glass-clad office towers. Since the 1970s, painters, sculptors, and writers have begun to explore and disclose these other Houstons—funky, marginal, subversive—in works that treat Houston as an archeology, a compilation of urban experiences heretofore unexcavated and unanalyzed. Architecture has hardly attempted to share this intro-spective tendency. Instead it reflects, as it customarily has, the city's extroversion. Because Houston has looked beyond itself for architectural direction, eclecticism and formalism have been recur-ring traits. Typological developments have depended more on externally imposed determinants, usually economic, than on pur-poseful architectural invention. Houston thus presents a broad array of typological and formal tendencies rather than well defined, patiently distilled, and consciously applied local tradi-tions. Such traditions have existed, but they fall into disuse, go unrecognized and uncatalogued, and so lose their connection to the present. This phenomenon occurs not over centuries, but well within an architect's span of practice.

The extent to which Houston's architecture has begun to be recovered and evaluated can be gauged by examining the atten-tion focused on Houston on the three occasions during the 20th century that the American Institute of Architects convened there. On the first occasion, in 1949, four then-new buildings obtained recognition: Donald Barthelme's parish hall and school for St. Rose of Lima Catholic Church, which won an AIA design award, first presented that year, Kenneth Franzheim's Foley's department store (which won a design award the next year), and MacKie & Kamrath's Temple Emanu El. These three buildings were overshadowed by a fourth, however, the Shamrock Hotel, which held its celebrated opening ceremonies just after the institute adjourned its convention. The Shamrock—which was demolished in 1987—was the object of obsessive attention and enormous ridicule; it was demonized as a symbol of resistance to modern architecture and was the only local building that Frank Lloyd Wright, who was awarded the institute's Gold Medal at the Houston convention, mentioned in his acceptance speech. Philip Johnson, who was then planning a modern house for Mr. and Mrs. John de Menil, best summarized the lack of curiosity about the city and its architecture (typical of its time and by no means restricted to Houston) when he quipped, in response to a reporter's query in 1950, "Must we dis-cuss architecture in Houston? It's so dull." (Johnson subse-quently remedied that circumstance.)

The next meeting of the American Institute of Architects in Houston, in 1972, was marked by a radical change in attitude. Peter C. Papademetriou's book, *Houston, An Architectural Guide*, the first guidebook to Houston architecture ever com-piled, contained his extended critical analysis of Houston's low-density urban form, the causes of its development, and the consequences that it portended for architecture. The book creat-ed a minor scandal in Houston because, rather than restricting itself to presentation of a limited number of recent buildings conforming to canons of established architectural taste, it addressed issues that the local profession chose to ignore, or to dismiss as subarchitectural. Papademetriou's overview, expanded upon in a series of essays that he published during the 1970s, took seriously the whole of Houston, the mess and the tawdriness. It focused on what Houston elites generally chose to suppress recognition of (and irritably rejected when called to their attention by outsiders): the characteristics and reasons for being of the city in between the architectural highlights and enclaves of privilege. It also demonstrated that the city that Houston had become did not evolve from natural circumstances but by historical actions, most often taken without regard for their architectural or urbanistic implications. Moreover, once it beheld, it did not condemn. Papademetriou was more interested in clarifying the conditions that stimulated the development of kitsch, for instance (as well as innovative building typologies and prestige design), than in discriminating between good and bad.

Through the guidebook, as well as his other writing, Peter Papademetriou identified Houston as a place worthy of critical inquiry and debate. He stimulated the beginning of scholarship on Houston's architectural and urban history, which was amplified by Drexel Turner, Howard Barnstone, Douglas Milburn, the American Institute of Architects, Houston Chapter, the Houston Public Library's Houston Metropolitan Research Center, *Texas Architect* magazine, and since 1982, *Cite, The Architecture and Design Review of Houston*, published by the Rice Design Alliance.

This guidebook, prepared for the meeting of the American Institute of Architects in Houston in 1990, is the beneficiary of these research efforts. It seeks to present the buildings of Houston in the context of the city's historical evolution and of its architectural-historical development. As such, it tends to look backward rather than forward, an unaccustomed point of view for writing about Houston, but one taken in the conviction that Houstonians, as well as visitors, can better understand the present and take responsibility for the future by learning about the past.

Stephen Fox
Fellow of the Anchorage Foundation of Texas

Downtown

Houston's downtown is the historic center. Like the city at large, though, it is an exploded landscape reorganized frequently with little attention to urbanistic continuity or consistency. Since 1905, when the first steel-framed skyscraper in Houston was built, downtown has undergone an irregular but dependable cycle of change. Each episode created a new skyline, overshadowing that which preceded it, and enlarged the boundaries of what is defined as downtown.

The latest manifestation of this cycle produced the gleaming office towers of the Smith-Louisiana corridor on the west side of downtown. These emblems of the city's major economic institutions dominate the landscape although they are newcomers to the downtown scene. Their shapes, colors, and spaces are audacious and exhilarating. Yet they lack density, their size notwithstanding. Persons accustomed to more traditional city centers are apt to find this section of downtown Houston disorienting. It is *all* new, with few traces of even the recent past (pre-1960) to ground the angled, curved, stepped, gridded, reflective towers that rise in proud isolation, one per block. The public way appears eerily underpopulated, since the buildings are linked to each other by an extensive but invisible network of pedestrian tunnels routed beneath the sidewalks and streets. But if this landscape is enigmatic, even unnerving, it is not boring. Its modernism is intensified by the presence of public art installations—works by Oldenburg, Nevelson, Dubuffet, Miró—that mediate between pedestrian scale and the engineering scale of the buildings to lyricize the experience of moving through these spacious precincts.

East of Louisiana Street lies what middle-aged Houstonians remember as downtown—a familiar composite of department stores, specialty shops, dime stores, cafés, and theaters, interspersed with tall office and hotel buildings. The eight blocks of Main Street between Texas Avenue and Clay Avenue were the operational and symbolic center of Houston from the 1920s through the 1960s, when the erosion of the Main Street retail district began in earnest. By now the erosion appears irreversible; not even the daily presence of approximately 180,000 workers downtown can compensate for the defection of shoppers to suburban malls. Main Street's loss of primacy is symbolized by the closed and empty Rice Hotel and Sakowitz store, and by the clearance of entire blocks for surface parking. The ultimate urbanistic consequences of this decay of downtown are visible east of Fannin Street, where the multiple-use Houston Center complex was launched in 1970 by clearing 32 blocks and then rebuilding portions of the site as an enclave of interconnected towers that stands aloof from the city.

From Texas Avenue north to Commerce Avenue is what remains of 19th- and early 20th-century Houston. The waterfront at the foot of Main Street, where barges and shallow-draft steamboats could dock and turn around, was a hub of commercial transport until the 1910s. Behind it, flanked to either side by Courthouse

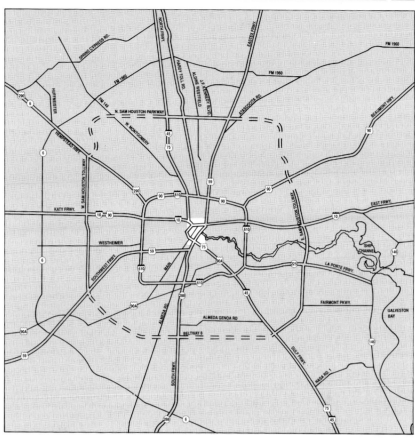

Square and Market Square, was the financial and commercial district. Yet even this small area was successively redeveloped: provisional construction (including large tents) gave way first to wooden, then brick and cast-iron storefronts, then to exuberant Victorian commercial buildings, and then to the first generation of skyscrapers. After the turn of the 20th century, the intensification of commercial traffic on both the bayou and the numerous railroads that entered Houston transformed the area north of Buffalo Bayou into a district of factories and warehouses. To the east of Main Street and Courthouse Square, new railroad construction penetrated the middle-income neighborhoods of Second and Third wards, and residential districts retreated southward up Main, Caroline, and Crawford into the streetcar suburbs of the South End.

Downtown is a historic record of Houston's attitude toward growth and development: what is coming will be of more value than what is here already. The result is a "dynamic" landscape unconstrained by those places, objects, or buildings that evoke memory and are used ritually to bind communities and generations together in loyalty to the city and its culture. For all its apparent disarray, this landscape does make sense. It is a testament to the priority that Houston's civic culture has always granted to individual speculation and its consequent reluctance to encumber the landscape with monuments whose permanence might obstruct the forward-looking gaze.

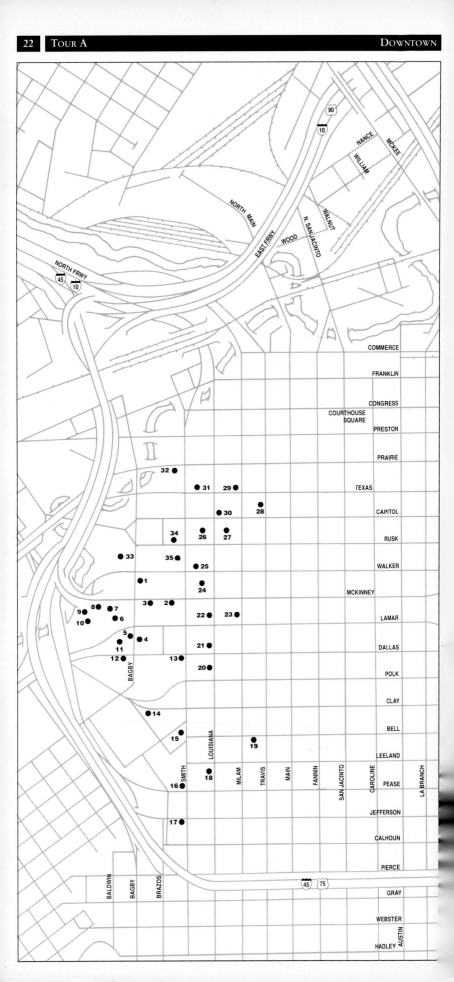

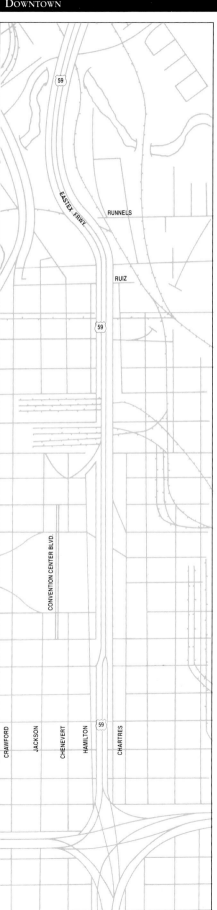

1. 901 Bagby Street
2. 500 McKinney Avenue
3. 600 McKinney Avenue
4. 1111 Bagby Street
5. 1100 Bagby Street
6. Sam Houston Park
   St. John Church
7. Sam Houston Park
   San Felipe Cottage
8. Sam Houston Park
   Staiti House
9. Sam Houston Park
   Pillot House
10. Sam Houston Park
    Old Place
11. Sam Houston Park
    Nichols-Rice-Cherry House
12. Sam Houston Park
    Kellum-Noble House
13. 500 Dallas Avenue
14. 500 Clay Avenue
15. 1400 Smith Street
16. 1600 Smith Street
17. 500 Jefferson Avenue
18. 1600 Louisiana Street
19. 800 Bell Avenue
20. 1200 Louisiana Street
21. 1100 Louisiana Street
22. 1000 Louisiana Street
23. 1010 Milam Street
24. 910 Louisiana Street
25. 611 Walker Avenue
26. 700 Louisiana Street
27. 711 Louisiana Street
28. 600 Travis Street
29. 701 Texas Avenue
30. 615 Louisiana Street
31. 615 Texas Avenue
32. 550 Prairie Avenue
33. 810 Bagby Street
34. 515 Rusk Avenue
35. 800 block Smith Street

these is Ruth Pershing Uhler's "The First Subscription Committee, 1854" (1935), at the first landing of the main stair. The building now houses the Library's Houston Metropolitan Research Center and the Texas and Local History Department, the principal repositories for publications, maps, and documents (including architectural drawings) on the history of Houston. Original furnishings in the reading rooms on the ground and second floors are still in use.

901 Bagby Street   **A-1**
Houston City Hall (1939) Joseph Finger

More stolid than soaring, despite its skyscraper aspirations, Houston's City Hall is resolutely official looking. Its solidly massed blocks are faced with Texas Cordova shell limestone, a favorite "regional" material for Texan public buildings in the 1930s and '40s. The allegorical sculpture is by Herring Coe and Raoul Josset; Finger's office detailed the aluminum screens above the principal entrances. The entrance lobby is colorfully finished with marble, nickel, and decorative plaster relief work. The main stair, on the west side of the building, and the Council Room, directly above the entrance lobby, are designed in a lighter, more streamlined manner. From the front of City Hall a series of paved terraces step down to **Hermann Square**, a block of ground bequeathed to the City of Houston in 1914 by the philanthropist George H. Hermann for use as a public park. In 1939, the Kansas City landscape architects Hare & Hare installed the reflecting basin that stretches out on axis with City Hall, as well as the broad grass terrace, hedgerows, and live oak trees that ring the pool. Simple in diagram, Hare & Hare's design has proved to be an exemplary urban garden that is intensively used.

500 McKinney Avenue   **A-2**
Julia Ideson Building, Houston Public Library (1926) Cram & Ferguson, William Ward Watkin and Louis A. Glover

Set on a tree-shaded block, this low, masonry building with its arched windows, clay tile roofs, and sculptural decoration provides a welcome contrast to the tall, brittle towers that now surround it. The Boston architect Ralph Adams Cram detailed the building with Spanish Plateresque ornament to insinuate a connection with Texas's architectural-historical past. The interiors, carefully restored in 1979 by S. I. Morris Associates, contain a series of Public Works Art Project murals; the most ingenious of

600 McKinney Avenue   **A-3**
Central Library Building, Houston Public Library (1975) S. I. Morris Associates

Eugene Aubry's Central Library Building is hardly contextual in the usual sense of the term, yet it pulls its surroundings into a civic whole, due chiefly to the scale of its giant portico and the breadth of its dark, bare, brick-paved plaza. Sally Walsh's subtle, stylish, and eminently usable interiors have been superlatively maintained. Claes Oldenburg's steel sculpture, "Geometric Mouse, Scale X" (1968), the first work of public art installed downtown, brightly punctuates the plaza.

1111 Bagby Street   **A-4**
Heritage Plaza (1987) M. Nasr & Partners

The boom in office building construction which reshaped the downtown skyline in the late 1970s and early '80s ended with this display of postmodern exhibitionism. Heritage Plaza's granite, stepped pyramid cap was inspired by architect Mohammed Nasr's vacation in the Yucatán. The elevator vestibule and a skylit lobby court are as compulsively activated as the exteriors, in order to absorb both the ramps that serve the 16 stories of parking above the lobby and the K-bracing which rigidifies the tower's partial framed tube structural system. A final flourish occurs at the plaza entrance, where a concave peristyle is deployed to reconcile the tower with the back of the ex-**Federal Land Bank Building** (1929, Hedrick & Gottlieb), which the developer, R. W. Wortham III, carefully preserved.

1100 Bagby Street   **A-5**
Sam Houston Park

After the giddiness of Heritage Plaza, it is refreshing to step across Bagby Street into Houston's oldest public park, Sam Houston Park, acquired in 1899. The grounds slope down to Buffalo Bayou, just as it is crossed by an elevated segment of Interstate 45, built through the park in the middle 1950s. Since 1956 Sam Houston Park has been administered by the Harris County Heritage Society, a non-profit preservation organization that has brought six historic buildings into the park to join one that has always stood in its grounds. Restored and appropriately furnished, they are maintained by the society as an open-air historical museum. Tour information is available in the Long Row building, which also contains a shop specializing in Houstoniana. In the adjoining annex is the Museum of Texas History, containing changing exhibitions.

Sam Houston Park   **A-6**
St. John Church (1891)

Built for a congregation of German Evangelical Lutherans and originally located amidst the farms of northwest Harris County, St. John Church is typical of 19th-century wooden church buildings in Texas. It is a gable-roofed box, its identity as a church signalled architecturally by its pointed arched openings and a broach spire. Moved to Sam Houston Park in 1968.

Sam Houston Park   **A-7**
San Felipe Cottage (1868)

San Felipe Cottage is representative of one of the most common house types built in Houston through the 1870s, the Gulf coast cottage, with its full-width porch inserted beneath a gabled roof. It was moved from

its original site on San Felipe Road, now West Dallas Avenue, just behind the Kellum-Noble House, in 1963 and restored by Harvin C. Moore.

Sam Houston Park   **A-8**
Staiti House (1905)

This large, turn-of-the-century house, described at the time of its completion as being in the California bungalow style, was moved here from Westmoreland Avenue in 1986. The identity of its architect has not been determined, but it is the mirror image of a contemporary house designed by the architects Jones & Tabor.

Sam Houston Park   **A-9**
Pillot House (1868)

The Pillot House indicates how the Gulf coast cottage was transformed by the taste for vertical emphasis, complex massing, and exuberant decoration which began to appear in Texas just before the Civil War and was firmly established in the 1870s. The interiors are furnished with high-style pieces of the 1860s, '70s, and '80s. The house was located at 1803 McKinney Avenue (now the site of the George R. Brown Convention Center) until its removal here in 1965. Restored by Denney & Ray in 1966.

Sam Houston Park   **A-10**
Old Place (c. 1825)

Old Place, originally located on Clear Creek, exemplifies the earliest type of house built in the Houston region after Anglo-

American settlement began in the 1820s. It is of rough-hewn cedar frame construction, surfaced with clapboards. A "mudcat" chimney stands to one side of the single-pen house, and a porch, a standard feature of Houston houses until the 1920s, is carried across the front. Adjacent to Old Place, with its back to the freeway, stands Louis Amateis's "Spirit of the Confederacy," set up in the park in 1908. This bronze statue of a mournful winged youth figured as the talisman of Robert Altman's enigmatic film "Brewster McCloud" (1970).

Heritage Society, which rescued the building and opened it to the public as a house museum in 1958, following restoration by Harvin C. Moore.

500 Dallas Avenue   **A-13**
One Allen Center (1972)
Wilson, Morris, Crain & Anderson

Sam Houston Park   **A-11**
Nichols-Rice-Cherry House (c. 1850)

The Nichols-Rice-Cherry House, an elite townhouse of the pre-Civil War period, is compact in plan but—without closets, kitchen, or bathrooms—amazingly spacious. The architrave and front doors are embellished with Greek revival detail that reappears inside along with fancy graining patterns. The house was built on Congress Avenue facing Courthouse Square. It was moved on its original site in 1886, then moved from that site to a new location in 1897 to become the studio of Houston's first resident artist, Emma Richardson Cherry. Following Mrs. Cherry's death, it was acquired by the Harris County Heritage Society and became the first building to be moved into the park. Restored in 1960 by Harvin C. Moore.

Sam Houston Park   **A-12**
Kellum-Noble House (1847)

The oldest surviving building in Houston, the Kellum-Noble House was built here, outside the original townsite in the "upper part" of Houston, adjacent to Nathaniel Kelly Kellum's brickyard. It is a double-pen house with a central dogtrot passage. The hipped roof, encircling galleries, and brick construction were all departures from conventional Houston house types. The house was included in the city's purchase of the park in 1899. A move to demolish it in 1954 led to the formation of the Harris County

Allen Center, named after the founders of Houston and begun by the Dallas developer Trammell Crow with Metropolitan Life Insurance Co., is the only downtown office complex where streets have been closed to create a superblock. The faceted brick planes of One Allen Center's base conceal two stories of pedestrian circulation and retail lease space that originally opened onto a walled plaza court facing Smith Street. After Century Development Corp. acquired Crow's interest, the company retained Lloyd Jones Brewer & Associates as architects of the not-quite-matching **Two Allen Center** (1977), the polygonal, aluminum-panelled **Three Allen Center** (1980), and the **Hotel Meridien** (1980, now the Doubletree). The firm disregarded WMCA's urbanistic strategy. Instead, they connected the office buildings with a network of air-conditioned pedestrian bridges that bypass the hotel and the suburbanized landscape installation at the center of the complex. In front of Two Allen Center, facing Polk Avenue, is Peter Reginato's "High Plains Drifter" (1973).

500 Clay Avenue   **A-14**
Antioch Baptist Church (1879) Richard Allen (1895) Robert Jones

Antioch Baptist Church, organized in 1866 for emancipated slaves, houses the oldest black Baptist congregation in Houston. The original church building by Richard Allen, a black master builder, was significantly enlarged in 1895 by Robert Jones and has

been expanded subsequently. It remains in what was once the heart of the city's oldest black community, despite attempts by real estate developers to acquire the property in the 1970s.

(best appreciated from the wall slit on Pease Avenue) are the work of The SWA Group. What might at first appear to be the entrance to a subway station at Smith and Ruthven is an air-conditioned passage that links 1600 Smith to the farthest extremity of the downtown tunnel system.

1400 Smith Street   **A-15**
Four Allen Center [now Enron Building]
(1983) Lloyd Jones Brewer & Associates

Aligned on the Fourth Ward grid rather than the South Side Buffalo Bayou grid that prevails downtown, the 50-story Four Allen Center tower is always seen in perspective. The density and thickness of its steel framed-tube perimeter is suppressed beneath a sleek membrane composed of alternating bands of silver reflective glass and white aluminum spandrel. At night, a neon halo atop the tower's summit outlines and emphasizes the building's smooth curves. The elevator lobby, surfaced in polished light gray granite, is refreshingly calm. At the corner of Smith and Andrews rises "Frozen Laces—One" (1980) by Louise Nevelson, installed in 1987 by Century Development Corp., Metropolitan Life Insurance Co., and American General Realty Co., the developers of Four Allen Center.

1600 Smith Street   **A-16**
1600 Smith Building (1984)
Morris*Aubry Architects

This pearl-gray, 52-story tower is faceted in plan, projecting the collision of street grids upward in tiered setbacks that culminate in a polygonal cap, which, like its neighbor at 1400 Smith Street, is illuminated at night. Conceived as half of a two-building complex, 1600 Smith departs considerably from the planning and architectural standards that prevailed in earlier phases of Cullen Center, of which it is a part. The jokey rolled-up sidewalk and the plaza fountain

500 Jefferson Avenue   **A-17**
500 Jefferson Building (1963)
Welton Becket & Associates

500 Jefferson and its companion, the ex-**Hotel America** (now the Whitehall, 1963, also by the Los Angeles architects, Welton Becket & Associates), were the initial buildings in Cullen Center, the first multiblock development in downtown Houston. The Becket office proposed a series of slab-shaped buildings, rotated to minimize obstruction of view, and interconnected with air-conditioned pedestrian bridges across the intervening streets. Precast concrete panels provide the architectural order; slender columns and a marble-revetted terrace in front of the hotel offered ground-level amenity (except that the marble is perpetually coming unstuck). Subsequent additions—the **Cullen Center Bank & Trust Co. Building** (1971) at 600 Jefferson and the 40-story **Dresser Tower** (1973) at 601 Jefferson, both by Neuhaus & Taylor—ignored the Becket master plan. As in other group developments, the chance to create a unified and distinctive whole lost out to the Houston penchant for individualism.

1600 Louisiana Street   **A-18**
Young Men's Christian Association
Building [now Downtown Branch YMCA]
(1941) Kenneth Franzheim

When Franzheim's 10-story, Tuscan Renaissance-detailed YMCA Building was built, it towered above a neighborhood of run-down late 19th-century houses to the

southwest of downtown. Encircled now by taller buildings, it appears a quaint reminder of the past, although the awning windows with which it has been crudely refitted considerably diminish the building's integrity.

1200 Louisiana Street   A-20

Hyatt Regency Houston (1972) JV III (Koetter, Tharp & Cowell, Caudill Rowlett Scott, and Neuhaus & Taylor)

Charles E. Lawrence of CRS was director of design for the first hotel that Hyatt built after it split with the Atlanta architect John Portman, whose hotels in Atlanta, Chicago, and San Francisco gave the corporation its singular architectural image. Portman's signature devices reappear here: a 30-story, 350-foot high lobby surrounded by balcony corridors, glass-cased elevator cabs, and a revolving cocktail lounge atop the hotel, whose name, Spindletop, is a punning tribute to the 1901 oil gusher from which 20th-century Houston's growth and good fortune stemmed.

The Hyatt lobby is the closest thing to an urban living room that downtown Houston possesses: tidy, air-conditioned, and access-controlled. Up the escalator past Charles Pebworth's heroically scaled, polished aluminum mural "Garden of the Mind," and across the runway above the indoor sidewalk cafe, the visitor will find glass doors that lead (during weekday business hours) to a steel box truss pedestrian bridge across the Louisiana-Dallas intersection. It provides a stunning vista of the Louisiana Street office corridor. At the opposite end of this bridge lies the ho-hum, 47-story **1100 Milam Building** (1973, JV III), for whose design KTC was chiefly responsible. The Hyatt Regency, the 2,750-car Regency Southwest Garage, and 1100 Milam were jointly developed by Tenneco and the Prudential Insurance Co. of America.

1100 Louisiana Street   A-21

First International Plaza [now 1100 Louisiana Building] (1980) Skidmore, Owings & Merrill and 3D/International

This pink granite-and-glass clad 55-story tower, developed by Gerald D. Hines Interests and PIC Realty Corp., pays homage to the Bank of America Building in San Francisco. SOM-San Francisco's designers, Edward C. Bassett and Lawrence S. Doane, use a diagonal array of triangular window bays to establish a geometrical theme that jumps from plan to section in the banking hall, 106 feet high at its summit. Unfortunately, the sculptural dynamism visible from the Smith-Dallas intersection is missing at Louisiana and

800 Bell Avenue   A-19

Humble Building [now Exxon Building] (1963) Welton Becket & Associates with Golemon & Rolfe and George Pierce-Abel B. Pierce

At 600 feet in height, the 44-story Humble Building, headquarters of the Humble Oil & Refining Co. (now Exxon Corp.), was briefly the tallest building west of the Mississippi River. Becket's designer, Louis Naidorf, strove to give the slender tower a pronounced regional identity—within the context of late 1950s corporate modern architecture—by emphasizing sun control. The tiers of horizontal aluminum sunshades encircling the building, together with the oversailing bands of aluminum fins at its summit, succeed in giving it a light, graceful appearance from a distance, although at close range the curtain wall is finicky in detail. The Humble Building gave Becket its first opportunity to exercise what it described as "total design." Thus, even the "sculpture" in the raised podium plaza (which conceals the employees' cafeteria and other large spaces that could not conveniently be wrapped around an elevator core) was the handiwork of the firm. Another innovative feature was the architecturally coordinated 1,300-car parking garage at 1602 Milam Street. This carries the air-conditioning equipment for the tower, leaving the top of the Humble Building free for the two-story Petroleum Club and an observation deck that has been closed since 1971, when One Shell Plaza out-topped Humble.

Lamar, where the building seems to ignore rather than shape the space of the plaza. The flush-set, reflective surfaces add considerably to this remoteness at ground level. Even Jean Dubuffet's "Monument au Fantóme" (1977), a whimsical, enigmatic allegory in painted fiberglass, installed under Doane's supervision in 1983, fails to bring this bleak and inhospitable plaza to life.

1000 Louisiana Street **A-22**
Allied Bank Plaza [now
First Interstate Bank Plaza] (1983)
Skidmore, Owings & Merrill and Lloyd
Jones Brewer & Associates

The second tallest building in Houston (71 stories, 970 feet), Allied is an extension of Bassett and Doane's predilection for having it both ways: buildings that are urbanistically responsive and sculpturally arresting. The tower is a vertical extrusion of two quarter circles slipped off-center in plan, a fractured cylinder sheathed in green reflective glass that has given rise to numerous quips: everything from Emerald City to an inflated dollar sign. Its great curves charge the surrounding space with a sense of movement and expansiveness; this perceptual sensation becomes perilously literal when the breeze picks up and wind action at the base of the building commences.

Bassett and Doane, with co-designer Richard Keating, acknowledged life along the street with a pair of basement level courtyards facing Louisiana, the one place downtown where a direct and visual connection is made between the street and the subterranean tunnel system. Mammoth-scaled balustrades of polished granite frame these courts, which are backed by thin

sheets of water pouring hypnotically over dark, speckled granite walls. The roofless pavilion between Louisiana Street and the front doors distracts from, rather than enhances, the building.

Inside, two double-decked sky lobbies offer views from different heights during business hours. Exposed trusses that emphasize the massive steel bundled-tube structure behind the tower's green glass skin are visible in the lower set of sky lobbies, on the 34th and 35th floors.

1010 Milam Street **A-23**
Tennessee Building [now Tenneco Building]
(1963) Skidmore, Owings & Merrill

The Tenneco Building is a classic, the standard against which all succeeding tall buildings in downtown Houston have been measured. It has yet to be surpassed. So much of what makes this building special derives from intangibles: proportions, light and shadow, surface and void. For instance, by slightly recessing the plane of the beams behind the plane of the columns, SOM's designer, Edward C. Bassett, created a sense of depth that one hardly notices. But the resulting play of shadows charges Tenneco's technologically conceived facades with the richness and animation ascribed in postmodern polemics to traditionally built buildings. The 50-foot high colonnade at the base of the tower achieves a degree of monumentality that no subsequent downtown building has quite been able to recapture. It provides a transition in scale from the street to the building that effortlessly lifts passersby to its heroic measure, without violating the logic of the building's constructional engineering. Even such questionable details as the ungenerous dimensions of the lobby and the way that the pink Texas granite paving of the plaza creeps up the outer wall do not detract from Tenneco's gravity. The fountain on the Louisiana Street side of the building was installed in 1984 to replace a line of drive-in bank kiosks. It is the work of Richard Keating of the Houston office of SOM.

910 Louisiana Street **A-24**
One Shell Plaza (1971)
Skidmore, Owings & Merrill and Wilson,
Morris, Crain & Anderson

The Shell Oil Co.'s decision to move its headquarters to Houston occasioned con-

struction of One Shell Plaza and precipitated Houston's rise to the status of America's energy capital. The 50-story, 715-foot high One Shell was the first downtown project of Gerald D. Hines Interests and the first for which Hines employed nationally-known architects in order to attract top corporate tenants and expedite financing. Architecturally, it is the result of a collaboration between SOM-Chicago's chief designer, Bruce J. Graham, and its engineer, Fazlur R. Khan. One Shell is the optimal high-rise office building: economically determined, efficiently planned, and architecturally detailed to express its engineering and constructional innovations. A pioneering application of Khan's framed-tube concept, One Shell's structure is concentrated in its perimeter walls and central service core, leaving the floors free of interior columns and dramatically reducing the amount of building material required. Graham treated the exterior wall surfaces of the poured-in-place concrete tower as a dense file of structural piers, thickening them near the corners of the building where structural loads are most intense to produce One Shell's distinctive rippling profiles. One Shell Plaza was the tallest concrete building in the world at the time of its completion. Despite its structural distinction, One Shell Plaza lacks the urbanistic and architectural presence of its immediate predecessors, Tenneco, Humble, and the First City National Bank Building. Drenched in polished travertine, it stands aloof from the surrounding city.

Diagonally across Louisiana Street at 777 Walker Avenue is a 26-story companion, **Two Shell Plaza** (1972, SOM and WMCA), also built by Hines Interests. The gradual deformation of the window grid into arch shapes on the lower floors expresses the distribution of gravity loads. The density of Skidmore, Owings & Merrill buildings in these blocks led Ann Holmes, fine arts editor of the *Houston Chronicle*, to dub this stretch of Louisiana Street "Skid Row."

611 Walker Avenue   A-25
Electric Tower (1968) Wilson, Morris, Crain & Anderson with Robert O. Biering

The 27-story Electric Tower, headquarters of Houston Lighting & Power Co., was the first of the office towers that would transform Smith Street into the downtown avenue of skyscrapers by the 1980s. The

slab-shaped office building, inspired by Eero Saarinen's CBS Building in New York, is prefaced on the Walker Avenue side by a dry moat detailed as a Japanese rock garden by Fred Buxton & Associates. The low block along Rusk Avenue was designed to contain HL&P's computer operations. To conserve energy, WMCA outfitted the Electric Tower with "sunglasses," panes of glass installed between the column lines that sit in front of the building's recessed curtain wall.

700 Louisiana Street   A-26
RepublicBank Center [now NCNB Center] (1983) Johnson/Burgee Architects and Kendall/Heaton Associates

RepublicBank tries valiantly to redress the urbanistic shortcomings associated with tall buildings of the 1960s. In an effort to avoid being sterile and unresponsive, it fills its one-block site to saturation point with elaborate details. The whole is monumental: from the rolled moldings at the base of the street walls to the vast Romantic Classical portals on the Louisiana and Smith street sides of the building; from the awesome internal volumes of its lobby, concourses, and banking hall, to the fantastically stepped skyline rising from the banking hall pavilion up the 56-story, 780-foot high office tower. Yet the RepublicBank building presents a troubling paradox—the more one experiences, the less one is satisfied. Philip Johnson and John Burgee tried to create a neo-1920s skyscraper, with all the richness of traditional buildings. Their exaggerations of scale and disregard for the realities of making the building are insufficient to reproduce that richness, however, and Republic Bank's desperate efforts to entertain and amaze have little substance behind them.

   Encased at the Louisiana-Capitol corner of the skylit, 125-foot high banking hall is a pre-existing 2-story building. This accounts for the extremely high level of the second floor. Gensler & Associates are responsible for interior design of the bank's spaces. Gerald D. Hines Interests, which built RepublicBank, installed the 1913 Seth Thomas clock in the concourse between the banking hall and the elevator lobby.

711 Louisiana Street   **A-27**
Pennzoil Place (1976) Johnson/Burgee Architects and S. I. Morris Associates

In the annals of late 20th-century skyscraper architecture, Pennzoil Place is as historically significant as One Shell Plaza—and much more appealing. It was built by Gerald D. Hines Interests for the Pennzoil Company, whose chairman, J. Hugh Liedtke, specifically wanted a building that did not look like One Shell Plaza. Philip Johnson and John Burgee, hastily brought in to replace Bruce Graham, responded to this directive by proposing two buildings instead of one, separated by a pedestrian path that crossed the square block site diagonally from corner to corner. This diagonal (which Philip Johnson describes as a "processional" route) imposed the 45-degree geometry visible in the dramatically splayed inner walls of both towers, their counter-sloped "roofs," and the tilted glass planes that enclose a pair of air-conditioned indoor plazas. The 36-story towers are held in tense equilibrium by the 10-foot wide slot that separates them; through this slot one can play peek-a-boo with the tempietto atop the Niels Esperson Building.

   Pennzoil became the harbinger of a new generation of American skyscrapers by flouting the engineering logic so perfectly expressed in One Shell Plaza. Its sharp angles, inflected planes, and tight bronze glass sheath appealed instead to a higher order of logic: profit. Pennzoil Place was so compelling that, despite the economic recession of the mid-1970s, Hines Interests added two floors to each tower during construction to meet the demand for lease space. Pennzoil decisively reoriented Johnson/Burgee toward developer architecture and it catapulted Gerald Hines to national recognition as a patron of adventurous—and profitable—architecture.

600 Travis Street   **A-28**
Texas Commerce Tower in United Energy Plaza (1981) I. M. Pei & Partners and 3D/International

Texas Commerce Tower, constructed by Gerald D. Hines Interests for Texas Commerce Bancshares, is the latest in a series of Houston buildings to claim the distinction of being tallest west of the Mississippi. It is 75 stories, 1,002 feet in height. The building is understated and precise in composition and detail but nonetheless aggressive, both in its height and in its site planning. In order to take advantage of its position on the skyline, the New York architect I. M. Pei backed it up to the main thoroughfare, Texas Avenue, and faced it toward the intersection of two less important streets, Milam and Capitol. The huge plaza tries to be both imposing and inviting. A raised terrace to the side contains an Islamic-influenced water garden which is genuinely charming, although a bit incongruous next to the building's massive granite shaft. A stepped causeway leading diagonally to the main entrance awkwardly fills out the block. The plaza also contains Joan Miró's "Personage and Birds" (1970), a marvelous, giant-scaled, painted bronze sculpture that Pei persuaded Hines and Texas Commerce to install in 1982. Inside, to the left of the elevator core, are Miró's small original and two alternatives. From the plaza one can glimpse the setback top of the Gulf Building, as well as Pennzoil Place at its bulkiest. And from the 60th-floor observation deck—accessible during business hours from the elevators that face the main entrance—a panoramic vista of southwest Houston is visible. Texas Commerce is the quintessential skyscraper in the polished gray granite suit. Good grooming and the public amenities generously provided by Texas Commerce Bank compensate for a lackluster personality.

701 Texas Avenue   **A-29**
Auditorium Hotel [now Lancaster Hotel] (1926) Joseph Finger

Joseph Finger's Auditorium Hotel had never been one of the city's more notable hostelries until it was acquired by General Leisure Corp. and transformed into a small, deluxe hotel called the Lancaster (1983,

Hightower-Alexander). It represents an intelligent act of urban conservation that is too rare in Houston.

615 Louisiana Street   A-30
Jesse H. Jones Hall for the Performing Arts (1966) Caudill Rowlett Scott

Jones Hall, home of the Houston Symphony Orchestra, is in the culture center style of the 1960s, a mix of architectural metaphors that was supposed to look both modern and classical. CRS conceived the building as a composite structure: a steel space-frame roof canopy, supported on reinforced concrete columns, would enclose the stage, auditorium, and lobby, all sheltered between two freely curved shells. Due to budgetary constraints the structural concept was simplified, but the forms stuck. Bland and scaleless externally and wallpapered in travertine, Jones Hall comes off at first glance as a provincial reflection of New York's Lincoln Center. This is unfortunate, for the building's formal image does not do justice to its ingenious planning or its technical innovations. Theatrical consultant George C. Izenour worked with CRS and acoustical consultant Robert Newman to devise an intricate moveable ceiling that allows the hall to be reconfigured for different types of performances. The teak-lined, 3,000-seat auditorium is serene and unpretentious while the lobby, animated by Richard Lippold's suspended stainless steel sculpture "Gemini II" (a tribute to Houston's identity in the 1960s as Space City), is exuberantly activated in section.

Jones Hall was built by Houston Endowment, a charitable foundation established by Mr. and Mrs. Jesse H. Jones, and presented to the City of Houston upon completion. Like other American cultural centers of its period, it was constructed within a purpose-made civic-cultural enclave intended to arrest the disintegration of downtown. Built simultaneously by the City of Houston were CRS's **Albert Thomas Convention and Exposition Center** (612 Smith Street, 1967), the raised plaza that lies between Albert Thomas and Jones Hall, and the 3-level, subterranean, 1,750-car Civic Center Garage. Time has demonstrated that this precinct functions more as an island of amenity than as a generator of urbanity. The street is ignored by a system of tunnels leading directly from the Civic Center Garage into the halls, a testament to Houston's overwhelming penchant for convenience and engineered efficiency.

615 Texas Avenue   A-31
Alley Theatre (1969) Ulrich Franzen & Associates with MacKie & Kamrath

The Alley Theatre is one of the best modern buildings in Houston, although its almost fortified appearance may appear too ominously defensive. The New York architect Ulrich Franzen was striving for a design that would be the antithesis of Jones Hall, expressing externally the complexities of planning, circulation, and servicing rather than submerging them within a simplistic formal package. Franzen overstated his case: the Alley's battered walls of poured-in-place concrete and its towers capped with gunnery turrets (actually penthouses for the air-handling equipment) are a bit aggressive from the perspective of the sidewalk. But inside the Alley has a magical ambience. The stairs that lead from the entrance vestibule to the second-floor lobby introduce a directed spatial flow that spirals volumetrically upward through the building and expands outward to the generous open-air terraces visible from the street. Jim Love's standing metal sculpture "Area Code" (1962) occupies the first landing of the main stairs. While Franzen's detailing bears no resemblance to that of Frank Lloyd Wright, the Alley's spatial compression and diminutive scale are definitely Wrightian. The building contains two theaters: an 800-seat thrust stage theater that fills the swelling bay at Texas and Smith, and the 300-seat Arena Theater in the basement, named in honor of Hugo V. Neuhaus, Jr., who chaired the Alley's building committee. The driveway through the building is a clever condensation of a typical Houston landscape feature.

Behind the Alley Theatre, at 600 Prairie Avenue, lies the 15-story **Alley Theatre Center** (1984, Morris*Aubry Architects with Peter D. Waldman), a 1,000-car parking garage built by Gerald D. Hines Interests to serve RepublicBank Center. The garage is handsomely faced with precast granite-aggregate concrete panels. Its top three floors are set aside for a third Alley theater space, and Peter Waldman alludes to Franzen's building with a curved balcony that forms (as Waldman puts it) a Jack-O'-Lantern face.

550 Prairie Avenue   **A-32**
Gus S. Wortham Theater Center (1987)
Morris*Aubry Architects

The Wortham, built to house the Houston Grand Opera and the Houston Ballet, contains two side-by-side theaters, one with 2,225 seats, the other with 1,102 seats. The building occupies municipal property but it was built entirely with private donations and, at its completion, turned over to the City of Houston. The Wortham had a long and troubled planning history, occasioned chiefly by unrealistically low initial cost estimates, which led to difficulties with funding and ultimately to controversy over the design of the exterior. The two performance spaces, planned with acoustician Christopher Jaffee and theatrical consultants Nananne Porcher and Clyde Nordheimer, work quite well. However, public circulation is awkwardly handled and the architectural detailing is garish and pretentious. The Wortham does contain one noble space—the Grand Foyer, a civic-scaled room that occupies the bridge spanning Prairie Avenue. The Grand Foyer and lobby offer marvelous framed views of the downtown skyline. A series of unfurling bronze banners by the sculptor Albert Paley (who also modeled the door pulls) line the escalator from the main entrance to the foyer. The SWA Group designed the plaza at Texas and Smith, punctuated with overscaled globes on blocky pedestals.

Between the plaza and Buffalo Bayou, which flows almost unnoticed around this segment of the Civic Center, is **Sesqui-centennial Park** (1989, TeamHou), the first phase of a beautification of the bayou's shore, won in a national competition by a trio of young Houston architects in 1986.

810 Bagby Street   **A-33**
Sam Houston Coliseum and Music Hall (1937) Alfred C. Finn

This was Houston's first major Public

Works Administration-funded building project, a symphony hall conjoined with a rodeo and convention arena, built under the auspices of Jesse H. Jones, the Houston entrepreneur who was then chairman of the Reconstruction Finance Corp. Unfortunately, Finn's smoothly faceted planar walls of light brown brick, punctured by vertically-aligned window bays, have been compromised by unsympathetic additions to the Music Hall (1955, Hermon Lloyd & W. B. Morgan). Still visible along the parapet lines of Finn's walls is an Art Deco chevron frieze.

515 Rusk Avenue   **A-34**
Federal Office Building and
U. S. Courthouse (1962) Staub, Rather
& Howze, Rustay & Martin, and
Harvin C. Moore

No building in downtown Houston better illustrates the unpredictability of history on questions of taste than the Federal Office Building. It was reviled and abominated from the time of its completion until its inadvertent rehabilitation as a precursor of postmodernism, after the Princeton architect Michael Graves produced a similar—albeit more effusive—design for the Public Services Building in Portland, Oregon in 1980. Since then, the Federal Building has come in for a bit more respect. Architect J. T. Rather, Jr. made the building's grid of four-foot square windows, set in fields of Texas Cordova shell limestone, the principal design element. Red tile covers the building at ground level. The lobby features two pairs of murals, commissioned in 1941 from the foremost Regionalist painters in Texas, Alexandre Hogue and Jerry Bywaters of Dallas. They depict historic (Hogue) and contemporary (Bywaters) scenes on Buffalo Bayou.

800 block Smith Street   A-35
Tranquillity Park (1979) Charles
Tapley Associates

Tranquillity Park was designed to tie
together the architecturally unrelated,
indifferently developed blocks that comprise the Civic Center. Covering three city
blocks (beneath two of which lies an extension of the Civic Center Garage), the park
is aptly characterized by its architect as a
"roof garden." Charles Tapley and Jerry
Lunow's thrusting diagonal walkways,
smoothly-shaped land formations, clustered
cylindrical fountains (the stainless steel
towers house the exhaust stacks for the
underground garage), and frequent grade
changes were intended to imbue the site
with a lively, intense atmosphere, a choice
that has always had its critics. The park's
name is derived from the lunar Sea of
Tranquillity, in commemoration of the fact
that the first word spoken from the moon
to earth was Houston: "Houston, the Eagle
has landed." (A wall-mounted plaque at the
Smith-Rusk intersection gives further
details.) Tranquillity Park offers a superlative prospect point, rare within downtown,
from which to survey the skyline.

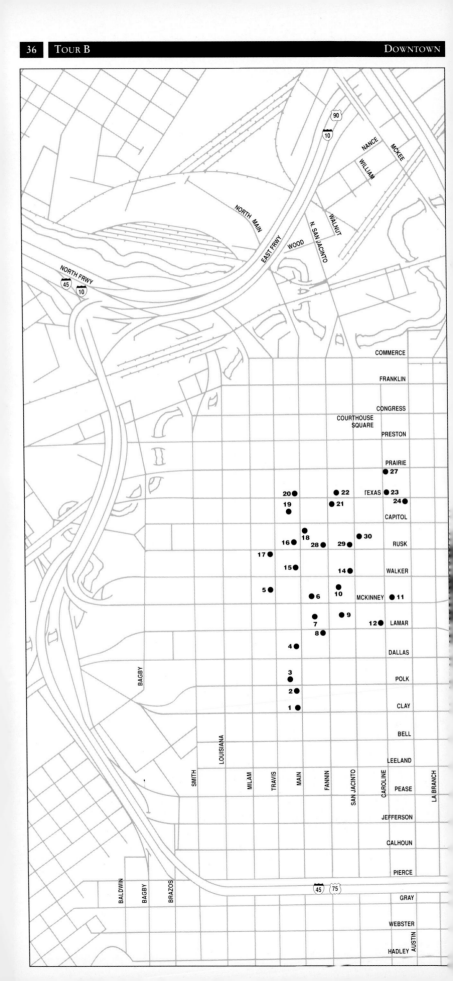

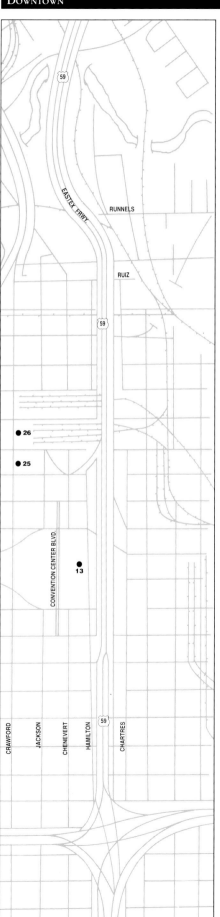

1. 1320 Main Street
2. 1300 Main Street
3. 1212 Main Street
4. 1100 Main Street
5. 910 Travis Street
6. 921 Main Street
7. 1001 Main Street
8. 1010 Lamar Avenue
9. 1001 Fannin Street
10. 909 Fannin Street
11. 1301 McKinney Avenue
12. 1221 Lamar Avenue
13. 1001 Convention Center Boulevard
14. 1121 Walker Avenue
15. 812 Main Street
16. 712 Main Street
17. 808 Travis Street
18. 705 Main Street
19. 601 Travis Street
20. Main Street and Texas Avenue
21. 1114 Texas Avenue
22. 1117 Texas Avenue
23. 1301 Texas Avenue
24. 1314 Texas Avenue
25. 1618 Texas Avenue
26. 501 Crawford Street
27. 1300 Prairie Avenue
28. 720 Fannin Street
29. 720 San Jacinto Street
30. 701 San Jacinto Street

1320 Main Street   **B-1**
First Methodist Church (1910)
Sanguinet, Staats & Barnes

It hardly seems possible today that when
the First Methodist Church moved to this
site from Texas Avenue, across from Texas
Commerce Tower, its new church building
went up amid large Victorian houses in
shaded gardens, set two or three to a block
behind cast iron fences. Now First Methodist sits on the edge of downtown
Houston, the point where continuous
building along Main Street stops and a
daunting new landscape of asphalt-surfaced
parking lots begins. Sanguinet & Staats's
design is not refined, but it is lively. The
tall, stout, corner tower with its attenuated
detail, the big, flat-arched windows filled
with murky stained glass, and the contrast
of brown brick with green tiles, cream terra
cotta, and dark marble decorative panels
make the church a welcome presence.
Urban change came swiftly: when the 6-
story educational building at Travis and
Clay (1929, James Ruskin Bailey) was erected, it was designed for possible future conversion into an office building.

1300 Main Street   **B-2**
Texas National Bank Building (1955)
Kenneth Franzheim

The Texas National Bank Building's quasi-
modern styling demonstrates the desperate
efforts of anxious eclectic architects to
assert stylistic currency in the 1950s. The
results were often problematic: in this
building, the gigantic eggcrate grid of aluminum louvers on the Polk Avenue side of
the building shields the second-floor banking hall from north light. Nevertheless, its
aggressively green curtain wall and rooftop
terraces make the Texas National Bank
Building an amusing period piece. The
building was originally topped with an illu-

minated revolving triangle (the logo of
Conoco, a major tenant) surmounted by a
globe that changed color to forecast the
weather. At 1322 Travis Street, across from
the back of the bank building, is its 10-story
parking garage, also by the Franzheim
office, notable for its sectionally exposed
fire stair.

1212 Main Street   **B-3**
Humble Building [now Main Building]
(1921) Clinton & Russell

The Humble Oil & Refining Co. completed
its first headquarters building at the foot of
the Main Street Victorian residence district,
demonstrating Houston's tendency to grow
by leaps rather than by increments and has-
tening the old residential district's demise.
When new, this 9-story office block must
have looked like a fragment of midtown
Manhattan dropped onto the prairie. The
New York architects Clinton & Russell
detailed the building quite handsomely with
a mixed blend of brown tapestry brick and
unobtrusive classical ornament, executed in
limestone. The principal facade of the
Humble Building faces the side street, Polk
Avenue, to facilitate daylighting and ventilation. Such considerations ceased to be
necessary after 1932, when the Humble
Building became the first office building in
Houston to be equipped with a central air-
conditioning system. At the corner of Main
and Dallas is a pavilion (originally an Air
France ticket exchange) set in a slate-paved
plaza (1963, Wilson, Morris, Crain &
Anderson). From the plaza one may survey
an annex to the Humble Building, the 17-
story Humble Tower (1936, John F. Staub
and Kenneth Franzheim), with its elegant
penthouse lantern in the style of the English
architect E. L. Lutyens. It contained the
cooling towers for the building's central air-
conditioning system.

1100 Main Street   **B-4**
Foley's (1947) Kenneth Franzheim

When Federated Department Stores opened
Foley's in 1947, it was the building of the
hour, the model of the postwar, downtown
American department store. Who would
have guessed that it was to be the last of its
kind? The store's major innovations were
total environmental control (therefore, no
windows except the ground-floor display
windows), interiors by Raymond Loewy
and William T. Snaith that stylishly rationalized the distribution of goods and cus-
tomers, and the 5-story parking garage at
Lamar and Travis, connected to the store by
an underground tunnel. Franzheim's office

detailed the exteriors of the building (which it expanded from 6 to 10 stories in 1957) with great assurance. The Main Street front, divided vertically into inset panels of orange Kasota stone studded with exposed aluminum bolts, appears neither blank nor busy. This is also true of the other three street faces, surfaced with patterned brickwork broken by strategically placed grills. The canopy that shades the sidewalk on all four sides of the building has the up-curved profile, back-lit with neon, that was characteristic in Houston from the late '30s through the early '50s. Despite retrenchment, Foley's has hung on. It is the only department store left in downtown Houston. Across from Foley's at 1111 Main Street is the ex-**Sakowitz Brothers** (1951, Alfred C. Finn), built for Houston's foremost locally-owned specialty store. Surfaced entirely in polished white Vermont marble, it projects an appropriately snob image.

910 Travis Street   **B-5**
Bank of the Southwest Building [now Bank One Building] (1956) Kenneth Franzheim

This 24-story building was the largest office building constructed downtown during the 1950s. Its bulky massing, clunky granite-veneered base, and bland curtain wall (the first all-aluminum curtain wall in Houston) make it clear why the First City National Bank Building and its successors were received locally with such relief. Franzheim's office was *trying* to be modern, as

the shallowly-curved facade facing Travis Street attests. The building initiated the downtown tunnel system with its underground connections to the Ten-Ten Garage and the Commerce Building. The second-floor banking hall, accessible during business hours via the escalators inside the Travis entrance, contains the major work of public art installed in Houston in the '50s: Rufino Tamayo's mural "America" (1956). Franzheim ardently championed the incorporation of works of art in his buildings. During the politically volatile 1950s this could be risky. The bank rejected a huge, already-fabricated cast aluminum sculpture by William Zorach, "The New State of Texas," which was to have been installed in the recess above the Travis entry, because it feared the piece's modernity would provoke public controversy.

921 Main Street   **B-6**
City National Bank Building (1947)
Alfred C. Finn

The 24-story City National Bank Building was the first tall office building constructed downtown after World War II. It looked back to the late 1920s with its stepped massing, its vertically-channelled window bays, and its odd L-shaped plan, which makes the most of very narrow Main Street frontage. As stodgy as it must have appeared at the time of its completion, the building exercises a strong positive influence on its surroundings today. Its determined profile, its piers of tan brick (a Southwestern standard from the 1920s through the '50s), and dark red-striped spandrels stand out against the slick, monochrome, reflective surfaces of the buildings that it is now seen against. The merger of the City National Bank and the First National Bank in 1956 set in motion plans for a new building that would overshadow Finn's building both architecturally and literally.

1001 Main Street   B-7
First City National Bank Building (1960)
Skidmore, Owings & Merrill with Wilson,
Morris, Crain & Anderson

Gordon Bunshaft of the New York office
of SOM designed the new First City
National Bank Building, a 32-story tower
paired with a free-standing aluminum and
glass banking pavilion. First City was the
first high modern office building erected in
downtown Houston. Its crisp, clean, airy
look set the style locally for image-con-
scious tall buildings of the 1960s. The tower
consists of a steel frame "exo-skeleton" (to
use SOM's terminology) faced with polished white Vermont marble (the masonry
reinforcing straps are crude additions of
1989), behind which the gray glass and aluminum curtain wall is recessed for sun
shading, the same strategy that would be
pursued at Humble and Tenneco. The New
York office's touch was not as deft as the
San Francisco office's, however. The tower
does not meet the ground with the stateli-
ness of Tenneco and the steel frame's marble
icing makes it seem diagrammatic and inert.

First City depended on contrast with the
masonry buildings around it for maximum
visual impact. As these have given way to
taller modern buildings, its clarity has come
to seem much less startling. The banking
hall still retains its impact: a lofty, free-
spanned modernist space animated by a
profusion of light and air, and the discreetly
luxurious finishes for which SOM is
famous. First City has the most outstanding
corporate art collection in Houston. Three
important color field paintings by Kenneth
Noland ("Graded Exposures"), Morris
Louis ("Delta Epsilon"), and Helen
Frankenthaler ("Blue North") are displayed
in the tower lobby, visible from Lamar
Avenue.

1010 Lamar Avenue   B-8
1010 Lamar Building (1981) Nasr Penton &
Associates and The Falick/Klein
Partnership

Mohammed Nasr's tutelage under the
Philadelphia architect Romaldo Giurgola is
evident in this 20-story office building,
ingeniously planned for a restricted site.
Nasr manipulated the building's section to
bring daylight in from above, as well as
from slots inset in its blind party walls. In
lieu of a plaza, he introduced a vertically
staged sequence of interior public spaces,
panelled in wood and treated as rooms
rather than an internalized exterior.
Intelligence and modesty pay off handsomely in this easily overlooked building.
Tony Rosenthal's "Bronco" hovers tensely
above the open, basement-level restaurant.

1001 Fannin Street   B-9
First City Tower (1981)
Morris*Aubry Architects

With this 49-story tower, built by First
City Bancorporation of Texas and Urban
Investment & Development Co., designer
Eugene Aubry fused urbanity and sculp-
tural presence to create a pair of triangular
plazas that open out and embrace the sur-
rounding city. Their intensity is reinforced
by First City's extraordinary installation of
art, notably the hypnotic nine-piece series
of bronze totems by Barbara Hepworth,
"Family of Man" (1970), choreographically
arrayed in the plaza at Fannin and Lamar.
In the lobby are Henry Moore's "Two-
Piece Reclining Figure No. 3," facing
Lamar, and Claes Oldenburg's "Inverted Q
Prototype" and Frank Stella's "York
Factory B," facing McKinney.

The building, a slab tautly deflected onto
the diagonal in plan, features a series of vertical notches that rise in a stair-step pattern
across its two angled faces and afford outside
views from the upper-floor elevator lobbies.
The flat plane of mottled gray soapstone,
with which the plaza and the lobby floor
surfaces are paved, the green tinted glass, and
the white aluminum wall panels used externally and internally make the airy, light-filled
lobby feel like a continuation of the plazas

rather than a separate, conditioned space, a sensation maintained at night by the cool white light that suffuses the interior. The result is an exhilarating urban room that encompasses both inside and outside.

909 Fannin Street   **B-10**
Two Houston Center (1974)
William L. Pereira Associates and
Pierce Goodwin Flanagan

In 1970 Texas Eastern Transmission Corp., a gas pipeline company, assembled 33 square blocks stretching from Fannin Street eastward along McKinney and Lamar avenues to the Eastex Freeway. For this 75-acre site, spotted with remnant buildings and surface parking lots, William L. Pereira Associates of Los Angeles prepared a master plan for that perennial 20th-century American urban fantasy, the city-within-the-city. Pereira and his designer, Frank Dimster, proposed a 4-level, 40,000-car parking megastructure that would cover the *entire* site, leaving only street intersections open to the sky. The upper surface of this Texas-sized garage was to be the landscaped promenade deck for a futuristic city of towers. So vast were the dimensions of the complex that it required an elevated loop road, tied directly to the Eastex Freeway, and a people-mover tram line. (The X-bracing visible on the Walker Avenue side of Two Houston Center marks what was to have been the people-mover's terminus.)

Two Houston Center, the only building for which Pereira's office was responsible, took seriously its role as gateway to Houston Center. At the Fannin-McKinney intersection there is a complex entry and ascent sequence (accessible only during business hours): up staggered rows of escalators from circular pavilion to circular pavilion, to the fourth-level promenade, a multilevel concourse through the 44-story tower, and finally to an open-air terrace spanning San Jacinto Street. This is the only segment of deck built according to the Pereira plan. The smooth glazed surfaces and curved corners with which Dimster shaped Two Houston Center's curtain wall reflect the impact of Cesar Pelli and Anthony Lumsden on the Los Angeles architecture scene of the early '70s. Further plans were halted by the recession of the mid-1970s and an unusual public outcry against covering the streets, while Pennzoil

Place upstaged Two Houston Center architecturally. The 46-story **One Houston Center** (1221 McKinney Avenue, 1978, S. I. Morris Associates, Caudill Rowlett Scott, and 3D/International) shows the transition from lavish showmanship to excessive caution. Its cavernous ground-floor lobby, accessible from the plaza facing McKinney, houses the **Museum of Art of the American West** (1984, Caudill Rowlett Scott).

1301 McKinney Avenue   **B-11**
Gulf Tower [now Chevron Tower] (1982)
Caudill Rowlett Scott

CRS's 52-story Gulf Tower, although square in plan, is treated sectionally as an exercise in geometric rotation. Its polished gray granite and silver reflective glass curtain wall is slickly detailed. Pedestrian through-traffic on the skybridge leading from One Houston Center (during business hours) is funneled through triangular scissor arches. Texas Eastern Corp. and Cadillac Fairview Corp., its partner from 1978 to 1986, settled on the air-conditioned skybridges as a compromise between Pereira's vision and economic and political realities. At street level, however, this compromise has an obvious consequence: an urban environment devoid of human presence.

1221 Lamar Avenue   **B-12**
The Park in Houston Center (1983)
Morris*Aubry Architects and
RTKL Associates

The Houston Center skybridge loop comes full circle in the curiously named Park in Houston Center. A two-block long elevated shopping mall spanning Caroline Street is bracketed by a 16-story office slab. This is the only major retail construction downtown since the opening of Sakowitz Brothers in 1951. The Park's 400-foot interior spine, a double-level shopping arcade capped by a glazed half vault, is tracked by a playful screen of freestanding colored pipes—part of it a fountain—designed by Kevin Shanley of The SWA Group. At the east end of the mall, where the bridge connections are made to the Gulf Tower and the 29-story, 430-room **Four Seasons Hotel-Houston Center** at 1300 Lamar Avenue (1981, Caudill Rowlett Scott), is the mall's "anchor," a food court that opens onto a balcony above Austin Street, overlooking Houston Center's zone of expansion and, in the distance, the George R. Brown Convention Center. At the west end are the escalators down to the street-level entrances on San Jacinto.

Like the Gulf Tower, The Park ignores the street. The original design called for a more open and variegated exterior, but as built it is an insulated fortress opening only at the predictably postmodern entrance portals on San Jacinto. Its hostility toward the street, doubly surprising in a retail center, is even more apparent since it faces Morris*Aubry's exemplary plazas at First City Tower. The emphasis on entry via skybridge or the downtown tunnels, both privately owned, limited access systems, suggests a dismaying utopian vision for Houston: a sharply divided world where salaried consumers are confined to secure islands of privilege and control while the streets below are abandoned to an excluded underclass.

servicing requirements for the 1.6 million square foot center. With admirable clarity he joined three, huge, double volume exhibition halls side-by-side, topped them with a third level of exhibition, meeting, and reception spaces, then prefaced the whole with a stacked set of public promenades that open out behind walls of glass, providing convention visitors with panoramic vistas of the downtown skyline. The exteriors express the big scale and straightforward organization of the center with effervescence and wit. Sad to say: in this exemplary public building the general public is not welcome. Arrangements to tour the center can be made, however, through the City of Houston Civic Center office.

In what has become a typical arrangement in recent decades, the site of the George R. Brown Convention Center was given to the City of Houston by Texas Eastern Corp. and Cadillac Fairview Corp. To take up the 3½-block interval between Convention Center Boulevard and Austin Street, Texas Eastern had the Slaney Santana Group and CRS Sirrine, with The Ehrenkrantz Group & Eckstut, lay out a landscape park that incorporates an existing line of live oaks along Lamar, a reminder that this was once the most respectable neighborhood in Victorian Houston. An earlier proposal by Emilio Ambasz (1982) for a representative public place, designed to give visitors a profound and intense experience of being in Houston, was rejected because it contained insufficient income-producing space.

1001 Convention Center Boulevard   **B-13**
George R. Brown Convention Center (1987) Houston Convention Center Architects & Engineers

The George R. Brown Convention Center is an extraordinary sight, whether viewed across the big expanses of cleared real estate characteristic of much of downtown, or from the Eastex Freeway, to which it is connected by purpose-made service ramps, or from the balcony affixed to the east end of The Park in Houston Center. It is big, bold, and very articulately designed by a consortium of architectural firms (Golemon & Rolfe Associates, John S. Chase, Molina & Associates, Haywood Jordan McCowan, and Moseley Associates with Bernard Johnson and 3D/International), under the guidance of Golemon's Mario Bolullo. Bolullo made architecture out of the programmatic, spatial, constructional, and

1121 Walker Avenue   **B-14**
Melrose Building (1952) Hermon Lloyd & W. B. Morgan

The first tall building in Houston to be designed with International Style attributes—applied though they were to a conventional U-plan building—was the 21-story Melrose Building, built by Melvin A. Silverman. A news report of the period stated that it looked to Rio de Janeiro, Mexico City, and Sweden for its modern architectural features. The original turquoise ceramic spandrel panels have been replaced with bronze anodized aluminum; otherwise the exteriors have suffered no major alterations.

812 Main Street   **B-15**
Battelstein's (1950) Finger & Rustay

Vacancy and neglect have not entirely dimmed the sophistication of Joseph Finger and George Rustay's additions to and refacing of the former Battelstein's specialty store. The horizontal strip windows let into the planar limestone facade and the inset second-floor balcony (originally intensively planted) were elements of a high-fashion retail look that also appeared in Kenneth Franzheim's transformation of the old Bender Hotel next door into the **San Jacinto Building** [822 Main Street, 1952] and in Alfred C. Finn's elegant refacing of **The Fashion** (917 Main Street, 1947, now Palais Royal—only the ground-floor storefront remains intact). Together with Foley's and Sakowitz Brothers, these projects date from the last episode of new construction along the Main Street retail and entertainment corridor, the traditional axis of downtown Houston.

712 Main Street   **B-16**
Gulf Building [now Texas Commerce Bank Building] (1929) Alfred C. Finn, Kenneth Franzheim, and J. E. R. Carpenter

The Gulf Building, with its striking chamfered corner bay dominating the intersection at Main and Rusk, is an urbane skyscraper in the best tradition of 1920s American city buildings. Constructed by the real estate magnate, banker, and newspaper publisher Jesse H. Jones, the 36-story, 450-foot high Gulf Building was the tallest skyscraper in Houston from 1929 until 1963. The profile of the tower, which rises

in stages to an attenuated vertical crown, and its prolific crypto-Gothic ornament were obviously inspired by Eliel Saarinen's never-built but much-copied Chicago Tribune Building design of 1922. What makes the Gulf Building so remarkable is that Franzheim and Finn gave substance to their borrowed image by thoroughly integrating the building into downtown Houston. Its six-story, limestone-clad base originally contained the Sakowitz Brothers store at Main and Rusk, several smaller shops, and a vaulted lobby that still extends from Main Street through the building to the majestic banking hall of Jones's National Bank of Commerce (now Texas Commerce Bank). The office tower above, faced with light brown tapestry brick, was the first in Houston to be treated architecturally on all four sides.

The Main Street lobby (accessible during business hours) is faced with polished Sienna travertine and floored in richly patterned terrazzo. It contains a series of murals by the New York painter Vincent Maragliatti depicting Texas historical scenes; the one entitled "Modern Houston" is especially entertaining. The Art Deco decorative detailing in polished Benedict nickel is the finest in Houston. When Franzheim remodelled the three-story high banking hall in 1959, he replicated the Art Deco balcony rails for new openings that he cut into the north wall of the room. He was also responsible for the installation of the stained glass panel over the Travis Street entry. In 1987 Texas Commerce Bank signalled completion of a $50 million certified rehabilitation of the Gulf Building (Sikes Jennings Kelly and CRS Sirrine) by relighting the upper stages of the tower's crown.

808 Travis Street   **B-17**
Niels Esperson Building (1927)
John Eberson

Mellie Keenan Esperson built the 32-story Niels Esperson Building as a memorial to her husband, a Danish-born real estate and minerals speculator. The architect, John Eberson of Chicago, had earlier designed for Niels Esperson the Majestic Theater (1923, demolished 1971) across the street at Rusk and Travis, the most opulent of Houston's three 1920s movie palaces and the one in which Eberson introduced his contribution to the genre, the "atmospheric" ceiling. The Italian Renaissance detail that Eberson liberally applied to the Majestic was also used to give the Esperson Building its architectural identity. Thus, the monumental entrance portal on Travis, framed by a pair of fluted Corinthian columns, and the high arched windows set into rusticated limestone walls and crowned by keystones bearing bucrania—the Roman version of a Texas steer skull—were matched high above the sidewalk with balustraded terraces, urns, obelisks, and the cylindrical, terra cotta-faced tempietto, a classical architectural monument *par excellence*. Mrs. Esperson maintained her offices on the 25th floor, where she and her friends were photographed having a tea party on one of the expansive setback-level terraces.

In 1939 Mrs. Esperson had Eberson and his son Drew add a 19-story annex to the Niels Esperson Building, which she named the **Mellie Esperson Building** (1941). Its Walker Avenue entrance portal and elevator lobby retain some Art Deco detail, although the interior has been altered. Unfortunately, the same is true of the elevator lobby and banking hall of the Niels Esperson Building. Nonetheless, the building's Westminster chimes still ring the hours and Esperson's crowning temple-like memorial is lit nightly, just as it was when the Niels Esperson Building dominated the downtown skyline.

center contains ground-floor shop spaces, an auditorium, a 2,000-car parking garage, five floors of offices, and a health club. Its Main Street sidewalk front is a shopping arcade, faced with a great piano-curved wall of butt-jointed glass inset behind bright red columns. It represents a badly needed vote of confidence in Main Street. Even the parking garage is urbanistically engaged; it affords great mid-level views of downtown to those spiraling up or down its ramps.

705 Main Street   **B-18**
S. H. Kress & Co. Building (1913)
Seymour Burrell

The Kress Building, constructed by S. H. Kress & Co. and occupied by it until 1980, is the only Houston building faced entirely with terra cotta. Burrell, Kress's corporate architect, dexterously used the material to produce a range of classical detail in a bright array of colors. The Kress Building has lost its cornice and its original storefront. The latter was replaced by a spirited postmodern storefront, part of a rehabilitation of the building carried out in 1983 by Ray Bailey Architects. This appropriately brings the architecture of the upper floors back down to the sidewalk.

601 Travis Street   **B-19**
Texas Commerce Center (1982) I. M. Pei & Partners and 3D/International

I. M. Pei and his associate Werner Wandelmaier made a major urban contribution with their design of the 19-story Texas Commerce Center, companion to Pei's Texas Commerce Tower at 600 Travis. The

Main Street and Texas Avenue   **B-20**
Rice Hotel (1913)
Mauran, Russell & Crowell

The Rice is Houston's traditional downtown hotel. It occupies the site where Houston's founders, in 1837, constructed a two-story wooden building that served until 1839 as temporary capitol of the Republic of Texas. This building was demolished and replaced by an ambitious Victorian hostelry, the Capitol Hotel, in 1883. The Capitol gave way in turn to the 17-story, 650-room Rice Hotel, a steel-framed, U-planned skyscraper built by Jesse H. Jones. The St. Louis architects Mauran, Russell & Crowell ornamented the red brick-faced building with ample, cream-colored terra cotta sculptural and architectural decoration. The classically detailed cast iron canopy with which they surrounded the ground floor of the hotel doubled as a terrace for public rooms on the second floor. Early photographs indicate that it was once fitted with rows of rocking chairs from which guests could survey the world at Main and Texas, traditionally considered the center of downtown Houston.

The hotel also provided both a "cooled, washed air ventilating system" and an open-air, pergola-covered roof garden for dining and dancing. Jones added a third wing to the hotel, at Texas and Travis (1926, Alfred C. Finn), and, by 1924, had installed a proto-air-conditioning system in the basement level cafeteria. The hotel's original "French" style interiors were continually altered; notable successors were Kenneth Franzheim's modernistic Empire Room (1938) and Staub, Rather & Howze's 18th-floor addition of the Petroleum Club (1951). The scene of numerous events of local historical significance, the Rice was closed in 1977.

1114 Texas Avenue   **B-21**
Post-Dispatch Building [now 609 Fannin Building] (1926) Sanguinet, Staats, Hedrick & Gottlieb

Despite brutal defacement of the lower two floors, the Post-Dispatch Building remains an authoritative classical presence on Texas Avenue. At 22 stories, it was the tallest reinforced concrete building constructed in Houston during the 1920s. It is faced entirely in limestone, and features monumental screens of Corinthian pilasters at the third and fourth floor levels and in its attic zone. The building was constructed by Ross S. Sterling, publisher of the *Post-Dispatch*, oil man, banker, future governor, and real estate developer, who in the 1920s challenged Jesse H. Jones for entrepreneurial supremacy. Since Jones had staked out Main Street, Sterling took on Texas Avenue. Across Fannin, he and his son-in-law, the architect Wyatt C. Hedrick, were responsible for the last of Houston's '20s style skyscrapers, the 21-story, Art Deco-style **Sterling Building** (1931). Now 608 Texas Tower, the building has lost its storefronts and its crowning pinnacles.

1117 Texas Avenue   **B-22**
Christ Church (1893) Silas McBee with J. Arthur Tempest

Christ Church, the oldest Episcopal parish in the city and now cathedral church of the Diocese of Texas, has occupied this site since 1839. McBee, a commissioner of endowments at the University of the South, was an ecclesiologist and amateur architect. His design for the church and the adjoining guild hall possesses neither the intensity of

High Victorian Gothic architecture nor the archeological precision of the emerging neo-Gothic movement. Yet the building's exceptional molded brickwork, its heavy, stepped, sandstone-capped parapets, and the firmly planted corner tower possess a compelling materiality that compensates for any deficiencies of composition or proportion. The nave is quite broad; consequently, the wide-span, darkly-stained timber trusses dominate the interior. The art glass windows are characteristic of the turn of the century. The Jeanette I. Ennis memorial window (1898), on the Fannin Street side of the nave next to the transept bay, is the one authenticated installation by Tiffany Studios in Houston. The guild hall, behind the arched cloister bays, contains the austere, exquisitely finished Golding Memorial Chapel (1939, William Ward Watkin). At the corner of Texas and San Jacinto is the Latham Memorial Hall (1952, Maurice J. Sullivan); facing Prairie Avenue is an extensive set of contextually deferential additions (1990, Ray Bailey Architects). The cathedral close, which opens onto Texas Avenue behind a traditional iron fence and a fringe of palm trees (a landscape feature essential to English-inspired Victorian buildings in hot, humid climates), is one of the most delightful outdoor spaces downtown.

1301 Texas Avenue   **B-23**
Federal Reserve Bank of Dallas Branch Building (1922) Sanguinet, Staats, Hedrick & Gottlieb

A compact neoclassical block decorated with Adamesque detail, the ex-Federal Reserve Bank Branch Building was stunningly transformed into a small, but monumental, office building for the Crispin Co. by Howard Barnstone in 1973.

1314 Texas Avenue   **B-24**

Petroleum Building [now Great Southwest Building] (1927) Alfred C. Bossom with Maurice J. Sullivan and Briscoe & Dixon

Bossom, a New York architect born and trained in England, proposed the Mayan stepped pyramids of Central America as an indigenous model for the American skyscraper. He gave form to this idea in one of the last buildings he completed before returning to England in 1926, the 22-story Petroleum Building. Built by the oil man J. S. Cullinan, the Petroleum Building has the limestone base and brown brick-faced shaft characteristic of 1920s Houston sky-scrapers. But it also features Mayan relief fig-ures protruding from the spandrel panels above the arched second-floor windows and more abstract pre-Columbian decoration in the spandrels of its three setback stages. Even the ceiling slab of the two-story garage facing Austin Street, which Bossom was pre-scient enough to append to the Petroleum Building, is embossed with a Mayan glyph.

1618 Texas Avenue   **B-25**

Annunciation Catholic Church (1871, 1884-1895) N. J. Clayton

Annunciation Catholic Church, which houses the oldest Roman Catholic parish in Houston, is the distinguished product of a long building history. The nave and the two low towers flanking the tall central tower were completed in 1871. By 1883 sizeable cracks had opened up in the nave walls and the towers were pulling away from the body of the church. The great 19th-century Galveston architect N. J. Clayton was

called in. During the next 11 years he com-pletely reconstructed and expanded the church. All visible fabric, externally and internally, bears the evidence of his involvement.

Clayton bolstered the nave walls with the arched buttresses visible from Texas Avenue. He reroofed the church and braced the front towers with twin entrance pavil-ions and the intense, slender central tower that they bracket. This tower, which exhibits the robust modelling of masonry surfaces that was one of Clayton's hall-marks, is 175 feet high. It was the tallest structure in Houston from its completion in 1889 until 1912. The interior of the church (open only during scheduled ser-vices) is quite lyrical. Clayton developed the figure of the arch into full volumetric expression in the apsidal sanctuary that he added to the nave in 1895. This receives the directional thrust of the vaulted nave ceiling and appears to expand to accommodate it. The spatial complexity of the sanctuary and the sense of upward movement that Clay-ton imparted to its symmetrically com-posed rear wall animate the interior of the church. Numerous minor alterations have been made to the church. The fine exterior brickwork was stuccoed in the early 20th century. On the south side of the nave, near the narthex, is a tiny added bay that con-tains the jewel-like Burkett Memorial Chapel of Our Lady of Perpetual Help (1925, Maurice J. Sullivan), with windows by Charles J. Connick of Boston.

Behind the church, at 608 Jackson Street, is the small, three-story **Annunciation Catholic School** (1906, N. J. Clayton). It exhibits exceptional molded brickwork, another Clayton characteristic. More restrained is **Incarnate Word Academy**, on the same block at 1611 Capitol Avenue (1905, N. J. Clayton). This is one of three buildings that Clayton designed for the girls' school, the oldest educational institu-tion in Houston. Unfortunately, the finest of these, the Auditorium (1899) at Jackson and Capitol, was pulled down in 1978. From Capitol Avenue, one has an especially good view of the downtown skyline.

501 Crawford Street   **B-26**

Union Station (1911) Warren & Wetmore

The construction of new union passenger and freight stations by the Houston Belt & Terminal Railway Co. between 1906 and 1911 drastically altered this section of Houston's Third Ward and precipitated its eventual annexation to the central business district. Warren & Wetmore, the New York architects best known for Manhattan's

Grand Central Terminal, produced a block-long station building with a high limestone base, surmounted originally by a red brick-faced attic story and a wide, flat, bracketed cornice. Because the need for office space was greater than had been anticipated, two extra floors were added to the building in 1912. Capped by a heavy cornice and balustraded parapet, this addition subverts the original compositional scheme and gives the building a blander appearance than it initially possessed. Finishes and details, however, are superlative. Windows sunk into two-story vertical channels are separated by steel spandrel panels decorated with exposed bolts in a sort of Beaux-Arts version of high tech. The three-bay Doric portico centered on the Crawford Street front of the station is a noble porte-cochere, vaulted with a ceiling of acoustically resounding Guastavino tile. The double volume waiting rooms inside, also similarly vaulted, were lit by the thermal windows visible above the porticos. Passenger service was discontinued in 1974. The interiors have been subdivided and are no longer accessible by the public.

capture the north light. These buildings also contained the offices of cotton exporters. Behind the Cotton Exchange, at 515 Caroline Street, is the charming, two-story, Italian-Mediterranean style showroom built for the **National Cash Register Co.** (1929, Joseph Finger).

720 Fannin Street   **B-28**
Texas State Hotel (1929) Joseph Finger

Joseph Finger emerged as something of a specialist in the design of multistory hotels during the boom years of the 1920s. The 16-story Texas State Hotel was one of his biggest commissions. As was typical, it featured historically derived decoration (in this case, of Spanish Plateresque origin) at the base level and the summit. Sandwiched between these layers of terra cotta were sheer walls of brown tapestry brick.

1300 Prairie Avenue   **B-27**
Houston Cotton Exchange and Board of Trade Building (1924) Sanguinet, Staats, Hedrick & Gottlieb

Despite the Cotton Exchange's importance in the economy of 19th and early 20th-century Houston, it erected a very straightforward and unpretentious 16-story office building to replace its Victorian exchange. Yet the limestone-faced base, with its paired Adamesque pilasters and double-height arched entrance portals on Prairie and Caroline, imbues the building with an urbane and decorous presence that still prevails. Metal-framed casement windows in the central bays of the Prairie Avenue facade provided clear north light for grading cotton. The attic zone, elaborately ornamented with cast concrete classical detail, originally contained the vaulted trading room of the Cotton Exchange. Wedged into the crook of the L-plan building is a two-story parking garage, one of the first to be structurally integrated into a Houston office building. From the Prairie-Caroline intersection one can see skylights atop the **Westheimer Building** (1217 Prairie) and the **Cotton Building** (502 Caroline), skewed to

720 San Jacinto Street   **B-29**
Texas Co. Building (1915)
Warren & Wetmore

The most princely of Houston's early 20th-century skyscrapers, the 13-story Texas Co. Building is an exceptionally fine example of classical architectural detail applied to a multistory office block. It was constructed to house the regional offices of Texaco, the first major oil company to establish its headquarters in Houston. The building makes its most notable contribution at ground level, where sidewalks are sheltered beneath grand limestone arcades supported on paired limestone columns armored with bronze bumper guards bearing the Texaco star. The arcades are vaulted with Guastavino tiles. At the top of the building another screen of paired columns is wrapped around its street faces. The Texaco Building was extended by three bays along San Jacinto Street by Warren & Wetmore in 1936. Kenneth Franzheim and Charles S.

Chase III added the stylistically respectful annex at 1111 Rusk in 1960 and S. I. Morris Associates was responsible for the limestone-faced garage of 1975. Except for the reglazing of windows and transfer of the main entry to the annex, the Texas Co. Building has been maintained externally without major alteration.

701 San Jacinto Street **B-30**
U.S. Post Office Building [now Sam Houston Station, U.S.P.O.] (1911)
James Knox Taylor, Supervising Architect of the Treasury

The U.S. Post Office and the Texas Co. Building mark this block of San Jacinto Street as a small but triumphant outpost of classical culture and a testament to the power of the City Beautiful movement at the turn of the century. The office of the Supervising Architect of the Treasury in Washington, D. C., headed by the Minneapolis architect James Knox Taylor, produced designs that adhered to consistently high architectural and constructional standards for hundreds of federal government buildings throughout the nation. Other American cities have near duplicates of Houston's elegant, limestone-faced, 18th-century French style post office. At the time of the building's construction, Rusk Avenue had just begun to relinquish its 60-year role as one of Houston's most elite residential avenues, where pillared Greek revival houses and turreted Victorian mansions sat securely in a landscape of mature domestic gardens. The lone street trees on the block just east of the post office, marking the site of the Houston Academy, the town's first public school, are the only natural features in what has become a barren asphalt prairie.

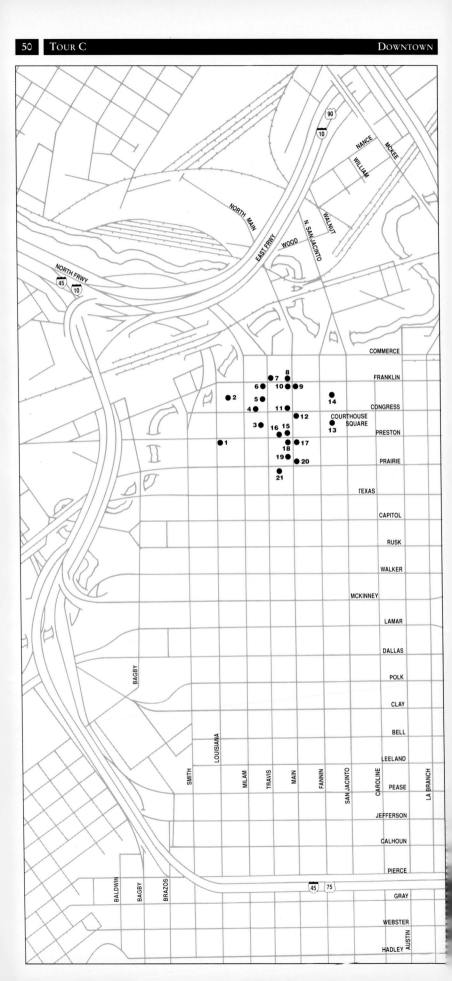

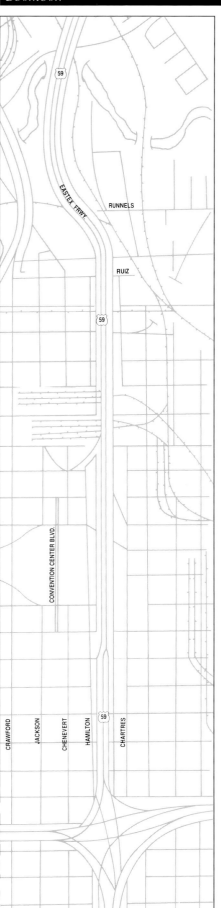

1. 401 Louisiana Street
2. 200 block Louisiana Street
3. 300 block Travis Street
4. 813 Congress Avenue
5. 214-218 Travis Street
6. 202 Travis Street
7. 913 Franklin Avenue
8. 116-120 Main Street
9. 201 Main Street
10. 202 Main Street
11. 218-220 Main Street
12. 301 Main Street
13. Courthouse Square
14. 1115 Congress Avenue
15. 320 Main Street
16. 911 Preston Avenue
17. 405 Main Street
18. 402 Main Street
19. 412 Main Street
20. 421 Main Street
21. 910 Prairie Avenue

401 Louisiana Street   **C-1**
Armor Building [now Hogg Building]
(1921) Barglebaugh & Whitson

Hogg Brothers, soon to develop the garden
suburb of River Oaks, built the eight-story
Armor Building as a combination auto
showroom and office building. The street
faces of the building acknowledge its reinforced concrete frame construction with a
simple grid of vertical piers and horizontal
spandrels, infilled with steel-sash industrial
windows. The architect, Charles Erwin
Barglebaugh of Dallas, had worked for both
Frank Lloyd Wright and Walter Burley
Griffin just after the turn of the century.
The ornamental panels set into the building's piers are in the style of Wright's mentor, the progressive Chicago architect Louis
H. Sullivan. On top of the building is a
penthouse, originally occupied by Hogg
Brothers and described at the time of the
building's completion as a "bungalow in the
clouds." Here Will and Mike Hogg hung
their Frederic Remington paintings above
their sister Ima's collection of 17th and
18th-century American furniture. In 1978
the Hogg Building was restored externally
to its original appearance by Harvin
Moore-Barry Moore Architects.

200 block Louisiana Street   **C-2**
Texas Commerce Motor Bank (1983) I. M.
Pei & Partners and 3D/International

A sleekly finished array of drive-in banking
stations configured in a pinwheel arrangement. This is where Harry Dean Stanton
spotted Nastassja Kinski in Wim Wenders's
"Paris, Texas" (1984).

300 block Travis Street   **C-3**
Market Square

Market Square is one of two public squares
that the brothers Augustus C. Allen and
John K. Allen set aside in their 1836 survey
of the City of Houston. From 1840 to 1929
it was the site of the city's public market
and from 1841 to 1939 site of the city hall.
Three ornate Victorian City Hall and
Market House structures occupied the

square between 1873 and 1960; all were
destroyed by fire. Throughout the 19th
century and into the first decades of the
20th, Market Square was the hub of retail
grocery, baking, and butchering operations
in Houston. The square was surrounded by
two and three-story brick buildings, most
constructed in the decade following the
Civil War. The east side of Travis Street still
gives an indication of the scale and architectural detail once characteristic of this neighborhood.

In 1986 DiverseWorks and the
Downtown Houston Association joined in
an effort to transform the square. Two
California sculptors, Doug Hollis and
Richard Turner, were commissioned to
work with three Texas artists, painter
Malou Flato, photographer Paul Hester,
and sculptor James Surls, to effect the transformation. What they propose is a square
within the square, paved with the history of
Houston—the rubble and fragments of its
demolished buildings. The proposal is a
memorial to the passage of time and a celebration of the everyday importance that
Market Square held for Houstonians.

813 Congress Avenue   **C-4**
Kennedy Bakery Building
[now La Carafe] (1861)

The narrow, two-story Kennedy Bakery
Building, one of the three oldest buildings
in downtown Houston and the only one
that has not undergone significant alteration, retains such notable details as the
rudimentary classical architrave that crowns
its front door and the decorative brickwork
visible in its cornice. The interior of what is
now a pub is dark, intimate, and full of
character. Its ground-floor window looks
out toward the towers of downtown, offer-
ing a contrast of old and new. Next to the
Kennedy Bakery, at 815-823 Congress, is

the three-story **Kennedy's Corner Building**, constructed at the same time as the bakery by John Kennedy, an Irish-born entrepreneur. Badly damaged by fire in 1888, Kennedy's Corner got a Victorian refacing. Succeeding epochs have not failed to leave their architectural traces on its two street faces.

214-218 Travis Street   **C-5**
W. L. Foley Dry Goods Co. Building
(1889) Eugene T. Heiner

The *Houston Daily Post* described the Foley dry goods store as "magnificent" and "palatial" at the time of its construction. The three-story building has two bays; the slightly lower third bay at 220 Travis is a refacing of part of Kennedy's Corner. Heiner detailed the store with High Victorian "constructive" ornament, including vertical incisions, sunk panels, frieze bands, and arched window heads. The building is of heavy timber construction, faced with yellow brick and limestone trim. It was seriously damaged by fires in 1976 and 1989. The sidewalk canopies and high-set curbs were once typical of downtown Houston. They tie the Foley Building seamlessly into the adjoining **Hermann Estate Building** (1917, F. S. Glover & Son) at 204-212 Travis Street.

202 Travis Street   **C-6**
Houston Cotton Exchange and Board of
Trade Building (1884) Eugene T. Heiner

This is Houston's outstanding High Victorian building. Erected by the Houston Cotton Exchange to house its quarters, the building sits, Chicago-like, on a high, raised basement. Heiner, one of Houston's foremost 19th-century architects, designed the Cotton Exchange as a vibrant High Victorian version of a Renaissance palazzo. But as American architects of the 1870s and '80s were wont to do, he expressively distorted conventional classical details to elicit contrasts of shape, color, texture, and depth. Hard, red, Philadelphia pressed brick, much of it molded and all of it laid

with the thin mortar joints typical of late 19th-century construction, is interspersed with sunk panels of buff brick and incised, carved, or molded ornamental details of limestone. Originally only three stories high, the building was enlarged with the addition of a fourth story in 1907. At that time the exchange floor was moved to the first floor of the building; it occupied the room at the corner of Travis and Franklin whose painted ceiling is visible through the big plate glass windows. The Cotton Exchange Building was rehabilitated in 1971 by Graham B. Luhn. It is now an office building.

913 Franklin Avenue   **C-7**
Southern Pacific Building (1911)
Jarvis Hunt

The Renaissance palazzo was also the model used by the Chicago architect Jarvis Hunt for this 9-story regional headquarters of the Southern Pacific Railway Co. Hunt's Progressive interpretation is so abstract that few overtly classical details are visible: the arabesques that frame the entrance portals and the horizontal bands of moldings staged at intervals between the second-floor window sills and the cornice. Patterned brick pendants and ornamental panels of brick and tile in the building's attic zone take the place of sculptural ornament. The Southern Pacific Building and the Texas Co. Building on San Jacinto illustrate the era's contrasting attitudes toward the use of conventional historical detail in tall buildings: progressive Chicago versus eclectic New York. The L-plan building is of reinforced concrete frame construction. Like several other contemporary tall buildings in Houston, it was originally equipped with a refrigerated air ventilation system. The building is still occupied by the Southern Pacific Transportation Co.

116-120 Main Street   **C-8**
Commercial National Bank Building
(1904) Green & Svarz

This six-story brown brick building, with

its rounded corner bay, was one of the first in Houston to display the return to classical architecture that succeeded the picturesque eclecticism of the Victorian era. Especially notable are the trio of colossal-arched openings centered on the Franklin Avenue and Main Street facades. This was the first skyscraper built in the financial district on lower Main Street. The building is of cage construction: load-bearing masonry perimeter walls envelop an interior steel frame.

201 Main Street   **C-9**
First National Bank Building (1905, 1909, 1925) Sanguinet & Staats

From 1866 until 1956 the First National Bank (now First City National Bank), the oldest chartered bank in Houston, occupied this corner. In 1904 the bank replaced its small, two-story building with the first steel-framed skyscraper built in Houston. This eight-story building was a long and narrow sliver. Its Main Street frontage included only the 25-foot wide corner bay at Main and Franklin; the additional three bays along Main Street were not added until 1909. In 1925 a third major addition carried the building through the block to Fannin Street. A double-height banking hall, installed in 1925, runs the entire depth of the building. Its detailing is rather coarse in comparison to the opulently classical, rusticated exterior, where the building's limestone base and buff brick, stone-trimmed shaft hold the Main-Franklin corner with authority. All three phases of the bank's building program were carried out by the Houston branch office of the Fort Worth architects, Sanguinet & Staats. Marshall R. Sanguinet and Carl G. Staats were the skyscraper kings of early 20th-century Texas.

202 Main Street   **C-10**
Houston National Bank Building (1928) Hedrick & Gottlieb

The last of the bank buildings constructed in the Main Street financial district was this formidable neoclassical block. Wyatt C. Hedrick, the Fort Worth architect who succeeded to Sanguinet & Staats's practice in 1926, and his Houston partner, R. D. Gottlieb, made up in massiveness and scale what they gave up in potential height. Rusticated limestone walls bracket screens

of fluted Doric columns on the building's main facades. High steel sash windows behind these screens are shielded by tall bronze railings. The architrave above the columns and the frieze and cornice atop the building are ornamented with sculptural decoration. The interior (not accessible) is as awesome as the exterior: the ceiling of the 56-foot high banking hall is a single vault finished with mosaic tile murals. Variegated marble floor, counter, and column surfaces are all intact. Visible from the rear, on Travis Street, is a miniature temple on the building's roof—it framed the bank's original proto-air-conditioning equipment. Hedrick clearly gave his father-in-law, Ross S. Sterling, the bank's chairman, the most that money could buy.

218-220 Main Street   **C-11**
Union National Bank Building (1912) Mauran, Russell & Crowell

The Main Street base of this 12-story, reinforced concrete framed building is detailed like a Roman commemorative arch, with freestanding Corinthian columns of Bedford limestone supporting ressauted architraves. The keystones above the arched ground-floor openings are carved with the likeness of Mercury, Roman god of commerce (and trickery). The office floors above the two-story base are faced with brown brick and topped with screens of alternating piers and pilasters. On the Congress Avenue face of the building, all the detail is flatter and more compressed. Mauran, Russell & Crowell were St. Louis architects with an extensive Texas practice. Most of their Houston work was done for Jesse H. Jones, who was a director of the Union National Bank.

301 Main Street **C-12**
Sweeney, Coombs & Fredericks Building
(1889) George E. Dickey

This narrow, three-story building is one of
the two surviving Houston works of
George Dickey, the city's most spirited
Victorian architect. The Main Street facade
features a corner turret, arched upper-floor
windows, molded brickwork, and thick,
flat, "constructive" ornament. Its intensity
contrasts so jarringly with the plain
Congress Avenue flank that preservationists
speculate Dickey reused parts of the W. A.
Van Alstyne Building (constructed on this
site in 1861) in the Sweeney building.
Rehabilitated by Welton Becket &
Associates in 1968, the Sweeney, Coombs &
Fredericks Building was almost demolished
in 1974 by the Harris County Commissioners Court to provide a site for the
adjacent, nine-story **Harris County
Administration Building** (1978, Kenneth
Bentsen Associates and Brodnax Phenix
Associates). The court was persuaded to
spare the building and it now provides
office space for the county engineer. Behind
it, at 1016 Congress Avenue, is the **Pillot
Building** (c. 1860), once a three-story brick
business block. All that remains of the original is the ground-floor cast iron store
front. The rest is a reconstruction (1990,
Morris*Architects with Barry Moore
Architects).

Courthouse Square **C-13**
Harris County Courthouse [now Harris
County Civil Courts Building] (1910)
Lang & Witchell

The county courthouse, either domed or
turreted and set in a centrally located, tree-
shaded square, is a recurring feature of the
Texas landscape. The Allen brothers
reserved this block of ground, two blocks
east of Market Square, as the site for a

county courthouse and it has been occupied
by the government of Harris County since
1837, when the congress of the Republic of
Texas designated Houston as the county
seat. This domed, classical courthouse is the
fifth to stand in the square. Although
superseded by a newer courthouse in 1952,
it remains the focal symbol of county government. Lang & Witchell, Dallas's most
prolific architects at the turn of the century,
won out over local competitors for the job
in 1907. A dome and columns were speci-
fied by the commissioners court. Lang &
Witchell's progressive, Chicago-trained
designer, Charles Erwin Barglebaugh,
revealed his preference for something less
conventional in the Wrightian detailing of
the piers between windows in the attic
story.

1115 Congress Avenue **C-14**
Harris County Family Law Center (1969)
Wilson, Morris, Crain & Anderson

This seven-story office and courtroom
building is WMCA's homage to Skidmore,
Owings & Merrill's American Republic
Insurance Co. Building in Des Moines. The
upper floors are constructed of widely can-
tilevered, prestressed, precast tees, neatly
balanced on pyramidally shaped steel
hinges atop the ground-floor columns.
Window glass is inset deeply within the
concrete frame. This is the most handsome
modern addition to the complex of county
government buildings that cluster around
Courthouse Square. From Walter A.
Quebedeaux Plaza at Congress and San
Jacinto, the original site of the Nichols-
Rice-Cherry House now in Sam Houston
Park, one can look eastward along
Congress and Franklin to Houston's most
elite neighborhood of the 1850s, Quality
Hill. It now consists almost entirely of sur-
face parking lots.

320 Main Street **C-15**
Kiam Building (1893) H. C. Holland

Ed Kiam's clothing store set a new standard
in Houston. Its five-story red brick build-

ing, featuring a bull-nose corner bay and a concave entrance alcove, ushered in the Main Street era of downtown urbanity that would prevail through the middle of the next century. Holland was an obscure English-born architect who practiced only briefly in Houston. He carefully differentiated the end bay on Preston Avenue to mark the access point to the upper office floors. He also battered the thick masonry piers along this side of the building, highlighting their structural role. The Kiam Building was restored in 1981 by Barry Moore Architects.

911 Preston Avenue   **C-16**
Ritz Theater (1926) William Ward Watkin

Houston's three great movie palaces of the 1920s—the Majestic, the Metropolitan, and Loew's State—were demolished in the 1970s. From that era, this side-street theater alone remains. Watkin's office gave it a delicately ornamented classical facade, finished in stucco. Rehabilitated in 1990 by Kirk Eyring with Barry Moore.

405 Main Street   **C-17**
Scanlan Building (1909)
D. H. Burnham & Co

The 11-story Scanlan Building was the tallest in Houston at the time of its completion. It was built by Kate Scanlan and her sisters as a memorial to their father, T. H. Scanlan, an Irish-born real estate and utilities investor who had been Houston's Reconstruction-era mayor. Miss Scanlan retained Daniel H. Burnham of Chicago to design the building, which exhibits finely-crafted classical ornament at its base, "Chicago" windows (a fixed pane of plate glass between two operable sash windows) on the second floor, and a series of terra cotta wreaths stationed between attic windows. Its broadly projecting roof-top cor-

nice is now gone. On this site Sam Houston's official residence, grandly called the President's House, was completed in 1838. After the national capital was transferred to the town of Austin in 1839, the President's House became a retail store.

402 Main Street   **C-18**
Public National Bank Building (1925)
James Ruskin Bailey

During the 1920s the financial district began to slide southward up Main Street as several new bank buildings, among them the Public National Bank, were constructed outside the confines of the old Victorian banking corridor. This is a restrained, classically detailed office block. Arched windows mark the ground floor and what was originally the topmost floor, which is ringed by a cantilevered balcony. Bailey added the setback ninth floor to the building in 1928. The clock that projects off the Main-Preston corner of the building was once a standard amenity in American downtowns.

412 Main Street   **C-19**
State National Bank Building [now State National Building] (1924) Alfred C. Finn

The 12-story State National Bank Building is a slender infill tower. Its rooftop penthouse is capped by a tile-roofed lantern and flanked front and back by broad terraces. The rusticated pink granite base was reconstructed when the building was rehabilitated in 1982 by Stuart L. Rothman.

421 Main Street   C-20
Burns Building (1883) E. J. Duhamel

One of the oldest buildings on Main Street
is the three-story Burns Building, which
now anchors its corner site in lonely isolation. The wide variety of arch configura-
tions visible above its second and
third-floor window openings is characteristic of the architect, Edward J. Duhamel,
who worked intermittently in Galveston,
Houston, and Austin between the middle
1870s and the late 1880s. The Burns
Building's facades exemplify American
High Victorian architecture at its least
inhibited. They were restored in 1965 by
Wirtz, Calhoun, Tungate & Jackson.

910 Prairie Avenue   C-21
Henry Brashear Building (1882)
Eugene T. Heiner

Tucked in behind the Rice Hotel is another
Victorian survivor, a narrow, but exuberant,
three-story commercial building. The fine
stucco-surfaced facade and cast iron cornice
again reveal Heiner's predilection for a
"constructive" deconstruction of
Renaissance classicism. Next door to the
Brashear Building are the **Scholibo
Building** (921 Prairie, 1880) and the
Stegeman Building (914 Prairie, c. 1877).

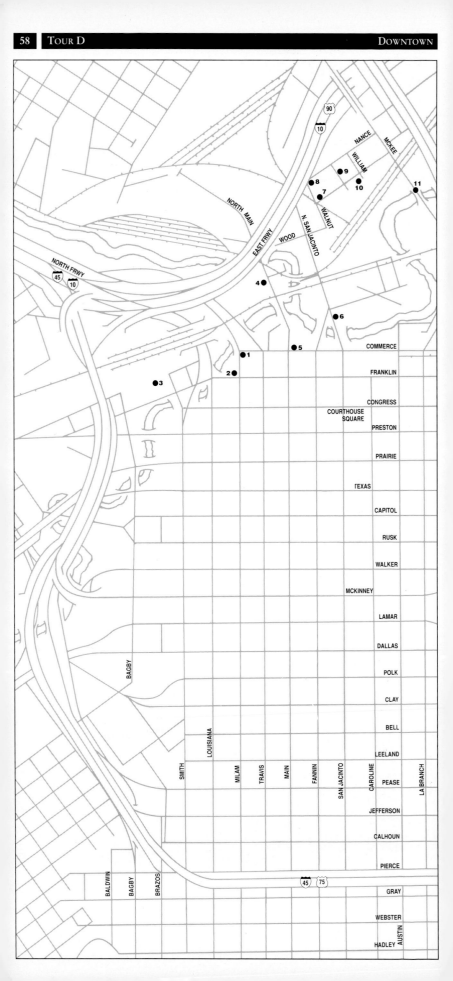

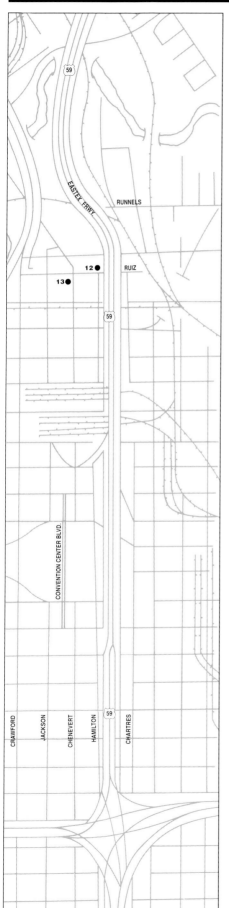

1. 800-806 Commerce Avenue
2. 719-721 Franklin Avenue
3. 401 Franklin Avenue
4. 1 North Main Street
5. 1000 block Commerce Avenue
6. 610 North San Jacinto Street
7. 802 Walnut Street
8. 1200 Rothwell Street
9. 1302 Nance Street
10. 701-711 William Street
11. McKee Street and Buffalo Bayou
12. 1901 Ruiz Street
13. 15 North Chenevert Street

800-806 Commerce Avenue   **D-1**
Siewerssen and Hogan-Allnoch Buildings
(1894 and 1906)

The little Sieverssen Building and the
Hogan-Allnoch Building, with its wide-
spanning arches, were conjoined in a rehabilitation (1975, Wilson/Crain/Anderson/
Reynolds) that transformed them into law
offices.

719-721 Franklin Avenue   **D-2**
Magnolia Cafe Building (1911)
Cooke & Co.

A rhythmically bracketed cornice and the
upswept corner parapet mark the Magnolia
Cafe Building, originally part of an extensive complex of brewery buildings that
spanned Buffalo Bayou. The cafe was located on the second floor; its handsome
Edwardian decor is still intact. Next door
to the cafe building, at 110 Milam Street, is
the company's ruined three-story cold storage and packing building (1906, Cooke &
Co.). Its rear section was washed away in
the flood of 1935 and it has stood in this
condition ever since.

401 Franklin Avenue   **D-3**
U. S. Post Office (1962) Wilson, Morris,
Crain & Anderson

Nominally a part of the Civic Center, the
central post office lies on the north side of
Buffalo Bayou, isolated from its environs
by street intersections, freeways, parking
lots, and railroad tracks. The five-story
administration building, a slab set on
columns and faced with white, precast con-

crete fins, projects the clean, detached look
of '60s modern American architecture.

1 North Main Street   **D-4**
Merchants & Manufacturers Building [now
University of Houston-Downtown] (1930)
Giesecke & Harris

This enormous 11-story building, designed
by a firm of Austin architects in the modernistic Perpendicular style, was constructed to serve as the Merchandise Mart of
Houston. Yet even before it was completed,
its fate was sealed economically by the
flood of 1929 and the stock market crash
five months later. Since 1974 the M&M
Building has been the downtown campus of
the University of Houston. Charles Tapley
Associates contributed the jazzy exterior
repainting and also converted the south
parking deck into a terrace, with pedestrian
access to Buffalo Bayou down below.

1000 block Commerce Avenue   **D-5**
Allens Landing Park (1967)
W. H. Linnstaedter

Through the early 1900s this was Houston's
public wharf area, the "foot of Main
Street." Across Buffalo Bayou, beneath the
Houston & Texas Central Railway trestle,
White Oak Bayou flows into Buffalo.
Houston's founders, Augustus C. and John
K. Allen, claimed this confluence of water-
ways as the head of navigation on Buffalo
Bayou. Upon this claim they staked the
future of their townsite speculation. At this
point, Main Street is deflected off-axis to
cross the bayou on the high, arched **Main
Street Viaduct** (1913, F. L. Dormant, City
Engineer), the largest single-arch concrete
span (150 feet) in Texas at the time of its
construction.

610 North San Jacinto Street   **D-6**
Peden Co. Building (1930)
James Ruskin Bailey

One of the last major buildings constructed
in the Fifth Ward "factory district" was this
four-story retail store and administration
building for the Peden Iron & Steel Co.,

whose extensive wholesale hardware operations were located across Baker Street in the one-story building with arched openings (700 North San Jacinto St., 1906, C. H. Page & Co.). The Peden Building is also in the modernistic Perpendicular style. Like other buildings along the bayou, it was constructed with additional floor levels below the street that could be served by commercial barge traffic.

1302 Nance Street   **D-9**
Erie City Iron Works Warehouse (1909)

This showroom and warehouse for a wholesale machinery business is of arcuated brick bearing wall construction, which shows to special advantage at the chamfered entrance bay and in the array of full-arched openings on the Sterrett Street side of the building.

802 Walnut Street   **D-7**
Patrick Transfer Co. Warehouse [now Texas Studios Building] (1911)

Faced with red brick laid up in decorative panels, this solid-looking building was constructed at the height of the building boom that transformed this section of Fifth Ward, where all the major rail lines entering Houston intersected.

701-711 William Street   **D-10**
James Bute Co. Warehouse (1910)
Olle J. Lorehn

Still occupied by the paint manufacturing and sales company for which it was built, this four-story brick building was the largest warehouse in Houston at the time of its completion.

1200 Rothwell Street   **D-8**
Henry Henke's Fifth Ward Store Building [now North San Jacinto Cafe Building] (1883)

A rare Victorian survivor in this section of Fifth Ward, this branch of the Henke grocery store on Market Square predated development of the factory district.

McKee Street and Buffalo Bayou   **D-11**
McKee Street Bridge (1932) James Gordon McKenzie, City Bridge Engineer

During his tenure as bridge engineer for the City of Houston, McKenzie put the ingenuity back into engineering. The undulating concrete girders bracketing the roadway expressively reveal the distribution of structural forces in their shapes, moment curves that rise above the piers beneath the roadway. The artist Kirk Farris coordinated the colorizing of the bridge and extensive landscape improvements to both the north and south banks of the bayou in 1985.

1901 Ruiz Street   **D-12**
J. L. Jones Warehouse (1930)
J. W. Northrop, Jr.

J. W. Northrop, Jr., best known for his
numerous houses in River Oaks and the
South End, designed this warehouse in a
slightly streamlined version of his characteristic neo-Georgian style.

15 North Chenevert Street   **D-13**
National Biscuit Co. Building (1910)
A. G. Zimmerman

This five- and six-story, brick and terra
cotta-faced, concrete-framed building is the
most monumental in the Second Ward
wholesale district, made more so by its corner stair tower. Zimmerman, Nabisco's corporate architect, produced similar
structures for the firm in Kansas City and
New York. Next door, at the corner of
Chenevert and Commerce Avenue, is
Nabisco's first production plant in Houston
(1902, Olle J. Lorehn). Its ashlar-faced
stone trim was a popular local decorative
feature at the turn of the century.

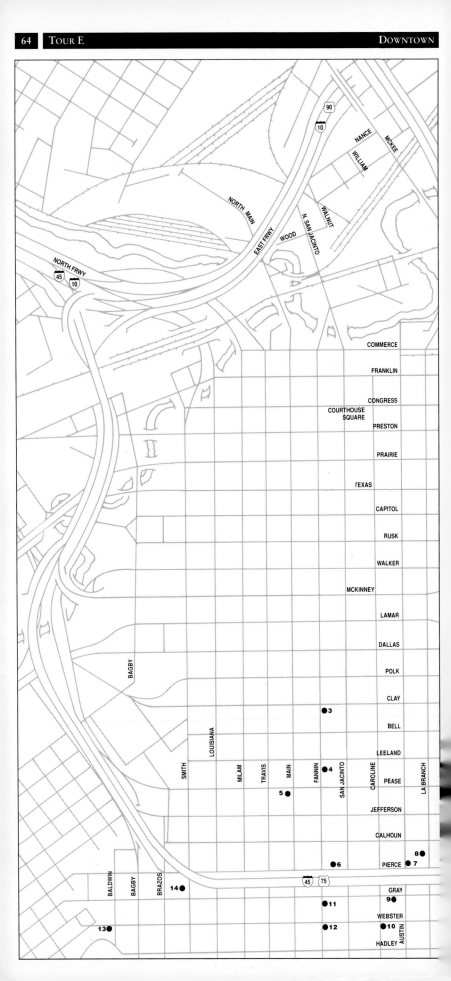

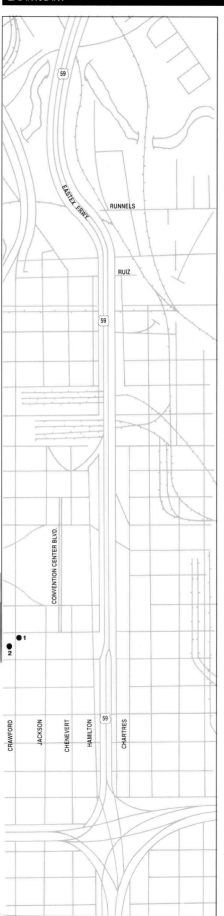

1. 1307 Crawford Street
2. 1313 La Branch Street
3. 1401 Fannin Street
4. 1617 Fannin Street
5. 1700 Main Street
6. 1111 Pierce Avenue
7. 1401 Pierce Avenue
8. 1902-1920 LaBranch Street
9. 1310 Gray Avenue
10. 2201 Caroline Street
11. 2111 Fannin Street
12. 2201 Fannin Street
13. 2204 Baldwin Street
14. 2006 Smith Street

1307 Crawford Street   **E-1**
Fire Station #8 (1968) Rapp Tackett Fash

Gerald Tackett's tautly detailed planes of
brown brick, penetrated by carefully proportioned panes of glazing and inset openings, demonstrate that even a fire station in
a decimated neighborhood can exert considerable architectural presence. Tackett's
design harmonizes with the adjacent
Energy Control Center, making a little
enclave of civic-spirited modern architecture along this formerly fashionable, residential thoroughfare.

1313 LaBranch Street   **E-2**
Houston Lighting & Power Co. Energy
Control Center (1972) Caudill Rowlett
Scott with Robert O. Biering

This is literally a high-profile building, with
its jutting cantilever bays (45 feet on the
Crawford Street side, 20 feet on the
LaBranch side) of poured-in-place, sand-
blasted concrete. Housed within the
Crawford bay is HL&P's central switching
and tracking operations room, where elec-
trical power supply to the entire city is
monitored and controlled. Industrial
designers Robert P. Gersin Associates
designed both this room and the 28-passen-
ger, glass-enclosed elevator gondola (visible
from Polk Avenue) that travels between the
lobby and the operations room. The
Energy Control Center was planned as a
public facility where the business of energy
supply was made visible. The high-ceilinged
lobby, minimally enclosed with glass walls
stiffened with glass mullions, was to have
been an exhibition area. Sadly, the corporation lost its nerve and the building has
never been used for these purposes. As a
result, it looks perpetually vacant. From the
plaza at Crawford and Polk one can see
HL&P's Polk Avenue substation, which CRS
turned into a vividly colored energy garden.

1401 Fannin Street   **E-3**
Masonic Temple Building (1924)
Alfred C. Finn

Finn's three-story Masonic Temple embod-

ies a degree of civility that in the 1920s was
taken for granted, yet today seems almost
unattainable. The wrought iron hardware at
the main entrance contributes to its self-
assured urbanity, which was reinforced
with a rehabilitation in 1981. Trying very
hard to do in the '80s what the Masonic
Temple achieved so effortlessly in the 1920s
is M. Nasr & Partners' 11-story **Fannin
Garage** (1112 Clay Avenue, 1984), faced in
granite aggregate precast concrete.

1617 Fannin Street   **E-4**
Houston House (1966) Charles M.
Goodman Associates with Irving R. Klein
& Associates

The Washington, D. C., architect Charles
M. Goodman's 33-story apartment slab,
with 400 units stacked atop a parking
garage and ground-level retail space, represents an effort to lure middle-income residents back downtown. Typologically it
appears better suited to a suburban location; one can hardly imagine a neighborhood of such buildings. The Houston
House has benefitted considerably from
removal of its original black-painted finish.

1700 Main Street   **E-5**
Beaconsfield Apartments (1911) A. C. Pigg

Alonzo C. Pigg was not a particularly brilliant interpreter of classical architecture.
Nonetheless, this 8½-story, 16-unit building is a domesticated high-rise, a real apartment house. Cleverly planned by E. C.
Lamb, the developer and builder, the apartment units are arranged around open-air
loggias (indicated by the wide central aper-
tures on the front and side elevations) that
ensured cross-ventilation in all rooms.
Rehabilitated in 1978, the Beaconsfield still
functions as a luxury apartment building.
Across Pease Avenue, half buried in the ex-
Savoy Field Hotel, is the 7½-story **Savoy**

Apartments (1906, C. H. Page & Co.), the first high-rise apartment building constructed in Houston. From the north, the battered profile of the Savoy's masonry bearing wall is visible. Both the Savoy and the Beaconsfield were built in the Main Street residence district, well uptown from the downtown business center.

1111 Pierce Avenue   **E-6**
Sacred Heart Church [now Sacred Heart Co-Cathedral] (1912) Olle J. Lorehn

Sacred Heart served the affluent suburban parish of the South End when its permanent church was built here, adjacent to the Main Street residence district. Lorehn's neo-Gothic detailing, executed in buff brick and limestone, was surprisingly academic for a Victorian architect. The church, co-cathedral of the Roman Catholic Diocese of Galveston-Houston since 1959, bears with stoic resignation its proximity to the Pierce Elevated Freeway (I-45).

1401 Pierce Avenue   **E-7**
St. Joseph Hospital. Cullen Family Building (1948) I. E. Loveless

Horizontal speed lines, disrupted by the stair-landing windows, and residual Art Deco ornament enliven this pink-colored, reinforced concrete building. It is authentically Southern Californian: Loveless was a

Beverly Hills architect whom the Sisters of Charity of the Incarnate Word retained for their work in Houston and Galveston from the mid '30s through the early '50s. He also designed the sedate, brick-faced convent at 1903 Crawford Street and Calhoun Avenue (1940).

1902-1920 LaBranch Street   **E-8**
St. Joseph Hospital. Maternity and Children's Building (1938) I. E. Loveless

Loveless's major contribution to the St. Joseph's complex is the conjoined four and five-story Maternity and Children's Building, occupying an entire block front between Calhoun and Pierce. Faceted corners, bands of Art Deco Christian ornament, and the vertically accentuated entrance bays to both wings are distinguishing features. Loveless pioneered the cross-street skybridge in Houston with the single-level passage that emanates from the Maternity wing. It has been joined by a triple-decker connecting the Children's wing to the main building (1964, Golemon & Rolfe), which replaced a group of earlier buildings, including the original main building of 1895 by N. J. Clayton & Co. of Galveston. Founded in 1887, St. Joseph's is the oldest hospital in Houston.

1310 Gray Avenue   **E-9**
Houston Teachers Credit Union Building [now Houston International University Building] (1964)
Howard Barnstone & Partners

A trimly designed office building that departs, somewhat hesitantly, from the official Miesian modernism of the 1950s.

2201 Caroline Street   **E-10**
Houston Typewriter Exchange Building
(1956) Joseph Krakower

As the nutty plaster soffit indicates, something is awry with what, at first glance,
seems to be a prosaic commercial building.
Herb Greene, Krakower's designer, was
responsible for injecting this touch of
whimsy into the building type—brick-
faced, windowless, and flat-roofed—with
which Houston was relentlessly suburbanized in the 1950s.

2111 Fannin Street   **E-11**
First City Motor Bank Building (1983)
Sikes Jennings Kelly

As is apparent from the Gray or Webster
avenue sides of this building, Frank S. Kelly
organized it in section, then extruded it laterally across the block to provide a double-
fronted but offset arrangement of drive-in
stations served by tellers inside the central
spine. Curved corners, a glossy white aluminum panel wall system, and green glass
give this building its cool look.

2201 Fannin Street   **E-12**
Paul House (1899) George E. Dickey

The wood and shingle-surfaced Paul House
is the only survivor of the Main Street residence district; its location one block off

Main identifies it as second tier in terms of
Victorian domestic grandeur. Yet it is an
absolute delight. Dickey's mischievous
pointed turret has earned the house its
affectionate designation as the "witch's hat
house." The Paul House was rehabilitated
by Phillip Martin Associates in 1984.

2204 Baldwin Street   **E-13**
The Cottage (1910) Sanguinet & Staats

A very sumptuous bungalow that has per-
sisted despite abuse and neglect. It was built
by the lawyer and horticulturalist, Edwin B.
Parker, and his wife Katherine, a co-founder
of the Houston Symphony Orchestra, as a
temporary home while their permanent residence, The Oaks (demolished in 1965), was
built on the wooded, five-acre site defined
by the curve of Oak Place.

2006 Smith Street   **E-14**
(1926) James Ruskin Bailey

Houston is a city of surprises. Here, next to
the Pierce Elevated Freeway, at the edge of
downtown, is a picturesquely massed, opulently decorated, neo-Jacobean country
house—in excellent condition. The house
was built for John Henry Kirby, a lawyer,
lumberman, and oil man from East Texas
who emerged at the turn of the century as
Houston's first tycoon. He and his family
had lived at this site since 1897, but in 1925
they replaced their florid Victorian house
with this rambling, 36-room, English
manor house, retaining part of the old
building's fabric because—it was said—
Kirby was superstitious about living in a
totally new house. Since 1948 the Kirby
House has been used as an office building,
but its major reception rooms have been
preserved. The house was rehabilitated in
1978. Unfortunately, the once-famous gardens have been converted to surface parking lots.

South End / Montrose

Houston is a city of boundless optimism. Yet this very expansiveness can have paradoxical spatial repercussions. Since everything seems possible and there are no public planning mechanisms to encourage the concentration of efforts toward any particular purpose or in any particular locale, activity is diffused. Where it ultimately will collect is unpredictable and land-use patterns are so volatile that long-term stability cannot be taken for granted even when concentrations do occur. Main Street, in the South End, illustrates this predicament. It was once Houston's most fashionable residential street, then its most fashionable suburban retail corridor. Now so few vestiges of either of these episodes survive that it is difficult to envision South Main in either urbanistic role. It remains a street of great potential, but there are many such streets in Houston.

Montrose Boulevard, to the west, has undergone a similar evolution. The Montrose Addition and surrounding neighborhoods succeeded to Main Street's role as the city's elite residential area in the early 20th century. Most of these were protected by restrictive covenants intended to guard against commercial encroachment and its destabilizing consequences. However, the inability of Montrose to resist these economic forces meant that the boulevard has relived the history of Main. Presently it is the most urbane street in Houston, its still visible suburban origins notwithstanding. Whether, in a city where change is the constant, it can consolidate its urbanistic assets and expand on them is problematic.

North of the Montrose neighborhoods lies the community now called Fourth Ward, the oldest black neighborhood in Houston. Fourth Ward is the antithesis of the popular image of Houston. It embodies everything the city is supposed to lack: tradition, history, a stable, rooted community culture. Fourth Ward, because it is black and poor, has endured official neglect for most of its history, yet it is the most moving place in the city. It is, as the novelist Olive Hershey observed, the soul of Houston.

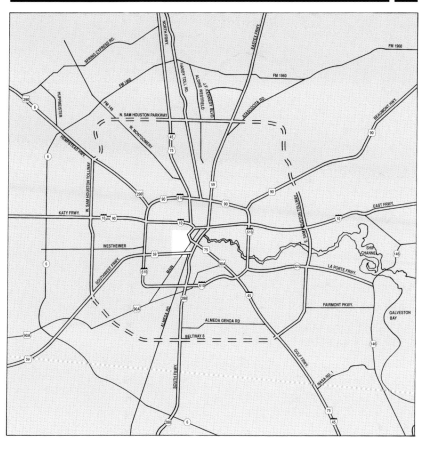

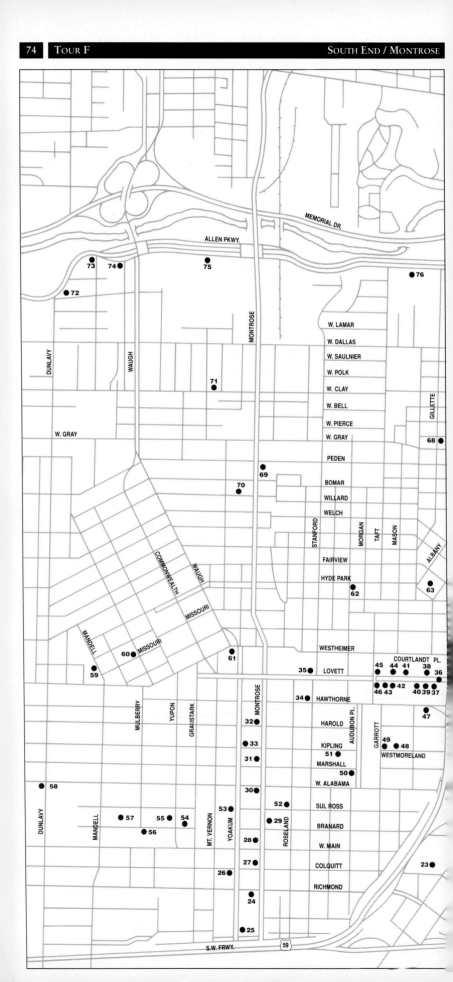

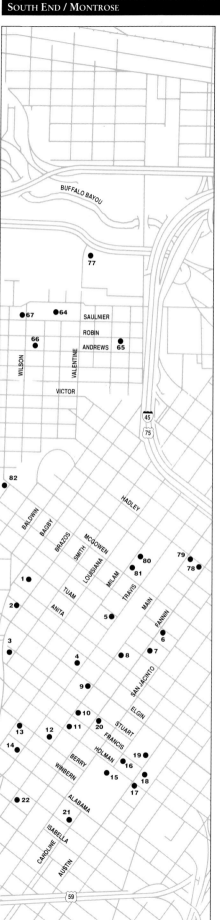

1. 401 Anita Avenue
2. 3106 Brazos Street
3. 3300 Smith Street
4. 3100 Travis Street
5. 2800-2816 Travis Street
6. 2701 Fannin Street
7. 2819 Fannin Street
8. 2935-2925 Main Street
9. 3200-3232 Main Street
10. 3303 Main Street
11. 3415 Main Street
12. 3512 Main Street
13. 3601 Milam Street
14. 3704 Travis Street
15. 1300 Holman Avenue
16. 1311 Holman Avenue
17. 3517 Austin Street
18. 3307 Austin Street
19. 3214 Austin Street
20. 3333 Fannin Street
21. 3816 Caroline Street
22. 1003-1005 Isabella Avenue
23. 4000 Main Street
24. 1035 Richmond Avenue
25. 4515 Yoakum Boulevard
26. 4204 Yoakum Boulevard and 1105-1107
    Colquitt Street
27. 4100 Montrose Boulevard
28. 4004 Montrose Boulevard
29. 3939 Montrose Boulevard
30. 3812 Montrose Boulevard
31. 3614 and 3600 Montrose Boulevard
32. 3410 Montrose Boulevard
33. 3520 Yoakum Boulevard
34. 804 Hawthorne Avenue
35. 802 Lovett Boulevard
36. Brazos Street and Courtlandt Place
37. 5 Courtlandt Place
38. 8 Courtlandt Place
39. 9 Courtlandt Place
40. 11 Courtlandt Place
41. 16 Courtlandt Place
42. 17 Courtlandt Place
43. 19 Courtlandt Place
44. 20 Courtlandt Place
45. 24 Courtlandt Place
46. 25 Courtlandt Place
47. 303 Hawthorne Avenue
48. 215 Westmoreland Avenue
49. 201 Westmoreland Avenue
50. 3702 Audubon Place
51. 607 Kipling Street
52. 3820 Roseland Avenue
53. 3812-3910 Yoakum Boulevard
54. 1300 Branard Avenue
55. 1409 Sul Ross Avenue
56. 1427 Branard Avenue
57. 1515 Sul Ross Avenue
58. 1715 West Alabama Avenue
59. 2512 Mandell Street
60. 1802 Missouri Avenue
61. 1801 Westheimer Road
62. 415 Hyde Park Boulevard
63. 100 block Tuam Avenue
64. 1207 West Dallas Avenue
65. 809 Robins Street
66. 1318 Andrews Street
67. 1402 Saulnier Street
68. 1501-1519 Victor Street
69. 1701 Montrose Boulevard
70. 1116 Willard Street
71. 1210 West Clay Avenue
72. 3401 Allen Parkway
73. 3301 Allen Parkway
74. 3201 Allen Parkway
75. 2727 Allen Parkway
76. 1801 Allen Parkway
77. 1 Allen Parkway
78. 2302 Fannin Street
79. 2301 Main Street
80. 2325 Milam Street
81. 2421 Milam Street
82. 2710 Albany Street

401 Anita Avenue   F-1
Lovett Square (1978) William T. Cannady & Associates

William T. Cannady envisioned Lovett Square as a low-rise, high-density proto-type for the devastated neighborhoods of the South End. Thirty-six condominium units are organized around six courtyards. The courtyards are stepped in section to give access to units entered at the second level and all open to a landscaped common that traverses the center of the block. Parking is confined to grade level, with direct access to all units. The stucco-sur-faced buildings were constructed without architectural supervision and show it. An unenthusiastic market response, coupled with escalation of real estate values in the area, discouraged replication of Lovett Square and reclamation of the South End.

3106 Brazos Street   F-2
Swenson Studio (1958) Swenson & Linnstaedter

Bailey A. Swenson's own house was a tower, twenty feet square in plan, that sand-wiched two levels of living space between a ground-floor patio and a fourth-floor roof garden. This was tacked on, in a very spon-taneous way, to an old garage-apartment building that contained Swenson's studio and, at various times, the studio of Donald Barthelme, the André Emmerich Gallery, and from the late 1950s to the mid-1960s Houston's most vanguard gallery, New Arts, operated by Swenson's wife Kathryn. Like Lovett Square, the Swenson studio-townhouse complex remains the single example of a potential prototype.

3300 Smith Street   F-3
Junior League Building [now Brennan's Houston] (1930) John F. Staub

John Staub's ex-club house for the Junior League of Houston provides yet another potential model of civilized urban living. The L-shaped building and its walled patio garden evoke the Creole architecture of New Orleans. Double-level galleries,

screened with louvered blinds (now glazed), originally served as open-air corridors on the courtyard faces of the building. Below the second-floor lunch room, facing Stuart Avenue, were retail spaces occupied by the shops of Junior League members and later by Staub's architecture studio. Brennan's transformation of the building into a restaurant (1967, Perez & Associates) was insensitive and heavy-handed. But the building has been preserved and is, for the price of a meal, publicly accessible. Mr. and Mrs. Robert Daniel and their son Jerry, who acquired the building when the Junior League vacated it, developed the surround-ing blocks into a slightly mistranslated Houston version of the Vieux Carré (1967-1976, Greacen, Houston & Rogers).

3100 Travis Street   F-4
Transcontinental Gas Pipeline Corp. Building [now 3100 Travis Building] (1951) Zimmerman & Bible

Transco's former home is a windowless three-story box (the top floor is a later addition) that relied upon central air-condi-tioning and fluorescent lighting for total environmental control. The patterned facades—horizontally banded brick framed with panels of limestone—suggest a mea-sure of design desperation over how to cope with windowlessness, an anxiety perhaps shared by the occupants. The highlight of the building is Edward Z. Galea's relief panel above the Travis Street entrance. Across the street, at 3100 Main Street, is the 12-story **Southwestern Bell Telephone Co. Building** (1965, George Pierce-Abel B. Pierce with Wilson, Morris, Crain & Anderson) in the clean style of the '60s.

2800-2816 Travis Street   F-5
Henke-Pillot South End Store [now Hoa Binh Shopping Mall] (1923) R. D. Steele

The original segment of this complex, fac-ing Travis Street, was resurfaced with the rest of the building in 1948 (Eugene Werlin with C. H. Kiefner), and the result has been modified piecemeal over the years. What

distinguishes this building is that it was the prototype of the 20th-century American suburban shopping center: it introduced the concept of off-street parking, toward which the grocery store itself was oriented. Its present role as an Indochinese retail center demonstrates the durability of the concept.

ers" in the jargon of the time. Finger's building for Ben Cohen was both more elaborate than others and considerably more exotic. Contemporary newspaper reports described it as detailed in the Chinese style.

2701 Fannin Street   **F-6**
Pacific Mutual Life Insurance Co. Building (1960) Neuhaus & Taylor

This was the first in a series of one-story office buildings straddling their own parking lots that Neuhaus & Taylor produced: a distinctly Houstonian building type. Here, the glass walls are screened by cantilevered fascia panels.

3200-3232 Main Street   **F-9**
Main & Elgin Building (1949) Kenneth Franzheim

Polychrome brick diapering and stone banding are used with dexterity to describe the internal organization of this block-long retail building.

2819 Fannin Street   **F-7**
Tuam Avenue Baptist Church [now Perfecto Cleaners] (1904) A. N. Dawson

Dawson's labored rendition of a Roman Corinthian temple for a suburban Southern Baptist congregation is in itself amusing. That the ex-church has housed Perfecto Cleaners since the congregation changed its name to South Main Baptist Church and transferred to a new site in 1920 only adds to the incongruity. The brown brick annex to the north (1928, Lamar Q. Cato) was built by Perfecto.

2935-2925 Main Street   **F-8**
Cohen Building (1929) Joseph Finger

The upper end of the Main Street residence district was redeveloped in the 1920s with one-story commercial buildings, "taxpay-

3303 Main Street   **F-10**
Houston Telephone Employees Federal Credit Union Building [now Communications Federal Credit Union Building] (1979) Urban Architecture and Sanders & Sanders

This is an intelligently conceived modern building that acknowledges its responsibilities to both function and site. Hossein Oskouie carefully adjusted the poured-in-place concrete frame, infilled with recessed walls of dark solar glass, to respond to particularities of solar orientation and internal spatial organization. The grand stairway and the raised terrace facing Main pay tribute to the importance of the street, and simultaneously shield at-grade parking. Unfortunately, the later replacement of an adjoining building with the motor bank has left the raised terrace awkwardly stranded in midair.

3415 Main Street   **F-11**
Trinity Church (1919) Cram & Ferguson
and William Ward Watkin

Ralph Adams Cram first made his mark on
American architecture in the 1890s with
suburban parish churches rendered in a
suave neo-Gothic style. Trinity, his
Houston example of the type, was designed
in collaboration with his former employee,
William Ward Watkin. Trinity demonstrates
that Texas Anglicans commanded much
more limited resources than their coreli-
gionists in the northern United States.
Nonetheless, its limestone facing, pinnacled
Ralston Memorial Tower (1921), and lofty,
simply finished interior give it the reassuringly churchly look that Cram championed.
The sculptor Oswald J. Lassig executed the
altar and reredos (1920). Cram and Watkin's
parish house at Fannin and Holman
burned. Its replacement (1949), as well as
additions grouped around the courtyard to
the north (1951), are by Cameron D.
Fairchild.

3512 Main Street   **F-12**
The Original Kelley's [now Christie's
Seafood Restaurant] (1936) H. K. Friedman

During the late 1920s the Spanish-
Mediterranean genre became the quasi-offi-
cial style of the South Main corridor,
Houston's smartest suburban retail strip
from the '20s until the early 1960s. Kelley's
was one of the last commercial buildings
designed in that style, and now is one of the
last reminders of that era in the street's history. Friedman was a restaurant designer.
His makeover of an existing root beer stand
was picturesquely underscaled and overstated.

3601 Milam Street   **F-13**
Holy Rosary Church (1933)
Maurice J. Sullivan

Holy Rosary is one of Sullivan's finest
churches, a disciplined neo-Gothic parish
church finished externally with Texas limestone and crowned by a slender copper
flèche. Holy Rosary's prismatic massing

and substantial but carefully proportioned
planar composition show the impact of
Ralph Adams Cram's former partner, the
New York architect Bertram G. Goodhue,
whose "modern" interpretation of traditional styles powerfully affected American
architecture during the 1920s. Sullivan was
also responsible for the rectory, facing
Travis Street behind the church. Oswald J.
Lassig executed the sculpture in the tympa-
num above the front door and the altar.

3704 Travis Street   **F-14**
LaMont Apartments (1919)

The three-story, six-unit LaMont
Apartments feature stacked solarium front
porches, oriented to the morning light and
the prevailing breeze. The top two floors
have been imaginatively remodeled to serve
as law offices (1988, William F. Stern &
Associates).

1300 Holman Avenue   **F-15**
South End Junior High School [now San
Jacinto Memorial Building, Houston
Community College Learning Resources
Center] (1914) Layton & Smith

One of Houston's most imposing City
Beautiful landmarks, South End Junior
High School (subsequently San Jacinto
Senior High School) is a monumental three-
story classical block. A screen of limestone
Doric columns is framed by pedimented
end bays in the style of the 18th-century
French architect Ange-Jacques Gabriel.
Alongside these end pavilions are mod-
ernistic setback towers with sculptural fig-

ures sprouting from the tops of piers, parts of two symmetrical additions made in 1928 (Hedrick & Gottlieb) and 1936 (Joseph Finger). Subsequent additions fail to do the complex justice. The *cour d'honneur*, which terminates Caroline Street, has been turned into a parking lot, and horizontal belt courses have been given very inappropriate, two-toned, high contrast accents. The Oklahoma City architects Layton & Smith won this commission in competition; they would go on to design the Oklahoma State Capitol.

1311 Holman Avenue   F-16
First Evangelical Church [now Central Congregational Church] (1927)
J. W. Northrop, Jr.

Despite his apprenticeship with Ralph Adams Cram, Northrop tended toward a rather mechanical treatment of the Lombard Romanesque, as the adaptation of the medieval brick architecture of northern Italy was known during the 1920s. A neat touch is the setback upper stage of the campanile; it evokes the skyscraper profiling that traditionalists used in the 1920s to connote modernity.

3517 Austin Street   F-17
Temple Beth Israel [now Erwin R. Heinen Theater, Fine Arts Department, Houston Community College] (1925) Joseph Finger

Finger applied what he described as Egyptian decorative motifs to the faceted, block-like masses of the temple building. Its hermetic look was reinforced when most of the exterior windows were sealed in 1950, at the time the building was air-conditioned. Behind the temple, at Holman and LaBranch, is the Abe M. Levy Community House, part of Finger's original design. To the south is the Freed Memorial Tower (1950, Irving R. Klein and Theo G. Keller), a spirited exercise in the modernistic Regency style; the stair hall is a delight. All interiors have been unsympathetically altered by the community college's architect, Charles Boelsen. Quick preservation

action by students and faculty in 1983 saved the buildings from being completely refaced by Boelsen.

3307 Austin Street   F-18
(1903)

Built for the cotton factor E. R. Richardson, this large columned house was one of the first of its type to be built in Houston. It was unusual among so-called Colonial revival houses locally because of the extent to which it replicated 18th-century architectural features, such as the pedimented ground floor windows and the corner pilasters. The Richardson House was moved to this site in 1926 from its original location on the block now occupied by the First Evangelical Church.

3214 Austin Street   F-19
[now Child Guidance Center] (1911)

Continuing a Victorian tradition, the wholesale grocer Edward W. Sewall created a family compound here in the South End. His daughter built her house next door at **3208 Austin** (1913), while a younger son built his house around the corner at **1304 Elgin Avenue** (1911). Together with the Richardson House across the street, these constitute a Colonial revival enclave that preserves an idea of what the South End must have been like during its heyday. Since 1959 the Sewall House has been occupied by the Child Guidance Center. Howard Barnstone & Partners completed a rehabilitation of the house in 1962. The large, white, stucco-surfaced building attached to the south side of the house is by William T. Cannady and Anderson Todd (1974). A residential building at the rear of the property, facing Caroline Street, is by Ziegler Cooper (1988).

3333 Fannin Street   F-20
Southwestern Bell Telephone Co. Building [now 3333 Fannin Building] (1958)
Joseph Krakower

The organic expressionist architect Herb Greene was Krakower's designer between

1954 and 1957. He detailed this two-story office building with concrete masonry units, deployed as relief ornament. During the building's occupation by a subsequent tenant, Uniroyal, the upper floor was painted black so that the decoration might read as tire treads.

3816 Caroline Street   **F-21**
Houston Light Guard Armory (1925)
Alfred C. Finn

By the time this National Guard Armory was built, the Houston Light Guard had ceased to be an elite social institution. Yet the use of the streamlined traditionalism associated with Bertram G. Goodhue gives the building an air of clubbiness. Finn's office detailed it to suggest 16th- and 17th-century English masonry buildings without incorporating Elizabethan or Jacobean features. Tapestry brick and limestone banding are combined in a composition of taut, faceted wall planes relieved by sculptural detail, notably relief panels exhibiting bellicose iconography.

1003-1005 Isabella Avenue   **F-22**
Isabella Court (1929) W. D. Bordeaux

The apogee of Main Street's Spanish episode occurred at the Isabella Court. Two floors of apartments, organized around a roofed, open-air courtyard, are stacked on top of ground floor shop spaces. Bordeaux introduced picturesque internal variations by inserting a 1½-story photography studio at 3911 Main (where the belt course between the first and second floors is arced) and carrying this sectional shift upward into second- and third-floor apartments. The central courtyard is not accessible but one can walk into the vestibule on Isabella; the original finishes are all preserved in a glorious state of seediness. Pierre D. Michael, who built the Isabella Court, also constructed the **Ironcraft Studio Building** next door (3901-3907 Main Street, 1927, Hiram A. Salisbury), a two-story Spanish precursor that featured apartments above shops and a Mediterranean courtyard. It is to be regretted that the courtyard has been filled in and the building crudely defaced.

4000 Main Street   **F-23**
South Main Baptist Church (1930)
Hedrick & Gottlieb

The successor to the temple-fronted Tuam Avenue Baptist Church is this high and mighty example of the Lombard Romanesque, executed in the brown tapestry brick characteristic of Houston in the 1920s. Multiple additions are by Wirtz & Calhoun. Its name notwithstanding, South Main did not gain access to frontage on Main Street until the 1960s, a consummation it celebrated with an expansive grass forecourt and fountain.

1035 Richmond Avenue   **F-24**
Burbridge Apartments (1958) G.A. Burbridge

Peter Papademetriou has called this wacky apartment building, visible from the Richmond-Montrose intersection, an allegory of the growth of Houston. The 8-unit, 3½-story structure is the improbable outgrowth of a perfectly normal garage-apartment building.

4515 Yoakum Boulevard   **F-25**
(1916, 1919) Alfred C. Finn

Ross S. Sterling built this house speculatively in Rossmoyne, a private place-type sub-

division that he began to develop in 1914. Two years after its completion he and his family moved in. It was then that Finn's designer, H. Jordan MacKenzie, produced the spectacular front porch: a wide-span, reinforced concrete structure bracketed by a cantilevered canopy on the north end and an inglenook on the south, framed by bulbous concrete columns. Centered above the front step is MacKenzie's signature device, an elongated cartouche. The Sterling House was rehabilitated by Stem Associates in 1981.

church available to the Houston Public Library for conversion into its Montrose Branch Library (1986, 1988, Ray Bailey Architects). Although one might quibble with some of the decisions (the minuscule front parking lot consumed a grove of mature trees), the Campanile represents an urbanistically responsible reuse of existing buildings that renews the city and its fabric instead of ripping it to shreds.

4204 Yoakum Boulevard and   **F-26**
1105-1107 Colquitt Street
Phillips Studio and Townhouses
(1977-1981) W. Irving Phillips, Jr.

This startling complex of buildings includes a 1920s Montrose house that sprouts both a vaulted extension and a four-story protrusion, a two-story garden house, a three-story row house whose rotated stucco mass is prefaced by a wooden facade screen, and a two-story row house set far back from the street. The existing house and its additions as well as the three-story house were originally occupied by the architect. Phillips was once a student of Colin Rowe and he incorporated into this group an array of rhetorical-analytical devices that range from the phenomenological to the contextual to the outrageous (the ostensibly modest two-story house has a swimming pool in the living room).

4100 Montrose Boulevard   **F-27**
Central Church of Christ
[now The Campanile] (1941 1947)
William Ward Watkin

Built in two stages, this Lombard Romanesque style church was the last to be designed by Watkin, who published two books on the subject of church architecture. It was also the first non-residential building to be constructed on the boulevard, following the expiration of deed restrictions in Montrose in 1936. After acquiring the property in 1981, the developer John Hansen had the educational wing transformed into shops and a restaurant and made the

4004 Montrose Boulevard   **F-28**
The Court at Museum's Gate (1985)
Compendium

Stepped, banded, and bichromatic, this 47-unit low-rise, high-density condominium is in the effusive postmodern style of the '80s. Designed by a group of young architects working for Compendium (which was both developer and architect), the complex is urban in intention. The result, however, is experientially schematic and formalistically overdetermined. Common spaces within the complex (not publicly accessible) remind one of the proletarian quarters of 19th-century industrial cities—before gentrification. The complex sits on a plinth, beneath which cars are parked, so that the only green spaces are along the street fronts. There Compendium happily retained the ornamental date palms, the original street trees of Montrose.

3939 Montrose Boulevard   **F-29**
3939 Montrose Building (1985)
Stem Associates

Typologically, 3939 is business as usual, a strip shopping center with parking out front. But its potentially deleterious effect on the boulevard is mitigated by Robert Stem's sensitive evocation of the 1920s commercial and industrial vernacular buildings spotted about the back streets of Montrose. As a result the center seems very

much at home, despite its suburban site planning. Bertha's Genuine Mexican Restaurant, at the Branard end of the center, contains a festively minimal interior by Kathy Heard (1986).

3812 Montrose Boulevard   F-30
[now Administration Building, University of St. Thomas] (1912) Sanguinet, Staats & Barnes

J. W. Link, who developed the Montrose addition in 1911, built this flamboyant, quasi-progressive style house on a square block site in the very middle of his subdivision. Its severe, set-back massing contrasts with the opulence of its surfaces, faced with vitrified buff brick, enameled terra cotta, glazed tile, and limestone. Since 1946 the house has been the administration building of the University of St. Thomas, which conscientiously maintains it, the original garage-apartment building, and the pergola that connects them. Unfortunately the university caved in to the temptation of a corporate identity package and permitted installation of the gratuitous brick and metal screen walls that disfigure the terraced lawn (1988, The SWA Group).

3614 and 3600 Montrose Boulevard   F-31
Parc IV and Parc V (1963, 1965) Jenkins Hoff Oberg Saxe

William R. Jenkins designed this handsome pair of 12-story apartment slabs. Their concrete frame construction, infilled with brick and sliding sash, is expressed without reservation. The careful proportioning of the

framed divisions gives the towers an urbane rather than an industrial aspect. Their relationship to the street is well considered, too, for while one edges the sidewalk, the other steps back to preserve a vestige of tree-shaded lawn.

3410 Montrose Boulevard   F-32
[now La Colombe d'Or] (1923) Alfred C. Finn

Walter W. Fondren, an oil driller and co-founder of the Humble Oil & Refining Co., built one of the last great houses on Montrose Boulevard. Its big scale, unsubtle frontality, and lack of specific historical derivation were traits more typical of the 1910s than the 1920s. Despite conversion into a restaurant, it retains a strong sense of its historic identity, including specimens of the palm trees that Link planted in 1911 to give his flat, treeless addition the Pasadena look, an arboreal analogy that would signify its aspirations to the status of a millionaires' community. Several of the boulevard lots were improved with houses by Finn, of which only the Westheimer House at **3704 Montrose** (1919) remains.

3520 Yoakum Boulevard   F-33
Annunciation Hellenic Eastern Orthodox Church [now Annunciation Greek Orthodox Cathedral] (1952) Peter E. Camburas

Camburas, a Chicago architect, designed this church for Houston's oldest Greek Orthodox parish in a stripped-down version of the Romanesque style. He faced it with limestone, however, rather than brick. The interior features a stone ikonostasis and a vaulted apse surfaced with mural work by the New York painter Stelios Maris.

804 Hawthorne Avenue   F-34
(1913)

Off the major boulevards—Montrose, Yoakum, and Lovett—the Montrose subdivision consisted primarily of two-story, four-square houses and large, one-story bungalows. This house, with its wide-span

front porch and big-scaled urns, is one of the more notable Montrose bungalows. It features a double volume living room, replete with musicians' gallery.

802 Lovett Boulevard   **F-35**
[now Lloyd Jones Fillpot Associates]
(1925) H. T. Lindeberg

Lindeberg, one of the most outstanding country house architects of the 1910s and 1920s, designed five houses in Houston; this was the only one not located in the neighborhood of Shadyside. The client, John Hamman, an independent oil man, permitted the builder to deviate from Lindeberg's specifications and drawings, as the shutters and roof tiles make clearly evident. Thus the house is not a consistent expression of Lindeberg's predilections. Since the 1940s it has been occupied by a succession of architectural firms—Kenneth Franzheim, the Houston branch of Welton Becket & Associates, and Lloyd Jones Fillpot Associates—which has ensured its survival. The one-story drafting room addition is by the Becket office.

Brazos Street and Courtlandt Place **F-36**
Courtlandt Place Wall (1988)
Eubanks/Bohn Associates

Courtlandt Place, platted in 1907, is a small neighborhood modeled quite literally on the private places of St. Louis. It consists of a boulevard divided by a landscaped median and bracketed at either end by colossal gate piers. The east end lost its concave screen of piers and spur walls to the construction of

the Southwest Freeway in 1969. This new wall of textured concrete block and cast concrete moldings belatedly replaces it. (If the entrance gate is closed, drive up to it and it will open automatically.)

5 Courtlandt Place   **F-37**
(1913) Sanguinet & Staats

The Colonial revival portico appears here at big scale, but with a homelike charm that is carried inside this house. The greenhouse and tennis court connoted high-status leisure activities. Across the street at **2 Courtlandt Place** is a discreet English manorial style house by John F. Staub (1926).

8 Courtlandt Place   **F-38**
(1911) Sanguinet, Staats & Barnes

Sanguinet & Staats had established themselves as architects of choice to Houston's elite by 1910, not only as designers of skyscrapers, but of pretentious suburban houses as well. These included the half-timbered house at **4 Courtlandt Place** and the New England Federal style house at **6 Courtlandt Place** (both 1910). This house is more ingratiating than the other two, although it shares with its neighbors the attributes of frontality, symmetry, big scale, and widely projecting eaves. The lattice work fence is by Eubanks/Bohn Associates (1987).

9 Courtlandt Place   **F-39**
(1914) Sanguinet & Staats

An Italian villa style was adopted for this house. The one-story porch wing on the east balanced by a porte-cochere on the west recur in most of the houses of Courtlandt Place. The preference given to the south and east exposures in order to catch the prevailing southeast breezes (and the corollary tendency to place serving spaces on the north or west) indicate the impact of climate on domestic planning in Houston. The balustraded terrace in front of the main entrance is a vestige of the front porch, a feature that would disappear altogether from stylish Houston houses in the 1920s.

11 Courtlandt Place   F-40
(1914) Birdsall P. Briscoe

Briscoe, in one of his earliest houses, gave evidence of the suave eclecticism that would mark his long career. The image is English picturesque, but the loggias, French doors, and low terrace that he introduced reconcile it to Houston's climate.

16 Courtlandt Place   F-41
(1912)

J. J. Carroll, who built this house, was managing partner of a lumber business begun by his father-in-law. According to family tradition, he was responsible for designing this house, with its big classical portico infilled with subsidiary classical porches. Birdsall P. Briscoe carried out later interior alterations. The Carroll House was part of a family enclave. Mrs. Carroll's mother, Mrs. W. T. Carter, Sr., lived at **14 Courtlandt Place** (1920, Birdsall P. Briscoe); her brother, W. T. Carter, Jr., lived at **18 Courtlandt Place** (1912, Olle J. Lorehn).

17 Courtlandt Place   F-42
(1916) Warren & Wetmore

At the same time that Warren & Wetmore designed the Texas Co. Building downtown, they produced this exquisite neo-Georgian house for the family of Thomas J. Donoghue, executive vice-president of Texaco. Like earlier Courtlandt Place houses, it is frontal and symmetrical. But the consistency and precision of its 18th-century English Adamesque detail, the ornamental enrichment of exterior surfaces, and the

lack of bulkiness and pretension demonstrate by contrast how provincial Houston's prevailing domestic architectural standards were. The bowed profile of the sun porch screening is a delightful touch.

19 Courtlandt Place   F-43
(1914) Birdsall P. Briscoe

Another early Briscoe house, a suburban pavilion with a Baroque front portal. The one-story wing is a later addition.

20 Courtlandt Place   F-44
(1916) Birdsall P. Briscoe

This is a sort of Georgianized version of Briscoe's house at 14, across the street. It was built for a fourth member of the W. T. Carter family. The striped awnings still in use here were once standard equipment in the South End.

24 Courtlandt Place   F-45
(1921) Alfred C. Finn

The stepped plan of this house, which exhibits nominal Tudor detail, enables the principal reception rooms to have access to the prevailing southeast breeze. Finn incorporated parts of the interior of the family's previous Victorian house in the Main Street residence district into their new home. The son of the family lived next door at **22 Courtlandt Place** (1917, Birdsall P. Briscoe).

25 Courtlandt Place   **F-46**
(1916) Sanguinet, Staats & Gottlieb

The impact of Warren & Wetmore is evident in Sanguinet & Staats's last house in Courtlandt Place, at the west end of the boulevard. Proportion, scale, detail, and plan configuration all defer to the authority of 17 Courtlandt Place and set this house apart from Sanguinet & Staats's earlier work.

303 Hawthorne Avenue   **F-47**
(1905)

A flamboyant airplane bungalow (so-called because the ridge of the second-floor roof usually runs perpendicular to that of the first floor), this was one of the earliest examples of this progressive middle class house type built in Houston. The rock-faced concrete work and the billowing roofs give this house a lilting character. The design is Design 775 from *Art and Architecture* (1902), one of the many catalogues of house designs published by the Knoxville architect George F. Barber. The late Victorian cottage next door at **219 Hawthorne** is also one of Barber's designs.

215 Westmoreland Avenue   **F-48**
(1907) Cooke & Co.

The Colonial revival at its most grandiose. This is one of the two great houses remaining in Westmoreland, the first of the South End enclaves to challenge the primacy of Main Street. As the name itself implies, Westmoreland was laid out in 1902 by the St. Louis engineer Julius Pitzman, whose master works are the most opulent of St.

Louis's private streets, Westmoreland and Portland places.

201 Westmoreland Avenue   **F-49**
(1905) Wilmer Waldo

Between 1902 and 1905 the civil engineer Wilmer Waldo dismantled his mother's elaborate Victorian house at Rusk Avenue and Caroline Street (1886, George E. Dickey) and reconstructed it, with modifications, here in Westmoreland, where the open prairie of Harris County spread out just beyond Garrott Street to the west. The Waldo House's Victorian proportions are evident, although Waldo modernized it by removing Dickey's tall tower and replacing the wooden porches with an arcaded brick loggia. Occupied by the Waldo family until the late 1960s, the house was subsequently owned by architect Clovis Heimsath and his family. Heimsath used the stable at the rear as his studio. He designed the dark, brick-faced row houses with the eyebrow windows at **3524 and 3526 Garrott** (1973).

3702 Audubon Place   **F-50**
(1924) E. H. Lightfoot

The impact of Pasadena as a trend-setter in American architecture during the 1910s and '20s is evident not only in the palm trees of Montrose and Yoakum boulevards but in the house types built in Montrose and other contemporary Houston subdivisions as well. This chalet style bungalow, with its bracketed eaves, stucco walls, and shingled second-story studio, appears to have been translated directly from southern California.

Ewart H. Lightfoot, who built this house for his family, was an architect-builder.

607 Kipling Street   **F-51**
(1919) (1938)William Ward Watkin

This house, purchased in 1922 by George Cohen, president of Foley Brothers department store, began modestly enough. But in the late '30s Cohen and his wife embarked on a series of alterations and additions, carried out by Watkin and his associate Nolan Barrick, which transformed it into a mini-mansion, replete with an Art Deco room that simulates a ship's interior.

3820 Roseland Avenue   **F-52**
(1914)

Mission type details—stucco wall surfaces and tile copings—are yet another echo of Pasadena. They give this rather severe house its distinctive image.

3812-3910 Yoakum Boulevard   **F-53**
University of St. Thomas. Welder Hall, Jones Hall, and Strake Hall (1958 and 1959) Philip Johnson Associates with Bolton & Barnstone

The University of St. Thomas is significant in Philip Johnson's career as his first realized multiple-building project and the last occasion on which he worked in the style of his mentor, Ludwig Mies van der Rohe. Johnson, who was commissioned to plan the university's campus in 1956 at the behest of Mr. and Mrs. John de Menil, combined the idea of a monastic community with the model of Thomas Jefferson's aca-

demic village for the University of Virginia. He devised a double-level, steel-framed walkway that circumscribes a rectangular green lawn at the center of the three-block site. Two-story rectilinear buildings attach to the walkway, whose steel columns describe the 10-foot, 4-inch planning grid with which Johnson organized the entire site. The careful composition of steel framing members and window units, infilled with panels of pink St. Joe brick, gives the campus buildings a strong sense of proportioned grace. Johnson modulated the intervals between his three initial buildings with brick screen walls. This lends a modest degree of spatial complexity to the ordered simplicity of the campus. **M. D. Anderson Hall** (1966, Howard Barnstone & Eugene Aubry) and the **Doherty Library** (1971, Eugene Aubry and Wilson, Morris, Crain & Anderson) upheld the precepts and maintained the subtleties of Johnson's buildings. **Cullen Hall** (1978, S. I. Morris Associates) does not. To the west of the central campus, the university and its architects abdicated all sense of responsibility in the siting and design of new buildings; they might as well be on a different planet.

During the 1960s St. Thomas was the center of vanguard culture in Houston, due largely to the connection of Mr. and Mrs. de Menil with its art department, run by Jermayne MacAgy from 1959 to 1964, and then by Mrs. de Menil until 1969. The second-floor gallery at Jones Hall was the setting for MacAgy's legendary exhibitions; the double-volume common room in Welder Hall (floored-over in 1977) was where local nabobs, students, priests, and artists rubbed shoulders with the luminaries of international culture. With his Miesian architecture, Philip Johnson provided a frame that was authoritative yet accessible; it was through this frame that the spirit of the new entered Houston. On loan from the Menil Foundation are three large steel pieces by Tony Smith, installed in the academic mall. From the upper deck of the walkway one can glimpse Philip Johnson's Transco Tower to the west. Across Yoakum Boulevard from Strake Hall is the Modern Languages Building, originally the childhood home of the reclusive Howard R. Hughes (**3921 Yoakum**, 1918, William Ward Watkin). Attached to the rear of the Hughes House is the university's chapel, a serene, sculpturally shaped room by Glen Heim with Howard Barnstone (1965).

1300 Branard Avenue   **F-54**
University of St. Thomas. Guinan Hall (1971) Howard Barnstone & Eugene Aubry

The university's dormitory is an inwardly turned building configured around a series of courtyards. The austere composition of splayed brick planes, into which voids sealed with obscured glass have been incised, lacks tension.

1409 Sul Ross Avenue   F-55
Rothko Chapel (1971) Howard Barnstone & Eugene Aubry

The Rothko Chapel, an ecumenical center built by Mr. and Mrs. John de Menil to contain 14 paintings executed especially for it by the abstract expressionist painter Mark Rothko, is a provocative building. Although built for the display of paintings, it is not a picture gallery. Although conceived as a chapel, it is not a church. Externally it is apt to appear contrived in its centrality and bland because it lacks constructive detail. Internally it profoundly embodies a sense of tragedy, reconciliation, and silence. The Rothko Chapel is a paradox—the building is mute, there is nothing to see in the paintings, yet this is an intensely moving place. The reflecting pool in front of the chapel contains Barnett Newman's Cor-ten piece "Broken Obelisk" (1967), installed by Mr. and Mrs. de Menil as a memorial to the Rev. Martin Luther King, Jr.

Philip Johnson was originally the chapel's architect. It was planned as part of the university, to be constructed on the site where the Doherty Library eventually was built. Rothko so strongly disapproved of Johnson's designs that Johnson withdrew from the project in 1967. Two years later Mr. and Mrs. de Menil parted company with the University of St. Thomas and chose a new site, adjacent to, but no longer on, the campus. Barnstone & Aubry adapted Johnson's ground plan and Johnson consulted with Eugene Aubry on the resolution of certain details, such as the location of the reflecting pool. The baffles that distribute skylight inside the chapel are a later modification by Aubry (1976, S. I. Morris Associates). Available at the chapel are publications documenting the wide array of religious, political, and cultural activities that have transpired here, as well as Susan J. Barnes's authorized history, *The Rothko Chapel, An Act of Faith*. The Rothko Chapel is open daily.

1427 Branard Avenue   F-56
Menil Foundation Business Office (1974) Howard Barnstone

A spirited conversion of a 1920s bungalow provided offices for one of the departments of the Menil Foundation. Anthony E. Frederick modified the building somewhat when it was transferred to this site from across the street in 1984; he also was responsible for the subtle but exhilarating transformation of two other bungalows for use as Menil outposts. One of these, the **Black Collection Office** (1519 Branard Avenue) is open to the public. During the late 1960s Mr. and Mrs. de Menil began to amass property in this neighborhood for construction of a museum and study center to contain their collection. In 1976, under the direction of Howard Barnstone, all the buildings in this precinct were painted gray-green with white trim, giving the area a distinctly Surreal aspect. Adjacent to the Business Office are Tony Smith's "New Piece" (1966) and "Marriage" (1965).

1515 Sul Ross Avenue   F-57
The Menil Collection (1987) Renzo Piano and Richard Fitzgerald & Partners

Dominique Schlumberger de Menil built this extraordinary building to contain the extensive collection of modernist, Byzantine, classical, and indigenous art and artifacts that she and her husband John (d. 1973) assembled. The Italian architect Renzo Piano, working with the English engineers Ove Arup & Associates, was commissioned in 1981 to design the museum building. (Louis I. Kahn and Howard Barnstone each had done preliminary schemes between 1973 and 1979.) Piano produced a building that is noble in scale, generous in dimension, and devoid of pretension. The broad terrace that circumscribes the museum frames views of—and imposes a sense of measure on—the flat Texas landscape. The Menil's crisp, rectilinear masses, framed with white-painted steel structural members and surfaced with gray-green painted cypress clapboards, provide a subtly proportioned backdrop for the intricate roof assembly, which consolidates skylighting, supporting structure, the graceful S-curve light baffles (Piano calls them "leaves"), lighting, and air-conditioning. The amplitude and luminosity of interior spaces make one realize that designing the "feel" of the place took priority over considerations of image. Nonetheless, Piano fused the rigorous yet delicate modernism of St. Thomas with the austerity of the Rothko Chapel and the distilled homeyness of the neighborhood's bungalows to construct an understated summation of Mr. and Mrs. de Menils' architectural patronage.

As interesting as the galleries and the promenade that joins them are the working spaces of the museum (not open to the public). Staff spaces and conservation and preparation areas are on the ground floor, behind the Branard elevation. Above is what Piano calls the "Treasure House," the isolated third-floor area that contains a series of spacious rooms where scholars can study pieces in the collection when not on exhibition. Mrs. de Menil's insistence on the importance of technical, curatorial, and scholarly activities meant that these parts of the museum were as attentively designed as were the public exhibition galleries.

Across Sul Ross from the front entrance to the museum is the Brazos Bookstore. Parking is a half-block away. A media center and restaurant are scheduled to be built in the vicinity. Sunk into the turf beneath the main approach walk to the museum is Michael Heizer's "Isolated Mass/Circumflex (#2)" (1968-78); across the street at Sul Ross and Mulberry is Mark di Suvero's "Bygones" (1976). **Richmond Hall**, an ex-Weingarten's grocery market (1934, Joseph Finger) at 1416 Richmond Avenue, has been transformed by Anthony E. Frederick into the Menil's own alternative gallery.

1715 West Alabama Avenue   **F-58**
Wilshire Village Apartments (1940)
Eugene Werlin

Of the three original FHA-insured garden apartment complexes built in Houston, Wilshire Village is the only one still extant. It offers many intelligent lessons in the planning of multiple unit housing, especially in the configuration of outdoor spaces and the inclusion of such amenities as the projecting window bays.

2512 Mandell Street   **F-59**
(1973) George P. Englert

Englert transformed an existing garage-apartment into his own house with a stucco screen wall that defines layers of deep and shallow space. Following Englert's death, the house was acquired by the architect Thomas M. Lonnecker, who has expanded it with great tact.

1802 Missouri Avenue   **F-60**
(c. 1922)

The "Alamo" parapet was a popular device for brick-faced bungalows.

1801 Westheimer Road   **F-61**
Tower Theater (1936) W. Scott Dunne

In the middle 1930s, Interstate Circuit, Inc. of Dallas, the major film distributor in Texas, moved out into the suburbs to develop neighborhood theaters and shopping center complexes. The Tower was its first such venture in Houston. Although the adjacent **Tower Community Center** between Montrose and Yoakum (1937, Joseph Finger) has had its flamboyant modernistic frontispieces embalmed in sprayed-on stucco, the theater itself, by the Dallas architect who specialized in this building type, retains its splendid pylon and illuminated front. Used for live performances since 1978, the Tower underwent exterior restoration by Barry Moore Architects in 1988.

415 Hyde Park Boulevard   F-62
L'Encore (1927) Frederick Leon Webster

This three-story Mediterranean tower house was designed, built, and occupied by Frederick Leon Webster, director of the Little Theater of Houston. It is a prime example of the fascination with the quaint, the diminutive, and the exotic that typified American architectural eclecticism in the 1920s. Occupying a 20-by-22-foot pad, it sits at one corner of a half-lot site to make room for the dense, intimate gardens that Webster planted. The other half of the lot, at 411 Hyde Park, is occupied by a shingled double house that Webster built in 1921 as his original studio and then expanded in 1927 with the addition of a small apartment.

100 block Tuam Avenue   F-63
Houston Lighting & Power Co.
Hyde Park Substation (1986)
Denny*Ray*Wines Associates

Neighborhood protest against the unsightliness of an HL&P installation paid off when the light company retained Denny*Ray*Wines to screen it with this lively brick, textured block, glass block, and chain link wall, incorporating a bus stop pavilion and ample planting.

1207 West Dallas Avenue   F-64
Beth Israel Cemetery
Temple of Rest (1935) Joseph Finger

Finger's modernistic classicism takes on an appropriately funereal note in this limestone-faced mausoleum. It is situated in Beth Israel Cemetery (originally Hebrew Cemetery), the oldest Jewish institution in Texas. The cemetery was founded in 1844, ten years after the organization of Congregation Beth Israel, the oldest Jewish congregation in Texas. Next to Beth Israel is Founders Memorial Park (originally City

Cemetery), where John K. Allen, one of the founders of Houston, is buried. Like other early cemeteries, Beth Israel and Founders were located on the outskirts of the Houston townsite, in this case along the main highway to San Felipe de Austin, another pioneer Anglo-American settlement, on the Brazos River.

809 Robin Street   F-65
(c. 1870s)

This tiny house is an archetypal example of the Gulf Coast cottage. Its side-facing gables, inset porch, and random width clapboards suggest that it is one of the oldest surviving houses in what has been variously known as Freedmantown or the San Felipe district, the neighborhood on the edge of Houston where emancipated slaves settled in the late 1860s. Comprising about 90 blocks, Fourth Ward, as the community is now known, once extended as far north as Buffalo Bayou (San Felipe Courts sits on what was the original site of Freedmantown) and as far east as Smith Street, where an institutional center existed around Antioch Baptist Church. West Dallas Avenue, the original San Felipe Road, was the main business corridor.

1318 Andrews Street   F-66
(c. 1870)

The Reverend John Henry Yates, pastor of Antioch Baptist Church, purchased the property on which he built this two-story wooden house in 1870. It is the oldest dateable building in Fourth Ward. The Yates

Homestead is a three-bay Southern town-house, typologically akin to the Nichols-Rice-Cherry House in Sam Houston Park. Across the street at 1319 Andrews is the raised cottage of another minister, Rev. Ned Pullam. Andrews Street contains some of the most substantial houses remaining in Fourth Ward. They contrast markedly with the towers of downtown Houston, which at this point loom dramatically over the neighborhood. Fourth Ward conserves a way of life once typical of Southern communities, white as well as black. Residents still spend time on their front porches socializing with passersby. It is not unusual for traffic in the narrow streets to be brought to a halt while a motorist converses leisurely with an acquaintance on a porch.

traditional explanation of the term "shotgun" is that if one fired a shotgun through the front door, the pellets would pass straight through the house and out the back door. This row of ten identical shotgun cottages is an illustration of the remarkable urbanistic impact that such simple vernacular houses can have when grouped in series.

1701 Montrose Boulevard   **F-69**
Montrose Veterinary Clinic (1989)
Leslie Barry Davidson

Davidson picturesquely extrapolated elements of the early 20th-century house types common in this neighborhood for a new veterinary clinic building.

1402 Saulnier Street   **F-67**
Good Hope Missionary Baptist Church
(1929) J. J. Hawkins

In the densely built confines of Fourth Ward the twin towers of Good Hope have the presence of a medieval cathedral in a small village. The architect, Jesse J. Hawkins, used stucco and rock-faced block to give the church's facade a sense of monumentality; his decorative detail is freewheeling, even slightly Art Deco, in character. Churches are still numerous in Fourth Ward, another 19th-century trait that persists here in the shadows of the downtown skyscrapers. Among them, Good Hope is architecturally preeminent.

1116 Willard Street   **F-70**
Jiménez Studio (1983, 1984, 1986)
Carlos Jiménez

The three stucco-surfaced buildings that comprise this group—the red, pyramid-roofed house, the blue, gabled studio, and the tall, thin *studiolo*—radiate an intensity that belies their apparent simplicity.

1501-1519 Victor Street   **F-68**
(c. 1900)

Of the housing types associated with Afro-American urban settlement in the South, the shotgun cottage is the best known. It is usually a long, narrow, one-story house prefaced by a porch, its rooms lined up in single file with all doorways aligned. The

1210 West Clay Avenue   **F-71**
Clarke & Courts Building (1936)
Joseph Finger

The continuous horizontal bands of steel sash, bulbous horizontal speed lines, curved corners, and above all the stepped-back pylon tower with architecturally integrated graphics make this one of the modernistic highlights of Finger's career. The building, a commercial printing plant, is built entirely of reinforced concrete.

3401 Allen Parkway   F-72
Rein Co. Building [now Allenpark Federal Savings & Loan] (1928) Howell & Thomas

The first increment of the Buffalo Bayou Parkway, a "pleasure drive" now called Allen Parkway, was built between 1925 and 1926 to the designs of the Kansas City landscape architects Hare & Hare. It ran from Sam Houston Park westward along the course of the bayou to the newly planned garden suburb of River Oaks. Will Hogg, the developer of River Oaks, had assisted the city with land acquisition for the parkway and he was determined that no inappropriate land use occur along its length. Hogg had no legal jurisdiction, but his influence must have been considerable, for the three printing plants built along the parkway in the late 1920s each adapted Spanish-Mediterranean attributes to conceal their industrial status. The area itself was euphemistically described as the "crafts district." The Rein Co., designed by a firm of Cleveland architects that specialized in printing plants, clearly distinguished the two-story office and advertising studio wing from the single-story plant wing. The clock tower is the pivot point about which both the building and the parkway drive rotate. Charles Tapley Associates was responsible for the building's conversion into a savings and loan institution in 1976; it added the pergola and cut new windows into the plant wing. Across D'Amico Street, to the rear, is the round-towered **Stedman Studio** (3327 D'Amico, 1927), built by a commercial artist as his studio and residence.

3301 Allen Parkway   F-73
Gulf Publishing Co. Building (1928) Hedrick & Gottlieb

Traffic engineering has brought Allen Parkway within a few feet of this sprawling, stucco-faced printing plant, the first to be completed in the area. The cast stone frontispiece facing Rochow Street bristles with *estípites*, twisted columns, and broken and scrolled curved pediments; it is appropriately florid. Alfred C. Finn designed extensive but harmonious additions (1936, 1939). The Gulf Publishing and Rein Co. buildings evidently won Hogg's approbation, since

the magazine he published, *Civics for Houston*, saluted them as "beautiful structures" of "unusually pleasant design."

3201 Allen Parkway   F-74
Star Engraving Co. Building [now 3201 Allen Parkway Building] (1930) R. D. Steele

Perched atop a bluff overlooking the parkway, this long-deserted Spanish style printing plant looks far better today than it must have when new. The snappy color combinations are particularly effective. Mainland Building and Development Group was responsible for the building's recycling as offices, temporary quarters for the Children's Museum, and the repertory theater, Stages (1985, W. O. Neuhaus Associates).

2727 Allen Parkway   F-75
American General Building [now Wortham Tower] (1965) Lloyd, Morgan & Jones

The 25-story American General Building was the first in a complex of office buildings developed by the American General Life Insurance Co. during the 1970s and

'80s. Arthur Jones designed the tower to stand on a terrace plinth (concealing the parking garage) above the rolling terrain alongside the bayou. The glass curtain wall is recessed behind a precast concrete grid, giving the tower its light, clean, '60s modern look. Other buildings in the complex are the 6-story **American General Life Building** (1979, Lloyd Jones Brewer & Associates) behind the Wortham Tower, the 15-story **LNG-Liberty Tower** at 2711 (1977, Lloyd Jones Associates), the 15-story **Riviana Building** at 2731 (1974, Lloyd Jones Associates), and the 42-story **America Tower** at 2929 (1983, Lloyd Jones Brewer & Associates). The American General Building remains the best.

1801 Allen Parkway   **F-76**
Jefferson Davis Hospital (1937) Alfred C. Finn and Joseph Finger

During the 1930s major public works projects were built along the Buffalo Bayou Parkway, which had been almost completely undeveloped prior to 1926. The tallest of these was the city-county public health hospital, Jefferson Davis, designed in 1931 but not begun until 1936 when Public Works Administration funding was obtained. It is a 12-story, cruciform, setback skyscraper, defaced however by the crude addition of stair towers in the 1980s. Closed in 1989, the 10-acre complex is unused and the fate of this fine modernistic building is in doubt. Across Allen Parkway from the hospital, on the crest of a low hill, sits Henry Moore's bronze "Large Spindle Piece," (1968, 1974), installed in 1979.

1 Allen Parkway   **F-77**
San Felipe Courts [now Allen Parkway Village] (1942, 1944) Associated Housing Architects of Houston

San Felipe Courts was the largest USHA-

financed, low-income housing community constructed in the South during the 1940s. It was also the most outstanding architecturally, due to the participation of MacKie & Kamrath as designers for Associated Housing Architects, a consortium of 12 Houston firms. Its precisely defined contours, cantilevered concrete canopies, and artful brick and tile banding represented a much higher standard of design and detailing than was customary for USHA housing. The landscape architect J. Allen Myers, Jr., laid out the *allée* of live oak trees defining the central lane and the densely planted garden courts between the apartment blocks to either side of it. Despite lack of maintenance by the Housing Authority of the City of Houston, San Felipe Courts remains a superlative example of public housing for low income families.

2302 Fannin Street   **F-78**
Gibraltar Building (1959) Greacen & Brogniez with J. Victor Neuhaus III

The five-story Gibraltar Building is a minor modern landmark; it was the first building in Houston to have walls faced entirely in heat absorbing, solar gray glass. Raymond H. Brogniez incorporated drive-in windows beneath the building; the double-volume banking hall occurred on the second floor. The building was originally lit at night to reveal its internal sectional organization. The Fannin front and the south-facing side walls have been refaced in silver reflective glass and both the double-height banking hall and the interiors by Knoll Associates have vanished.

2301 Main Street   **F-79**
Knoll Building Houston (1984) Tigerman Fugman McCurry with Ray Bailey Architects

Stanley Tigerman's transformation of an old auto showroom into a showplace of corporate design included the application of a snappy red grid to the exterior and a superimposed "negative" pediment to mark the main entrance. The parking lot is a *cour d'honneur*, studded with trees and more axially-aligned virtual pediments. The interior is much less exceptional, despite a skylight that parallels the axial central runway, changes in floor level, and wavy cross walls.

2325 Milam Street   **F-80**
Fire Station #7 [now Houston Fire Museum] (1899) Olle J. Lorehn

The oldest fire station remaining in city ownership, Fire Station #7 was built to serve the South End neighborhoods that flanked upper Main Street. Rough-faced stone trim contrasted with smooth pressed brickwork and the decorative roundels above the square-headed stall openings were characteristic of Lorehn. Since 1982 the building has contained a museum documenting the history of the Houston Fire Department.

2421 Milam Street   **F-81**
(1911) George Freuhling

The house that Freuhling designed and built for Mr. and Mrs. R. C. Duff was once a South End showplace, famous for the international musical celebrities whom Mrs. Duff entertained and the terraced formal gardens which extended to the corner of McGowen Avenue and Travis Street. The Colonial Revival style house itself originally faced McGowen; it was turned to face Milam and moved to one corner of its site in 1937, when the property was subdivided. R. C. Duff built the three-story **Sheridan Apartments**, across McGowen at 2603 Milam Street, in 1922. They are typical of the many apartment buildings constructed in the South End suburbs along the trolley car lines that tied the area to the downtown core. Across Milam from the Duff House was another grandiose neighborhood landmark, St. Paul's Methodist Church (1909,

R. D. Steele and E. J. Fountain). The domed classical building later became Second Baptist Church; it was pulled down in 1969.

2710 Albany Street   **F-82**
DePelchin Faith Home (1913) Mauran & Russell

Above the arcaded loggia that runs across the ground floor of what was built as an orphanage are two floors of sleeping porches—originally enclosed only with screening and a wide, bracketed eaves. The Italianate imagery of this graceful building perhaps owed something to the new buildings of the Rice Institute.

Hermann Park / Medical Center

Despite Houston's reputation as an unplanned city, there are precincts where civic planning has produced memorable public landscapes. The most impressive of these lies along Main Street in its passage between The Museum of Fine Arts, and the Texas Medical Center, near Hermann Park and the campus of Rice University. The park and boulevard improvement scheme carried out in 1916 and 1917 under the direction of the St. Louis landscape architect George E. Kessler responded wholeheartedly to the initial impetus for large scale planning in the neighborhood: the new Rice Institute campus, laid out by the Boston architects Cram, Goodhue & Ferguson, which opened in 1912. The staged rows of live oak trees that flank this segment of Main Street, the lanes of the Rice campus, and streets in many of the neighborhoods developed nearby in the 1920s give the public way here a strong sense of spatial definition. Streets are positive spaces that have been transformed through use into distinctive public places. The voluntary cooperation of various institutions and individuals in shaping this civic landscape has resulted in a collective realm, one that provides a coherent spatial frame for the buildings and sites connected to it.

On the doorstep of this exemplary district, the Texas Medical Center comes as a shock. The lesson in civic decorum that Main Boulevard offers has gone unheeded here. In this district devoted to human well-being, contempt for the environment prevails, reducing this dense cluster of hospital, teaching and research, office, hotel, and parking buildings to a competitive, hostile, and—to outsiders—incoherent agglomeration, garnished around the edges with inconsequential bits of suburban shrubbery. The act of vandalism that the medical center's administrative agency, the Texas Medical Center, Inc., committed in 1987 when it demolished one of Houston's most popular landmarks, the Shamrock Hotel, bespeaks the elementary failure of this public institution to accept the responsibility of citizenship, of being part of the city. As Richard Ingersoll noted in 1989, "unless the Texas Medical Center, Inc. instills in its members a sense of greater public responsibility, the confusion will continue..."

At what seems like, but isn't, the end of Main lies the ultimate popular Houston landmark, the Astrodome. Here the Texan condition of vast space can be powerfully experienced in its immeasurable parking lot and in the giant, introverted well of space within, an exaggerated contrast of emptiness and plentitude characteristic of Texas, but very different from the spatial tunnels of Main Boulevard.

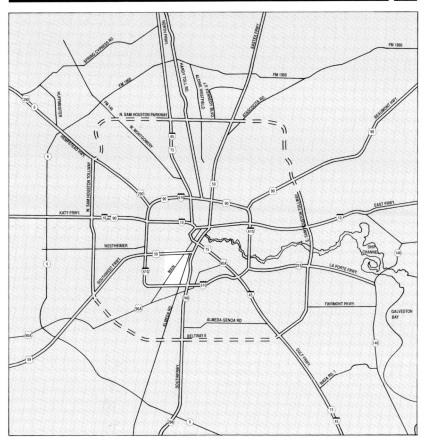

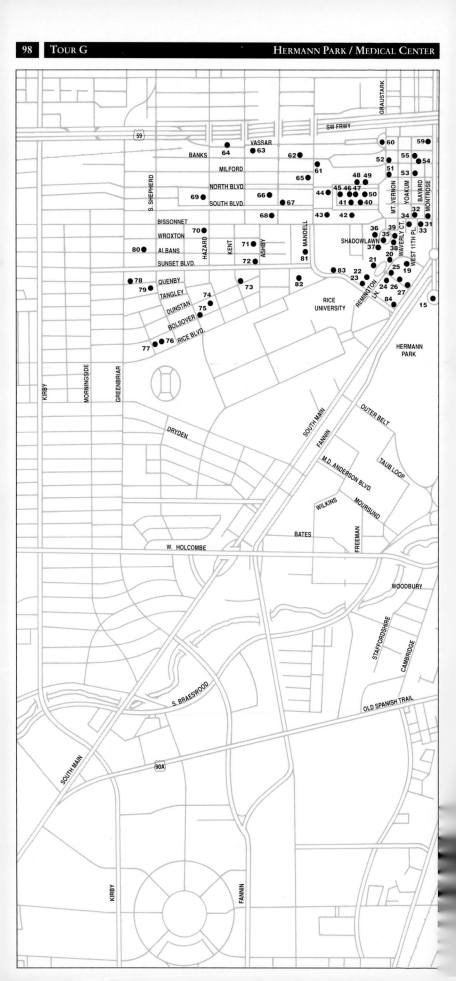

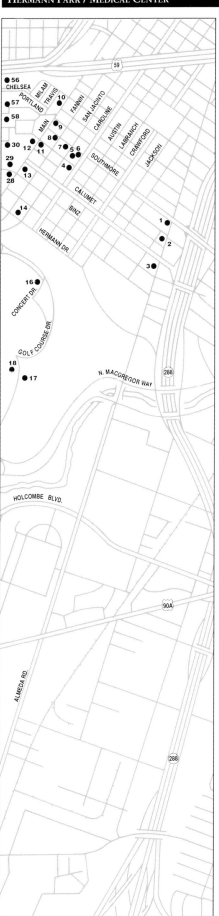

1. 5202 Almeda Road
2. 5302-5314 Almeda Road
3. 5516 Almeda Road
4. 5300 Caroline Street
5. 5220 Caroline Street
6. 1220 Southmore Avenue
7. 1112 Southmore Avenue
8. 5210 Fannin Street
9. 5115 Main Street
10. 4912 Main Street
11. 5315 Main Street
12. 5300 Main Street
13. 5501 Main Street
14. 1111 Hermann Drive
15. Hermann Park
16. 100 Concert Drive
17. 6200 Golf Course Drive
18. 1513 Outer Belt Drive
19. 3 Remington Lane
20. 8 Remington Lane
21. 10 Remington Lane
22. 12 Remington Lane
23. 14 Remington Lane
24. 9 Remington Lane
25. 6 Longfellow Lane
26. 4 Longfellow Lane
27. 4 Longfellow Lane
28. 1001 Bissonnet Avenue
29. Bissonnet Avenue and Montrose Boulevard
30. 5101 Montrose Boulevard
31. 5216 Montrose Boulevard
32. 5215 Yoakum Boulevard
33. 1 West 11th Place
34. 2 Waverly Court
35. 17 Shadowlawn Circle
36. 11 Shadowlawn Circle
37. 9 Shadowlawn Circle
38. 6 Shadowlawn Circle
39. 5 Shadowlawn Circle
40. 1324 South Boulevard
41. 1400 South Boulevard
42. 1405 South Boulevard
43. 1515 South Boulevard
44. 1505 North Boulevard
45. 1411 North Boulevard
46. 1405 North Boulevard
47. 1323 North Boulevard
48. 1324 North Boulevard
49. 1318 North Boulevard
50. 1317 North Boulevard
51. 4923-4927 Graustark Street
52. 1220 Milford Street
53. 4949 Yoakum Boulevard
54. 1110 Milford Street
55. 1117 Banks Street
56. 4611-4621 Montrose Boulevard
57. 216-222, 238-242, 243, and 302
    Portland Street
58. 4911 Montrose Boulevard
59. 4704 Montrose Boulevard
60. 1303 Vassar Place
61. 4901-4903 Mandell Street
62. 1638 Banks Street
63. 1731-1733 Vassar Place
64. 1906 Vassar Place
65. 1601 Milford Street
66. 1705 North Boulevard
67. 1660 South Boulevard
68. 1707 South Boulevard
69. 5100 Hazard Street
70. 2003 Bissonnet Avenue
71. 1807 Wroxton Road
72. 1802 Sunset Boulevard
73. 1828 Dunstan Road
74. 2007 Dunstan Road
75. 2032 Bolsover Road
76. 2217 Bolsover Road
77. 2229 Bolsover Road
78. 2246 Quenby Road
78. 2229 Quenby Road
80. 2238 Albans Road
81. 5326 Mandell Street
82. 1601 Sunset Boulevard
83. 1500 Sunset Boulevard
84. 2 Sunset Road

5202 Almeda Road G-1
Houston Turn-Verein Clubhouse (1929)
Joseph Finger

Reduced by neglect and vandalism to a seriously deteriorated state, the former clubhouse of Houston's oldest German social
club sports lively Art Deco detail, notably
the relief plaques above the piers of what
originally was an open gallery and the
slightly intimidating Teutonic insignia.
Finger described the architecture as being a
"modification of German Secession and Art
Nouveau."

5300 Caroline Street G-4
[now Clayton Library Center for
Genealogical Research] (1917)
Birdsall P. Briscoe

Briscoe designed this well-proportioned
neo-Georgian house for Susan Vaughan and
William L. Clayton. Clayton, co-founder of
the cotton exporting firm of Anderson,
Clayton & Co. and Under-Secretary of
State for Economic Affairs during the
Truman administration, and his wife had
Briscoe alter and expand the house on several occasions. Briscoe converted the original
garage at Oakdale and San Jacinto into a
delightful guest house in 1932 and in 1936
transformed a sun porch into a panelled
library, replete with wood carving by the
Austin craftsman Peter Mansbendel that cel-
ebrates iconographically the source of Clayton's wealth. Since 1966 the house has been
open to the public as the Houston Public
Library's genealogical research center.

5302-5314 Almeda Road G-2
Patio Shops (1931) B. W. Holtz and H. M.
Sanford

The Patio Shops are a vintage strip shopping center organized to take advantage of a
wedge-shaped site and liberally decorated
with Spanish detail.

5220 Caroline Street G-5
Winslow Court (1929) Russell Brown Co.

At first sight the Winslow Court appears to
be a slightly eccentric mansion. Presumably
the intention was for it to blend with its
context, since it was the first apartment
building to be constructed along what had
been a boulevard of single-family houses.

5516 Almeda Road G-3
Third Church of Christ, Scientist (1928)
Henry F. Jonas & Tabor

J. Rodney Tabor's Mediterranean style
church pays homage to the First Church of
Christ, Scientist in Palo Alto, California by
the architect Elmer Gray. With its octagonal
lantern, tile roofs, and pink-colored stucco
walls, it is a distinctly Californian amalga-
mation of north Italian and Byzantine
detail.

1220 Southmore Avenue G-6
(c. 1915)

This stucco-surfaced, tile-roofed house, one
of the earliest built in the Southmore
Addition, appears to have been a sympa-

thetic reaction to the Mediterranean style residential halls on the nearby campus of the Rice Institute. Like them it has a three-story belvedere tower.

1112 Southmore Avenue   G-7
(1923) Maurice J. Sullivan

Sullivan designed this house for his family and it is due to filial piety that it survives in good condition. It represents a combination of attributes often seen in the 1920s: the English-influenced picturesque manor house prominently displaying an Italian loggia, a cultural conjunction that must have been especially welcome in sultry Houston.

5210 Fannin Street   G-8
First Unitarian Church (1952)
Thomas E. Greacen II

Greacen configured the church and its educational building around a central courtyard entered directly from the street. The influence of Eliel Saarinen's Middle Western churches of the 1940s is evident in this understated complex. Subsequent additions have not adhered to the quality of the original.

5115 Main Street   G-9
Bank of Houston Building (1967) Wilson, Morris, Crain & Anderson

John Bertini, who designed this steel-framed, glass-walled pavilion, paid tribute to Ludwig Mies van der Rohe's National Gallery in Berlin. However, as one of

Bertini's partners observed, the homage was completed before the original.

4912 Main Street   G-10
Weldon's Cafeteria [now Massey Business College] (1949) MacKie & Kamrath

The taut horizontals, precise stone copings, and cantilevered balcony display the Kamrath touch, which transformed what might otherwise have been a nondescript storefront into a spirited exposition of modern design. Next door, at 4910 Main, is Joseph Finger's Art Deco **Barker Brothers Studio** of 1931.

5315 Main Street   G-11
First Congregational Church [now St. Matthew Lutheran Church] (1927) J. W. Northrop, Jr.

Northrop employed both a Lombard Romanesque stylistic formula and materials quite similar to those of his First Evangelical Church, which was designed and built at the same time as First Congregational. Their effect has proved compelling; the extensive additions for St. Matthew Lutheran by Bailey A. Swenson (parish hall, 1942) and Harry A. Turner & Charles E. Geyer (the chapel and cloister extension on Prospect and the school wing on Oakdale, 1955) are almost indistinguishable from the original structure.

5300 Main Street   G-12
First Presbyterian Church (1949) Hobart Upjohn and Maurice J. Sullivan

In its isolated setting, the big scale of First Presbyterian is not as monumental as it ought to be, although the austere classical detail framing the Main Street entrance portal is quite grand. Herring Coe executed the sculptural work. Upjohn, a New York architect, was the last in a dynasty of American church architects, each member of which designed a Texas church. The grandfather, Richard Upjohn, was responsible for St. Mark's, San Antonio; the father, Richard M. Upjohn, for St. James, La Grange; the grandson for First

Presbyterian, which could easily hold the other two. Extensive additions to the rear are by Ray Bailey Architects (1987).

The bridge levels spanning between the towers contain living rooms in the most deluxe apartment units.

5501 Main Street   G-13
St. Paul's Methodist Church (1930)
Alfred C. Finn

Pious competition asserted itself along Main Street in the late 1920s. St. Paul's, a slick, neo-Gothic, cathedral-style church, was clearly the winner. Like so many in that decade, the church owes much to the influence of the New York architect Bertram G. Goodhue. The lofty interior of the steel-framed church is as impressive as the limestone-clad exterior, although the insertion of a Protestant preaching box surmounted by a choir, in place of the expected high altar, is a bit disconcerting.

1111 Hermann Drive   G-14
The Warwick Towers (1983) Golemon & Rolfe and Werlin, Deane & Associates

Allen Rice was responsible for this handsome pair of 30-story condominium apartment towers, built of precast concrete.

Hermann Park   G-15
Sam Houston Statue (1925)
Enrico F. Cerracchio, sculptor,
J. W. Northrop, Jr., architect

Cerracchio's bronze equestrian statue of Sam Houston, the frequently outrageous adventurer, statesman, and soldier for whom the city is named, faces east; his outstretched arm points toward the San Jacinto battlefield, 19 miles away, where Houston's victory over the army of Mexico in 1836 ensured the independence of Texas. This was the major work of public art erected in Houston during the heyday of the City Beautiful movement, a set piece that now seems to direct incoming traffic toward the park's central parking lot.

The monument terminates the view up Montrose (or at least it did until the Mecom Fountain was installed in what had been the Sunken Garden at Montrose and Main in 1964). Its location is pivotal since it deflects traffic off-axis onto the curving loop roads that originally subdivided the 410-acre park. This was all part of the master plan devised by the St. Louis landscape architect George E. Kessler in 1916, two years after the property had been donated to the city by George H. Hermann. Kessler's master plan included the conversion of Main Street, from McGowen all the way south to Bellaire, into Main Boulevard. It was under Kessler's direction that the magnificent *allée* of live oak trees was planted along Main between Bissonnet and University. After Kessler's death in 1923, the master plan was carried out by the Kansas City landscape architects Hare & Hare into the 1950s. Since the 1970s, however, Kessler's and Hare & Hare's improvements have been whittled away in an effort to accommodate increasing use, increasing traffic, and the growth of various cultural institutions located in the park.

100 Concert Drive   **G-16**
Hermann Park Miller Outdoor Theater
(1968) Eugene Werlin & Associates

The dramatic canopy shielding fixed seating is composed of three triangular folded plates of Cor-ten steel that span 95 feet between support points. Across Hermann Circle Drive from the theater hill is the **Houston Museum of Natural Science** with its Burke Baker Planetarium (1964, George Pierce-Abel B. Pierce and Staub, Rather & Howze) and Wortham IMAX Theater (1989, Hoover & Furr and 3D/International).

6200 Golf Course Drive   **G-17**
Hermann Park Clubhouse
(1933) Arthur E. Nutter

Nutter's clubhouse is a picturesque Mediterranean style building composed around a flagstone paved common room. Broad *portales* face the golf course.

1513 Outer Belt Drive   **G-18**
Hermann Park Houston Zoological Gardens Concourse and Concession Building (1950) Hare & Hare, landscape architects, Irving R. Klein & Associates, architects

The concourse of the Houston Zoo is one of the most beautiful public open spaces in Houston. Hare & Hare demonstrated how compelling Houston can be when plantings,

water, and architectural structures are coordinated to give form to a place in what is too often a flat, monotonous landscape. The central water channel is flanked by rows of live oak trees and low, stepped terraces faced with benches. Defining the outer edges of the concourse are a pair of free-standing concrete canopies that run the entire length of the water channel. At the right of the head of the channel lies Klein's elegant **Concession Building**, which forms an open air circle adjacent to a shallow lagoon containing two mature cypress trees. Regrettably, the exceptional quality of this space has not been respected and preserved by the city's Parks and Recreation Department. The original gates were demolished to build the intrusive **Kipp Aquarium and Entrance Building** (1982, Pierce Goodwin Alexander) and the viewing stand for the Seal Pool at the foot of the concourse (1988) departs considerably from Hare & Hare's and Klein's architectural standards. The **Primate House** (1950, Irving R. Klein & Associates), the concourse's terminal feature, is slated for demolition. Other additions to the zoo grounds do adhere to original design standards, especially the **Large Cat Facility** (1984, Caudill Rowlett Scott), an ambitious piece of landscape architecture, and the **George R. Brown Education Center** (1988, Ray Bailey Architects), which incorporates Herring Coe's cast stone plaques (1952), salvaged from the demolished entry gate piers.

3 Remington Lane   **G-19**
(1938) John F. Staub

Staub's particular gifts as an architect are admirably demonstrated in this house. Its splayed plan responds to the curvature of the street, its shallow depth allows through ventilation, and its assured composition gracefully disguises the fact that major rooms are oriented toward the private rear garden rather than the street. The house is a condensation of early 19th-century English Regency architectural themes, "regionalized" in a Louisiana Creole interpretation. The house was designed for the daughter of J. S. Cullinan, the founder of the Texas Co. (Texaco). Cullinan developed this small enclave neighborhood, Shadyside, in 1916. He retained George E. Kessler to lay out the subdivision and then invited his friends and business associates to build their houses here. Across the street lies the site of Cullinan's own house, a huge brick pile demolished in 1972.

8 Remington Lane   **G-20**
(1923) H. T. Lindeberg

Harrie T. Lindeberg was one of New York's foremost "country house" architects when he was commissioned to design four houses in Shadyside in the early 1920s. Lindeberg displayed his considerable versatility by designing each in a different style. This pink stucco surfaced, tile-roofed Spanish farmhouse turns its arcaded loggia toward the prevailing breeze. Consequently, the front door ends up in the backyard, an environmentally-sanctioned breach of convention frequently employed by John F. Staub, who came to Houston in 1921 to supervise construction of the four houses for Lindeberg and remained to start his own practice.

10 Remington Lane   **G-21**
(1925) H. T. Lindeberg

This very restrained English Regency style house is a work of considerable architectural stature: quite grand but extremely understated, in the best country house tradition. One of Lindeberg's trademarks, the spider-in-the-web iron grille, is visible at the front entrance. Delicate wrought iron pergolas create a complex play of shadows on the lower half of the textured stucco walls.

12 Remington Lane   **G-22**
(1920) Alfred C. Finn

When Lindeberg arrived in Shadyside, this is what local architects were producing: big-scaled, unsubtle versions of the country house look, here of remote English Jacobean derivation.

14 Remington Lane   **G-23**
(1924) Briscoe & Dixon

Not all of J. S. Cullinan's friends were rich; those who weren't demonstrated that it was possible to live with propriety and grace in such modest houses as this French manorial style dwelling. Briscoe cleverly pulled the garage into the architectural composition to make the building mass seem larger.

9 Remington Lane   **G-24**
(1923) H. T. Lindeberg

Generally considered Lindeberg's outstanding work in Houston, this spectacular house is in the picturesque cottage style with which he made his reputation. The roof of closely-lapped shingles that imitate the texture of thatch is called a Lindeberg roof. As was customary of American country house architects, Lindeberg took careful note of climate and planning, organizing the L-plan house so that major rooms open toward a rear garden and the prevailing southeast breeze. The client, the investment banker Hugo V. Neuhaus, was so enthusiastic that he secured for Lindeberg his other Shadyside commissions. Neuhaus's eldest son, the modernist architect Hugo V. Neuhaus, Jr., grew up in this house.

6 Longfellow Lane   **G-25**
(1926) Birdsall P. Briscoe

Briscoe seems to have learned from Lindeberg's Shadyside houses by the time he designed this Jacobean style house for J. S. Cullinan's son, Craig Cullinan. It is a richly, but subtly, ornamented house, as a close look at its decorative brick bonding, stained glass windows, and wood carving—by Peter Mansbendel—reveals.

4 Longfellow Lane   **G-26**
(1923) Briscoe & Dixon

A formal neo-Georgian production; like all good country house architects, Briscoe was necessarily a master of many styles.

2 Longfellow Lane   **G-27**
(1924) H. T. Lindeberg

The stucco-faced wing that advances closest to the street is a late addition to a mannerist version of an English Georgian style house. It is symmetrical on its garden elevation, but asymmetrical on its motor court side. There Lindeberg juggled divergent axes of approach and composition to compensate for the fact that the house faces the side property lines to facilitate ventilation, rather than facing the street.

1001 Bissonnet Avenue   **G-28**
The Museum of Fine Arts, Houston (1924, 1926)William Ward Watkin; Ralph Adams Cram, consulting architect (1958, 1974) Ludwig Mies van der Rohe with Staub, Rather & Howze (1958) and the Office of Ludwig Mies van der Rohe (1974)

The Museum of Fine Arts, the first public art museum to be built in Texas, was designed to sit opposite Shadyside and the entrance to Hermann Park in order to comprise (along with the campus of Rice University) a new precinct on the edge of the city in the 1920s, planned in accord with the precepts of the City Beautiful movement as exemplifying the best of Houston. Watkin's limestone-faced museum—a screen of Ionic columns framed by slightly angled wings—is a paradigmatic City

Beautiful temple of high culture, taking its place alongside the large Gothic and Romanesque churches of Main Street in a kind of textbook presentation of great moments in architectural history.

When additions were needed, they were made by encasing the rear of Watkin's building; as has become the case elsewhere, what was once the front door no longer admits visitors to the museum. The magisterial **Brown Pavilion** and **Cullinan Hall**, by the great German-American architect Ludwig Mies van der Rohe, form the new front. Mies, once director of the Bauhaus and a founder of the Modern Movement in

20th-century architecture, was commissioned in 1954 to prepare a plan for the expansion of the Watkin building. He proposed filling in a rear courtyard with Cullinan Hall, an awesome double-volume space a half-level above the main entrance on Bissonnet, and wrapping around its north face the two-story Brown Pavilion. This plan was carried out in two stages, the second completed five years after Mies's death in 1969. The Mies building is one of those great moments in architectural history for which the 1920s buildings surrounding it are stand-ins. It is a classic: precise, subtle, serene, and charged with spatial grandeur, full of the "nothing" to which Mies paradoxically aspired to reduce architecture. It is the finest modern building in Houston.

**Bissonnet Avenue and Montrose
Boulevard**   **G-29**
Lillie and Hugh Roy Cullen Sculpture
Garden (1986) Isamu Noguchi
with Fuller & Sadao

The Japanese-American sculptor, Isamu
Noguchi, made here a solemn place in
which to contemplate the Museum of Fine
Arts's sculpture collection, a walled garden
that does not so much shut out Houston as
it edits, condenses, and intensifies it. The
broad granite causeways replicate the essential flatness of Houston; walls, hillocks, and
free-standing granite planes modulate this
horizontally extensive, slow-moving space.
In the Cullen Sculpture Garden Noguchi
came to terms with Houston. His interpretation is utterly unlike Hare & Hare's at the
Houston Zoo. But its subtlety (the way an
angled gravel bed along the Montrose wall
seems to have been thrust into the garden
by the Contemporary Arts Museum across
the street) and intensity are profound and
powerfully affecting.

5101 Montrose Boulevard   **G-30**
Alfred C. Glassell, Jr., School of Art (1978)
S. I. Morris Associates

Eugene Aubry, who designed the museum's
art school building, exposed its poured-in-
place concrete frame externally and internally, filling it with a gridded, reflective
membrane of insulated glass block. The
central gallery, where changing exhibitions
are mounted, is a double-volume, skylit
spine that slices the building in two.
Illuminated at night, the Glassell School
becomes an inhabited cut-away section,
revealing its contents and occupants.

5216 Montrose Boulevard   **G-31**
Contemporary Arts Museum (1972)
Gunnar Birkerts & Associates with
Charles Tapley Associates

The pointy, knife-edged corners and reflective stainless steel sheathing of the
Contemporary Arts Museum represent the
attempt of the Michigan architect Gunnar
Birkerts to deflect the building away from

Mies's museum across the street. The parallelogram-shaped exhibition space inside
never quite came off as the warehouse loft
that it was intended to resemble; it was considerably improved with a remodeling carried out by Morris*Architects in 1987.
Down below are a smaller gallery and the
museum shop. Mel Chin's "Manila Palm"
(1978) is installed behind the museum.

5215 Yoakum Boulevard   **G-32**
Helmet House (1985) Alan Hirschfield

Hirschfield described this aggressively
composed infill house as a Teutonic knight.

1 West 11th Place   **G-33**
(1925) William Ward Watkin

A compact French provincial style house
(minus its shutters, unfortunately) that sits
at the foot of a small private street laid out
by the architect J. W. Northrop, Jr., in 1920.
Northrop was responsible for the houses at
2, 4, 5, and 6 West 11th Place.

2 Waverly Court   **G-34**
(1952) Wilson, Morris & Crain

This small-scaled contemporary house,
closed off from the traffic along Bissonnet,
is focused on a series of internal garden
courts. The propylaeum astride the garden

path is a late addition by Morris*Aubry Architects (1987).

conceived, disciplined development of the precepts of Ludwig Mies van der Rohe.

17 Shadowlawn Circle   G-35
(1926) John F. Staub

Shadowlawn, like Waverly Court and West 11th Place, took advantage of its proximity to Shadyside to offer itself to discriminating home builders on what, in the 1920s, was the edge of Houston. Staub's marvelous French Breton style manor house seems slightly incongruous with its steep shingled roofs and almost windowless walls. But like so many Staub houses, it opens at the rear through French doors and arched loggias to a private garden and the prevailing breeze. Additions in 1990 by Cannady, Jackson & Ryan precipitated demolition of Staub's free-standing garage apartment.

6 Shadowlawn Circle   G-38
(1933) H. A. Salisbury

Salisbury exploited the curve of the street to extend this manorial style house laterally on its shallow site.

5 Shadowlawn Circle   G-39
(1934) H. A. Salisbury & T. G. McHale

The pastoral allusions of this house take on urbanistic overtones as it continues the siting and stylistic strategies of the Salisbury-designed house next door.

11 Shadowlawn Circle   G-36
(1926) William Ward Watkin

A formidably-scaled neo-Georgian house offset with palm trees.

9 Shadowlawn Circle   G-37
(1961) Anderson Todd

Holding its own among the 1920s eclectic country houses is this unobtrusive but generously proportioned courtyard house of steel, brick, and glass, a rigorously

1324 North Boulevard   G-40
(1926) John F. Staub

One of six houses that Staub designed in Broadacres, a small private place neighborhood rendered extraordinary by the staggered rows of live oak trees that William Ward Watkin had planted when he laid out the neighborhood in 1922. This austere manorial style house recedes in plan so that all the major rooms have access to the prevailing breeze. The front door is on the west side of the house, beneath a corbelled brick archway inspired by the work of the English architect E. L. Lutyens.

1400 South Boulevard   G-41
(1929) John F. Staub

Sumptuously detailed with molded brick and terra cotta shingle tiles, this manorial style house was acclimatized with oversized window bays equipped with leaded casements; stylistic consistency was maintained without choking off the breeze. To the left of the protruding gabled bay, the ornamental brickwork patterns vary from panel to panel around the second-floor windows.

1405 South Boulevard   G-42
(1925) Briscoe & Dixon

Briscoe's version of the English manorial genre complements the Staub houses across the street. Fleming & Sheppard designed the gardens, which are still maintained.

1515 South Boulevard   G-43
(1928) Birdsall P. Briscoe

Briscoe considered this Tuscan villa style house one of his most accomplished works. It was restored in 1989 by Ray Bailey Architects; The SWA Group was responsible for landscape improvements. Across the street at **1505 South Boulevard** is another Briscoe-designed house (1927), now almost invisible behind the dense vegetation installed, along with the street wall facing

South, by the New York landscape architect Ellen Shipman in 1937.

1505 North Boulevard   G-44
(1927) John F. Staub

Staub essayed considerable virtuosity in this neo-Georgian house by asymmetrically arranging windows in a symmetrically composed front facade. The big arched window lights the front stair; reception rooms all look out to a rear garden where the topiary arches, planted to the designs of the landscape architect J. Allen Myers, Jr., still bracket a central grass terrace.

1411 North Boulevard   G-45
(1928) Birdsall P. Briscoe

Briscoe reduced the front elevation of this restrained house to a manipulation of oversized window openings framing an inset central loggia. C. C. Fleming designed the gardens.

1405 North Boulevard   G-46
(1924) John F. Staub

This Connecticut Valley colonial style house was the first that Staub designed in Houston. Its stylistic provenance was rationalized by arranging the rooms one-deep, in a long, thin file, so that all were permeated by the prevailing breeze. Anthony E. Frederick restored the house in 1984. The front gate is not original.

1323 North Boulevard   **G-47**
(1927) Birdsall P. Briscoe

Of 17th-century French manorial derivation, this symmetrically composed house is
set in formal gardens designed by Fleming
& Sheppard.

1324 North Boulevard   **G-48**
(1927) Birdsall P. Briscoe

Briscoe abstracted the manorial genre to its
geometric essence in this taut, planar house
faced with inset triangular gables.

1318 North Boulevard   **G-49**
(1926) William Ward Watkin

Despite having planned the subdivision and
its landscaping, Watkin got the opportunity
to design only one house in Broadacres. It
was, however, one of the most assured that
he produced, a planar, white stucco-surfaced Spanish house, framed by almost
identical end bays. The arched second-floor
windows are a later alteration.

1317 North Boulevard   **G-50**
(1930) John F. Staub

Staub's version of the formal French manorial style was imposing but, character-

istically, he integrated major rooms with a
rear garden through oversized, triple-hung
windows.

4923-4927 Graustark Street   **G-51**
Graustark Family Townhouses (1972)
Howard Barnstone

Barnstone designed this trio of row houses
as an exercise in doing the most with the
least. Each is 16 feet wide but so cleverly
organized in section that the interiors seem
quite spacious. Externally, his low key
urban vernacular incorporates such witty
touches as glass garage doors that permit
the car to be admired even when indoors.

1220 Milford Street   **G-52**
Milford Townhomes (1984) Arquitectonica

Packed tightly together on a single lot,
these row houses are ingeniously planned
to ensure internal spaciousness. The gabled
turquoise monitor admits skylight into a
three-story high stairwell at the center of
each house; the grid of glass blocks visible
outside continues into the interior to filter
skylight from the stairwells into adjoining
rooms. The brash (and now picturesquely
fading) colors are a trademark of the Miami
architects.

4949 Yoakum Boulevard   **G-53**
(1983) Skidmore, Owings & Merrill

SOM's one house in Houston was designed
by, and for, the partner in charge of its local
office from 1976 to 1986, Richard Keating.
In the best tradition of Keating's native

California, the house is very self-effacing from the street—and quite opulent inside.

rather than the parked car. It was developed in part by the architect, John H. Kirksey.

1110 Milford Street   G-54
(1926) J. T. Rather, Jr.

Rather worked for, and eventually became the partner of, John F. Staub. Here he produced the quintessential suburban dream house of the 1920s, a compact, Regency style brick house with a latticed loggia to the side. Rather also designed the picturesquely composed house next door, at **1112 Milford**, with its expansive bay window (1926).

216-222, 238-242, 243, and 302   G-57
Portland Street
Gramercy Gables (1928-1950)
F. Stanley Piper

The homebuilder C. C. Bell, Jr., had his brother-in-law, the Bellingrath, Washington, architect Stanley Piper, design the Gramercy Gables, a complex of manorial style apartment buildings constructed over a 25-year period along this would-be private place boulevard. At the opposite end of the street, the architect Joseph Finger built the brick-faced, tile-roofed duplex at **120 Portland** (1926) where he and his family lived. Next to it is MacKie & Kamrath's clinic and house for Dr. Coole at **102 Portland** (1941).

1117 Banks Street   G-55
(1931) J. T. Rather, Jr.

The last to be built in this trio of Rather houses (for the families of two brothers and a sister) was also the finest, a superb example of disciplined composition and exquisite detail in the Staub manner. Rather executed the classical ornament of this little French manorial style house in molded brick.

4611-4621 Montrose Boulevard   G-56
Chelsea Market (1985)
Kirksey-Meyers Architects

Notable for its urban design, this specialty retail center emphasizes pedestrian amenity

4911 Montrose Boulevard   G-58
Holland Lodge No. 1 (1954)
Milton McGinty

The centerpiece of this windowless box (from the heroic age of air-conditioning) is William M. McVey's inset mural sculpture. Executed *in situ*, it depicts the founding of Masonry and its transmission to Texas.

4704 Montrose Boulevard   G-59
Palacio Tzintzuntzan (1989)
George O. Jackson, Jr.

Exuberant stencilling has transformed the modernistic Piazza Building (1941) into a Meso-American hot spot, a tribute to the

power of paint. The courtyard and drive-through aqueduct are by Rafael Longoria (1989).

inserting it onto a street of conventional suburban houses.

1303 Vassar Place   **G-60**
Vassar Place Apartments (1965)
Howard Barnstone

Barnstone's gift for working spatial miracles in confined circumstances is exemplified by this set of apartments, which radiates around the foot of Vassar Place. Intricately planned units are configured around private gardens and terraces that open, in a staged sequence, to a common green space at the back of the site.

1731-1733 Vassar Place   **G-63**
Vassar Place Townhouses (1983)
William F. Stern & Associates

This group of four brick-faced row houses defers to the neighborhood by maintaining the existing front setback line and preserving mature trees already on the site. Stern's elevations are urbane. Inside, generous living lofts occupy the second floor, with bedrooms clustered on the ground floor behind the garages—a recurring pattern of organization among Houston infill row houses.

4901-4903 Mandell Street   **G-61**
Mandell Residences (1985) Arquitectonica

Brown brick, white tile, and giant-scaled geometric incisions are used to induce a sense of spatial depth and individual identity in this row of four houses. Arquitectonica's shapes are a tongue-in-cheek salute to the metaphysical geometries of the Philadelphia architect Louis I. Kahn, just the sort of insider's irreverence that sets their critics to steaming. The backs of the houses (visible from Banks Street) zigzag in plan: something buildings aren't supposed to do.

1638 Banks Street   **G-62**
(1960) Wilson, Morris, Crain & Anderson

Ralph A. Anderson, Jr. designed this modern, flat-roofed courtyard house as his own residence, confidently but unobtrusively

1906 Vassar Place   **G-64**
(1989) Wittenberg Partnership Architects

In a tribute to the unorthodox Los Angeles architect Frank O. Gehry, Susan and Gordon Wittenberg adroitly managed the collision of shapes and mixture of despised materials in this lively house. Its big windows overlook the Southwest Freeway.

1601 Milford Street   **G-65**
(1937) Campbell & Keller

A determinedly functionalist modern villa, flat-topped, stucco-surfaced, with pipe-rail-

lined roof decks and glass block corner windows.

1705 North Boulevard   **G-66**
(1938) H. A. Salisbury & T. G. McHale

Salisbury & McHale mixed Regency and regionalist metaphors in this graceful house, faced with symmetrical chimney stacks and cast iron galleries.

1660 South Boulevard   **G-67**
(1929) Katharine B. Mott with
Burns & James

Katharine Mott, a house builder and designer from Indianapolis, settled in Houston in 1927. For the next four years she and her husband, Harry, a real estate broker, built houses speculatively in Houston's newest subdivisions, most of which she designed in association with the Indianapolis architects Burns & James. Mrs. Mott's houses were in the picturesque manorial style and exhibited skillful decorative detail in brick and stone, executed by a crew of craftsmen who built all the houses. Across the street, at **1659 South Boulevard**, is an earlier house by Mrs. Mott (1928).

1707 South Boulevard   **G-68**
(1927) J. W. Northrop, Jr.

Built for the banker and suburban real estate developer George F. Howard, this house was in the neo-Georgian genre at which Northrop excelled. Note how Northrop preserved the symmetry of the front facade by varying the sill heights of the first-floor windows; such legerdemain

was especially admired in the 1920s. Northrop carried this penchant for architectural gamesmanship up the street by designing a series of houses in which the composition of the Howard House is varied, but never beyond recognition: **1715 and 1749 South Boulevard** (1928), **1813 South Boulevard** (1929), and **1817 South Boulevard** (1931).

5100 Hazard Street   **G-69**
Edgar Allen Poe Elementary School (1929)
Harry D. Payne

Payne came to Houston in 1925 from the office of the St. Louis architect William B. Ittner, the foremost school design expert in the Middle West, as a consultant to the Houston school district. Poe is one of a series of neighborhood schools that Payne designed, all based on the same plan but varied in their stylistic details. Spirited additions to the rear are by Kendall/Heaton Associates (1986).

2003 Bissonnet Avenue   **G-70**
(1968) William J. Anderson

The first in a series of modern houses with which Anderson and his partner Tom Wilson architecturally reinvigorated the 1920s neighborhood of Southampton Place. This inwardly-focused house, built for the architect's family, faces a busy intersection. Yet despite its closed aspect, it has a strong figural presence due to its shingled wall surfaces and shapely profiles.

1807 Wroxton Road   G-71
(1970) Charles Tapley Associates

The modernist strategy for inserting new houses in Southampton generally entailed construction of a privacy wall insulating new from old. Behind this brick wall is a fascinating collection of little buildings strung together along a central causeway. All that is visible from the street, however, are the thrusting hoods and skylights of this architectural conclave.

1802 Sunset Boulevard   G-72
(1951) David D. Red

Designed for the architect's family, this climatically responsive organic house features screened porches angled toward the prevailing breeze. The roof surfaces originally were sodded.

1828 Dunstan Road   G-73
(1970) Anderson Todd

The chocolate-colored paint on this very restrained brick and steel courtyard house is not original. Todd played the rectilinearity of the architecture against the curvature of Kent Street with assurance.

2007 Dunstan Road   G-74
(1970) Anderson/Wilson

Behind the angled wooden plane is a house built of concrete tilt wall, with ceilings of exposed steel bar joists inside. It is set into the midst of suburban conventionality without too much ado, in contrast to the

overscaled Georgian-burgers that began to go up in Southampton in the middle 1980s.

2032 Bolsover Road   G-75
(1989) Tom Wilson

This sculpturally massed house of stucco-surfaced concrete block, a late but confident assertion of faith in modern design, aggressively confronts the neighborhood context.

2217 Bolsover Road   G-76
(1985) Morris*Aubry Architects and Charles Keith Associates

Multiple gables, a recurring theme in Eugene Aubry's residential design, are used to domesticate this modern house.

2229 Bolsover Road   G-77
(1985) Michael Underhill

Underhill reinterpreted what was originally a typical Houston house of the 1930s by stressing centrality and figuration and reiterating the existing pyramidal roof on two added pavilions, lined up along Whitley Street.

2246 Quenby Road G-78
(1972, 1982) William T. Cannady & Associates

The initial house, barely visible on the east, is a three-story, flat-roofed, wooden cube (now stucco-surfaced) that sits far back on what was originally a wooded greensward. Ten years after its completion, the architect-owner built a second version near the front property line that stylistically registered the changed spirit of the age.

2229 Quenby Road G-79
The Bachelors Club (1926)

Although Southampton Place was restricted to single-family houses from its inception in 1923, the Bachelors Club existed for ten years before its building too became a single-family residence. The house is a delightful English cottage configured around a miniature great hall.

2238 Albans Road G-80
(1987) Ziegler Cooper Architects

Ziegler Cooper concluded 20 years of modern residential architecture in Southampton with a new house that attempts to reconcile modernity with suburban conventionality.

5326 Mandell Street G-81
(1927) Drink Milner

Architectural attributes of old Virginia were consolidated into this suburban cottage.

1601 Sunset Boulevard G-82
First Christian Church (1958)
Brown & McKim

Although it is the shape of the church's roof that is most prominent externally, what one experiences inside are the walled gardens flanking the church, visible through the nave's entirely glazed perimeter. Donald Barthelme, who was originally associated with Hamilton Brown on this project, conceived this building as a "church without walls," a notion that Brown carried through after Barthelme withdrew from the project. The landscape architect Ralph Ellis Gunn installed the plantings; Seymour Fogel was responsible for the glazed brick and stained glass mural on the front of the church.

1500 Sunset Boulevard G-83
Congregation Emanu El Temple (1949)
MacKie & Kamrath and Lenard Gabert

Temple Emanu El marks one of the high points of MacKie & Kamrath's career. Shunning historical imagery, they architecturally embodied the idea of a house of

worship. The building's dominant horizontals are rhythmically countered by the
gentle rise of the tent-like, steel-framed roof
structure. The use of thin Roman brick
with horizontally raked joints and stone
coping and the detailing of the entrance
show the influence of Kamrath's mentor,
Frank Lloyd Wright, who bestowed official
approval on the newly-completed temple
when he came to Houston in 1949 to accept
the Gold Medal of the American Institute
of Architects. Attached to the northeast
side of the temple is a free-standing chapel
by Clovis Heimsath Associates (1975).

2 Sunset Road   **G-84**
(1920) William Ward Watkin

Facing Main Street behind a stucco-faced
wall (installed by John F. Staub in 1936),
this tile-roofed Mediterranean villa style
house was designed by Watkin to harmo-
nize stylistically with the Rice Institute
campus buildings next door.

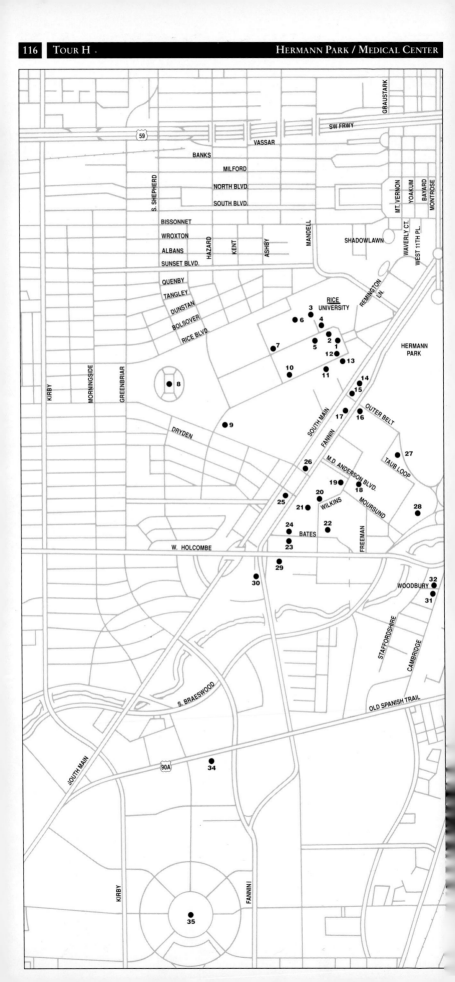

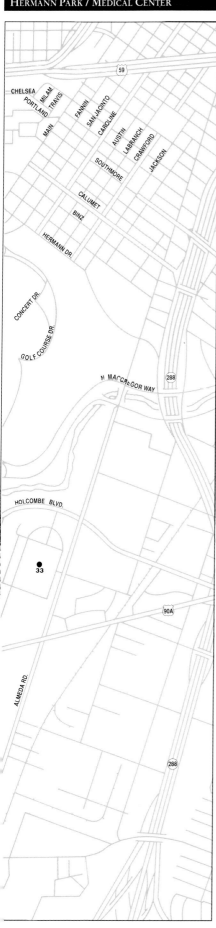

1. 6100 Main Street
   Rice University
2. Rice University
   Physics Building
3. Rice University
   Mechanical Laboratory
   and Power House
4. Rice University
   Abercrombie Laboratory
5. Rice University
   M.D. Anderson Hall
6. Rice University
   Seely G. Mudd Computer Laboratory
7. Rice University
   M.D. Anderson Biological
   Laboratories,
   Keith-Wiess Geological Laboratories,
   Space Science and Technology
   Building
   Hamman Hall
8. Rice University
   Rice Stadium
9. Rice University
   Media Center
10. Rice University
    Herring Hall
11. Rice University
    Institute Commons and South Hall
12. Rice University
    Cleveland Sewall Hall
13. Rice University
    Cohen House
14. 6221 Main Street
15. 6265 Main Street
16. 6411 Fannin Street
17. 6410 Fannin Street
18. 1200 Moursund Avenue
19. 1130 M.D. Anderson Boulevard
20. 1129 Wilkins Street
21. 6565 Fannin Street
22. 1515 Holcombe Boulevard
23. 1100 Bates Avenue
24. 1101 Bates Avenue
25. 1709 Dryden Street
26. 6900 Fannin Street
27. 1502 Taub Loop
28. 1115 North MacGregor Drive
29. 1100 Holcombe Boulevard
30. 6910 Fannin Street
31. 1920 Woodbury
32. 1911 Woodbury
33. 2002 Holcombe Boulevard
34. 1500 Old Spanish Trail
35. Loop 610 and Kirby Drive

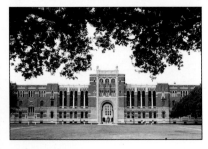

6100 Main Street   **H-1**
Rice University
Administration Building [now Lovett Hall]
(1912) Cram, Goodhue & Ferguson

When the Boston architect Ralph Adams
Cram was commissioned in 1909 to plan
the campus of the newly-organized William
M. Rice Institute (Rice University since
1960), he devised an architectural style
appropriate to an institution of high culture
set on an immense plain in a hot, humid,
Southern locale. Although Cram was best
known as a champion of the revival of
Gothic architecture, he deemed this utterly
unsuitable for Houston. So, in one of the
most inspired episodes in the history of
20th-century American eclecticism, Cram
formulated a "southern" analogue of
Gothic for the architecture of Rice. He
shaped long, thin, screen-like buildings to
defer to the prevailing breeze, undercut
them with arched, cloistered passageways,
and encrusted them with Byzantine,
Venetian, and northern Italian detail. Faced
with brick, limestone, and colored marbles,
these buildings outlined sequences of quadrangular and axially-elongated courts
defined spatially by massed ranks of trees.
    The Administration Building (now called
Lovett Hall after the university's first president, Edgar Odell Lovett, a professor of
astronomy from Princeton who retained
Cram) was the first and most elaborately
finished of Cram's buildings. It sits astride
the main axis of the campus, which penetrates the building's arched portal, the
Sallyport, and proceeds into the Academic
Court. Because it initially contained not
only the administrative offices of the university but most of its classrooms, faculty
offices, a library, and the double volume
Faculty Chamber, Cram varied the pattern
of window openings within the building's
symmetrically composed ranges to indicate
differences in internal arrangements. The
cloister on the Academic Court side of the
building is ceiled with Guastavino tile
vaults. Note the jokey collegiate iconography on column capitals and at the bases of
the Sallyport arch. Oswald Lassig, an
Austrian stone cutter, executed the figural
sculpture on the Administration Building.

Rice University   **H-2**
Physics Building (1914) Cram,
Goodhue & Ferguson

Next to the Administration Building and
connected to it by a free-standing extension
of the cloistered walkway is the Physics
Building. Cram varied the degree and character of architectural decoration on the

exteriors of this three-part building to relate
its faces to different sectors of the campus:
an elaborately detailed south facade facing
the Academic Court, a stripped-down
north elevation facing the Court of
Engineering across the street, and transi-
tional decoration for the Physics
Amphitheater, a semidetached block containing a large lecture hall. Mary Chase
Perry and the Pewabic Pottery Co. of
Detroit were responsible for the decorative
tilework above the main entrance from the
cloister. Inside this entrance is a vaulted
vestibule ceiled with exposed Guastavino
tiles bearing scientific insignia.

Rice University   **H-3**
Mechanical Laboratory and Power House
(1912) Cram, Goodhue & Ferguson

Situated at the head of one of the cross-axes
that intersects the main axis is the
Campanile, the symbolic theme structure
with which Cram's office provided the university. It was a smokestack for the university's power plant, not a bell tower, but it
possessed the typological-historical-vertical
associations that Cram felt a college campus
required. The Mechanical Laboratory, to
which the Campanile is attached, represents
the pared-down version of Cram's Rice
style that he considered appropriate to the
lesser status of the Court of Engineering.
Redressing this cultural estimation are the
three slabs of pink Texas granite installed
by the New York sculptor Michael Heizer
in 1984, "45°, 90°, 180°."

Rice University   **H-4**
Abercrombie Laboratory (1948) Staub &
Rather, William Ward Watkin, consulting
architect

J. T. Rather, Jr., attempted to modernize
Cram's Rice style with exaggerated horizontality. The relief sculpture next to the
entrance portal is "Man Drawing Power
From the Sun and Transforming It into
Energy" by William M. McVey, an instruc-
tor of sculpture at the Cranbrook Academy

of Art and a graduate of Rice's architecture department in the 1920s.

Rice University H-5

M. D. Anderson Hall (1947) Staub & Rather, William Ward Watkin, consulting architect; (1981) James Stirling, Michael Wilford & Associates with Ambrose/McEnany

J. T. Rather, Jr., designed this inoffensive classroom building just after the end of Rice's heroic age of architectural patronage (Cram died in 1942; Lovett retired in 1947). Thirty-two years later, with the addition of the Brochstein Wing to Anderson Hall (which had become the architecture building), Rice embarked on a second age of patronage by commissioning James Stirling and Michael Wilford of London as architects. Stirling & Wilford's addition to Anderson Hall causes it to conform to Cram's General Plan of 1910. Internally they opened a concourse through both the existing building and its added wing (the segment of the building closest to the street), marked at either end by conical skylights that salute Cram's Venetian Gothic tabernacles atop the Physics Building. Midway along the concourse, they made two double-volume spaces, the top-lit Jury Room (part of the new addition) and the Farish Gallery (a reclaimed space). Internal porthole windows and clerestories give the interiors a light, open feeling. Externally, Stirling & Wilford playfully inverted the compositional codes of Rather's building, sometimes subtly, other times boldly, always with wit. The off-center bull's eye window on the west elevation of the Brochstein Wing is a clue to the sectional organization of the interior.

Across the street is the **Chemistry Building** (1925) by Cram & Ferguson and William Ward Watkin, designed in a slightly too conventional rendition of the Lombard Romanesque style. Watkin was a draftsman in Cram's office who was sent to Houston in 1910 to supervise construction of the initial buildings. President Lovett invited him to remain at Rice and begin a school of

architecture, which Watkin headed from the institute's opening in 1912 until his death in 1952.

Rice University H-6

Seely G. Mudd Computer Laboratory (1983) Charles Tapley Associates

Mudd Laboratory is a postmodern interpretation of the Rice style.

Rice University H-7

M. D. Anderson Biological Laboratories, Keith-Wiess Geological Laboratories, Space Science and Technology Building, Hamman Hall (1958, Anderson, Keith-Wiess, Hamman), (1966, Space Science) George Pierce-Abel B. Pierce

This row of three laboratory buildings and the 500-seat Hamman Hall auditorium (visible through the sallyport of George R. Brown Hall) represent a conscientious attempt by Pierce-Pierce's designer, Edwin J. Goodwin, Jr., to distill a modernist version of Cram's Rice architecture. What they lack is the scale and depth of Cram's originals and their defining presence in the landscape. David G. Parsons modeled the special bricks that appear in shiner courses, stamped with insignia appropriate to the various disciplines. The laboratories have benefitted from the remedial planning strategy evident in the adjacent **George R. Brown Hall** (1991) by Cambridge Seven Associates and RWS Architects. Like Stirling & Wilford, Cambridge Seven's Charles Redmon attentively studied Cram's General Plan when it came to placing this exceptionally well detailed building on its site next to the Chemistry Building.

Rice University H-8

Rice Stadium (1950) Hermon Lloyd & W. B. Morgan and Milton McGinty

Dominating the asphalt prairie at the western end of the campus are the upper decks of the 70,000-seat Rice Stadium. Built in only nine months, the stadium is an undisguised exposition of reinforced concrete construction technology made graceful by

the lithe, 30-inch diameter columns supporting the upper decks. In Cram's General Plan this entire portion of the campus was designated as the site of a Persian garden. Just across the parking lot from Rice Stadium, isolated for the time being from the center of the campus, is **Alice Pratt Brown Hall**, home of the school of music (1991, Ricardo Bofill and the Taller de Arquitectura with Kendall/Heaton Associates). Designed by the Barcelona architect known for his boldness, the building is genuinely Texan in its magnitude.

Rice University   **H-9**
Media Center (1970)
Howard Barnstone & Eugene Aubry

Mr. and Mrs. John de Menil built the Media Center and the adjacent ex-Rice Museum (now insensitively altered) to contain the Institute for the Arts, which they moved from the University of St. Thomas to Rice in 1968. Aubry's low-tech, shed look—finished off with galvanized sheet iron siding—was intended to symbolize the provisional status of this delightful building.

Rice University   **H-10**
Herring Hall (1984)
Cesar Pelli & Associates

Cesar Pelli, the New Haven architect, essayed a rigorous, disciplined, and very provocative interpretation of Rice's architectural heritage at Herring Hall, acknowledging both Cram and his successors. The three-story, gable-roofed classroom block and the offset reading room wing, with its

odd truncated vault, are typologically derived from Rice's earliest buildings. The masonry curtain walls are treated as elaborate coded surfaces articulating the building's spatial organization and supporting structure. Herring Hall was built in a grove of mature live oak trees, a building site set aside in Cram's General Plan.

Across the central greensward from Herring Hall is the Rice Memorial Center, with its **Ley Student Center** addition by Pelli (1986), a far less satisfying endeavor than Herring Hall.

Rice University   **H-11**
Institute Commons and South Hall
[now Baker College and Will Rice College]
(1912) Cram, Goodhue & Ferguson

Cram reserved the south side of the campus for the residential group for men and accorded it a distinct sub-style, based on the urban vernacular building traditions of Genoa. These buildings (originally a unit, now incorporated in two separate residential colleges) were faced with stucco; the cloister arches are brick with only limited stone work. The towers were provided so that students might have cool places to study on warm, humid evenings. East Hall (also part of Baker College) and West Hall (now part of Hanszen College) were added in 1914 and 1916.

Rice University   **H-12**
Cleveland Sewall Hall (1971)
Lloyd, Morgan & Jones

Facing the Physics Building across the Academic Court and adjoining the Administration Building to the north, Sewall Hall is a near-copy of Physics by instruction of the donor, Blanche Harding Sewall, an ardent admirer of Cram's architecture. Lloyd, Morgan & Jones brought this bit of literal contextualism off without anxiety, even where they had to improvise. Ross Coryell executed the decorative sculpture work. At the center of the Academic Court is a bronze statue of the founder, William M. Rice, modeled by the English sculptor John Angel and mounted on a pink Texas granite base by Cram & Ferguson (1930). Behind the Founder's Memorial is the ponderous **Fondren Library** (1949, Staub & Rather, William Ward Watkin, consulting architect), which, to satisfy university politics at the time of its planning, broke with Cram's General Plan and was built atop the main axis, prematurely terminating it. It has constituted a monumental obstruction in the center of the campus ever since.

Rice University　　　　**H-13**
Cohen House (1927) William Ward Watkin

Watkin employed Greek Byzantine ornament copiously in the small-sized, big-scaled "house" for the institute's faculty club.

6221 Main Street　　　　**H-14**
Edward Albert Palmer Memorial Chapel [now Palmer Memorial Episcopal Church] (1927) William Ward Watkin

Designed and built at the same time as Cohen House, this Lombard Romanesque style church adds to the Main Street parade. It is decorated eclectically with exuberant Venetian Renaissance ornament in the style of Pietro Lombardo; his Church of Santa Maria dei Miracoli in Venice inspired the arrangement of the chapel's interior, with its high set chancel and sanctuary. Watkin was also responsible for the campanile. John F. Staub designed the parish house of 1930, which occasioned another exuberantly decorated portal, to the north of the church.

6265 Main Street　　　　**H-15**
Autry House (1921) Cram & Ferguson and William Ward Watkin

Autry House, next door to Palmer Chapel, was built as a community house where Rice students could study and socialize between classes. It lay next to the streetcar stop (on what is now Fannin Street) where students alighted to head into the campus. Cram and Watkin detailed the building to correspond to the architecture of Rice's residential group for men, launching in the process the Main Street Mediterranean look. The present front entrance is by Bailey & Belanger (1975). Inside is a little great hall; mounted above the fireplace is Pompeo Coppini's bronze relief portrait plaque of James L. Autry, in whose memory the building was constructed.

6411 Fannin Street　　　　**H-16**
Hermann Hospital [now Cullen Pavilion] (1925) Berlin & Swern and Alfred C. Finn

George H. Hermann, who gave the City of Houston the property that became Hermann Park, left the bulk of his estate to a foundation charged with building, equipping, and operating a charity hospital. The lavishly detailed Spanish-influenced hospital opened 11 years after Hermann's death, alongside his park at the very edge of Houston. The first floor lobby and corridors retain the brilliantly colored decorative tilework installed by Berlin & Swern, a firm of Chicago architects. These were restored along with the exterior of the building in 1990 by David Hoffman with Wayne Bell.

To the south of the original building lies a newer Hermann Hospital (now the **Robertson Pavilion**), built in the first phase of the development of the Texas Medical Center (1949, Kenneth Franzheim and Wyatt C. Hedrick). The nine-story distension in light precast concrete, the Jones

Pavilion, is an addition to Hermann Hospital that turns into **The University of Texas Health Science Center at Houston** (1977, Brooks, Barr, Graeber & White). This phase of expansion also included the Dunn Memorial Chapel, David Graeber's version of Skidmore, Owings & Merrill's Air Force Academy Chapel, with stained glass by Cecil Casebier, located in front of the Robertson Pavilion.

6410 Fannin Street   **H-17**
Hermann Professional Building (1949)
Kenneth Franzheim and Wyatt C. Hedrick

The 15-story Hermann Professional Building was the first high-rise office building constructed in Houston outside downtown. It was built to entice doctors to relocate their practices to the Texas Medical Center, conceived in the early 1940s by a group of Houston businessmen as an economic development venture and financed by the M. D. Anderson Foundation. The foundation acquired 133½ acres of Hermann Park from the city in 1943, chartered the Texas Medical Center, Inc., and awarded grants that enabled several local hospitals, one out-of-town medical school, and the state legislature to set up new facilities on the heavily wooded tract. In 1945 the independent oil man Hugh Roy Cullen made substantial donations to most of these institutions; by the late 1940s a building boom was underway that still continues. The Hermann Professional Building represented the last gasp of the Main Street Mediterranean attempt to design in a unifying civic style. Its bullnosed corners, wrap-around windows, and stepped profile indicate that red tile roofs and scrolled windows alone were insufficient. The relief sculpture depicting medical emergencies that flanks the Fannin Street entrance is by Edward Z. Galea. In 1958 the building was doubled in size with a westward extension toward Main Street (Kenneth Franzheim with John H. Freeman, Jr.). The Finnish sculptor Mauno Oittenen was responsible for the amusing abstract relief sculpture around the Main Street entrance portal.

1200 Moursund Avenue   **H-18**
Baylor College of Medicine Cullen Building (1947) Hedrick & Lindsley

The first building to open in the Texas Medical Center was this four-story, late modernistic, stone-sheathed slab, terminating the axis at the head of M. D. Anderson Boulevard with its convex entrance bay.

Edward Z. Galea executed the panels of relief sculpture. Ray Bailey Architects designed the porte-cochere, motor court, and Alkek Fountain (1982), which take some of the edge off Hedrick & Lindsley's original.

1130 M. D. Anderson Boulevard   **H-19**
Texas Women's University
Mary Gibbs Jones Hall
(1969) Freeman, Van Ness & Mower

A precisely detailed, trimly proportioned essay in the aesthetics of cast-in-place concrete frame construction, spoiled by the subsequent addition of a bulbous penthouse story.

1129 Wilkins Street   **H-20**
Garden Club of Houston Park (1982)
Charles Tapley Associates

This exquisitely detailed garden court seeks valiantly to compensate for the mean, chaotic, indifferent treatment of public spaces within the Texas Medical Center. The fountain is a rewarding demonstration of what can be accomplished with thoughtfulness and ingenuity. Unfortunately, the garden was conceived as an isolated retreat rather than the model for a more amenable public environment within the medical center.

6565 Fannin Street   **H-21**
Methodist Hospital (1951) Watkin, Nunn,
McGinty & Phenix 1989 Morris*Architects

Between the late modernistic original
(which faces Bertner Avenue) and the postmodern gabled Dunn Tower addition of
1989, Methodist Hospital has doubled in
size every decade; the pink granite aggregate concrete-faced Dunn additions were
built in what had been the spaces *between*
buildings. This sort of architectural history—where style is completely subsumed
by the programming, servicing, and management of space—explains why the Texas
Medical Center is such a harried and bewil-
dering place. It is a landscape of expanding
or shrinking factories competing for advantage in the health industry, not a campus
occupied by institutions dedicated to high-
minded research. On the Fannin Street face
of Methodist's west wing (1959, Milton
McGinty) is "The Extending Arms of
Christ" by Bruce Hayes.

1515 Holcombe Boulevard   **H-22**
The University of Texas M. D. Anderson
Hospital and Tumor Institute
[now The University of Texas M. D.
Anderson Cancer Center]
(1954) MacKie & Kamrath, Schmidt,
Garden & Erickson, consulting architects

M. D. Anderson, the University of Texas's
cancer research hospital, was the medical
center's resplendent champion of modern
design when it opened. MacKie & Kamrath,
reacting against modernistic compositional
formulas, shaped the building as a series of
off-set slabs extended horizontally into the
landscape in response to programmatic
requirements. Windows were keyed to solar
orientation and internal use: wide bands,
undergirded by corrugated aluminum spandrels, faced north and south to light
patients' rooms. MacKie & Kamrath revetted the exteriors with flamboyant gray-
veined Georgia Etowa pink marble. The
Knoll Planning Unit planned and furnished
the interiors. Like so much of the Texas
Medical Center, M. D. Anderson has suf-

fered stylistically from overexpansion.
MacKie & Kamrath enlarged the building
through the 1960s in accord with the original design. Then came the huge, polygonal
towers of the Lutheran Pavilion and the
Dunn Memorial Chapel (1976, MacKie &
Kamrath and Koetter, Tharp & Cowell),
built in front of the Holcombe face of the
patient wing, followed by the anarchitec-
tural R. Lee Clark Clinic (1987, Pierce
Goodwin Alexander), which finished off
that side of the building. The Bertner
Avenue wing is all that remains visible of
the original.

1100 Bates Avenue   **H-23**
Children's Nutrition Research Center
(1989) 3/D International and Bernard
Johnson, Inc.

It is the detailing of the curtain wall—thin
panels of pink Texas granite alternately
flame-finished and polished—that gives this
ungainly building its strong visual presence.
At night the stars atop the building's parapet light up.

1101 Bates Avenue   **H-24**
Texas Children's Hospital (1954)
Milton Foy Martin

Succeeding the modernistic in architectural
currency in the medical center was the contemporary, visible in Foy Martin's Texas
Children's. The tubular aluminum *brise-
soleil* is extruded horizontally; vertical
pylons (containing the dynamically off-center fire stairs) provide the element of contrast and signal the location of the front
door. Martin tripled the building's height in
1971, at which time it was joined laterally to
St. Luke's Episcopal Hospital, facing
Bertner (1954, Staub, Rather & Howze and
H. A. Salisbury), its 26-story brown brick
tower, and the **Texas Heart Institute** (1971,
Staub, Rather & Howze and Milton Foy
Martin, Caudill Rowlett Scott, consulting
architects). The stair-stepped surgical care
wing was added in 1991 (Kenneth Bentsen
Associates).

1709 Dryden Street   **H-25**
Medical Towers Building (1957)
Golemon & Rolfe, Skidmore, Owings
& Merrill, consulting architects

SOM's first Houston building was the 18-
story Medical Towers, an example of the
Lever House design Houstonized by con-
verting the floating horizontal base at the
bottom of the building into a parking
garage. The building has been respectfully
treated and it retains its original turquoise
porcelain-enameled curtain wall. Next
door, at 6624 Fannin Street, is **St. Luke's
Medical Tower** (1991, Cesar Pelli &
Associates and Kendall/Heaton Associates).
Ominously, the St. Luke's tenant brochure
illustrates a clone supplanting the Medical
Towers Building in the development's ultimate phase.

6900 Fannin Street   **H-26**
Smith Tower (1989) Lloyd Jones
Fillpot & Associates

Having already built the 22-story **Scurlock
Tower** at 6560 Fannin (1980, S. I. Morris
Associates) and the 25-story **Houston
Marriott Medical Center** at 6580 Fannin
(1984, Sikes Jennings Kelly), Methodist
Hospital, with Century Development
Corp., added another tower to its burgeon-
ing real estate empire. The 25-story Smith
Tower is a sleekly detailed precast concrete-
faced tower backed by an even sleeker alu-
minum-clad parking garage.
Air-conditioned pedestrian bridges join the
various components to the medical center.

1502 Taub Loop   **H-27**
Ben Taub General Hospital (1989)
CRS Sirrine and Llewelyn-Davies Sahni

Close attention was paid to Cesar Pelli's
Herring Hall at Rice University when it
came to the design and detailing of the cur-

tain wall of this monster building for Harris
County's public health hospital. At 1510
Outer Belt Drive, in front of the earlier Ben
Taub Hospital, is **The Daughters of the
Republic of Texas Log House Museum**,
constructed here to celebrate the centennial
of Texas independence (1936, Harry
Weaver). At the intersection of Outer Belt
Drive and North MacGregor Drive is the
statue of Houston's Confederate hero,
Lieutenant Dick Dowling, an Irish-born
saloon keeper who held off the Yankees at
the Battle of Sabine Pass (1905, Frank W.
Teich, sculptor).

1115 North MacGregor Drive   **H-28**
City of Houston Department of Public
Health Building (1963) MacKie & Kamrath

Horizontality is the compositional motif of
this handsome building complex. Next
door, at 1441 Moursund Avenue, is the
rather contrived **University of Houston
Pharmacy Building**, also by MacKie &
Kamrath (1978).

1100 Holcombe Boulevard   **H-29**
Prudential Building [now The University of
Texas Health Science Center] (1952)
Kenneth Franzheim

Like the lamented Shamrock Hotel, which
sat nearby at Holcombe and Main, the 18-
story Prudential Building represents an
architectural paradox: it is extremely stodgy
in composition yet extraordinarily impressive in detail. The first local corporate high-
rise office building constructed outside
downtown, it was one of a series of regional
headquarters buildings erected by the
Prudential Insurance Co. in the late 1940s
and early 1950s that introduced new levels
of amenity for office workers. In Houston
these included convenient parking, generous landscaped grounds, tennis courts, and
a beautifully detailed swimming pool ter-

canted wall planes. Interior spaces expand fluidly into a double-volume, top-lit court on the second floor, originally a restaurant. It is to be regretted that the building was never completed and that street widening and nearby construction have crowded so close by. But even in its partial state the APC is impressive and delightful.

1920 Woodbury   **H-31**
(1930) Katharine B. Mott
and Burns & James

One of Mrs. Mott's largest houses, it occupies an entire block front in the subdivision of Devonshire Place.

1911 Woodbury   **H-32**
(1946) C. D. Hutsell

The Dallas architect and builder C. D. Hutsell was responsible for this spirited, idiosyncratic example of Spanish style suburban design.

race located in the southeast corner of the building. The entrance sequence from Holcombe through the lobby is a marvel of spatial orchestration. It begins at the Azalea Forecourt, where Wheeler Williams's "The Family" is installed in a fountain, proceeds beneath a splendid, skylit porte-cochere outfitted with sinuous benches and planting troughs, then through the double-volume, cylindrical entrance vestibule, where Peter Hurd's American Scene genre piece, "The Future Belongs To Those Who Prepare For It" occupies a curved panel, and ends at the elevator lobby, where those awaiting cabs can look into the tropically planted swimming pool court. Since acquiring the building in 1975 the University of Texas has maintained it with the consideration that it deserves. Only the pair of illuminated signs stationed in the blank panels atop the tallest slab that depicted the Rock of Gibraltar have been removed. The interior and exterior public spaces of the Prudential show the Franzheim office at its best. From 1955 until 1969 the Contemporary Arts Museum occupied a small but ingeniously designed building by MacKie & Kamrath, a triangle in section, which stood on the grounds of the Prudential Building facing Fannin. It no longer exists.

6910 Fannin Street   **H-30**
Adams Petroleum Center (1957)
Donald Barthelme and Hamilton Brown

Because it never acquired the 17-story tower that was to have ridden atop its canonical '50s floating base, the APC is easily overlooked. It is a marvelous example of Barthelme's attempt to develop a responsive modern architecture, one obviously indebted to contemporary Scandinavian design. The four elevations are different, reflecting their solar orientations. Public spaces are finished with polished wood, veneered onto

2002 Holcombe Boulevard   **H-33**
Veterans Administration Hospital (1944)
Alfred C. Finn, (1991) 3/D International
and Stone, Marracini & Patterson

Finn's complex for what originally was the 1,000-bed U. S. Naval Hospital is in the monumental modernistic style, or, as it was described at the time of its completion, "conservative contemporary." It has been superseded by an even more overwhelming example of bureaucratic organizational design, a vast complex of interlocking rotated square bays that step up in section to a central spine. A system of interstitial floors devoted entirely to servicing this 1,047-bed hospital is hidden behind the building's horizontally banded face of precast concrete panels.

1500 Old Spanish Trail   **H-34**
Shell Information Center (1972) Welton Becket & Associates

This pristine, white, six-story office building was built to anchor Plaza del Oro, a 525-acre mixed-use real estate development of the Shell Oil Co. Unfortunately, by the time the center was completed South Main Street's status as Houston's prime suburban development axis had passed decisively to Post Oak.

Loop 610 and Kirby Drive   **H-35**
The Astrodome (1965) Hermon Lloyd & W. B. Morgan and Wilson, Morris, Crain & Anderson

With typical Texan bravado, Judge Roy Hofheinz, the expansive promoter who built the Astrodome (largely with public monies), called it the Eighth Wonder of the World. It was the first permanently enclosed, air-conditioned sports arena built to accommodate baseball and football games. The 642-foot clear span of the steel lamella trussed roof structure, 218 feet high at the dome's summit, was the second longest in the world at the time of completion. The Astrodome originally had a maximum seating capacity of 66,000. This included the 53 Skyboxes that ringed the summit of the stadium, entertainment suites outrageously decorated in both Old World and Space Age themes. The scoreboard, 474 feet long and 4 stories high, blazed into action every time one of Judge Hofheinz's Astros hit a home run. In 1966, AstroTurf, developed especially for the dome, was installed on the playing field to replace mere natural grass.

The Astrodome sits in the center of a flat, paved, 260-acre tract where 30,000 cars can be parked. Adjacent to the dome is the Astrohall, an exhibition and livestock arena. Hofheinz developed both the Astrovillage,

a complex of four motels, including the flagship **Astroworld Motor Hotel** with its fabled, top-floor Celestial Suite, continuing the Skybox decorating aesthetic (1969, Brodnax, Phenix & Associates), and **Astroworld**, a 57-acre amusement park (1968, Randall Duell & Associates, designers, Linesch & Reynolds, landscape architects), all connected by a bridge constructed across Loop 610. In 1968 the Hofheinz interests asserted that the Astrodomain's 13,600 tons of air-conditioning not only exceeded the total tonnage of many northern U. S. cities, but that of entire nations!

The Astrodomain has always evoked strong responses. The Italian critic Vicky Alliata wrote in 1974 that "the whole thing far surpasses all current definitions of kitsch, obscenity, and bad taste." Robert Altman transformed it into a theater of sinister obsession in his film "Brewster McCloud" (1970). Guru Maharaj Ji and his devotees attempted to levitate the dome in 1973. In 1970, Peter Papademetriou wrote that the Astrodomain enshrined late 20th-century American values just as the Vatican complex celebrated those of the Counter-Reformation for Renaissance Rome. In observance of the Astrodome's 21st anniversary in 1986, the journalist David Kaplan had the last word: "Let it rain."

In 1989 the historic integrity of this Houston landmark was ruthlessly destroyed by its owner, Harris County. The scoreboard was demolished to provide space for more seating and four, giant, cylindrical drums were added to the perimeter of the dome to contain new circulation ramps (CRS Sirrine, Wilson/Griffin, John S. Chase, and Haywood Jordan McCowan).

West University Place / Braeswood

D uring the 1920s Houston began to be transformed by the impact of the privately-owned automobile. The broad prairie north of Brays Bayou came to be dotted with middle-income subdivisions that gravitated toward the campus of the Rice Institute and the small elite neighborhoods near it. Provision of paved thoroughfare streets, such as the new Kirby Drive (a continuation of the Buffalo Bayou Parkway) linked these subdivisions to the center of Houston, although by the late 1930s the emergence of suburban shopping districts, such as the Village, relaxed dependence on the merchants of Main Street. The Village is downtown as transformed by the car. Off-street parking has been provided without abandoning the linear, street-related building typology characteristic of downtown. These are just pushed farther back from the curb line and stretched out laterally.

The subdivisions of West University Place eventually opted for incorporation in 1925, as did their tiny neighbor, South Side Place. Today they are autonomous enclaves within Houston. The ethnic and economic homogeneity, zoning codes, and low taxes that they offer have enticed the newly affluent to settle there, inciting speculative building on a scale not seen since the communities' initial development. Although carried out under existing planning controls, this new building has exerted such a profound impact upon these towns that it is decried even by the gentrifying residents.

The post-World War II infilling of the numerous gaps between the subdivisions of the 1920s accounts for the string of subdivisions along Holcombe-Bellaire Boulevard (its dual designation a result of differing municipal jurisdictions) that stretches south to Brays Bayou. The model that the postwar subdivisions tried to emulate was Braeswood, a 1920s garden suburb with a curvilinear street network and substantial houses on large lots. But because Braeswood's initial development fell afoul of the Great Depression, it ended up emulating the imitators. Its northwest quadrant, bordering Kirby Drive, was developed in the early 1950s with the long, low, one-story ranch houses that dominated Houston residential construction during the late 1940s and 1950s.

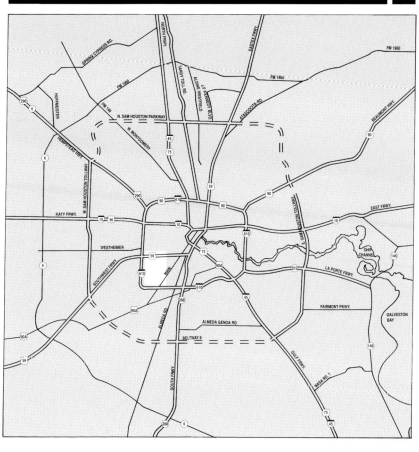

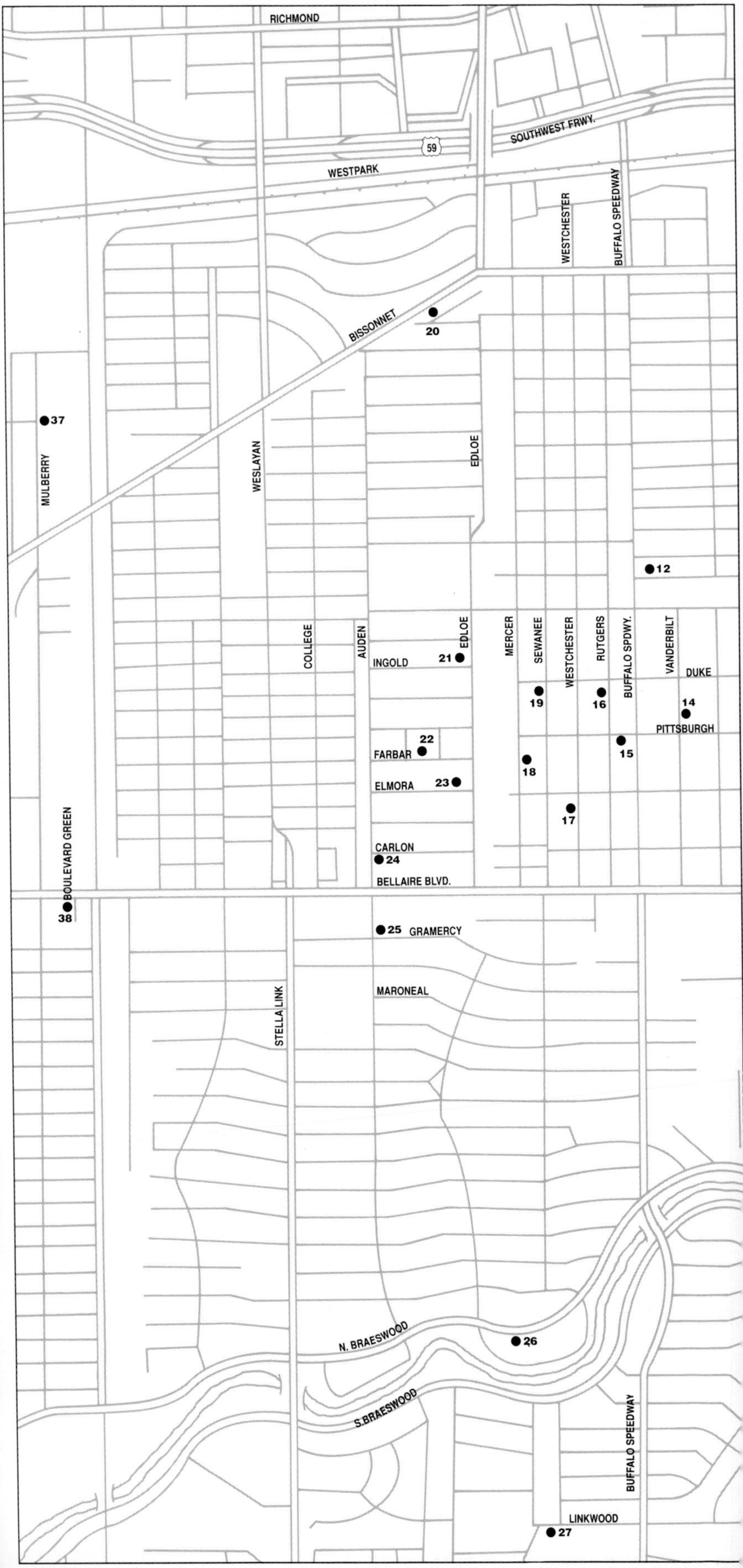
RICHMOND
SOUTHWEST FRWY.
59
WESTPARK
WESTCHESTER
BUFFALO SPEEDWAY
BISSONNET
20
37
MULBERRY
WESLAYAN
EDLOE
12
COLLEGE
AUDEN
INGOLD
21
EDLOE
MERCER
SEWANEE
WESTCHESTER
RUTGERS
BUFFALO SPDWY.
VANDERBILT
DUKE
19
16
14
PITTSBURGH
22
FARBAR
15
18
ELMORA
23
17
BOULEVARD GREEN
CARLON
24
BELLAIRE BLVD.
38
25
GRAMERCY
MARONEAL
STELLA LINK
N. BRAESWOOD
26
S.BRAESWOOD
BUFFALO SPEEDWAY
LINKWOOD
27

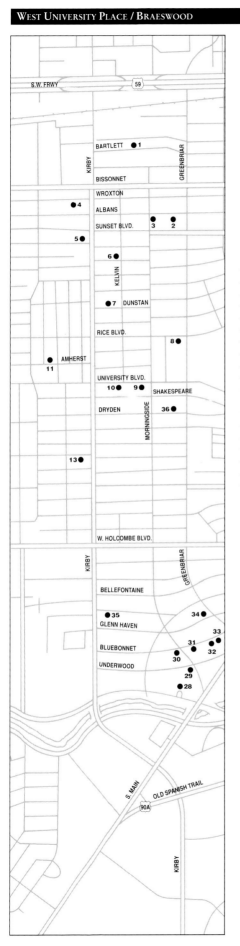

1. 2344-2348 Bartlett Street
2. 2311-2315 Albans Road
3. 2347 Albans Road
4. 2621-2629 Wroxton Road
5. 2600 Nottingham Road
6. 4916 Kelvin Drive
7. 2500 Dunstan Road
8. 2353 Rice Boulevard
9. 2439 University Boulevard
10. 2501 University Boulevard
11. 2812 Amherst Street
12. 3124 Amherst Street
13. 2621 Pittsburgh Street
14. 6435 Vanderbilt Avenue
15. 3211 Pittsburgh Street
16. 6428 Rutgers Avenue
17. 6638 Westchester Avenue
18. 6533 Mercer Avenue
19. 6416 Sewanee Avenue
20. 3742 Wroxton Road
21. 3708 Ingold Street
22. 3730 Farbar Street
23. 3716 Elmora Street
24. 3783 Carlon Street
25. 3780 Gramercy Boulevard
26. 3615 North Braeswood Boulevard
27. 3511 Linkwood Drive
28. 2322 North Braeswood Boulevard
29. 2333 Underwood Boulevard
30. 2337 Bluebonnet Boulevard
31. 2329 Bluebonnet Boulevard
32. 2309 Bluebonnet Boulevard
33. 2307 Bluebonnet Boulevard
34. 2308 Glenn Haven Boulevard
35. 2523 Maroneal Boulevard
36. 2330 Dryden Street
37. 701 Mulberry Lane
38. Bellaire Boulevard
    and Boulevard Green

2344-2348 Bartlett Street   **I-1**
Bartlett Townhouses
(1981) Alan Hirschfield

Hirschfield offset these three row houses in
response to a curve in the street that marks
its transition from a commercial to a residential thoroughfare.

West University Place, Stern paired row
houses to conform to the city's zoning
code. The use of brick and wood clapboard
siding, gabled roofs, and front porches are
intended to connote "home."

2311-2315 Albans Road   **I-2**
Albans Townhouses (1982)
William F. Stern & Associates

Tubular oriel windows capped by gabled
bays mark this pair of blue stucco-surfaced
row houses.

2600 Nottingham Road   **I-5**
Triangle Refineries Building (1951)
Lenard Gabert & W. Jackson Wisdom

Wisdom's use of orange Roman brick with
horizontally raked joints and horizontal
bands of coping betrays the influence of
MacKie & Kamrath. The giant-scaled louvers on the south side of the building, facing Nottingham, are a signature detail that
Wisdom was to repeat in other projects.

2347 Albans Road   **I-3**
Southampton Court Townhomes (1980)
Ziegler Cooper

Ziegler Cooper arranged these brick-faced
row houses in a mews, hanging the firebox-
es and cylindrical flues of the prefabricated
fireplace units off the upper floor as a sign
of domestic habitation. Diagonally across
the street at 4614 Morningside Drive are the
peach-colored **Morningside Townhomes**
(1986), also by Ziegler Cooper. One block
to the south at 2401-2403 Sunset Boulevard
and Morningside are the white stucco,
round-cornered **Sunset Terrace Houses**
(1979, William T. Cannady & Anderson
Todd).

4916 Kelvin Drive   **I-6**
Kelvin Design Group Studio (1960)
David D. Red

For an advertising and graphics studio Red
provided a two-story office building bracketed by a single-story wing which is lit by
sloped panes of north-facing glass.

2500 Dunstan Road   **I-7**
University Savings Association Building
[now President and First Lady Spa
Building] (1964). Bank Building
Corp. of America.

Wenceslao A. Sarmiento, the Peruvian-born
designer for the St. Louis-based Bank
Building Corp., let himself go with this
delightfully wacky six-story building in the
Village. Its interiors were completely

2621-2629 Wroxton Road   **I-4**
Wroxton Road Residences (1982)
William F. Stern & Associates

Here, in the independent municipality of

reconstructed following its conversion into a health spa.

Village, a suburban, auto-oriented version of a downtown shopping district begun in 1938.

2501 University Boulevard   I-10
Craig's (1955) Eugene Werlin

Craig's dates from the Village's heyday. With its mixture of Roman brick and ledgestone and its angularly inflected planar facade, it survives unaltered as an ebullient example of 1950s contemporary commercial design. Nearby, although not in quite so pristine a condition, is the ex-**Butler-Grimes Co. Building** at 2507 Times Boulevard, also by Werlin (1950). Inappropriate paint colors mar the ex-**Meyer Bros. The White House** at 2525 University (1950, Lenard Gabert & W. Jackson Wisdom), described at the time of its construction as an example of "ranch style architecture."

2353 Rice Boulevard   I-8
Christ The King Lutheran Church (1982)
Charles Tapley Associates

Alongside H. A. Salisbury's existing split-faced limestone education building (1949), Gerald Moorhead designed the long-delayed second phase, a church and free-standing belfry. Externally, this is a postmodern interpretation of Salisbury's cozy suburban Cotswold style. Internally, it is spacious yet intimate, and bracingly austere. Nearby are several other examples of interpretive contextualism: **Village Square** at 2370 Rice Boulevard, a rehabilitated 1955 office and retail building (1983, William T. Cannady & Associates), and **Morningside Square** around the corner at 5555 Morningside Drive (1984, Barry Moore Architects), which also combines retail with office uses.

2812 Amherst Street   I-11
(1937)

A cubic modernistic box, rehabilitated and expanded by Carlos Jiménez (1989). Next door, at **2808 Amherst**, is a suburban cottage tactfully expanded by Alfonso Varela (1985).

2439 University Boulevard   I-9
Peterson's Pharmacy Building (1940)
Bailey A. Swenson

Although deprived of its original painted finish, Peterson's retains Swenson's modernistic graphics and fenestration. It was one of the first buildings constructed in the

3124 Amherst Street   I-12
(1986) Anthony E. Frederick

The undemonstrative exterior conceals a cool, generously proportioned interior, hinted at by the casement-filled kitchen

window bay projecting from the house's east side.

conventional images of "traditional" domesticity.

2621 Pittsburgh Street **I-13**
(1946)

It required only three months to erect this delightful pink modernistic house, which is constructed entirely of welded structural steel. Even the streamlined garage is steel.

6428 Rutgers Avenue **I-16**
(1951) Gosta Sjolin

This modest two-story house, faced with wood shakes, was designed by the Swedish-born and trained Sjolin for the Houston landscape architect Ruth London.

6435 Vanderbilt Avenue **I-14**
(1984) Leslie Barry Davidson

To cope with the demand for houses much larger in size than those built in West University Place in the 1930s, '40s, and '50s, Leslie Davidson has ingeniously retrieved traditional Southern house types. This house is derived from the suburban raised cottages of New Orleans and Galveston. Its high, arched porch, which wraps around the principal reception room, is a neighborly feature. String courses on the south side of the pink stucco-faced house describe its stepped-sectional organization. Davidson demonstrates the relevance of traditional typologies for urbanizing suburban neighborhoods, an intelligent alternative to the conspicuous overbuilding whose consequences are omnipresent in West University Place.

6638 Westchester Avenue **I-17**
(1982) Alan Hirschfield

Major spaces in this house are grouped beneath two pyramidal roofs. They are joined by a narrow kitchen-corridor overlooking a central courtyard, enclosed by a third, screened pyramid. The lantern that crowns the foremost blue metal-roofed pyramid is Hirschfield's salute to James Stirling and Michael Wilford's work at Rice University.

3211 Pittsburgh Street **I-15**
(1984) Taft Architects

Built on a mid-block sliver site, this vertically organized house wittily deconstructs

6533 Mercer Avenue **I-18**
(1985) Leslie Barry Davidson

The Gulf coast cottage, Houston's fundamental house type, is here neatly transformed into a suburban house, a much more civil and gracious addition to the neighborhood than the hulking Georgianburgers that have proliferated in West University since the middle 1980s.

6416 Sewanee Avenue   **I-19**
(1977) Anderson/Wilson

Tom Wilson also followed Southern precedent in the siting, if not the architectural design, of this low-key, medium-tech house. The Charleston single house, with rooms aligned behind a narrow street front and facing south toward a long side garden, appears here as a pre-engineered steel structure, surfaced with metal and wood panels. In place of a side gallery, Wilson substituted a wooden deck and lap pool, screened from the street by a latticed privacy wall that doubles as a front porch.

3742 Wroxton Road   **I-20**
(1980) Lonnecker+Papademetriou

A shallow extension of the front of this previously nondescript one-story house occasioned Papademetriou's witty excursion into imagery-intensive planar manipulation. Plantings now obscure the pergola-porch, with its residual "Alamo"-front shaped gable, and the nonchalance with which Papademetriou clipped his stucco-surfaced addition onto the existing shingle-sided house.

3708 Ingold Street   **I-21**
(1988) Carlos Jiménez

Receding planar surfaces of metal, peach-colored stucco, and exposed concrete block subtly establish the presence of this courtyard house while minimizing the impact of its front-facing garages. The metal canopy above the garden gate imparts a jaunty touch.

3730 Farbar Street   **I-22**
South Side Place Bath House (1983)
Taft Architects

South Side Place, the smallest incorporated municipality in Harris County, is one block wide and ten blocks long. The public swimming pool is its civic center, a fact that Taft Architects acknowledged with the mock-heroic wall of polychrome concrete block, which provides backing for two changing rooms.

3716 Elmora Street   **I-23**
(1986) Val Glitsch

A postmodern version of an old Houston favorite, the suburban "country house" in the style of England's great early 20th-century architect, E. L. Lutyens.

3783 Carlon Street   **I-24**
(1930)

This Mediterranean style suburban house is one of the historic architectural landmarks of South Side Place.

3780 Gramercy Boulevard   **I-25**
(1947) Harry B. Grogan

A late but spirited modernistic house,

incorporating such contemporary details as the solarium's canted green glass windows. This was the home of Harvey R. Houck, Jr., who began development of this subdivision, Braes Heights, in 1945 according to plans by the landscape architects Hare & Hare.

pavilion to frame the site. The stone chimney pylon features a window inserted in the back of the firebox at ground level. Brochstein, a custom woodwork manufacturer, also executed the fittings and furniture for this house, making it a virtual museum of locally-produced modern design.

3615 North Braeswood Boulevard   I-26
(1957) Joseph Krakower

Herb Greene's hand is evident in this low-slung house, especially in the vertical slot windows that take the place of corners and the tense profile of the hipped roof. Next door, at **3611 North Braeswood**, it is the attenuated Japanese-like eaves that point to Greene's involvement (1957, Joseph Krakower).

2333 Underwood Boulevard   I-29
(1950) Eugene Werlin

Yet another example of 1950s contemporary design, with its combination of brick, dark-stained shingles, and Texas shell limestone. The juxtaposition of an angled stone plane with the vertical expanse of glass at the entrance is particularly striking. The roof's perforated eaves and the combination sun screen-planting ledge on the Morningside face of the house are "organic" touches. Werlin dominated this little corner of the world; he was responsible for **2329 Underwood** (1936), **2338 Underwood** (1935), and designed **2330 Underwood** (1930) while a draftsman for Cameron Fairchild.

3511 Linkwood Drive   I-27
Bethany United Methodist Church
(1953, 1958) Gehring & Reichert

The modern style of Eliel Saarinen, with its emphasis on crafted decoration rather than engineering, influenced the design of this church complex. The pierced block screens and the cast stone detailing, especially the Saarinen-like bell tower pylon, make Bethany a strong presence in the neighborhood.

2322 North Braeswood Boulevard   I-28
(1951) I. S. Brochstein

Situated at the head of Braeswood Court in the subdivision of Braeswood (laid out by the landscape architects Hare & Hare in 1927) is this contemporary house, its wings angled forward from a modishly off-center

2337 Bluebonnet Boulevard   I-30
(1937) Wirtz & Calhoun

This was the most famous modern house built in Houston in the 1930s. White stucco walls, flat roofs, terrace decks, glass block panels, and tubular metal railing brought the spirit of the new to Braeswood. The steel-framed house retains its original furnishings, designed especially for it by J. Herbert Douglas. The architects L. M.

Wirtz and Harold Calhoun were as adroit with traditional styles as they were with advanced ones. For the business partner of L. D. Allen, who built this house, they produced a very carefully detailed American Georgian house around the corner at **2356 Underwood Boulevard** (1936).

2329 Bluebonnet Boulevard   I-31
(1929) Carl A. Mulvey

This picturesque manorial style house, one of four that Mulvey designed for the Braeswood Corp., demonstrates his attentive study of contemporary houses by John F. Staub. The molded brick chimney and the brick nogging in the timber-faced front porch are notable details.

2309 Bluebonnet Boulevard   I-32
(1929) Carl A. Mulvey

Mulvey had worked for Birdsall P. Briscoe before starting his own practice, a fact which is evident in the composition and proportions of this graceful house. The Braeswood Corp. described the house as being in the French colonial style.

2307 Bluebonnet Boulevard   I-33
(1955) Bolton & Barnstone

Howard Barnstone achieved critical recognition in the mid-1950s with this two-story steel-framed modern house. Closed off from the street by a garage and a walled entrance court, the house is opened at the back with walls of glass two stories high. Interiors by Florence Knoll are no longer

intact and only portions of the landscape design by Thomas D. Church remain.

2308 Glenn Haven Boulevard   I-34
(1987) Michael Underhill

This is the most prepossessing of a number of adventurous houses designed by young Houston architects and built in Braeswood in the 1980s. Its brick terrace gives the tripartite stucco-faced house a monumental aspect. The denticulated-ventilated cornice is a clever postmodern paraphrase of a traditional architectural detail.

2523 Maroneal Boulevard   I-35
(1952) Paul László with Howard Barnstone

In its contrast of house types, Braeswood distinctly exhibits the two periods of its development. This low, remarkably long house, on a block of low, long houses, was designed by the Hungarian-born Beverly Hills architect Paul László. Its cantilevered entrance canopy, north-facing *brise-soleil*, and vertical redwood siding are organized beneath a continuous fascia. László incorporated a front-facing garage into this arrangement and, in the best California tradition, made it seem like a civilized amenity rather than a necessary evil.

2330 Dryden Street   I-36
(1936) Bailey A. Swenson

A modern house that displays great aplomb despite its minuscule size.

701 Mulberry Lane   **I-37**
(1988) Victor A. Lundy

A modest modern house and studio for the architect and his wife, a painter.

Bellaire Blvd. and Boulevard Green   **I-38**
Boulevard Green (1981) Alan Hirschfield

Built on a two-acre lot formerly occupied by a single house, this group of 16 houses refracts, rather than mirrors, conventional signs of domesticity. Hirschfield condensed images from the local scene, then abstracted and reconstituted them. The free-standing white stucco screens are intended to introduce what Hirschfield describes as a "community scale" to the street.

Riverside / Universities

Houston is a Southern city. Whatever connotations of graciousness and civility this characterization may evoke, it also raises the issue of race. Houston's ex-Third Ward, as it expands southward into Riverside Terrace, is a landscape that spatially depicts the development of Houston's Afro-American community from a culture formed under the impact of legal segregation to one that has won nominal equality but persists as a distinct subculture, not just as a matter of ethnic pride, but because of continuing social and economic disparities that sharply divide black from white. Dowling Street, the main street of the old Third Ward, is in ruins. The end of segregation in the 1960s meant that the external political forces that gave the street cohesion dissipated. With these have gone the portion of the community that could afford to leave, moving southward over the old color barriers into neighborhoods developed in the 1920s and 1930s as white middle- to upper-middle income subdivisions. Texas Southern University, the central institution of black culture in Houston today, sits on this old color line. To the north are Third Ward and Cuney Homes, the first low-income public housing complex in Houston; to the west and south are the middle-class cottage neighborhoods of Washington Terrace.

Stretching along the Brays Bayou Parkway that connects Hermann Park and MacGregor Park are the elite neighborhoods of black Houston, Riverside Terrace and its ancillaries. From the 1930s through the early 1960s these were where Houston's most established Jewish families were concentrated. The decision of almost all of these and other white households to abandon Riverside Terrace in the 1960s, documented in Jon Schwartz's film, "This Is Our Home, It Is Not For Sale" (1987), marks almost the only occasion in Houston's history when insulated middle-class whites had to come to terms with the negative consequences of a system of racial privilege in which they were supposed to be beneficiaries. That Jewish families settled in Riverside Terrace in the 1930s because they were not welcomed in River Oaks has ensured that this episode is one of the few instances of real estate transition that has not merely been absorbed into the collective amnesia of a city where real estate volatility is the norm.

The University of Houston has encapsulated itself from urban demographic changes. Through purchase and exercise of its power of eminent domain, it has surrounded itself with a swath of territory that buffers the campus on all four sides. Displaced neighborhoods and apartment complexes have been replaced with suburban institutional landscaping, a noncommittal approach to urban design typical of Houston's largest university.

Just to the north of the university's campus, the Gulf Freeway, the first intercity freeway in Texas, was built along the right-of-way of the Galveston-Houston Electric Co.'s Interurban railroad, a poetic symbol of the triumph of the private car over rapid mass transportation. Completion of the Gulf Freeway in 1952 sparked

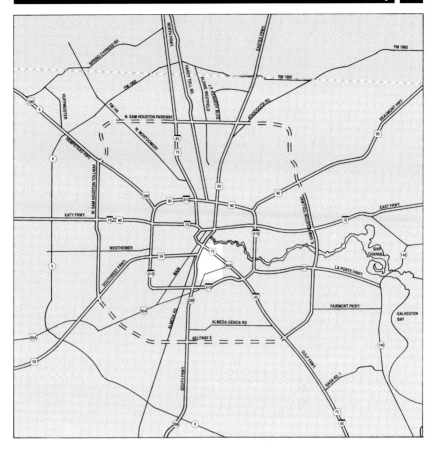

Houston's first episode of freeway-related development. It was along this corridor that the first suburban corporate office complex and regional shopping mall were built, forecasting a future that has now bypassed many of these pioneer installations.

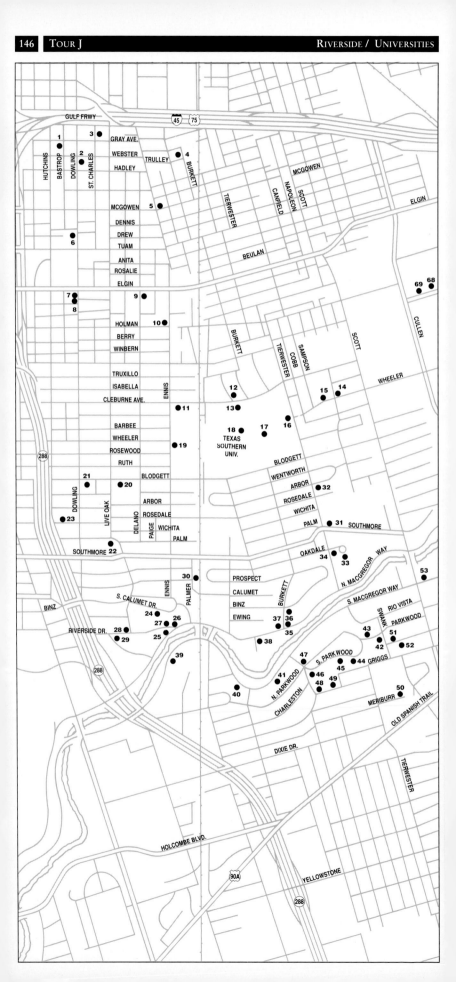

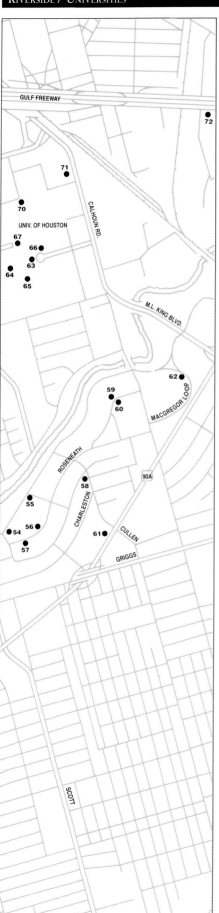

1. 2222 Gray Avenue
2. 2209 Dowling Street
3. 2009 St. Charles Street
4. 3201 Trulley Street
5. 3005 McGowen Avenue
6. 2702 Dowling Street
7. 3206 Dowling Street
8. 3212 Dowling Street
9. 2802 Elgin Avenue
10. 3204 Ennis Street
11. 3002 Cleburne Avenue
12. 3201-3315 Cleburne Avenue
13. 3100 Cleburne Avenue
14. 3601 Wheeler Avenue
15. 3535 Wheeler Avenue
16. Texas Southern University
    Science Building
17. Texas Southern University
    Ernest Sterling Student Center
18. Texas Southern University
    Martin Luther King
    Humanities Center
19. Texas Southern University
    Health and Physical Education
    Building
20. 2802 Blodgett Avenue
21. 2602 Blodgett Avenue
22. 2504 Wichita Avenue
23. 2221 Rosedale Avenue
24. 2620 South Calumet Drive
25. 2555 North MacGregor Way
26. 2627 Riverside Drive
27. 2623 Riverside Drive
28. 2521 Riverside Drive
29. 2506 Riverside Drive
30. 5401 Palmer Street
31. 3501 Southmore Avenue
32. 3502 Arbor Avenue
33. 3512 Oakdale Court
34. 3504 Oakdale Court
35. 3401 North MacGregor Way
36. 3402 Binz Avenue
37. 3315 North MacGregor Way
38. 3226 North MacGregor Way
39. 3028 South MacGregor Way
40. 3126 South MacGregor Way
41. 3314 South MacGregor Way
42. 3612 Parkwood Drive
43. 3611 Parkwood Drive
44. 3430 South Parkwood Drive
45. 3418 South Parkwood Drive
46. 3402 South Parkwood Drive
47. 3403 North Parkwood Drive
48. 3403 Charleston Street
49. 3417 Charleston Street
50. 3605 Meriburr Lane
51. 3711 Charleston Street
52. 3716 Charleston Street
53. 3807 South MacGregor Way
54. 3904 South MacGregor Way
55. 4000 South MacGregor Way
56. 3939 Roseneath Drive
57. 3912 Roseneath Drive
58. 4216 Fernwood Drive
59. 4511 North Roseneath Drive
60. 4506 North Roseneath Drive
61. 4343 Old Spanish Trail
62. South MacGregor Way and
    MacGregor Loop Drive
63. 4800 Calhoun Road
    University of Houston
64. University of Houston
    Cullen Family Plaza
65. University of Houston
    Student Life Plaza
66. University of Houston
    University Center
67. University of Houston
    Philip Guthrie Hoffman Hall
68. University of Houston
    Agnes Arnold Hall
69. University of Houston
    Science & Research Center
70. University of Houston
    Architecture Building
71. University of Houston
    Bates College of Law
72. Schlumberger Well Services Headquarters

cottage was one of the more pretentious houses built in this section of Third Ward.

2222 Gray Avenue   **J-1**
St. John Baptist Church (1946)
James M. Thomas

St. John's nave, elevated above a raised basement, and its twin towers exemplify a church building type favored by local black congregations in the 1930s, '40s, and '50s. Vertical strips of glass block are used here as architectural decoration. The builder, James M. Thomas, specialized in church construction and design.

3201 Trulley Street   **J-4**
Greater Zion Missionary Baptist Church (1955) John S. Chase with David C. Baer

The neo-Romanesque was a favored style for Houston churches. Chase's application represents a late, and very flat, interpretation of this ecclesiastical genre. This was one of the architect's first major building projects.

2209 Dowling Street   **J-2**
Wesley Chapel A. M. E. Church (1926)
W. Sidney Pittman

This high-set, vertically attenuated, brown brick-faced church is the only extant work in Houston of W. Sidney Pittman. A son-in-law of Booker T. Washington, Pittman was the first professional black architect to practice in Texas. Pittman's use of a towered church front and an elevated nave seems to have established the prototype for such churches as St. John Baptist. Located just a few blocks apart, these two churches still preside with authority over the deteriorating center of what was once a thriving community in Third Ward. H. D. Frankfurt was responsible for additions to Wesley Chapel in 1946.

3005 McGowen Avenue   **J-5**
Blue Triangle Branch Y. W. C. A. Building (1951) Hiram A. Salisbury and
Birdsall P. Briscoe

The semicircular entrance portico, faced with limestone and decorated with a running fret pattern, is a device that Briscoe frequently employed on his public building projects of the 1930s and '40s. The contrast between high style (stone facing) and low style (steel sash casement windows) was a favorite theme of the '40s, as was the raised brick banding used to decorate the walls of the rear gymnasium wing. John Biggers's mural "The Negro Woman in American Life and Education" (1953) is inside.

2009 St. Charles Street   **J-3**
(c. 1907)

Occupied by the family of a porter employed by the Pullman Co., this turreted

2702 Dowling Street   **J-6**
St. John Missionary Baptist Church (1948)
Beckmann, Williams & Williams

The San Antonio architects Beckmann, Williams & Williams produced the grandest of the Dowling Street churches. St. John, with its Ionic temple front, is curiously

anachronistic—more typical of the 1920s than the late '40s. Even so, it ennobles its surroundings.

3206 Dowling Street   **J-7**
Eldorado Ballroom (1939) Lenard Gabert

Gabert's streamlined modernistic nightclub and commercial building for the jazz impresario C. W. Dupree is another Third Ward landmark, although rather different in character than the magisterial churches of Dowling Street. The bull-nosed corner at Dowling and Elgin and the second-floor slot windows, framed by horizontal speed lines, still distinguish the Eldorado. Across Elgin at 3018 Dowling is **Emancipation Park**, 10 acres acquired as a public gathering place by Houston's black community in 1872 and donated to the City of Houston in 1916 as the first public park in Houston open to blacks. The annual celebration of Juneteenth, the anniversary of the enactment of the Emancipation Proclamation in Texas on 19 June 1865, began in Emancipation Park. Its modernistic buildings, a recreation center, amphitheater, and bath house (1939, William Ward Watkin), are indifferently maintained.

3212 Dowling Street   **J-8**
Progressive Amateur Boxing Association Rev. Ray Martin Boxing and Community Center (1988) Padilla Associates

John Padilla ingeniously used glazing to describe the sectional organization of this prefabricated metal building. Its upbeat

image attempts to ward off the gloominess of the depressed surroundings.

2802 Elgin Avenue   **J-9**
Progressive New Hope Baptist Church (1942)

Yet another example of the twin-towered church type, surfaced in red tapestry brick. The double volume arched loggia of the adjoining educational building gives the complex an unexpectedly monumental scale.

3204 Ennis Street   **J-10**
Houston Negro Hospital [now Riverside General Hospital] (1926) Hedrick & Gottlieb. (1931). Maurice J. Sullivan

J. S. Cullinan built both the three-story hospital, facing Elgin, and the two-story School of Nursing Building, facing Holman Avenue. Both are pared-down examples of Mediterranean architecture. Unfortunately, the School of Nursing, the more engaging of the two, is a burned-out shell.

3002 Cleburne Avenue   **J-11**
Congregation Adath Emeth Synagogue [now Charles P. Rhinehart Music Center Auditorium, Texas Southern University] (1948) Irving R. Klein & Associates

The tautly inflected brick planes of Klein's synagogue show the influence of Eliel Saarinen on modern architecture in Houston in the late 1940s and early '50s. The stepped section and telescoped plan are coordinated to produce a delightful rounded bay at the east end of the building. From the 1920s to the early 1950s Alabama Avenue was the dividing line between the black neighborhoods of Third Ward and what developed as a middle-income neighborhood, with a pronounced Jewish presence, to the south, a historic distinction preserved in the contrast between the wood frame rent houses of the one and the brick suburban cottages of the other. As the congregation's sale of its synagogue to Texas Southern University in 1958 attests, this color line dissolved, presaging the end of legal racial segregation in Houston.

3201-3315 Cleburne Avenue   J-12
Cuney Homes (1940) Stayton Nunn-Milton McGinty with John F. Staub (1942) Associated Housing Architects of Houston

Cuney Homes, the first U. S. Housing Authority-financed low income housing complex constructed in Houston, was built in two stages. Nunn and McGinty's original section is fairly spartan, although site planning by the Kansas City landscape architects Hare & Hare downplayed the repetitiveness of the apartment blocks by skillful use of curved and angled streets and by preserving existing trees. The second phase, for which MacKie & Kamrath were responsible, employed brick banding, thin concrete canopies, and horizontal slot windows to give the housing blocks a distinctly modern look.

3100 Cleburne Avenue   J-13
Texas Southern University Administration, Classroom, and Auditorium Building [now Mack H. Hannah Hall] (1950) Lamar Q. Cato

Cato's three-part main building recalls Italian state architecture of the 1930s, especially its crypto-classical porticoes with their flat roof slabs and thin, square piers. Replacement of steel sash windows with bronze solar glass has taken some of the edge off the contrast between industrial glazing and the requisite material of regional monumentality, Texas shell limestone. This was the first permanent building to

open on Texas Southern's new campus. The university began in 1927 as Houston Colored Junior College, a racially segregated institution whose establishment and development paralleled that of the University of Houston.

3601 Wheeler Avenue   J-14
Texas Southern University Thurgood Marshall School of Law Building (1976) John S. Chase

The combination of white precast concrete panels, bronze solar glass, and bronze anodized aluminum produces a high contrast color scheme that is simple yet forceful. The protruding second-story bay curves outward to interact with the curve of Wheeler Avenue, making the building's presence felt despite its confined site.

3535 Wheeler Avenue   J-15
Newman Hall (1968) Clovis Heimsath Associates

Heimsath and his designer W. Irving Phillips, Jr., used an extensive array of wall and roof shapes to indicate the interior spatial composition of this chapel and student center building. Across the street at 3530 Wheeler Avenue is **St. Luke The Evangelist Church** (1961, John S. Chase), as ebullient on its terms as is Newman Hall.

Texas Southern University   J-16
Science Building [now Samuel M. Nabrit Science Center] (1958) Wyatt C. Hedrick

Hedrick's no-nonsense '50s contemporary look (orange brick and horizontally aligned windows) was reinterpreted with considerable panache in Cavitt McKnight Weymouth's addition of 1984, at the corner of Wheeler and Tierwester. The relief panel next to the principal entrance is "Man and the Universe" by Carroll Simms; inside is John Biggers's mural "Web of Life."

Texas Southern University   **J-17**
Ernest Sterling Student Center (1976)
John S. Chase

Since the mid-1970s Chase has given the center of the TSU campus a new architectural identity. The most distinctive of the several buildings for which his office is responsible is the Sterling Student Center. Like the law school, the long, low student center is faced with vertically striated white precast concrete panels and bronze solar glass. It is crowned by a glazed penthouse hovering dramatically between four vertical towers. The architecture is not refined, but the building's bold shapes and sharp chromatic contrasts compel attention. Also by Chase is the adjacent **School of Education Building** (1981).

announced by this sports arena, which is handsomely surfaced in earth-toned concrete tiles.

2802 Blodgett Avenue   **J-20**
Riverside Service Station (c. 1940)

A neighborhood convenience detailed with suburban Mediterranean attributes.

2602 Blodgett Avenue   **J-21**
Riverside National Bank Building [now Unity National Bank Building] (1963)
John S. Chase

This glass-, brick-, and marble-faced bank is notable for its jaunty folded-plate roof structure. The first black-owned bank in Texas, it became a symbol of community pride and achievement in Third Ward.

2504 Wichita Avenue   **J-22**
(1930) W. D. Bordeaux

Bordeaux had worked in Los Angeles before coming to Houston in the late 1920s. Here he produced one of the first local examples of an American regional style that

---

Texas Southern University   **J-18**
Martin Luther King Humanities Center (1969) John S. Chase

With its oversailing cylindrical pavilion serving as pivot point for two symmetrically extended wings, this forceful building marked the first departure from TSU's previously unambitious architectural work. Stationed in front of the building is Carroll Simms's "African Queen Mother" (1968).

Texas Southern University   **J-19**
Health and Physical Education Building (1989) Haywood Jordan McCowan

TSU's aggressive move into surrounding residential neighborhoods in the early 1980s made Ennis Street the campus's new western boundary. The campus presence is

was to become quite popular in the 1930s, based on the mid-19th-century buildings of Monterey, California.

2221 Rosedale Avenue   **J-23**
(1929) Joseph Finger

This house is not subtle but it stands out by virtue of its scale, massing, and arcaded loggia. It is located in the first section of Riverside Terrace, a middle-income neighborhood that was opened in 1924 and developed along both sides of Brays Bayou.

2620 South Calumet Drive   **J-24**
(1936) Burns & James with Lenard Gabert

North and South Calumet and Riverside drives were the elite streets within the 1920s sections of Riverside Terrace. After the deed restrictions were allowed to lapse in the early 1960s, the large lots invited redevelopment. This French manorial style house survives, although no longer as a single-family dwelling. Designed by a firm of Indianapolis architects, its asymmetrical massing is a typical '30s touch. Across Riverside Park, the colonnaded house at **2619 North Calumet Drive** (1930) is by J. M. Glover.

2555 North MacGregor Way   **J-25**
(1929)

The prevailing eclectic genre in this section of Riverside Terrace was the picturesque manorial style. This example occupies a pivotal site at the confluence of the MacGregor Parkway and Riverside Drive.

2627 Riverside Drive   **J-26**
(1929) Katharine B. Mott with Burns & James

Katharine and Harry Mott were especially active in Riverside Terrace in the late 1920s, building speculative houses in which Mrs. Mott's characteristic mixture of ornamental brickwork and stone was always evident. She and Burns & James produced **2620, 2612, and 2417 Riverside Drive**, as well as **2519 North MacGregor Way**, in 1928-1929.

2623 Riverside Drive   **J-27**
(1936) Birdsall P. Briscoe

Briscoe's only house in Riverside Terrace conformed to the manorial mode. It was in fact his last foray into that particular genre. The graceful Regency-style porch is a charming anachronism, just the sort of historical "mistake" that eclectic architects of the 1920s and '30s committed with delight.

2521 Riverside Drive   **J-28**
(1929) Charles Dieman

The corner turret and the three-story tower make this house a local landmark.

2506 Riverside Drive   **J-29**
(1936) Bailey A. Swenson

Horizontal speed lines framing second-floor windows and an inset bull-nosed corner send this white stucco-surfaced, flat-roofed modern house around the sharply curved Riverside Drive-North MacGregor Way intersection. This was the

rizes many characteristics of the 1950s contemporary look in Houston.

first of a series of modern houses that Swenson was to design for Mr. and Mrs. Ben Proler and their children.

3512 Oakdale Court   J-33
(1959) John S. Chase

The architect's own house is bisected by a two-story glass wall lighting a cantilevered stair that dramatically spans a fountain trough.

5401 Palmer Street   J-30
(1941) MacKie & Kamrath

Taut planar facades, a flat roof, and slot windows still mark this house as modern, despite unsympathetic alterations.

3504 Oakdale Court   J-34
(1949) Wilson, Morris & Crain

WMC's designer, Ralph A. Anderson, Jr., set the horizontally aligned windows of this flat-roofed contemporary house into recessed panels above lengths of corrugated industrial siding.

3501 Southmore Avenue   J-31
Congregation Beth Yeshurun Synagogue [now Lucian L. Lockhart Elementary School] (1949) Finger & Rustay

Only the education wing of Finger & Rustay's formidable modernistic Regency style complex for Houston's oldest Orthodox congregation was built. Its limestone-banded, tapestry brick-faced walls and bronze accoutrements are impressive, especially the torcheres shaped like menorahs that flank the main entrance.

3502 Arbor Avenue   J-32
(1959) John S. Chase

With its flared roof, solar screens, and orange Roman brick, this house summa-

3401 North MacGregor Way   J-35
(1956) Lenard Gabert & W. Jackson Wisdom

This flat-roofed house, with its stone base and vertically boarded upper story, steps down in section as it fans out in plan. Closed to the street, it opens to a rear garden replete with period landscape fixtures, including a kidney-shaped pool spanned by an arched bridge. Note the loblolly pine tree that grows through a hole in the soffit above the front porch, a classic '50s organic touch.

3402 Binz Avenue J-36
(1968) John S. Chase

Chase was extremely deferential to the architectural context of the Timber Crest enclave when he designed this large house, with its stone base, boarded upper story, and widely projecting eaves with curved stucco soffits.

3315 North MacGregor Way J-37
(1948) Bailey A. Swenson

Swenson's version of the French manorial has a definite '40s swing.

3226 North MacGregor Way J-38
(1949) MacKie & Kamrath

This austere, hard-edged house with its glazed corner bay exhibits neither the pronounced horizontality nor the Wrightian ornament one expects of MacKie & Kamrath.

3028 South MacGregor Way J-39
(1936) Robert C. Smallwood

This Regency style country house projects the image of stately suburbanity that was to

characterize the southern sections of Riverside Terrace.

3126 South MacGregor Way J-40
(1952) Bailey A. Swenson

Riverside Terrace is known especially for its uninhibited contemporary style houses of the 1950s. This trim house, contained beneath a monopitch roof plane, is a subdued example.

3314 South MacGregor Way J-41
(1984) Haywood Jordan McCowan

Despite its three-story height and geometrically configured projections, this house recedes visually into its site, due in part to its dark-stained wood surfaces.

3612 Parkwood Drive J-42
(1938) Joseph Finger

A handsomely composed and proportioned house, detailed in a suburban rendition of the traditional architecture of Charleston, South Carolina. In siting the house, Finger's office made the most of the low promontory that it occupies. Across the street at **3615 Parkwood** is another house by Finger (1940), a stylistic companion to 3612.

3611 Parkwood Drive J-43
(1953) Bolton & Barnstone

Howard Barnstone placed all the major rooms behind the south-facing front of this house to ensure adequate ventilation. The pop-up clerestory was apparently included to satisfy the subdivision's restrictive covenants mandating two-story houses.

3430 South Parkwood Drive J-44
(1942) Lenard Gabert

This attenuated Regency-style house was the biggest that Gabert designed in Riverside Terrace. Its long front elevation conceals the shallow depth of the house. Large Houston houses of the 1920s, '30s, and '40s were frequently extended in plan in order to open them to the prevailing southeast breeze.

3418 South Parkwood Drive J-45
(1938) Henry A. Stubee

The "southern colonial" plantation image struck a very responsive chord in affluent new Houston neighborhoods of the 1930s. This was the first house to be built in the Parkwood section of Riverside Terrace.

3402 South Parkwood Drive J-46
(1951) Philip G. Willard

The counterthrust roof plane of the glazed second-story bay gives this low-slung con-

temporary house, set on a broad, undulating site, the dynamic look so prized in the early '50s.

3403 North Parkwood Drive J-47
(1953) Philip G. Willard & Lucian T. Hood, Jr.

This concrete-framed, '50s modern house, one of the most exuberant in Riverside Terrace, looks as though it is about to take flight. The protruding second-story bay, a concession to the restrictive covenants, is a typical neighborhood feature that was jokingly called the mother-in-law room.

3403 Charleston Street J-48
(1952) Bailey A. Swenson

Another of the Proler family houses, this appears to have been Swenson's belated tribute to the Prairie school work of Frank Lloyd Wright.

3417 Charleston Street J-49
(1950). Bailey A. Swenson

The tubular steel struts upholding the

porch canopy add a bravura touch to this Riverside contemporary.

3605 Meriburr Lane **J-50**
(1956) Herb Greene

The idea of an organic architecture liberated from all convention inspired Greene's design of this house for a single person. A triangle in plan, it was built around a tree (which has not survived). The walls are surfaced with roofing tiles and the thin roof, folded down and strung from cables, sailed above a carport. The house is now in an advanced state of deterioration; the cables have snapped and the carport roof is propped with lengths of timber.

3711 Charleston Street **J-51**
(1940) C. D. Hutsell

Hutsell was a Dallas architect and builder who specialized in a quirky, Texanized version of the Mediterranean style. He and his brother A. E. Hutsell built this house and the one next door at **3707 Charleston** on speculation. Both have been altered, but Hutsell's distinctive touch is still visible.

3716 Charleston Street **J-52**
(1907)

This turn-of-the-century cottage was the home of the carpenter Theo H. Kuhlman, whose family's dairy farms covered much of what became Riverside Terrace. Kuhlman's house originally sat on South MacGregor Way near Scott Street. He had it moved here in 1937, after development of that section of the subdivision began.

3807 South MacGregor Way **J-53**
(1953) Flatow, Moore, Bryan & Fairburn

The Albuquerque architect Max Flatow designed this house for his brother's family. The cantilevered entrance canopy and the panelled walls exude the optimistic spirit of '50s modernism. Flatow engineered the flat roof so that it would retain rain water to provide evaporative cooling. Next door at **3819 South MacGregor Way** is one of Bailey A. Swenson's best houses, completed in 1954 for his patron, collaborator, and business associate, Leon Green.

3904 South MacGregor Way **J-54**
(1936) John F. Staub

Despite extremely insensitive alterations, this house still radiates a modest charm. It was one of Staub's first ventures into the Texas regional style, a move inspired by the Dallas architect David R. Williams, the proponent of a regionalist movement in Texas architecture.

4000 South MacGregor Way **J-55**
(1939) Joseph Finger

Finger designed the biggest house in Riverside Terrace, a French manorial style suburban chateau, for the family of grocery chain magnate Joe Weingarten.

3939 Roseneath Drive **J-56**
(1978) O'Neil Gregory, Jr.

A discreet cluster of box-like shapes that turn in on each other, this wood-sheathed house was built for the architect's family.

Across the street, discretion clearly was not a priority with the aggressively bow-windowed house at **3934 Roseneath Drive** (1949, Bailey A. Swenson).

Bailey A. Swenson), with the mother-in-law room thrust above the long ground-floor wing.

3912 Roseneath Drive   **J-57**
(1956) Leo Kern

Kern, a home builder, pulled out all the stops when it came to building his own house, which incorporates every possible feature of the '50s contemporary look.

4506 North Roseneath Drive   **J-60**
(1954) Bolton & Barnstone

Barnstone's superior rebuke to the excesses of contemporary styling took form with this brick, stucco, and wood-surfaced house. The street-face is closed, while the south-facing rear garden elevation is extensively glazed. The maid's room was stacked on top of the garage to beat both the deed restrictions and the mother-in-law room.

4216 Fernwood Drive   **J-58**
(1949) Bailey A. Swenson

Yet another Proler house, this one is drawn out in an extremely long wing facing Fernwood that is deftly pivoted in plan and activated in section to respond to the Cullen Boulevard intersection. The lurid paint job notwithstanding, this is a remarkable demonstration of the Swenson office's facility with contemporary design.

4511 North Roseneath Drive   **J-59**
(1952) Philip G. Willard &
Lucian T. Hood, Jr.

The glazed void of the staircase, executed in curved corrugated glass, is superlative, as is the crisp precision of the eaves lines. This house echoes the formula visible next door at **4505 North Roseneath Drive** (1950,

4343 Old Spanish Trail   **J-61**
Alamo Plaza Motel (1948)

It is a tribute to its quintessentially Texan image that this motel, located along what was once the main east-west highway through Houston, is still in operation. Architecturally, the scalloped gable (actually the product of a mid-19th-century repair to the famous mission church in San Antonio) has been used to screen a multitude of sins in chauvinistic Texas.

South MacGregor Way and   **J-62**
MacGregor Loop Drive
MacGregor Park Clubhouse (1931)
A. E. Nutter

The first of three delightful Mediterranean style park clubhouses that Nutter designed in the early 1930s was built in the park that Peggy Stevens MacGregor donated to the City of Houston in 1926 as a memorial to her husband, the real estate developer

Henry F. MacGregor (commemorated in a cenotaph, across from the clubhouse, by William Ward Watkin of 1937). She also provided funds for the city to acquire the rights-of-way along Brays Bayou for the linear park between MacGregor and Hermann parks and its flanking drives, which became North and South MacGregor ways. All were laid out by the landscape architects Hare & Hare.

a ceremonial, representative place. Hare and Hare's master plan used architecturally defined quadrangular spaces to form a coherent whole. Unfortunately, a new approach was initiated across the campus in 1966 in the hope of achieving informal, natural, and spontaneous arrangements. The suburban residential plantings installed here only detach the plaza from its surroundings.

4800 Calhoun Road   J-63
University of Houston
Ezekiel Cullen Building (1950)
Alfred C. Finn

A tall, frontal central block flanked symmetrically by low wings was the established formula for modernistic public buildings. Finn did not deviate from convention when his office produced the architectural set piece of the university's campus, the administration building. A fan-shaped auditorium (restored in 1987 by Barry Moore Architects) projects off the east front of the building, on axis with the Calhoun Road entrance drive. Shell limestone facing, allegorical relief sculpture, and decorative cast aluminum work completed the package. The Cullen Building fit into Hare & Hare's 1937 campus master plan, joining the pair of shell limestone-faced, tile-roofed buildings to either side, **Science** and **Roy Gustav Cullen** (both 1939, Lamar Q. Cato). Reglazing has robbed Ezekiel Cullen of the aluminum screens that once filled the central register above the west entrance doors.

University of Houston   J-64
Cullen Family Plaza (1972) Fred Buxton & Associates and Cornell, Bridges & Troller

Replacing an oval reflecting basin installed in 1939, this sculpturally activated fountain pool is bridged by a series of concrete plateaus with which Lee Kelly's stainless steel piece "Waterfall, Stele, and River" (1972) has been integrated. Conceived as a "people place" rather than an architectural focus, Cullen Family Plaza establishes itself as an autonomous activity zone rather than

University of Houston   J-65
Student Life Plaza (1971) John Zemanek and Fred Buxton

A small, charming garden incorporating water, paving, and trees that evokes the contrasting colors and textures of each, the Student Life Plaza is a precious interlude in an otherwise oppressively banal landscape that denies the campus a sense of definition and identity. Adjacent to the plaza is the **Student Life Building** (1968, Richard S. Colley and Ford, Powell & Carson), where the Texas modern regional look associated with Colley and O'Neil Ford has been turned into a routine formula.

University of Houston   J-66
University Center (1967) George Pierce-Abel B. Pierce

Sectionally activated public buildings organized around collective spaces were an innovation in Houston in the 1960s. The University Center's engineering aesthetic— long spans infilled with repetitive wall systems and the use of concrete as a finish material— lacks the fine-grained detail needed to enliven such spaces. The University Center and the adjoining **Conrad N. Hilton College of Hotel and Restaurant Management and Continuing Education Center** (1974, Pierce Goodwin Flanagan) seem scaleless and anonymous, despite the visible evidence of architectural design that they present.

University of Houston   J-67
Philip Guthrie Hoffman Hall (1974)
Kenneth Bentsen Associates

A homage to I. M. Pei in poured-in-place concrete, the six-story Hoffman Hall is the one building that masters the spatial concepts inherent in the replanning of the campus after 1966. Its height, breadth, and solid, well-proportioned, well-detailed frame enable it to control architecturally the laterally expansive space of Anne Garrett Butler Plaza, an immense, inclined lawn free of the busy plantings that disfigure other campus spaces. Hoffman Hall sits on a raised terrace that counters the topographical variation of the lawn. It also frames an important pedestrian connection architecturally, creating a sense of having arrived at a significant place. In the center of Butler Plaza is Peter Forakis's tall Corten piece, "Tower of the Cheyenne" (1972).

University of Houston   J-68
Agnes Arnold Hall (1966)
Kenneth Bentsen Associates

This six-story concrete frame and brick infill classroom building was the first on the campus to engage in sectional manipulation and the integration of outdoor with interior space. The estimation of Houston's potential to sustain open-air balcony corridors

proved overly optimistic and retrofitting was necessary to control wind turbulence through the building. Yet despite these experiential shortcomings, Agnes Arnold Hall is one of the liveliest venues on campus.

University of Houston   J-69
Science and Research Center (1969)
MacKie & Kamrath

MacKie & Kamrath's inflation of Wrightian details to huge scale may seem bizarre at first sight. But their effort to control the elevations of this overwhelmingly big building by introducing staged levels of horizontal banding, contrasting window alignments, and articulation of vertical shafts can only be appreciated when the building is compared to its listless neighbors. A second generation annex to the Science and Research Center, the **Houston Science Center Addition** (1991, Houston Science Center Architects), is an intelligently conceived and articulately detailed building designed by Gilbert Hoffman of White Budd Van Ness Partnership and Mario Bolullo of Harry Golemon Architects.

University of Houston   J-70
Architecture Building (1986)
Johnson/Burgee Architects and
Morris*Aubry Architects

Philip Johnson's *jeu d'esprit* at UH was to expropriate the 18th-century French architect C.-N. Ledoux's never-built design for a House of Education in the ideal town of Chaux, inflate it to Texan proportions, and then drop it on axis with the campus's major parking lot entrance to become the university's new architectural set piece. The frontality, figuration, and symmetry of the building are a relief compared to its trivial or merely anonymous neighbors. But in its perfunctory detailing and concern with superficial image, it is more like its neighbors than it would have us believe. Stacked trays of studio space are organized around an interior court, centered beneath the roofless stone temple atop the building. The arched windows on the third floor afford

fine views of both the university and the
downtown skyline. Installed to either side
of the south entrance are hieratic granite
benches by the sculptor Scott Burton
(1985).

University of Houston   **J-71**
Bates College of Law [now Law Center]
(1969) Freeman, Van Ness & Mower

Clarity, proportion, and restraint characterize the assembly of exposed, poured-in-
place concrete components that make up
the law center's several buildings. These are
arranged around a paved agora, beneath
which the college's main library is located.
The northern-most classroom building is an
addition by Pitts, Phelps & Mebane (1975).
Situated at the approach to the college is
Gerhard Marcks's seated bronze figure
"Albertus Magnus" (1955).

5000 Gulf Freeway   **J-72**
Schlumberger Well Services Headquarters
(1953) MacKie & Kamrath

The Gulf Freeway was completed in 1952,
along the right-of-way of the Interurban
trolley line between Houston and
Galveston. Schlumberger was the first corporation to construct a suburban headquarters complex along the new freeway. In
designing the two- and three-story front
office building, MacKie & Kamrath adopted the modern industrial vernacular that the
Walter Kidde Co. had used for the research
and testing buildings in the complex: low,
flat-roofed buildings with alternating horizontal bands of brick spandrel, window
glass, and corrugated aluminum spandrel
and header panels. The entrance is marked
by a slender brick pylon that visually counters the building's horizontality and a dramatic cantilevered porte-cochere canopy.
These features indicate Karl Kamrath's
indebtedness to Frank Lloyd Wright and
also to the Dutch architect W. M. Dudok.

North Side / East End

That railroad lines largely bypassed downtown Houston and the South End accounts in part for their historic identification as high-status districts. The presence of the rail lines that made Houston the railroad center of the Texas Gulf Coast by the late 1850s gave quite a different character to the parts of the city that they traversed—north of Buffalo Bayou along the old Montgomery Road (now North Main Street), and east of Houston along the old Harrisburg Road. The North Side, which lay largely in Houston's Fifth Ward, was the site of the Southern Pacific Company's railroad car shops and yard. This was an employment center that attracted subsidiary industries and a large working-class population, occupying residential neighborhoods between White Oak Bayou, Quitman Street, and Elysian Street, today home to a large Hispanic community.

The portion of Third Ward due east of what is now downtown was also a working-class residential neighborhood, bounded on the east by the diagonally aligned rail yards of the Galveston, Houston & Henderson Railroad. This was totally redeveloped between the 1920s and the 1950s as a warehouse district tied to the San Antonio & Aransas Pass railroad line. Since the early 1950s, a light sprinkling of Asian-owned retail businesses have been operated here.

The East End, on the east side of the G. H. & H. yards, was developed for moderate income housing, beginning in the early 20th century. This is also where industrial manufacturing and oil field equipment and servicing operations began to be located in the 1930s and '40s, infilling between residential areas along the major east-west streets: Leeland, Polk, McKinney, Harrisburg, Canal, and Navigation. These replaced the last bits of open countryside that, in the 19th century, separated Houston from the town of Harrisburg, 5$^1/_2$ miles away, where dairy farms, fruit orchards, and the country houses of the Lockart and Brady families had been located.

Modernization of the waterfront along Buffalo Bayou commenced with the completion of Navigation Boulevard and Clinton Drive in the late 1920s. This was where the new, planned industrial districts of the 1930s and '40s were located. Farther east still is Magnolia Park, laid out in 1909 near the site of the Turning Basin of the Houston Ship Channel as a large, working-class neighborhood. When Mexican-Americans began to settle in large numbers in Houston during the 1910s, they established *barrios* on the North Side and the East End, especially in Magnolia Park. Just south of Magnolia Park, on South Wayside Drive, are the original grounds of the Houston Country Club (now Gus S. Wortham Park). Its opening here in 1909, along the banks of Brays Bayou, sparked development of several adjacent suburban neighborhoods. These treated the bayou as a scenic amenity rather than a commercial thoroughfare, the role it shared with railroads in Houston throughout the 19th century.

The North Side and the East End are the traditional workshops of Houston. They possess a certain gritty texture that has survived.

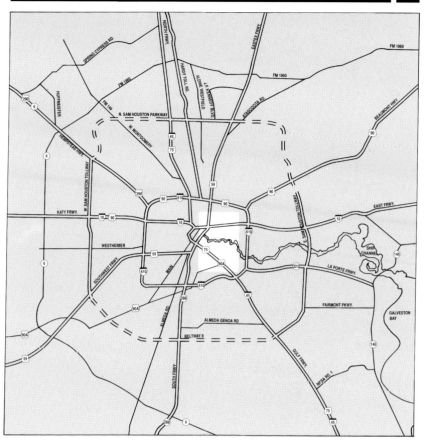

The presence in these areas of working class Hispanic Houstonians results in a degree of popular street life that is missing from the city's more affluent precincts.

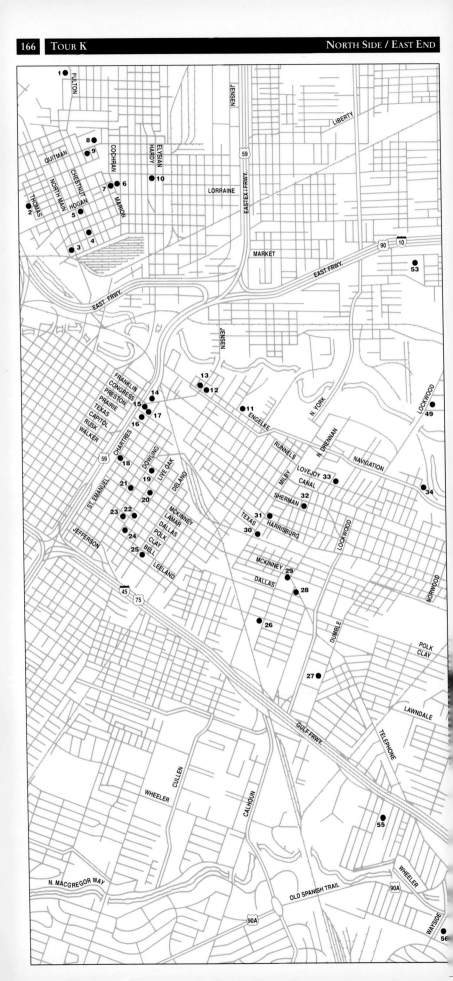

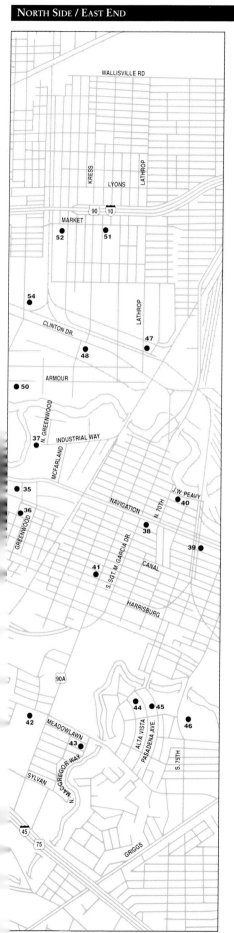

1. 3725 Fulton Street
2. 2015 Thomas Street
3. 1615 North Main Street
4. 1703 Chestnut Street
5. 702 Hogan Street
6. 1906 Cochran Street
7. 1920 Marion Street
8. 1200 Quitman Street
9. 1050 Quitman Street
10. 2102 Hardy Street
11. 2809 Engelke Street
12. 2405 Navigation Boulevard
13. Runnels Street and Jensen Drive
14. 121 St. Emanuel Street
15. 2018 Franklin Avenue
16. 2017 Preston Avenue
17. 2109-2111, 2113-2117, and 2119
     Congress Avenue
18. 801-811 Chartres Street
19. 701 Dowling Street
20. 908 Live Oak Street
21. 2300-2310 McKinney Avenue
22. 2501 Polk Avenue
23. 2400-2420 Polk Avenue
24. 2508 Clay Avenue
25. 1507 Delano Street
26. 4200 Leeland Avenue
27. 1700 Dumble Street
28. 4411 Dallas Avenue
29. 100 Telephone Road
30. 711 Milby Street
31. 3801 Wilmer Street
32. 4015 Sherman Street
33. 4401 Lovejoy Street
34. 5303 Navigation Boulevard
35. 235 North Norwood Street
36. 5801 Canal Street
37. 501 North Greenwood Street
38. 6902 Navigation Boulevard
39. 7320 Navigation Boulevard
40. J. W. Peavy Drive and
     North 70th Street
41. 1001 Wayside Drive
42. 6510 Lawndale Avenue
43. 6740 Meadow Lawn Drive
44. 1724 Alta Vista Avenue
45. 1766 Pasadena Avenue
46. 541 South 75th Street
47. 1441 Lathrop Street
48. 5800 Clinton Drive
49. 750 Lockwood Drive
50. 5520 Armour Drive
51. 6402 Market Street
52. 5910 Market Street
53. 4910 Market Street
54. 1024 Lockwood Drive
55. 2401 Munger Street
56. 2999 South Wayside Drive

3725 Fulton Street   **K-1**
Moody Park, "Vaquero" (1978)
Luis Jiménez, sculptor

Jiménez's brilliantly colored, action-packed molded fiberglass cowboy is one of the liveliest and most popular public art installations in Houston. The statue also provides a marvelous vantage point from which to survey the downtown skyline.

2015 Thomas Street   **K-2**
Sunset Hospital [now Thomas Street Center] (1911) Department of Buildings and Bridges, Galveston, Houston & San Antonio Railway

Built by a subsidiary of the Southern Pacific Railway as a staff hospital (the Southern Pacific's shops, Houston's major industrial employer at the turn of the century, are nearby), the Sunset Hospital has been remarkably well preserved. The combination of three colors of brick, molded brick decoration, and red roof tiles gives the building a rich but subdued aspect. The palm trees, the street fence, and the pergola-covered entry gate remain intact.

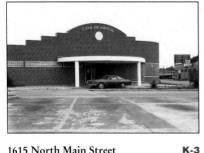

1615 North Main Street   **K-3**
Casa de Amigos Community Health Center (1983) Urban Architecture

This neighborhood health center, built by

Harris County, is a lively building that pays special attention to its down (but not out) surroundings. In giving shape to the streamlined brick- and glass block-faced building, Hossein Oskouie took note of both nearby modernistic warehouse and industrial buildings and the incomparable Pan América Ballroom next door at 1705 North Main. Oskouie ensured that the building functions as the gateway to the North Side by positioning it diagonally on its site. Here he demonstrated how sympathetic concern for context can lead to a building that draws its environs into a greater whole. Immediately behind, at 1620 Keene Street, is the studio of artist Noah Edmundson, where "It's Always 8:05 AM In Hell."

1703 Chestnut Street   **K-4**
Mission German Methodist Episcopal Church, South [now Templo Jerusalén] (c. 1892)

This Victorian cottage church is characteristic of this North Side neighborhood in the city's ex-Fifth Ward, a working-class district dependent on the Southern Pacific yards just south of Burnett Street. The building's uses illustrate demographic transitions within the area. From 1938 to 1961 it was the parish seat of St. George Syrian Orthodox Church and the cultural center of Houston's Arab community. Since 1961 it has been the home of a Spanish-language Protestant congregation. Just across Harrington Street, at 1626 Chestnut, is an unexceptional house that has begun to petrify, reflecting the popularity of decorative concrete work in the 1930s and '40s.

702 Hogan Street   **K-5**
Fire Station No. 9 (1971) W. Irving Phillips, Jr., & Robert W. Peterson

Phillips used brick and precast concrete to shape this box-like fire station. Incisions of various depths and widths imbue the building with a sense of tension and spatial complexity.

1906 Cochran Street   **K-6**
Casa de Amigos Health Center (1974)
Dennis Kilper and Harry Ransom

Dennis Kilper differentiated the brick end walls of this city health clinic from the stucco-surfaced cross panels, exhibiting the building's steel bar joist roof structure along the latter. The building is not well maintained: nor is the ex-**North Side Methodist Church** (1923, 1928, Alfred C. Finn), to which Kilper and Ransom's building is attached.

1920 Marion Street   **K-7**
Holy Name Church (1926)
Frederick B. Gaenslen

Gaenslen's twin-towered church, detailed, as is his All Saints in the Heights, with French Romanesque motifs, exerts a strong presence in this neighborhood of modest houses. The church is finished with dark red tapestry brick.

1200 Quitman Street   **K-8**
Jefferson Davis Senior High School (1927)
Briscoe & Dixon and Maurice J. Sullivan,
William Ward Watkin, consulting architect

Cast stone detail of Georgian provenance imparts a strong semblance of classical order and decorum to this high school. Together with **John Marshall Junior High School**, across Quitman at 1115 Noble Street (1925, Hedrick & Gottlieb), it forms an enclave of public buildings near the center of the neighborhood.

1050 Quitman Street   **K-9**
Carnegie Branch, Houston Public Library (1982) Ray Bailey Architects

Although a part of the civic arena formed by the two school buildings, this branch library was designed in response to other factors. The building's east elevation faces a small park behind a gridded surface of bronze solar glass. (The classical colonnade set up in the park is all that remains of the original Carnegie Branch Library of 1925.) The west elevation is a stucco screen, painted in bright pastel colors. The library succeeds at being an unintimidating public building, but its lack of a clearly distinguishable facade makes it seem rather equivocal in a setting where other public buildings are unambiguously frontal. The interior is light, airy, and enjoyable.

2102 Hardy Street   **K-10**
George W. Bergstrom Grocery Store
Building (c. 1905)

Rock-faced cast concrete surfaces were a specialty of the Swedish-born Houston architect Olle J. Lorehn, for whom George W. Bergstrom worked as a draftsman several years before opening this grocery, feed, and beer emporium. As was customary, Bergstrom occupied the apartment above his business premises.

2809 Engelke Street   **K-11**
Martínez House and Garden

Timoteo Martínez, a Mexican-born plasterer, moved into this house in the former Second Ward in 1934. He began embellishing the cottage and its surroundings, continuing this delightful program of home improvements into the mid-1980s, by which time he had passed the age of 90.

2405 Navigation Boulevard **K-12**
Our Lady of Guadalupe Catholic Church (1923) Leo M. J. Dielmann

During his long career, the San Antonio architect Leo Dielmann produced an extraordinary number of Roman Catholic churches all across Texas. After designing Our Lady of Guadalupe Church in San Antonio for a Spanish-speaking parish, he was commissioned to design churches for parishes of the same dedication in Laredo and Houston. The Houston church is an enlarged version of the San Antonio prototype; it is detailed with Lombard Romanesque features and finished in light red brick. Subsequent additions, such as the front porch, detract from the church's integrity. Dielmann's building replaced a wooden frame structure dating from the founding of the parish in 1912. Our Lady of Guadalupe, located in Second Ward, was an important community center for Mexican Americans in Houston.

Runnels Street and Jensen Drive **K-13**
Guadalupe Plaza (1988)
Hispanic Consortium

The City of Houston installed this generously-scaled, Mexican-themed plaza across from Our Lady of Guadalupe, in the parking lot of the ill-fated Mercado del Sol, a would-be festival marketplace occupying the old Lottman Manufacturing Co. mattress plant (1904, 1910, 1926). The simple but effective spatial organization, substantial construction, bright colors, and such details as tropical plantings, the encircling pergola, and the large fountain make it as urbane a space as could be hoped for in the middle of a parking lot. The plaza seems to have been conceived as the site for ceremonial public occasions; because of its distance from neighborhood houses, it is not intensively used for informal recreation. On the

north side of the parking lot, across the railroad track, is a *placita* that steps down the bank of Buffalo Bayou to become a water gate. Luis Bodmer and the landscape architect George S. Porcher were the park's designers.

121 St. Emanuel Street **K-14**
Gribble Stamp & Stencil Co. Building (1948) C. R. Berry & Co.

The two-story glass block cylinder functions as the pivot point for this building's diverging wall planes, which are finished with red and tan brick banding.

2018 Franklin Avenue **K-15**
Standard Brass & Manufacturing Co. Building (1937) John F. Staub

Staub's associate, J. T. Rather, Jr., emphasized the planar walls of this industrial building with horizontally banded steel sash windows. Deep and shallow volumetric incursions provide for vehicular and pedestrian access.

2017 Preston Avenue **K-16**
Cheek-Neal Coffee Co. Building (1917)
Finger & Bailey

Joseph Finger and James Ruskin Bailey were responsible for this now ill-maintained five-story building, which forthrightly expresses its reinforced concrete frame construction. The Cheek-Neal Coffee Co. manufactured Maxwell House Coffee here.

2109-2111, 2113-2117, and   **K-17**
2119 Congress Avenue

These three buildings, dating from the late 1890s and early 1900s, exhibit details characteristic of local commercial construction of the time. The red brick building at 2109-11 has window openings handsomely framed by round arches. The central building at 2113 shows remnants of a brick cornice. And the corner building, at 2119, retains its ground-floor cast iron front. The upper stories of these buildings were rented to boarders; at the turn of the 20th century, this section of Second Ward was almost entirely residential. Its conversion into a warehouse and industrial district did not begin until after the opening of Union Station in 1911.

801-811 Chartres Street   **K-18**
On Leong Chinese Merchants Association Building (1951) Irvine & Hoyt

This three-story retail, office, and apartment building was the first institutional expression of Houston's Chinese community. Designed in a self-consciously Sino-modernistic style, it became the nucleus of a small Asian business center that expanded dramatically in the 1980s with the opening of Indochinese establishments nearby.

701 Dowling Street   **K-19**
Herrin Transfer & Storage Co. Building (1937) Harvin Moore & Hermon Lloyd

A compact business building decked out with such modernistic devices as the porthole window.

908 Live Oak Street   **K-20**
Wald Transfer & Storage Co. Building (1949) Irving R. Klein & Associates

This block-long building is one of the highlights of the East End warehouse district. The contrast of horizontal strip windows with the vertical pylon, the two-toned masonry finishes, and the use of concrete framing strips and canopies are handled with great flair.

2300-2310 McKinney Avenue   **K-21**
Standard Sanitary Manufacturing Co. Building (1924) Alfred C. Finn

Finn's use of dark brick makes this four-story warehouse—quite large by Houston standards of the time—a brooding presence. Close by, at 2205 McKinney, is Finn's stylistically similar **Crane Co. Building** (1926).

2501 Polk Avenue   **K-22**
Houston Lighting & Power Co. Substation (c. 1948)

Minimally detailed with louvered openings, identifying graphics, and a centered doorway, this two-story planar building is a very spirited example of modernistic design.

2400-2420 Polk Avenue   **K-23**
Houston Post Building (1955) Herbert Voelcker & Associates

Voelcker made his reputation as an architect of modernistic county courthouses in north and west Texas. The ex-Houston Post

Building is in a late, heavy rendition of the style; its street fronts have been sealed.

2508 Clay Avenue   **K-24**
St. Nicholas Catholic Church (1923)
Leo M. J. Dielmann

Dielmann produced a vaguely Spanish mission image for St. Nicholas, the black Roman Catholic parish. Its quirkiness is representative of his work.

1507 Delano Street   **K-25**
Tien Hou Temple, Sino-Indochinese Association of Texas (1987)

Although this Taiwanese temple complex would appear exotic anywhere in Houston, here, in this depressed neighborhood, it seems almost like a mirage. The construction materials were imported from Taiwan, although some of the carving was executed in Houston by Chinese artisans.

4200 Leeland Avenue   **K-26**
City of Houston Water Customer Service Building (1984) Kendall/Heaton Associates

Kendall/Heaton sleekly retrofitted the ex-East End State Bank Building to become a service and operations center for the city's water department.

1700 Dumble Street   **K-27**
Stephen F. Austin Senior High School (1937) Birdsall P. Briscoe, Maurice J. Sullivan, Sam H. Dixon, Jr., and Joseph Finger

The Public Works Administration financed the construction of two public high schools in Houston which were virtually identical in plan but strikingly different in outward appearance: Austin and Lamar (on Westheimer Road). Austin's conservative architectural imagery is enlivened with imaginative ornamental brick detailing.

4411 Dallas Avenue   **K-28**
Church of the Redeemer, Episcopal (1952)
Tellepsen Construction Co.

Tom Tellepsen, a general contractor who was a parishioner of Redeemer, built a new church based on a vision he had had in a dream. At the time of its completion, the concrete building was described as the first windowless church in Houston. It was centrally air-conditioned and the nave was illuminated with concealed fluorescent lighting. Behind the altar is John Orth's mural "Christ of the Workingman."

100 Telephone Road   **K-29**
Eastwood Elementary School [now Dora Lantrip Elementary School] (1916)
Maurice J. Sullivan

Eastwood, where this school and the Church of the Redeemer are located, was developed in 1911 by the William A. Wilson Co., developers of Woodland Heights. The company donated this site near the center of the subdivision for a school, planned by Maurice Sullivan, then City Architect of Houston. Designed in the Spanish mission style, with arcaded loggias and patios, it was described at the time of its construction as being the first school in Houston arranged on the "cottage plan," with classrooms occupying a series of free-standing pavilions. In 1927 sympathetic additions by Harry D. Payne and James Ruskin Bailey were made at the rear of the complex.

711 Milby Street   **K-30**
Cameron Iron Works Building (1935)

This elaborately detailed modernistic office building was nonchalantly plugged onto an existing industrial installation.

3801 Wilmer Street   **K-31**
(c. 1860) **Demolished in 1991**

It is dismaying to realize that behind the wooden fence and in front of the asbestos-shingled second-floor balcony is an antebellum Greek Revival house. The fluted Doric columns and the dog-eared door and window frames on the first floor reveal the house's true identity. John Thomas Brady, the builder, was an entrepreneur who owned 2,000 acres between Houston and Harrisburg that he attempted to develop. After his death, his heirs subdivided the family enclave along Milby Street into the Brady Addition, naming streets after family members. In the early 1920s, the Brady House, which originally sat across the street facing Milby, was moved into the front yard of Brady's son's house, the raised brick cottage at 3803 Wilmer.

4015 Sherman Street   **K-32**
Blessed Sacrament Church (1924)
Frederick B. Gaenslen

This is the best of Gaenslen's Houston churches and one of the finest of his career. Its distinguishing feature is its ornamental brickwork, a conspicuous attribute of San Antonio architecture of the 1920s. Next door is the original church and parish house, designed by Lewis Sterling Green and Birdsall P. Briscoe (1910). It was constructed on a site that the Brady family donated in the Brady Addition.

4401 Lovejoy Street   **K-33**
Ripley House (1940) Birdsall P. Briscoe and Maurice J. Sullivan

Mrs. Daniel Ripley, whose husband built the Savoy Apartments on Main Street, endowed a foundation to build and operate this community center, where residents of surrounding lower-income neighborhoods could have access to recreational and educational programs and low-cost health care. Briscoe and Sullivan planned the building as a series of functionally discreet zones, as the massing and elevations imply. Monumentality was reserved for the entry bay, a quarter-circular drum faced with a file of thin brick piers. Greek-inspired relief figures decorate spandrel panels within this drum.

5303 Navigation Boulevard   **K-34**
Parker Bros. & Co. Building (1939)
Joseph Finger

Mellie Esperson developed the Esperson Industrial District along the south shore of Buffalo Bayou just upstream from the turning basin of the Houston Ship Channel. Navigation Boulevard curves sinuously through the slightly rolling terrain of the Esperson Industrial District, its entrance marked by this small but prepossessing modernistic office building for a construction products supply company.

235 North Norwood Street   K-35
J. A. Folger Coffee Co. Building [now Continental Coffee Products] (1938, 1947) Robert J. Cummins, engineer

Set at the highest point in the Esperson Industrial District is the five-story manufacturing plant for Folger's coffee, designed by Cummins's associate Frank Zumwalt. The horizontally banded brick elevations feature two kinds of glass block interspersed with operable steel sash windows.

5801 Canal Street   K-36
"The Rebirth of Our Nationality" (1972-1973) Leo Tanguma, painter

Leo Tanguma directed dozens of local Chicano artists in creating a work of community art on the side of the Continental Can Co. building. Tanguma purposefully deployed the rhetorical style of the great Mexican muralists for this long reflection on the condition of poor Mexican Americans in Houston in the 1970s. Unfortunately, the surface is deteriorating.

501 North Greenwood Street   K-37
Republic Steel Corporation Buildings (1941) Joseph Finger

Finger's little head office building is, as one might expect, modernistic. Of far more interest is the adjoining production plant,

faced entirely with a modular steel panel wall system.

6902 Navigation Boulevard   K-38
Fire Station No. 20 (1972) W. Irving Phillips, Jr., & Robert W. Peterson

Phillips used the same materials for this fire station that he and Peterson had used at Fire Station No. 9 on Hogan Street. Here, however, a thinner, tenser sensation was sought, aided especially by differentiating between recessed and flush-set glazing.

7320 Navigation Boulevard   K-39
Sociedad Mutualista Benito Juárez Casino Hall (1928)

This modest wooden building was the first purpose-built non-religious public institution constructed in Houston's East End by local Mexican Americans. It provided a place for theatrical performances and Mexican American community events in Magnolia Park, one of the neighborhoods where Mexican immigrants settled en masse in the 1920s and 1930s. Magnolia Park had been part of John T. Brady's real estate holdings, and was developed in the 1910s as a working-class neighborhood in proximity to the Houston Ship Channel.

J. W. Peavy Drive and North 70th Street   K-40
Hidalgo Park Kiosk (1935) Vidal Lozano

This high-set kiosk is built entirely of molded concrete: its stone base, its writhing tree trunk and branch vertical supports, and its conical thatched roof. Mexican

Americans raised the money to purchase this small piece of property facing Buffalo Bayou and within sight of the turning basin of the Ship Channel, turned it over to the City of Houston as a public park, and sponsored the construction of Lozano's kiosk.

1001 Wayside Drive   **K-41**
Park Memorial Baptist Church (1951)
Dixon & Greenwood

A late example of the Lombard Romanesque style that had been so dominant in Houston in the 1920s. Big in scale and finely detailed, the church loses nothing by comparison with its predecessors.

6510 Lawndale Avenue   **K-42**
Conventual Chapel of the Villa de Matel
(1928) Maurice J. Sullivan

The Villa de Matel, the mother house and novitiate of the Sisters of Charity of the Incarnate Word, who operate St. Joseph Hospital, was Sullivan's first major commission after he began his own practice in 1919. The complex, designed in the Lombard Romanesque style, is set on a 72-acre site. The Conventual Chapel, which lies south of the mother house, is the grandest church built in Houston during the 1920s. It is detailed with neo-Byzantine decor. Sullivan employed exposed aggregate concrete mosaic for the wall surfaces and Guastavino tile vaults for the chapel's ceiling. Numerous varieties of polished colored marbles are used. Sullivan designed the stained glass windows, which were

fabricated in Munich. Seating in the chapel is in collegiate choir arrangement.

6740 Meadow Lawn Drive   **K-43**
(1941)

Indicative of the high standards of domestic design that prevailed in Houston in the 1930s and early 1940s is this modest one-story, brick-faced house. It is located in the subdivision of Idylwood, developed in 1928 along an extension of the Brays Bayou Parkway. Next door at **6748 Meadow Lawn** is a modernistic house (1940), somewhat the worse for coarse alterations.

1724 Alta Vista Avenue   **K-44**
(1912) Cooke & Co.

The architect W. A. Cooke designed this expansive Mission bungalow, faced with stucco and red roof tiles, for his family. It is located in Forest Hill, planned in 1910 by the Kansas City landscape architects Hare & Hare as the first subdivision in Houston with a curvilinear street plan. Forest Hill was laid out across Brays Bayou from what was then the Houston Country Club (now Gus S. Wortham Park). The Cooke House was one of three large houses built there; these did not presage Forest Hill's future, however, and during the 1920s they came to be surrounded by much more modest houses.

1766 Pasadena Avenue   **K-45**
(1911) Lang & Witchell

This Colonial revival house was the largest built in Forest Hill. Designed in the Houston branch office of Dallas's most prolific architects, it sits on a small hillock looking out to Brays Bayou.

541 South 75th Street   **K-46**
Mason Park Shelter House (1932)
A. E. Nutter

Nutter designed the simpler of these two stucco-surfaced, tile-roofed Mediterranean buildings. It is similar to his shelter houses in Hermann and MacGregor parks. The second, by H. A. Salisbury & T. G. McHale (1950), is joined to Nutter's original by a tile-roofed Doric colonnade.

1441 Lathrop Street   **K-47**
Rice Hotel Laundry (1966)
Neuhaus-Wingfield Associates

For a commercial laundry, Hugo V. Neuhaus, Jr., and Magruder Wingfield, Jr., produced this straightforward but carefully ordered and detailed steel-framed building.

5800 Clinton Drive   **K-48**
Ford Motor Co. Building (1947)
Giffels & Vallet

The Detroit architects Giffels & Vallet shaped this late modernistic style building for the Ford Motor Co.'s service and parts operation with curved corners, streamlined ribbon windows, and a high, glazed central bay. The building is set on a spacious lawn, an indication of the suburbanizing trend that was even beginning to affect standards for design in industrial districts.

750 Lockwood Drive   **K-49**
National Steel Products Co. Building
[now Electric Wire & Cable Co.] (1950)

Not only the production plant but the head office advertised this corporation's foremost product, the semicircular corrugated steel structural shell—a Quonset hut in all but name.

5520 Armour Drive   **K-50**
Pittsburgh Plate Glass Co. Building (1955)
Milton McGinty

As was often the case with Houston industrial buildings of the 1940s and '50s, masonry of contrasting types, textures, and colors was skillfully combined here to elicit an appearance that was economical but not merely utilitarian. McGinty's building programmatically differentiates between office and production space. It also incorporates that favorite modernistic device, the pylon.

6402 Market Street   **K-51**
Denver Harbor Park Recreation Building
(1949) Staub & Rather

Along Market Street one encounters a succession of public buildings that employed brick and tile banding to induce decorative wall patterns. On this stepped, boxy building, organized around a central gymnasium, J. T. Rather, Jr., combined maroon glazed brick with buff brick and concrete coping.

5910 Market Street   **K-52**
John L. McReynolds Junior High School
(1956) Stayton Nunn

Stayton Nunn ventured a bright array of colors as well as decorative grillwork on this large complex of buildings. The stairwells are marked by projecting V-shaped bay windows, which, in combination with the polychrome brick, anticipate Cesar Pelli's work at Rice University by nearly 30 years.

4910 Market Street　　　　　　K-53
Phyllis Wheatley Senior High School (1949)
MacKie & Kamrath

Kamrath emphasized the horizontal and dispensed with fields of colored tile or glazed brick. But this large school complex, built originally as the high school for black students in Fifth Ward, shares with McReynolds Junior High and the Denver Harbor Park Recreation Building the virtues of solid construction and conscientious detailing. As a result, these three buildings have aged without display of strain or deterioration. Behind Wheatley, in the 5100 block of Sonora Street, is MacKie & Kamrath's **Finnigan Park Recreation Building** (1949), which has not fared quite so well.

1024 Lockwood Drive　　　　　　K-54
Howard Flint Ink Co. Building (1940)
Harley & Ellington

A small modernistic office building, designed by a firm of Detroit architects. Across the street, at 1111 Lockwood, is MacKie & Kamrath's **Thornhill-Craver Co. Building** (1949).

2401 Munger Street　　　　　　K-55
The Orange Show (1979) Jeff D. McKissack

Jeff McKissack, a retired postal worker, began the Orange Show in 1968 and worked on it until just before his death in 1980. He dedicated this open-air compound to his belief that the orange functioned as a privileged transmitter of energy from the sun to humankind. Its museum, maze-like passages, arenas, and viewing pavilions, were all intended to focus on didactic spectacles about orange power. McKissack built the compound himself, using concrete block and scavenged materials for decoration. His colorful metal work, both stationary and mobile, animates the Orange Show. Following acquisition of the property in 1981 by the Orange Show Foundation, it was restored by Barry Moore Architects. The Orange Show is open to the public on weekends between mid-March and early December, and on weekdays between Memorial Day and Labor Day.

2999 South Wayside Drive　　　　K-56
Farnsworth & Chambers Building [now City of Houston Department of Parks and Recreation Building] (1957)
MacKie & Kamrath

Another in the series of suburban corporate office buildings that MacKie & Kamrath produced in the 1950s, the critical decade of Houston's suburbanization. Battered walls of randomly-coursed green Arizona mint stone are contained by insistent horizontals, a Kamrath trademark. Indicative of the status of the automobile, the front entrance is identified with a weighty porte-cochere. Given the park-like setting, lush interior garden courts, and the building's color, it is fitting that it now serves as headquarters for the city parks department. The building also functioned as temporary headquarters for NASA while the Manned Spacecraft Center at Clear Lake City was under construction.

The Heights

L ike the North Side and the East End, the Heights is a working-class area of Houston, its fortunes historically tied to railroad lines. The route of the Houston & Texas Central, the pioneer Houston railroad, parallels the old Washington Road. Along the railroad tracks were industries of various kinds. At Chaneyville, near the intersection of Washington Avenue and Studemont, one such concentration is still marked by the silos of the Blue Ribbon Rice Mills. It was also along the roads leading out of Houston that cemeteries were established in the 19th century. Washington provides access to the opulent Glenwood Cemetery and, next door, solemn Washington Cemetery, originally Deutsche Gesellschaft. Germans comprised the largest bloc of resident immigrants in 19th-century Texas and their presence in Houston is still evident in the Baker Addition in what had been the Sixth Ward, now the city's oldest intact residential neighborhood.

Electrification of the street car lines in 1890 allowed real estate developers to expand much farther out from the compact centers of American cities. Houston Heights, a new community developed by Middle Western investors in the early 1890s, took advantage of this technical advance. The chief investor went so far as to purchase the Houston street car system to ensure its extension to Houston Heights, $2^1/_2$ miles from Market Square, then used the profits the system generated to keep the Heights afloat economically during the Panic of 1893. Houston Heights was no mere "addition" to the city of Houston. It was the first large, planned community undertaken locally and its central thoroughfare, Heights Boulevard, was the first divided boulevard to be laid out in the Houston area. Although it was never a high status neighborhood, the Heights introduced a much more comprehensive and rationalized approach to community planning than had ever been tried before in Houston. It also demonstrated that suburban communities could exist in proximity to, but without being a part of, the central city, at least until its eventual annexation by Houston.

The subsequent extension of streetcar lines from downtown also accounted for the development of Brooke-Smith Addition and Woodland Heights, which infilled between the Heights and Houston proper. Woodland Heights adopted the symbols and strategies of more elite neighborhoods, providing landscape amenities, a no longer extant gateway, and restrictive covenants (which are still enforced) upon opening in 1907, the better to compete for moderate-income house buyers.

The Heights, as this whole area is now collectively known, has become a mixture of old-time working-class families, both Anglo- and Mexican-American, younger families seeking relatively inexpensive housing, and specialized groups, most visibly artists. Like much of Houston, the Heights has a slightly ragged look, appealing to some as homey while appearing to others as merely run-down. With this aspect goes a small-town ambience typical of many Houston neighborhoods, which could easily be in East Texas or at some crossroads on the coastal plain, far removed from skyscrapers and freeways.

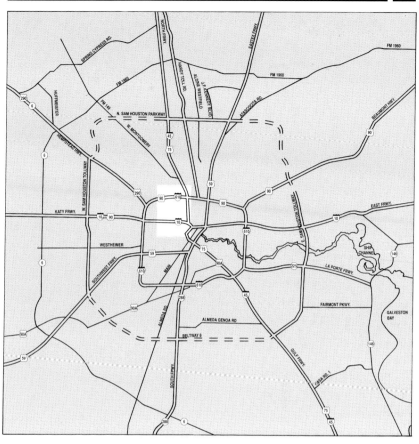

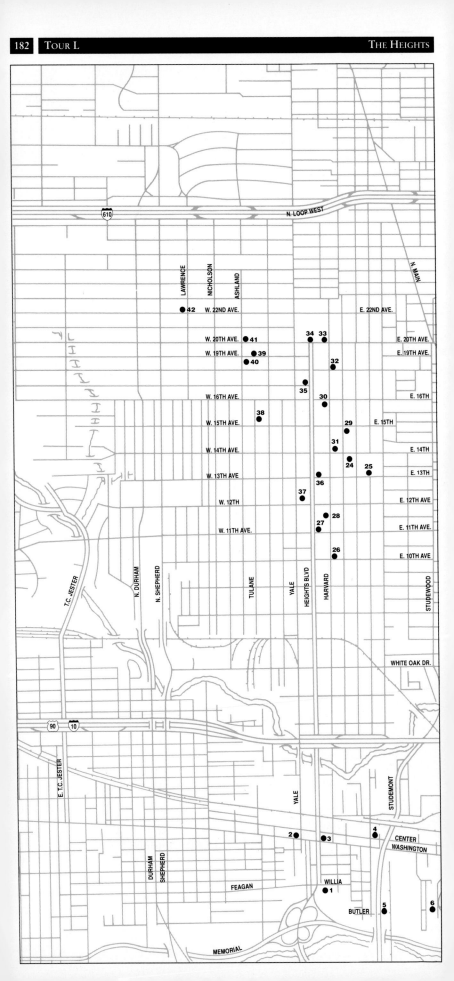

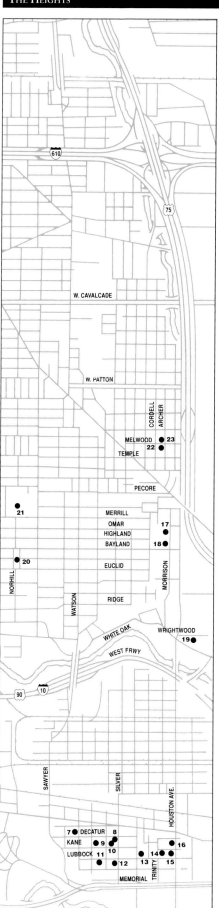

1. 3615 Willia Street
2. 3800 Washington Avenue
3. 3620 Washington Avenue
4. 3122 Center Street
5. 3000 Butler Street
6. 2525 Washington Avenue
7. 2212 Decatur Street
8. 1909 Decatur Street
9. 2018 Kane Street
10. 1910 Kane Street
11. 2017 Lubbock Street
12. 617 Silver Street
13. 1718 Lubbock Street
14. Kane Street and Trinity Street
15. 1505 Kane Street
16. 815 Houston Avenue
17. 3301 Morrison Avenue
18. 205 Bayland Avenue
19. 1215 Wrightwood Avenue
20. Norhill Street and Euclid Street
21. 1100 Merrill Street
22. 308 Cordell Street
23. 403 Archer Street
24. 300 East 14th Avenue
25. 401 East 13th Avenue
26. 1002 Harvard Street
27. 1102 Heights Boulevard
28. 1123 Harvard Street
29. 306 East 15th Avenue
30. 120 East 16th Avenue
31. 1400 Harvard Street
32. 1802 Harvard Street
33. 119 East 20th Avenue
34. 139 East 20th Avenue
35. 1703 Heights Boulevard
36. 1302 Heights Boulevard
37. 107 West 12th Avenue
38. 1528 Tulane Street
39. 341 West 19th Avenue
40. 350 West 129th Avenue
41. 347 West 20th Avenue
42. 611 West 22nd Avenue

3615 Willia Street   **L-1**
Carroll Sterling Masterson Downtown
Branch and Metropolitan Offices, Young
Women's Christian Association (1979)
Taft Architects

Taft's first major building in Houston consists of a long two-story bar parallel to
Willia Street, which sprouts an angled rear
wing containing a double-volume gymnasium that overlooks the Buffalo Bayou
Parkway. Gridded stucco planes, stepped
tile banding, and square sectioned windows
give the building a toy-like aspect. Inside, a
sinuous ramp leads from the main entrance
past the gymnasium and swimming pool to
the second floor in a spirited architectural
promenade. The YWCA was a cheaply constructed building and the results of initial
economies have begun to show.

was rehabilitated in 1978 by Taft Architects.
At the same time they cleverly transformed
the interior into a nightclub, respecting the
old without attempting to conceal their
own interventions.

3122 Center Street   **L-4**
Damascus Baptist Church (1937)

This was the first independent work of
James M. Thomas, a contractor who specialized in building churches. It is an example of the twin-towered church type
especially popular in Houston from the
1920s into the 1950s. The Damascus Baptist
Church is located in a small black neighborhood in Chaneyville, a settlement along the
historic Washington Road that led northwest from Houston to Washington-on-the-
Brazos. At **1015 Court Street**, just in front
of the church, is an extravagantly roofed
bungalow built in 1927.

3800 Washington Avenue   **L-2**
Heights State Bank Building [now NBC
Bank-Houston] (1962) Wilson, Morris,
Crain & Anderson

This concrete and glass pavilion lost some
of its precision when two bays were added
along its Washington Avenue frontage.
Ralph A. Anderson, Jr., stacked radial precast concrete "trees" above a grid of cast-in-
place concrete columns, topping the whole
thing off with a cast-in-place roof slab. This
was the one locally designed Houston
building that Arthur Drexler included in his
"Transformations in Modern Architecture"
exhibition at The Museum of Modern Art
in 1979.

3620 Washington Avenue   **L-3**
Citizens State Bank Building [now
Rockefeller's] (1925) Joseph Finger

The previous home of Heights State Bank
illustrates how drastically attitudes about
appropriate architectural imagery changed
between the 1920s and 1960s. Finger's classically detailed facade stands out from, yet
is still a part of, the strip of commercial
buildings along Washington. It is closed and
secure looking, but it doesn't try to distance
itself from the street. The handsome facade

3000 Butler Street   **L-5**
Blue Ribbon Rice Mills (c. 1958-1965)
Barton-Chalmers Corp.

Chaneyville was the point at which the
Galveston, Harrisburg & San Antonio
Railway line crossed Buffalo Bayou to
intersect the Houston & Texas Central
Railroad line. Around this juncture there
developed in the late 19th century a small
industrial enclave whose presence is monu-
mentalized in this complex of reinforced
concrete tubular rice elevators. Although
built in the late 1950s and early 1960s, these
structures, especially the long stand of
white silos that parallels Studemont, possess

an archetypal aspect. Their height, regularity, and industrial scale make them a double of the downtown skyline, visible just to the east. Closed and stripped of their internal mechanism in 1986, the elevators now stand (for how long is uncertain) as a brooding presence on the landscape.

2525 Washington Avenue   **L-6**
Glenwood Cemetery "Solitude" (1926)
Marcel Bouraine, sculptor

Dr. Ethel Lyon Heard acquired this Bouraine figure in Paris, when it was exhibited there in 1927, and brought it to Houston to be installed on her husband's grave. The Heard monument is one of many in Glenwood Cemetery, laid out in 1871 by the English horticulturalist, Alfred Whitaker, on what was then the western edge of Houston. Glenwood is Houston's Victorian landscape cemetery. It was the first professionally designed and landscaped public space in the city. Because of its proximity to Buffalo Bayou, the 65-acre site is topographically varied and heavily wooded. Along its curving drives lies everyone who was anyone in Houston, including the architects Henry C. Cooke, Kenneth Franzheim, John F. Staub, and Hugo V. Neuhaus, Jr.

2212 Decatur Street   **L-7**
(c. 1897)

The wooden gingerbread brackets beneath the porch lintel are profiled to look like birds on the wing. Such distinctive bits of decoration recur on the modest wooden houses of this neighborhood, the W. R. Baker Addition in what had been the city's Sixth Ward. This is Houston's oldest intact neighborhood, a working-class district developed in the late 1850s near the shops of the Houston & Texas Central Railroad Co., which lay north of Washington Avenue.

1909 Decatur Street   **L-8**
(c. 1880)

As the twin front doors imply, this is a

double house, a type built for the rental market. Its solemn symmetrical front elevation is enlivened with bird brackets beneath the porch roof.

2018 Kane Street   **L-9**
(1908)

Henry R. Lighthouse, a brick manufacturer, built this Colonial revival house, the most pretentious in Sixth Ward, on the site of his wife's childhood home. The combination of tan brick and red mortar is a detail visible on other Houston buildings of the 1910 period. One block to the east, at **1920 Kane Street**, is a two-story I-house, so called because of its rectangular plan configuration and narrow width. This house, sitting in a fenced garden, strongly conveys a sense of what Sixth Ward must have been like at the end of the 19th century.

1910 Kane Street   **L-10**
(c. 1895)

The largest Victorian house in Sixth Ward, this features a gable surfaced with fish-scale shingles, a favorite ornamental finish in the 1890s.

2017 Lubbock Street   **L-11**
Rubenstein Group Building (1984)
Rubenstein Group

Built by the architect Larry Rubenstein to house his architectural studio, this two-story building is of wood post-and-beam construction, surfaced externally with corrugated metal. Roger Detherage, the art cabinet maker, oversaw construction of the

studio, which is evident in its meticulous but simple finishes and carefully worked-out joinery. The sawtooth skylights admit north light into the second-floor production space.

617 Silver Street   **L-12**
(c. 1894)

This simple house, raised high on piers, is redolent of Galveston or New Orleans. Like so much of Sixth Ward, it bespeaks a way of life at variance with the image of Houston that its downtown skyline projects, an image that can be appreciated in its full splendor from the generous front porch of this house.

1718 Lubbock Street   **L-13**
Albert F. Keller Grocery Store Building
(c. 1913)

The corner store, with apartment above, is executed here in brick. This building was rehabilitated and expanded by Richard Roeder to house his interior design studio. One block to the south, at **1720 State Street**, is a similar structure, the Witt Grocery Store (c. 1908).

Kane Street and Trinity Street   **L-14**
Sixth Ward Community Park (1989)
Slaney Santana Group, landscape architects

The design of this small park grew out of a collaboration between the St. Joseph Multi-Ethnic Cultural Arts Committee and a landscape architecture studio from Texas A & M University, translated into reality under the guidance of Scott Slaney. The

park's most remarkable features are the walled courtyard at Kane and Trinity, which contains painted tiles and face masks made by residents, working with the artists Paul Kittleson and Carter Enst, and the splendid cactus water fountain by Tim Glover. The mural on the side of the parish school building is "A United Community" (1985, Sylvia Orozco and Pio Pulido).

1505 Kane Street   **L-15**
St. Joseph's Catholic Church (1902)
Patrick S. Rabitt with George E. Dickey

Patrick Rabitt was a Galveston architect trained by N. J. Clayton, whose influence is apparent in the exceptional ornamental brickwork with which this church is profusely detailed. St. Joseph's was the German parish in Houston. Across the street, at 800 Houston Avenue, is **Trinity Lutheran Church** (1954, Travis Broesche), the oldest German Lutheran congregation in the city. The two churches testify to the strength of the German presence in Sixth Ward during the late 19th and early 20th centuries.

815 Houston Avenue   **L-16**
Knapp Chevrolet Co. Building (1941)
R. Newell Waters with E. Kelly Gaffney

Waters differentiated the showroom bay, with its bull-nosed corners framing plate glass display windows, from the low, unadorned service bay. The two are divided by a glass block-filled modernistic pylon that identifies the building on top and admits the public down below.

3301 Morrison Avenue   L-17
(1910)

The William A. Wilson Co., developers of this neighborhood, Woodland Heights, built many of the houses here speculatively and publicized them in *Homes,* a monthly magazine that it issued during 1911 and 1912. This fine Craftsman bungalow was one such house. It retains its porch piers of concrete, cast to look like stone, and the division of its external wall surfaces into contrasting zones of shingles and clapboard. The ganged windows in the broad roof dormer and the exposed rafter ends beneath the porch roofline are other identifying traits. This house is flanked by equally notable productions, **3305 Morrison** (1911) to the north, and **3215 Morrison** (1910) to the south. The latter, originally occupied by a cement contractor, has suffered numerous ill-advised alterations.

205 Bayland Avenue   L-18
(1911)

William Wilson's own house was the largest on Woodland Heights's main thoroughfare, Bayland Avenue, which Wilson lined with live oak trees. His propensity for planting street trees, especially unusual for the developer of a lower middle-income subdivision, led to his appointment to the City of Houston's first Board of Park Commissioners in 1910. The Wilson House is "progressive" in style. Lack of historically derived detail and pronounced horizontality ally it with the progressive school of Chicago. The house has suffered inappropriate alterations.

1215 Wrightwood Avenue   L-19
(c. 1920)

This Mission style bungalow, with its scalloped "Alamo" gable, is finished with stucco and faced with an arcaded porch. Just to the east, at the center of a vacant lot over-

looking the North Freeway, is a giant banana (David Adickes, sculptor).

Norhill Street and Euclid Street   L-20
Norhill Esplanades (1920)

One of Will C. Hogg's earliest ventures in suburban real estate development was this neighborhood, Norhill, laid out in several sections on the former dairy farm of his partner, Henry W. Stude. Like Woodland Heights to the east, Norhill was a lower middle-income subdivision. Nonetheless, it was planned with civic amenities: two-block-long esplanades landscaped as small parks that bring a measure of garden city charm to this modest neighborhood.

1100 Merrill Street   L-21
James S. Hogg Junior High School (1926)
Briscoe & Dixon and Maurice J. Sullivan,
William Ward Watkin, consulting architect

In place of an esplanade park at Norhill and Merrill, Hogg and Stude's Varner Realty Co. donated property for the construction of a public school, which was named in honor of Hogg's father, Texas governor J. S. Hogg. The school building, as was customary, was functionally planned. But it also served as a neighborhood civic monument, lined up on the axis of Norhill Street and decorated with Jacobean architectural detail.

308 Cordell Street   L-22
(1910)

Frank R. Reed, a plasterer, built this bungalow house in the Brooke Smith Addition.

Reed clearly saw the advertising potential that his own house offered for business and took full advantage of it.

403 Archer Street   **L-23**
(c. 1910)

The grandest house in Brooke Smith Addition is this temple-fronted Colonial revival, which lords it over more modest surrounding houses.

300 East 14th Avenue   **L-24**
Arlington Court (1985)
William F. Stern & Associates

Taut, rounded bays, high pitched roofs, and pale lavender-colored stucco walls distinguish this complex of 18 row houses, aligned along a central greensward. Houses turn their backs to the street and the complex is secured from within. But Stern handled these attributes with such delicacy that the complex does not project a paranoid or forbidding aspect. The gate house, facing East 14th, is a tribute to the Scottish Arts and Crafts architect Charles Rennie Mackintosh. Next door to Arlington Court, at **1317 Arlington**, is the brightly painted and profusely landscaped studio of the artist Sharon Kopriva.

401 East 13th Avenue   **L-25**
John H. Reagan Senior High School (1927)
John F. Staub and Louis A. Glover, William Ward Watkin, consulting architect

The Tudor style of 16th-century England was a favorite for educational buildings from the 1890s through the 1920s. As is to be expected, Staub applied it to this rationally planned school building with great aplomb. The original building has been outflanked with numerous additions, none of which is comparable in quality to the original.

1002 Harvard Street   **L-26**
All Saints Catholic Church (1927)
Frederick B. Gaenslen

Gaenslen, a San Antonio architect who specialized in Roman Catholic churches, had a number of commissions in Houston during the 1920s. All Saints was the largest of these. Its French Romanesque detail is very attenuated.

1102 Heights Boulevard   **L-27**
(c. 1896)

The suburban town of Houston Heights was laid out in 1891 by the Omaha & South Texas Land Co., a syndicate of investors from Omaha, Nebraska. Its street grid was bisected by this grand avenue, Heights Boulevard, the first divided boulevard in

Houston. Although the Heights was an industrial working-class suburb, a number of large houses were built along Boulevard (as the street was called in its early years) by individuals connected with the development company. This is the only one of those houses that survives. It was built speculatively by Henry F. MacGregor and sold to John A. Milroy, a company official who served as mayor of Houston Heights. (The Heights was an independent municipality from 1896 until 1918, when it allowed itself to be annexed by Houston.) The design is adapted from Design No. 30 in the *Cottage Souvenir No. 2* of 1891, a pattern book by the Knoxville architect George F. Barber.

1123 Harvard Street   **L-28**
(1912)

Harvard Street contains the largest concentration of rehabilitated houses of any street in the Heights. This "Alamo" bungalow, the most substantial and elaborate of its kind in Houston, is one of the most notable of these houses. It was built by Joseph Schleser, a brick contractor, for his own family.

306 East 15th Avenue   **L-29**
Immanuel Lutheran Church (1932)

This small church, raised on a high basement, exhibits the hard-edged planar interpretation of Gothic architecture characteristic of the 1920s and '30s. It is handsomely finished and detailed. Unfortunately, its future is not secure.

120 East 16th Avenue   **L-30**
Heights Church of Christ (1925)
Alfred C. Finn

Rejecting conventional religious imagery, Finn detailed this small but imposing boxlike church with an extremely reduced neo-Georgian vocabulary. The location of the nave atop a raised basement was characteristic of Protestant churches in the 1910s and '20s, as can be seen time and again in the Heights.

1400 Harvard Street   **L-31**
Second Church of Christ, Scientist
(1922)

In a part of town where the bungalow was the predominant house type of the 1910s and '20s, it seems only suitable that there should be a bungalow church.

1802 Harvard Street   **L-32**
(1896)

This Victorian towered villa is a variation on the house at 1102 Heights Boulevard. One of the remaining grand houses in the Heights, it has been restored by Bart Truxillo.

119 East 20th Avenue   L-33
(1918)

A two-story concrete porch, consisting of a stepped roof parapet, thick, tapered columns, and cut-out balusters, gives this two-story brick house an archaic appearance. This was not an uncommon trait for Texan buildings of the 1900-1920 period, when historically derived stylistic images were deliberately rejected for various kinds of progressive experimentation.

139 East 20th Avenue   L-34
Heights High School [now Alexander Hamilton Middle School] (1920) Maurice J. Sullivan

Sullivan was serving as official architect for the Houston city government when he designed this school, the quintessential suburban public building type. It terminates the vista at the north end of Heights Boulevard and is decorated with Tudor detail.

1703 Heights Boulevard   L-35
Heights Christian Church (1927) C. N. Nelson

To judge by the number and prominence of its churches, the Heights seems to have been an exceptionally pious community. The Christian Church is the most outstanding of these religious buildings, by virtue of its elevated situation, overscaled, slightly chunky proportions, and the stone Doric column screen with which Nelson decorated the exterior.

1302 Heights Boulevard   L-36
Heights Branch, Houston Public Library (1925) J. M. Glover

As Nelson was to do at the Heights Christian Church, Glover used big scale to give a sense of presence to this, one of the first two branch libraries constructed in Houston. Italian Renaissance detail, executed in cast stone, marks the entrance bay, which projects slightly forward of the tile-roofed library building. Ray Bailey Architects rehabilitated the building and added a large extension that complements, but does not mimic, the original (1979). The library contains a well-stocked archive on the history of the Heights.

107 West 12th Avenue   L-37
Houston Heights City Hall and Fire Station [now Fire Station No. 14] (1915) A. C. Pigg

The consolidation of municipal offices with a fire station gave rise to a distinctive public building type that became widespread in small Texas towns during the 1920s. Houston Heights's city hall and fire station is a very early example of this type.

1528 Tulane Street   L-38
(c. 1899)

This diminutive wooden house was built by Frederick Moeller, a carpenter who worked for the Houston & Texas Central Railroad. It was tactfully but imaginatively rehabilitated by Val Glitsch.

341 West 19th Avenue   **L-39**
Heights Theater (1925, 1941, 1990)

West 19th is the Heights's downtown retail district and its architectural centerpiece is this neighborhood movie theater, rescued from dereliction and rehabilitated by architect Robert Morris for Sharon and Gus Kopriva. Its modernistic exuberance animates the street. In 1988 West 19th became one of the first two urban demonstration projects of the Texas Historical Commission's Main Street program, leading to its economic revitalization through the conservation and reuse of its historic buildings.

350 West 19th Avenue   **L-40**
Harold's (1960) Brooks & Brooks

This pert one- and two-story commercial building is West 19th's outstanding modern landmark. The sales area, treated as a glass pavilion, is differentiated from the closed service block.

347 West 20th Avenue   **L-41**
(c. 1907)

The two-story curved veranda of this wooden house, set back in an enclosed yard, communicates the homey, old fashioned ambience of the Heights. The property was owned by Stephen R. Zagst, a carpenter and builder.

611 West 22nd Avenue   **L-42**
Oriental Textile Mill [now W. R. Grace & Co. Zonolite Construction Products Division] (c. 1892)

Built as a mattress factory, this brick industrial building was located in the Heights's factory district, in the town's northwest corner. It bespeaks the Omaha & South Texas Land Co.'s conception of the Heights as an industrial suburb. The original has had numerous additions, of which the most visible is the six-story clock tower facing Lawrence Street.

West End / River Oaks / Greenway

Because Houston has grown at ever accelerating rates of diffusion, sites that began on, or beyond, the edge of town often find themselves migrating closer and closer toward the center. River Oaks, Houston's highest status residential neighborhood, is a case in point. It began not only beyond the edge of Houston in the early 1920s, but on the wrong side of downtown for an ambitious garden suburb. The provision of a direct connection to downtown in the form of the Buffalo Bayou Parkway, the first in a series of Olmsted-like bayou parkway corridors planned by the landscape architects Hare & Hare for the City of Houston, overcame River Oaks's isolation. By the late 1930s its pre-eminence had become so firmly established that it began to influence development patterns downtown; the first office buildings to be constructed west of the Main Street district went up on the cross street that connected Main to the bayou parkway drive, Allen Parkway. River Oaks now lies at the geographic center of Houston, with downtown to the east and Post Oak to the west.

Privately instituted and administered planning controls, conspicuous amenities, and access were key to River Oaks's success and long-term durability. Over time, these lessons have been absorbed by developers of nonresidential properties also. The district south of River Oaks, between Kirby Drive and Weslayan Avenue, illustrates spatially the sequence from roadside strip developments along secondary streets to corporate installations along major thoroughfares to comprehensively managed office parks tied to the regional freeway network. Where Buffalo Speedway (an evocative name dating from the 1920s) and Richmond Avenue intersect, these three stages are juxtaposed.

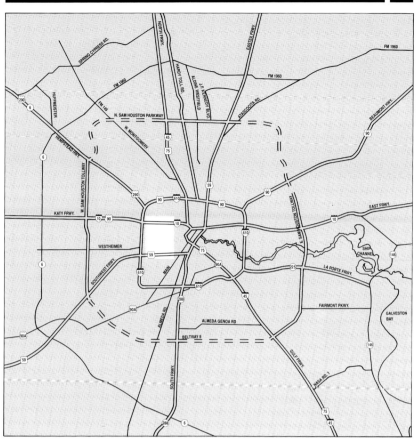

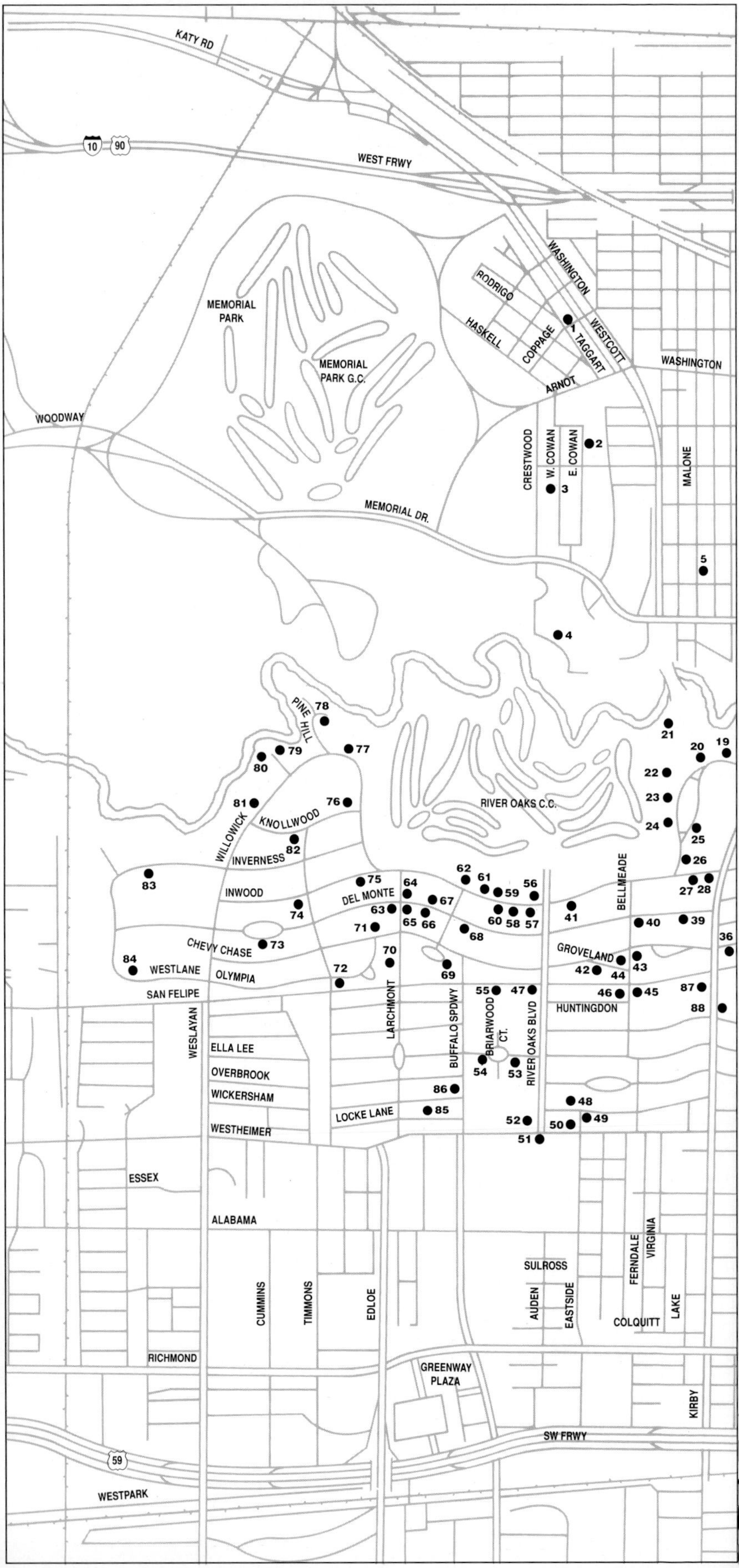

KATY RD

10 90

WEST FRWY

WASHINGTON

RODRIGO
WESTCOTT
HASKELL
COPPAGE
TAGGART
ARNOT

MEMORIAL PARK

MEMORIAL PARK G.C.

WOODWAY

CRESTWOOD
W. COWAN
E. COWAN

MALONE

MEMORIAL DR.

1
2
3
4
5

PINE HILL
78
79
80
77
81
KNOLLWOOD
76
WILLOWICK
INVERNESS
82
83
INWOOD
75
DEL MONTE
64
62
61
56
59
60 58 57
63
65 66 67
68
71
74
73
CHEVY CHASE
70
84
WESTLANE
OLYMPIA
72
69
SAN FELIPE

RIVER OAKS C.C.

21
20 19
22
23
24
25
26
27 28
BELLMEADE
41
40 39
36
GROVELAND
42 44 43
46 45
87
88
HUNTINGDON

WESLAYAN
ELLA LEE
OVERBROOK
WICKERSHAM
WESTHEIMER

LARCHMONT
BUFFALO SPDWY
BRIARWOOD CT.
RIVER OAKS BLVD

55 47
54 53
86
85
LOCKE LANE

48
52 50 49
51

ESSEX

ALABAMA

CUMMINS
TIMMONS
EDLOE

SULROSS
AUDEN
EASTSIDE
FERNDALE
VIRGINIA
LAKE
COLQUITT

KIRBY

RICHMOND

GREENWAY PLAZA

59

SW FRWY

WESTPARK

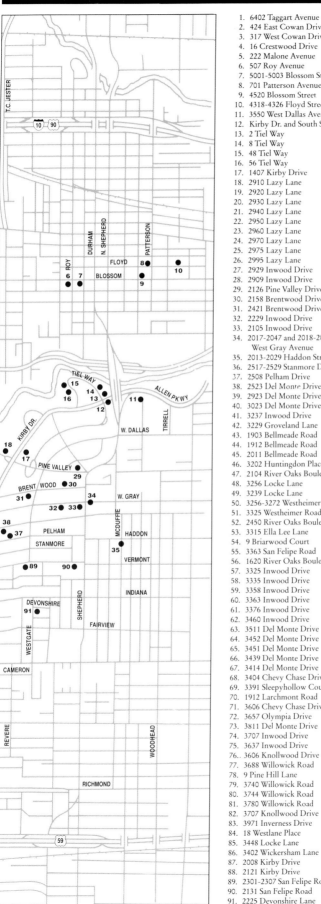

1. 6402 Taggart Avenue
2. 424 East Cowan Drive
3. 317 West Cowan Drive
4. 16 Crestwood Drive
5. 222 Malone Avenue
6. 507 Roy Avenue
7. 5001-5003 Blossom Street
8. 701 Patterson Avenue
9. 4520 Blossom Street
10. 4318-4326 Floyd Street
11. 3550 West Dallas Avenue
12. Kirby Dr. and South Shepherd Dr.
13. 2 Tiel Way
14. 8 Tiel Way
15. 48 Tiel Way
16. 56 Tiel Way
17. 1407 Kirby Drive
18. 2910 Lazy Lane
19. 2920 Lazy Lane
20. 2930 Lazy Lane
21. 2940 Lazy Lane
22. 2950 Lazy Lane
23. 2960 Lazy Lane
24. 2970 Lazy Lane
25. 2975 Lazy Lane
26. 2995 Lazy Lane
27. 2929 Inwood Drive
28. 2909 Inwood Drive
29. 2126 Pine Valley Drive
30. 2158 Brentwood Drive
31. 2421 Brentwood Drive
32. 2229 Inwood Drive
33. 2105 Inwood Drive
34. 2017-2047 and 2018-2048
    West Gray Avenue
35. 2013-2029 Haddon Street
36. 2517-2529 Stanmore Drive
37. 2508 Pelham Drive
38. 2523 Del Monte Drive
39. 2923 Del Monte Drive
40. 3023 Del Monte Drive
41. 3237 Inwood Drive
42. 3229 Groveland Lane
43. 1903 Bellmeade Road
44. 1912 Bellmeade Road
45. 2011 Bellmeade Road
46. 3202 Huntingdon Place
47. 2104 River Oaks Boulevard
48. 3256 Locke Lane
49. 3239 Locke Lane
50. 3256-3272 Westheimer Road
51. 3325 Westheimer Road
52. 2450 River Oaks Boulevard
53. 3315 Ella Lee Lane
54. 9 Briarwood Court
55. 3363 San Felipe Road
56. 1620 River Oaks Boulevard
57. 3325 Inwood Drive
58. 3335 Inwood Drive
59. 3358 Inwood Drive
60. 3363 Inwood Drive
61. 3376 Inwood Drive
62. 3460 Inwood Drive
63. 3511 Del Monte Drive
64. 3452 Del Monte Drive
65. 3451 Del Monte Drive
66. 3439 Del Monte Drive
67. 3414 Del Monte Drive
68. 3404 Chevy Chase Drive
69. 3391 Sleepyhollow Court
70. 1912 Larchmont Road
71. 3606 Chevy Chase Drive
72. 3657 Olympia Drive
73. 3811 Del Monte Drive
74. 3707 Inwood Drive
75. 3637 Inwood Drive
76.. 3606 Knollwood Drive
77. 3688 Willowick Road
78. 9 Pine Hill Lane
79. 3740 Willowick Road
80. 3744 Willowick Road
81. 3780 Willowick Road
82. 3707 Knollwood Drive
83. 3971 Inverness Drive
84. 18 Westlane Place
85. 3448 Locke Lane
86. 3402 Wickersham Lane
87. 2008 Kirby Drive
88. 2121 Kirby Drive
89. 2301-2307 San Felipe Road
90. 2131 San Felipe Road
91. 2225 Devonshire Lane

6402 Taggart Avenue   **M-1**
Taggart Park Townhouses (1984)
Arquitectonica

Taking advantage of a square corner site,
Arquitectonica grouped these four houses
in an unorthodox arrangement: the blue
house is L-shaped in plan and wraps
around the pink house at the corner.
Perforated screen walls and pastel colors
allow these houses to exert a big presence
on the street.

424 East Cowan Drive   **M-2**
(1941) MacKie & Kamrath

A splendidly detailed and maintained modern house, planned to take advantage of the
prevailing breeze.

317 West Cowan Drive   **M-3**
(1941) F. Talbott Wilson and S. I. Morris, Jr.

Slightly more conservative than the MacKie
& Kamrath house, Wilson's courtyard
house for the photographer Paul Peters
incorporated a photo studio.

16 Crestwood Drive   **M-4**
(1959) George Pierce-Abel B. Pierce (1974)
S. I. Morris Associates (1980) Gwathmey,
Siegel & Associates

The New York architect Charles
Gwathmey had the last word in this much-
remodeled house. The two-story box is an
addition by Eugene Aubry. Gwathmey
completely reworked the interiors and

added the screen walls, lap pool, brilliant
colors, and the grass driveway.

222 Malone Avenue   **M-5**
Beer Can House (1974)

John Milkovisch, a retired upholsterer who
had worked for the Southern Pacific Railway, proudly claimed to have drunk the beer
from every can that he used to festoon his
modest house. The grounds also came in for
considerable improvement. The result is an
enthusiastic paean to the virtues of recycling.

507 Roy Avenue   **M-6**
Roy Avenue Townhouses (1974)
S. I. Morris Associates

Eugene Aubry and Hossein Oskouie
returned to the corrugated galvanized sheet
iron siding that Aubry had used at the Rice
Media Center for this pair of houses. As a
result, they blend almost imperceptibly into
the landscape of Brunner, a working-class
neighborhood that once was briefly an
independent municipality.

5001-5003 Blossom Street   **M-7**
Tin Houses (1984) Ian Glennie
and Urban Architecture

Ian Glennie designed this pair of corrugated
metal-surfaced townhouses as a tribute to
the Roy Avenue Townhouses, a block away.
His vertically elongated proportions, studio
windows, and the dramatic exposed stair on
the west side make them more visible, and

exceptional, within the context of the neighborhood.

701 Patterson Avenue   M-8
Lauricella Grocery Store Building (1921)

A traditional corner grocery store building, with the proprietor's living quarters above. Such buildings were once common in the suburbs of Southern towns and cities. This is a rare, functioning survivor.

4520 Blossom Street   M-9
Butler Gallery (1989) Phillips/Ryburn

Robert Van Buren designed this precisely detailed wood shed building to fit as unobtrusively as possible into Brunner. Most of the block-front site is used to display sculpture. At **601 Patterson Avenue** is an 1880s-era house restored in 1989 by William H. McDugald, Jr.

4318-4326 Floyd Street   M-10
Grove Court Townhouses (1980)
Taft Architects

The staggered siting of these six houses per-

mitted the inclusion of both private walled gardens and a central common green, differentiated by undulating walls. The tile detailing retrieves a type of architectural graphics common in Houston in the 1910s and '20s. Interiors at Grove Court consist of open lofts, where daylight and internal vistas create a sense of spaciousness.

3550 West Dallas Avenue   M-11
Harris County Center for the Retarded (1966) Howard Barnstone & Eugene Aubry

This complex of buildings is constructed of overscaled, articulated concrete structural members infilled with brick and glass. It backs up to Allen Parkway, where it appears austere and almost intimidating. A closer look shows that it is actually a village-like campus of elemental buildings linked by covered passageways on a sloping site. Adjoining the center is the six-story **Cullen Residence Hall** (1978, S. I. Morris Associates).

Kirby Dr. and South Shepherd Dr.   M-12
River Oaks Gate Piers (1926) John F. Staub

When Staub's biographer, Howard Barnstone, called these pink stucco-faced piers the "gates of Paradise," he succinctly characterized the status of River Oaks, Houston's most elite residential neighborhood. This pair was built to mark the entrance to River Oaks from the Buffalo Bayou parkway drive (now called Allen Parkway), which links the neighborhood directly to downtown Houston. River Oaks was begun in 1923 by lawyer Will C. Hogg, his brother Mike, and their friend Hugh Potter. Hogg envisioned River Oaks as an exemplary planned residential community that would provide a model for the rest of Houston to follow. In Hugh Potter he found the perfect executive to carry this vision into reality. Potter, who bought the Hogg family's interest in the development in 1936, ran the River Oaks Corporation until its dissolution in 1955. He and Herbert A. Kipp, the engineer who laid out the community, oversaw the initial development of its entire 1,100-acre extent. Despite Hogg's advocacy of civic planning, River Oaks did not set a Houston pattern. Instead it became *the* exception to Houston's reputation for unplanned expansion—and a much-coveted reward for those who profited from that expansion.

2 Tiel Way   **M-13**
(1961) MacKie & Kamrath

A concrete block-built house with Japanese overtones, very closed and secure in appearance. The extraordinary plantings are the work of A. J. Ballantyne.

8 Tiel Way   **M-14**
(1953) MacKie & Kamrath

Kamrath's multiple-level house for his own family nestles securely into its sloping site between a deep ravine and Buffalo Bayou. The railing along the street is also by Kamrath.

48 Tiel Way   **M-15**
(1958) MacKie & Kamrath

Planned on a 30°-60° reflexive geometric grid, this angled house is wedged into a small hillock on its street side, while the rear is opened to a view of Buffalo Bayou. As is characteristic of Kamrath's work, organic decorative detail contributes substantially to the character of the building. Also by MacKie & Kamrath are **59 Tiel Way** (1949) and **67 Tiel Way** (1950).

56 Tiel Way   **M-16**
(1952) Cowell & Neuhaus

This early work of Hugo V. Neuhaus, Jr., bespeaks his training at the Harvard Graduate School of Design in the early 1940s. The small wood house turns into a glass-walled pavilion at the rear, overlooking Buffalo Bayou. Restored by Leslie Elkins in 1991.

1407 Kirby Drive   **M-17**
(1930) Charles W. Oliver

Oliver, staff architect for the River Oaks Corporation from 1926 to 1931, designed numerous houses in a wide variety of styles. This picturesque manorial style house, located on an undulating site along the parkway drive that leads downtown, was one of his best.

2910 Lazy Lane   **M-18**
(1950) Cowell & Neuhaus

Hugo V. Neuhaus, Jr., designed this stunning modern house for his own family. A U-shaped pavilion configured around a garden court, it brought high-style Miesian modernism into the Homewoods section of River Oaks, a stronghold of eclectic design.

2920 Lazy Lane   **M-19**
(1991) Robert A. M. Stern Architects and Richard Fitzgerald & Partners

A very large reaffirmation of Homewoods's

allegiance to the eclectic country house tradition.

2930 Lazy Lane   M-20
(1964) Howard Barnstone & Partners

Barely visible from the street, this is an austere yet grand modern house organized on two levels to take advantage of the site's downward slope toward Buffalo Bayou. The living and dining room, on the back side of the house, occupies a glass pavilion framed with steel trusses that rides above the garage.

2940 Lazy Lane   M-21
Bayou Bend (1928) John F. Staub with Birdsall P. Briscoe

Will and Mike Hogg built Bayou Bend (which is not visible from the street) as a house for their sister Ima. Miss Hogg loved the Creole architecture of New Orleans, which led Staub to design this house in a style that she called "Latin Colonial," a mixture of early 19th-century American Federal, early 19th-century English Regency, and Louisiana Creole. Surfaced with pale pink stucco, green louvered blinds, and a copper roof, it is a tripartite classical country house that sits with assurance—and warmth—at the end of the entrance drive. Parts of the 14-acre site have been left in their natural condition. The East Terrace Garden was designed by the landscape architect Ruth London; the Diana Garden, a series of terraces that step down from the north side of the house toward Buffalo Bayou, is the work of Fleming & Sheppard.

Since 1966, the house has contained the decorative arts collection of The Museum of Fine Arts, acquired and installed under Miss Hogg's guidance. This comprises an important collection of 17th, 18th, and 19th-century American furniture, paintings, silver, and ceramics. Bayou Bend is open to the public by prior appointment. Access to the museum is from a parking lot at the south end of Westcott Drive, off Memorial Drive.

2950 Lazy Lane   M-22
Dogwood (1928) Birdsall P. Briscoe with John F. Staub

Built by the Hoggs' friend Frederick C. Proctor, this Norman manorial style house with its circular entrance tower is not visible from the street. It subsequently was the home of Mr. and Mrs. Mike Hogg. The gardens were designed by C. C. Fleming.

2960 Lazy Lane   M-23
(1933)John F. Staub

J. Robert Neal and his father sold the family business—manufacturers of Maxwell House Coffee—to General Foods in the late 1920s. With his share of the proceeds Neal built this opulent, limestone-faced, chateau-style house, detailed with Louis XV ornament. It is distended in plan to take advantage of the prevailing breeze. Staub incorporated thick, flat aluminum window sash, which gives the house a distinctive '30s edge. Olmsted Brothers designed the original gardens.

2970 Lazy Lane   M-24
(1934) James C. Mackenzie with Charles W. Oliver, Birdsall P. Briscoe, consulting architect

This attenuated neo-Georgian house is not visible from the street. Mackenzie, a New York architect, planned the house around a landscaped motor court, framing the opposite side of the court with a long garage and service building that mirrors the configuration of the house. The gardens were designed by Louis Frothingham; Ellen Shipman designed the camellia garden.

2975 Lazy Lane   M-25
(1939) John F. Staub

Staub's version of a Natchez plantation house, blown up to Texan scale. The gardens were designed by C. C. Fleming.

2995 Lazy Lane   M-26
Ravenna (1935) John F. Staub

A large but exquisite house that is English

Georgian on the front and Deep South on the back, where a double-height Tuscan portico overlooks gardens designed by Ellen Shipman with Ruth London.

2929 Inwood Drive   **M-27**
(1934) John F. Staub

Staub excelled at austere design, as is evident in this disciplined house, with its elliptical-arched openings and its slender chimney stacks.

2909 Inwood Drive   **M-28**
(1936) John F. Staub

Staub virtually repeated the plan diagram of the house next door in this somewhat more expansive neo-Georgian house, faced with cast aluminum balconies. The *allée* of live oaks on the garden side of the house was laid out by C. C. Fleming.

2126 Pine Valley Drive   **M-29**
(1936) Claude E. Hooton

Hooton, a member of the first generation of Houston architects to be trained locally at

Rice, worked in Finland in the late 1920s and was conversant with Scandinavian modern architecture. This is one of the best of a series of modernized traditional houses that he produced in the middle 1930s. It still impresses, despite subsequent alterations.

2158 Brentwood Drive   **M-30**
(1933) F. McM. Sawyer

Sawyer was an obscure architect who designed two quirky Spanish style houses in Houston built of reinforced concrete. This one survives in good condition.

2421 Brentwood Drive   **M-31**
(1929) Katharine B. Mott with
Burns & James

This charming house, with its arched loggia entrance way, was the first of ten houses that Mrs. Mott built in River Oaks.

2229 Inwood Drive   **M-32**
(1935) H. A. Salisbury & T. G. McHale

The crisp detail and assured proportions of this compact house show Salisbury & McHale at their best. The clapboard-faced house front framed by brick chimney end walls derives from New England.

2105 Inwood Drive   **M-33**
(1966) P. M. Bolton Associates

With this house, located at the intersection of two busy streets, Bolton gave form to the preferred River Oaks house type of the '70s: the inwardly focused dwelling walled off from its surroundings. The oversized

panelled doors were an attempt to compensate with monumental urban scale for the house's anti-suburban introversion.

2017-2047 and   **M-34**
2018-2048 West Gray Avenue
River Oaks Community Center (1937)
Stayton Nunn-Milton McGinty,
Oliver C. Winston, consulting architect

Hugh Potter, president of the River Oaks Corporation, developed the community center as a model of suburban convenience shopping that would enhance, rather than threaten, River Oaks. The two crescent-shaped retail buildings, framing the western terminus of West Gray, remain in their original condition. Winston, a Washington, D. C., architect, introduced the backlit, upcurved canopy detail to Houston. This original feature is now obscured by canopies installed in 1975. The corporation added to the center through the 1950s. Consequently, it stretches along West Gray as far as Driscoll Street. In 1979 Weingarten Realty had the center's various components painted white and installed the Washingtonia palm trees along West Gray (S. I. Morris Associates). The silly post-modern clock faces atop 1964 and 1973 West Gray, tacked on in 1988, detract from the center's cool, assured look.

2013-2029 Haddon Street   **M-35**
Haddon Townhouses (1983) Arquitectonica

Arquitectonica's first Houston project consisted of this terrace front of ten row houses symmetrically flanking modest little

McDuffie Street. All stops were pulled out to advertise externally the internal spatial organization of the narrow three-story houses and the two expansive studio houses that bracket the terrace at either end. A restrictive covenant protects the color scheme for a term of years.

2517-2529 Stanmore Drive   **M-36**
(1936) Cameron D. Fairchild

In 1935 Herbert A. Kipp, vice president of the River Oaks Corporation, platted a series of greenway courts along the south side of Stanmore and the east side of Sharp Place. This was a remedial effort aimed at salvaging the lots that otherwise would face directly onto San Felipe Road and South Shepherd Drive. Houses now back up to those busy streets and face common greens instead. Cameron Fairchild was commissioned by the corporation to design all the houses on the first of the Stanmore courts to be developed.

2508 Pelham Drive   **M-37**
(1927) Charles W. Oliver

Oliver, the corporation's architect, designed in all styles. But his own favorite was the Mediterranean, as evidenced by the house he designed for his family. It shows the influence of one of the most persuasive interpreters of the Mediterranean genre, the Pasadena architect Wallace Neff. Today, Oliver's house is nearly upstaged by the fantastic live oak tree in front of it.

2523 Del Monte Drive   **M-38**
(1936) Armon E. Mabry

The formal French manorial style seems to have been Mabry's preferred genre. This

well designed, if not expensive, houses. Briscoe transcribed details from the architecture of 18th-century Charleston onto this suburban neo-Regency house. The combination of Southern detail and English domestic type appealed to Ima Hogg, under whose tutelage the nine houses were built. On account of the decorative panel in the first floor window grills, this house was known as the Redbird House.

relatively small house represents his most engaging rendition of the type.

3229 Groveland Lane   **M-42**
(1936) Birdsall P. Briscoe

Another neo-Georgian production by Briscoe, deftly proportioned, with classical architectural detail executed in molded brick. The tripartite Wyatt windows effectively counter the closed aspect of the central register.

2923 Del Monte Drive   **M-39**
(1934) Birdsall P. Briscoe

Here Briscoe essayed a Southern version of the Georgian style, incorporating oversized windows to admit light and breezes.

3023 Del Monte Drive   **M-40**
(1938) Birdsall P. Briscoe

With this design Briscoe paid tribute to the early 19th-century LeCarpentier-Beauregard House in the French Quarter of New Orleans. He suburbanized the original without sacrificing its neoclassical dignity.

1903 Bellmeade Road   **M-43**
(1926) Charles W. Oliver

The advertising man Pierre L. Michael, who built the Isabella Court on Main Street, had Oliver design this diminutively scaled, intricately planned Mediterranean house for his family. It was sensitively rehabilitated by William F. Stern & Associates in 1987.

3237 Inwood Drive   **M-41**
(1925) Briscoe & Dixon

Of the nine houses built by the River Oaks Corporation in 1925 and 1926 to promote the development of Country Club Estates, its first section, this is the only small house that remains intact. It preserves Will Hogg's vision of River Oaks as a community of

1912 Bellmeade Road   **M-44**
(1926) John F. Staub

A New England colonial style house set in a lush Houston garden. The house was tactfully expanded in 1987 by Larry Davis. Across the street, at **1915 Bellmeade**, is a

contextual salute by Charles W. Oliver
(1928).

2011 Bellmeade Road   **M-45**
(1927) Charles W. Oliver

The River Oaks Corporation built this
splayed-wing patio house, calling it (for
obvious reasons) the River Oaks
Mediterranean Villa.

3202 Huntingdon Place   **M-46**
(1972) Ford, Powell & Carson

The San Antonio architect Chris Carson
shaped this high-set brick house around
internal courtyards, so that from all direc-
tions it presents a closed aspect.

2104 River Oaks Boulevard   **M-47**
(1940) Armon E. Mabry

A grand Georgian style house that is surprisingly delicate in scale. The clapboards
are detailed to emulate stone blocks, an
18th-century conceit.

3256 Locke Lane   **M-48**
(1966) Neuhaus-Wingfield Associates

Behind the low street wall is an exceptional
small house, a crisply detailed pavilion that
also manages to be an urbane town house.
Hugo Neuhaus provided privacy here

without transforming the house into a
fortress.

3239 Locke Lane   **M-49**
(1937) Harvin Moore & Hermon Lloyd

A delightful modernistic house that preserves its jaunty original features. The firm
designed over 80 houses in River Oaks
before the war.

3256-3272 Westheimer Road   **M-50**
Lamar-River Oaks Community Center
(1948) William G. Farrington Co.

Raymond H. Brogniez, Farrington's
designer, made the most of masonry detailing and the bow-front pavilion and pylon
tower when designing this strip center.

3325 Westheimer Road   **M-51**
Mirabeau B. Lamar Senior High School
(1937) John F. Staub and Kenneth
Franzheim with Louis A. Glover, Lamar Q.
Cato, and Harry D. Payne

Terminating the south end of River Oaks
Boulevard is this PWA-built public school

building, notable for its streamlined modernistic detail. The auditorium bay is fronted with a screen of fossilated Texas limestone bearing a relief map of the State of Texas executed by Nino Lenarduzzi. Franzheim expanded the complex in 1950. Sympathetic additions and a rehabilitation of the existing buildings are by Ray Bailey Architects (1989). It was once said, in reference to Lamar, that River Oaks Boulevard was the only street in Houston with a country club at either end.

2450 River Oaks Boulevard   M-52
St. John The Divine Church (1954)
MacKie & Kamrath with
H. A. Salisbury & T. G. McHale

MacKie & Kamrath repackaged traditional liturgical arrangements in this finely crafted modern building. The architects ultimately succeeded in the dubious task of modernizing, without really changing, accepted conventions. To the west of the church is the large but self-effacing **Parish House** (1979, Ray Bailey Architects). Behind the Parish House is **St. John's School** (1947-1948, H. A. Salisbury & T. G. McHale) with additions by MacKie & Kamrath (south campus, 1953), Neuhaus Associates (Winston Hall, 1971), and Caudill Rowlett Scott (1980). The free-standing chapel facing River Oaks Boulevard is by H. A. Salisbury & T. G. McHale with MacKie & Kamrath and Birdsall P. Briscoe (1941).

3315 Ella Lee Lane   M-53
(1938) J. T. Rather, Jr.

This small house features the shallow layering of wall planes that Rather used frequently.

9 Briarwood Court   M-54
(1970) Keith Kroeger Associates

Designed by Ulrich Franzen's partner, the New York architect Keith Kroeger, this white stucco-faced house is composed with

a series of faceted wall planes dramatically intersected by large glass panels. A walled motor court separates the front of the house from the street.

3363 San Felipe Road   M-55
(1950) Philip C. Johnson Associates with Landes Gore and Cowell & Neuhaus

Architecturally and culturally, this large, flat-roofed house is the modernist equivalent of Bayou Bend. It was Philip Johnson's first work in Houston and with it he established the architecture of his mentor, Ludwig Mies van der Rohe, as the high style of Houston modernism. The house turns a nearly blank brick wall, capped by a white-painted Miesian fascia, toward the street. The principal reception rooms are arranged around an internal garden court, roofed over with an intersecting barrel-vaulted canopy installed by Howard Barnstone & Eugene Aubry (1965).

1620 River Oaks Boulevard   M-56
(1935) John F. Staub

This limestone-faced Regency villa was the most expensive house built in Houston during the Great Depression. According to his biographers, the independent oil man Hugh Roy Cullen was motivated to build it partly to provide much-needed jobs. Staub turned the garden face of the house south, toward Inwood Drive (from which it can best be seen); as in many Staub houses, the front door is in the back yard. It faces a very grand motor court. Staub laid out the once-famous gardens, transplanting specimen trees from Louisiana to Houston to give it instant maturity. Next to the entrance gate, at the head of River Oaks Boulevard, is the overbearing clubhouse of the **River Oaks Country Club** (1966, Golemon & Rolfe), which replaced Staub's too-modest, too-understated original.

3325 Inwood Drive   **M-57**
(1930) Katharine B. Mott with
Burns & James

Katharine Mott built this whitewashed brick and timbered house to be her family's home.

3335 Inwood Drive   **M-58**
(1926) John F. Staub

A setting of live oaks draped with Spanish moss has always made this picturesque English manorial style house, with its angled service wing, especially beguiling.

3358 Inwood Drive   **M-59**
(1930) Charles W. Oliver

This was the first of many plantation style houses to be built in River Oaks. It was intended to celebrate the provenance of its owner, Theodosia Campbell Christie, who was from Natchitoches, Louisiana.

3363 Inwood Drive   **M-60**
(1933) J. T. Rather, Jr.

Rather designed this shingled and gabled house as an outsized version of John F. Staub's own house at 3511 Del Monte. It

was built for the geologist and contractor George R. Brown and his family.

3376 Inwood Drive   **M-61**
(1924) Briscoe & Dixon

This was the first house in River Oaks, built by the cotton exporter Will Clayton as a summer house for his family. Briscoe used Mount Vernon as the organizing image; amusingly, the kitchen is "correctly" placed in one of the twin dependencies connected to the main house by curved hyphens. In addition, Briscoe also installed a swimming pool and tennis courts. Since 1930 the house has been occupied year-round by Clayton's descendants.

3460 Inwood Drive   **M-62**
(1926) Cram & Ferguson with
Stayton Nunn

Blanche Harding Sewall was so enamored of Ralph Adams Cram's buildings at Rice University that she commissioned him to design this house for her and her husband. Cram worked from Mrs. Sewall's own sketches in designing the stucco-faced, tile-roofed Spanish style house. Interior detail is based on the House of El Greco museum in Toledo. Mrs. Sewall travelled to Spain with Mildred Stapley and Arthur Byne to acquire artifacts and furniture. Ellen Shipman designed gardens for the small estate in the middle 1930s, but they no longer survive. The house was rescued from dereliction and superlatively restored in 1979 by Charles Tapley Associates.

3511 Del Monte Drive   **M-63**
(1926) John F. Staub

Staub designed this much-copied New England colonial style house for his own family; he chose the style to remind his wife of her native Massachusetts. At the time it was completed the house stood on the western edge of Houston. Still occupied by the architect's descendants, it was extended in 1984 by Charles Keith Associates.

3452 Del Monte Drive   **M-64**
(1931) John F. Staub

Here Staub wittily produced an American colonial style house with two fronts that don't match, one formal (facing the street), the other picturesque (facing a rear motor court). The projecting wing to the right is a carefully detailed addition by Anthony E. Frederick (1982).

3451 Del Monte Drive   **M-65**
(1930) J. W. Northrop, Jr.

Completing the neo-colonial lineup at the Del Monte-Larchmont intersection is this large American Georgian style house.

3439 Del Monte Drive   **M-66**
(1937) Birdsall P. Briscoe

Briscoe demonstrated his gift for discreet

mannerism in this asymmetrically composed neo-Regency house.

3414 Del Monte Drive   **M-67**
(1938) Birdsall P. Briscoe

A somewhat more archeological approach to the Regency genre, this house is faced with a bowed portico and framed by recessed polygonal wings.

3404 Chevy Chase Drive   **M-68**
(1978) S. I. Morris Associates

Eugene Aubry compressed this large house into a hard-edged, gable-roofed village.

3391 Sleepyhollow Court   **M-69**
(1929) Frank J. Forster

The New York architect Frank Forster specialized in extravagantly picturesque recreations of French Norman farmhouses, often incorporating salvaged materials that he acquired in periodic trips to Europe to give them an authentic ambiance. This house, built for Mr. and Mrs. Haywood Nelms, was one of his largest. It is very long and quite thin, organized around a neo-medieval great hall decorated with a mural by the Santa Fe artist Gerald Cassidy depicting characters from Robin Hood. Forster also designed a garage, stable, kennel, and play-house, as well as the dovecote at the rear gate, facing San Felipe. The clinker brick-work was originally whitewashed. The house was rehabilitated in 1979 by Langwith Wilson King & Associates, who designed the wall along San Felipe.

1912 Larchmont Road   **M-70**
(1936) John F. Staub

Staub adapted the design of this house from the Kellum-Noble House in Sam Houston Park, the oldest building in Houston. He emphasized the Kellum-Noble House's vernacular origins by bas-ing this house on its L-plan rear elevation rather than its symmetrical front elevation. This enabled him to orient the principal rooms to a south-facing side garden. Additions were sensitively added in 1957 by Harvin C. Moore.

3606 Chevy Chase Drive   **M-71**
(1951) Birdsall P. Briscoe

Briscoe came to favor this planar, composi-tional type, prefaced by a flat-roofed iron porch, in the houses he designed near the end of his long career.

3657 Olympia Drive   **M-72**
(1941) Donald Barthelme

Barthelme found his version of the Staub Regency so satisfying that he never felt

compelled to design in the traditional styles again.

3811 Del Monte Drive   **M-73**
(1969) Howard Barnstone & Eugene Aubry

Behind the self-effacing, cypress-sheathed exterior of this flat-roofed house lies one of Barnstone's master works.

3707 Inwood Drive   **M-74**
(1950) Birdsall P. Briscoe

A delicately scaled Charleston single house transplanted to River Oaks.

3637 Inwood Drive   **M-75**
(1940) John F. Staub

An austere, planar distillation of a Georgian house, compact in massing but grandly detailed. The formal gardens were designed by Fleming & Sheppard.

3606 Knollwood Drive   **M-76**
(1942) Birdsall P. Briscoe

Briscoe eclectically grafted long Regency

windows and a French roof and dormers onto what is basically a Georgian style house.

3688 Willowick Road **M-77**
(1952) Edward Durell Stone
with Thomas E. Greacen II

This contemporary style house by the New York architect Edward Durell Stone—designed prior to his fixation with masonry solar screens—was an important model locally for architects who wanted to go modern but were not willing to commit themselves unreservedly to the precepts of Frank Lloyd Wright or Ludwig Mies van der Rohe. The house is not visible from the street.

9 Pine Hill Lane **M-78**
(1989) Carlos Jiménez

This brilliantly colored complex represents a total reconstruction of a small house by the San Antonio architect O'Neil Ford (1957). Its multi-hued component parts and square windows presage a beautifully modulated and lit interior. The house is tucked back on Pine Hill, a private lane that (like Tiel Way) is reminiscent of Los Angeles, with houses set close to the narrow, winding street yet buffered by luxuriant vegetation and motor courts. Also on this street are houses by Frank Welch & Associates at **2 Pine Hill Lane** (1976) and Wilson, Morris, Crain & Anderson at **3700 Willowick Road** (1956).

3740 Willowick Road **M-79**
(1957) Staub, Rather & Howze

Into the 1950s Staub continued to adapt historic Southern prototypes to contemporary domestic programs. Here a Greek revival cottage is merged with a classic '50s ranch house.

3744 Willowick Road **M-80**
(1955)

This is a '50s condensation of the early 19th-century Baltimore country house,

Homewoods. Next door, at **3760 Willowick**, is a trim, contemporary style house by Hermon Lloyd & W. B. Morgan (1953). Facing out to Willowick, at **3734**, is a limestone-faced *maison de plaisance* (1964, Robert W. Maurice & Richard M. Wilkins).

3780 Willowick Road **M-81**
(1952) Wylie W. Vale

Unlike Riverside Terrace, River Oaks rarely let itself go all the way for 1950s contemporary design. This house, set far back on an undulating site, is an uninhibited exception. Vale designed a slightly more sedate contemporary style house at **3723 Knollwood Drive** (1955) for the daughter of the clients for this house.

3707 Knollwood Drive **M-82**
(1940) Birdsall P. Briscoe and
George W. Rustay

This large house is set behind a monumental portico supported by fluted Doric columns.

3971 Inverness Drive **M-83**
(1984) Ray Bailey Architects

Constructed on a sliver site excerpted from a larger lot, this house is a graceful postmodern interpretation of a New England farmhouse—as it might have been romantically reinterpreted in the 1880s. Across the street at **3970 Inverness Drive**, and barely visible, is a redwood-sheathed modern house by Frank Welch & Associates (1973), a simple composition of carefully propor-

tioned rectangular planes and voids organized beneath a shallow hipped roof. The rolling site was once part of the Hogg brothers' weekend camp, Tall Timbers, from which this section of River Oaks takes its name.

ing breeze. Privacy was ensured by the low garden wall. The house exemplifies the high standard of domestic planning in Houston at the end of the eclectic era, just before central air-conditioning abolished the need for climatic responsiveness.

18 Westlane Place   **M-84**
(1957) Bolton & Barnstone

A testament to the persuasive example of Philip Johnson's house on San Felipe, this flat-roofed, steel-trimmed (but wood-framed) modern house is very much in the Miesian-Johnson mode. Thomas D. Church, the San Francisco landscape architect, designed the axial brick causeway that visually penetrates the house and organizes open space adjoining it in a subtle but powerfully architectonic way.

2008 Kirby Drive   **M-87**
River Oaks Elementary School (1929)
Harry D. Payne

Another of the state-of-the-art elementary schools that Payne produced in the late 1920s.

3448 Locke Lane   **M-85**
(1939) MacKie & Kamrath

Karl Kamrath's first house for his family was built in the "poor" part of River Oaks, in one of the sections developed in the late 1930s closest to Westheimer Road. Its modernity has been somewhat diluted by exterior alterations, especially the lapped wood screen wall and lean-to patio shed that Kamrath himself appended. MacKie & Kamrath also were responsible for the house next door at **3444 Locke Lane** (1939).

3402 Wickersham Lane   **M-86**
(1938) F. Talbott Wilson & S. I. Morris, Jr.

This Monterey style house is offset in plan so that all rooms have access to the prevail-

2121 Kirby Drive   **M-88**
The Huntingdon (1983) Talbott Wilson

The 34-story Huntingdon condominium tower, despite its height and slender profile, does not quite live up to the expectations aroused by its pretentious baroque gate piers. Next door at 2001 Kirby Drive is the 13-story **River Oaks Bank & Trust Co. Building** (1970, Wilson, Morris, Crain & Anderson), which, up close, suffers from the same finicky detailing as The Huntingdon.

2301-2307 San Felipe Road   **M-89**
Chilton Court Apartments (1939)
F. Talbott Wilson & S. I. Morris, Jr.

An ingeniously conceived pair of apartment

buildings, offset in plan so that each unit seems like a detached two-story house, with light and air entering from all four sides. The eight units flank a common green space. This was one of three apartment complexes built on the periphery of River Oaks by the River Oaks Corporation.

2131 San Felipe Road   **M-90**
Hamman Exploration Co. Building (1940)
Harvin Moore & Hermon Lloyd

Here the '30s Regency is streamlined with a stainless steel portico and glass block strip windows.

2225 Devonshire Lane   **M-91**
(1982) Frank Welch & Associates

This row house is composed with planes of rose-colored brick. Its aloofness is tempered by balcony railings designed in a sort of Texas version of Chinese Chippendale. Next door at **2224 Salisbury Lane** is a gray, stucco-finished row house by Kenneth Bentsen Associates (1988).

KATY RD.

10 90

WEST FRWY

MEMORIAL PARK

MEMORIAL PARK G.C.

RODRIGO

WASHINGTON

WESTCOTT

TAGGART

HASKELL

COPPAGE

ARNOT

WASHINGTON

WOODWAY

CRESTWOOD

W. COWAN

E. COWAN

MALONE

MEMORIAL DR.

WESTCOTT

PINE HILL

RIVER OAKS C.C.

WILLOWICK

KNOLLWOOD

INVERNESS

INWOOD

DEL MONTE

BELLMEADE

CHEVY CHASE

GROVELAND

WESTLANE

OLYMPIA

SAN FELIPE

LARCHMONT

BUFFALO SPDWY.

BRIARWOOD CT.

RIVER OAKS BLVD.

HUNTINGDON

WESLAYAN

ELLA LEE

OVERBROOK

WICKERSHAM

WESTHEIMER

LOCKE LANE

ESSEX

15

14

ALABAMA

2

11

3

12

9 8

10

13 7

FERNDALE

VIRGINIA

23

25

22 24

SULROSS

CUMMINS

TIMMONS

EDLOE

AUDEN

EASTSIDE

COLQUITT

LAKE

27

28

RICHMOND

16

21

18

20 26

GREENWAY PLAZA

17

19

KIRBY

59

SW FRWY

WESTPARK

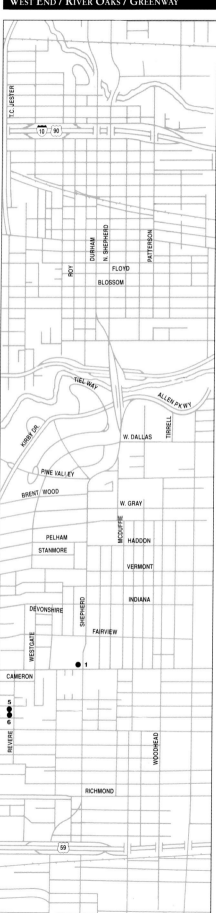

1. 2140 Westheimer Road
2. 2503 Westheimer Road
3. 2615 Cameron Street
4. 2801 Kirby Drive
5. 2902 Revere Street
6. 2930 Revere Street
7. 2719 Kipling Street
8. 2800 Kipling Street
9. 2819 Ferndale Street
10. 2905 Kipling Street
11. 2709-2713 Ferndale Street
12. 2814 Virginia Street
13. 2911-2913 Ferndale Street
14. 3471 Westheimer Road
15. 3915 Essex Lane
16. 3830 Richmond Avenue
17. 3600 block Cummins Lane
18. 3700 block Richmond Avenue
    8-12 and 9-11 Greenway Plaza
19. 3500 block Richmond Avenue
    1, 2, 3, and 5 Greenway Plaza
20. 3333 Richmond Avenue
21. 3336 Richmond Avenue
22. 3102 Buffalo Speedway
23. 3120 Buffalo Speedway
24. 3121 Buffalo Speedway
25. 3230 Sul Ross Avenue
26. 3323 Richmond Avenue
27. 2990 Richmond Avenue
28. 2627 Colquitt Street

2140 Westheimer Road   **N-1**
St. Anne's Catholic Church (1940)
Maurice J. Sullivan

The staged bell tower of St. Anne's and its
gabled planar facade, punctuated with
restrained Renaissance classical detail, are
the elements that make this church such a
distinctive landmark. In contrast to its
Spanish exterior, the vaulted basilican interior of the church is decorated in the neo-
Byzantine style that Sullivan had earlier
used at the Conventual Chapel of the Villa
de Matel. Sullivan employed exposed aggregate concrete mosaic for the interior finish
of the church. This is pink in color and contrasts with the rows of dark green polished
plaster-faced columns dividing the nave
from the side aisles. Sullivan designed the
adjacent school, built in stages between
1930 and 1953, and the free-standing parish
house facing South Shepherd, the first
increment of the complex to be completed
(1929).

2503 Westheimer Road   **N-2**
Forum of Civics Building [now River Oaks
Garden Club Building] (1910) (1927)
John F. Staub, Birdsall P. Briscoe, and
J. W. Northrop, Jr.

For Will C. Hogg, Staub remodeled the ex-
John Smith County School into a "New
England town hall," a community center
from which Hogg's Forum of Civics could
promote the benefits of planned urban
development. Hogg's ideals for Houston
were not generally shared and after his
death in 1930 the organization lapsed. Since
1942 the building has been the headquarters
of the River Oaks Garden Club, which
installed a series of handsome gardens
behind the Forum of Civics (1955, J. Allen
Myers, Jr., and Herbert Skogland). The
building was restored in 1986 by Graham
B. Luhn.

2615 Cameron Street   **N-3**
Schudy Clinic (1955) MacKie & Kamrath

Hidden away on a dead-end street, this is
an absolutely delightful building, tiny in

scale but incorporating a range of "organic"
amenities.

2801 Kirby Drive   **N-4**
Hard Rock Cafe (1986) Tigerman Fugman
McCurry and Ray Bailey Architects

Designed to appear like a Garden District
mansion, Stanley Tigerman's Hard Rock
Cafe is very tame. It is in fact almost nondescript and is rescued from anonymity
only by "Save The Planet," the soaring '63
T-bird on a stick by Doug Michels, Hudson
Márquez, and Chip Lord.

2902 Revere Street   **N-5**
Penguin Arms Apartments (1950)
Arthur Moss

Tigerman's conventionality at the Hard
Rock Cafe is all the more surprising given
that this is the startling context. Moss's
zany Penguin Arms Apartments, a take-off
on a much publicized California house by
Harwell Hamilton Harris, was one of the
original examples of "Googie" architecture
decried by Douglas Haskell in a famous
satiric diatribe of 1952. As John Kaliski
aptly described this building: "It seems
either poised for take-off or imploding even
as one views it."

2930 Revere Street   **N-6**
Frost Office Building (1985)
Ray Bailey Architects

This compact office and apartment building, with structured parking tucked below,
is a colorful homage to the work of Taft
Architects.

2719 Kipling Street   **N-7**
Kipling Apartments (1956)
Burdette Keeland

The framed wall plane at the end of the
motor court and the obscured glass balcony
rails are subtle touches that distinguish this
low-key complex of garden apartments. Its
density and the prominence accorded the
automobile bespeak the influence of Los
Angeles on Houston in the 1950s.

2800 Kipling Street   **N-8**
Kipling Townhouses (1974)
Burdette Keeland & Associates
with Donald C. Reese

By manipulating shallowly layered planes
and degrees of transparency within openings, Keeland created a complex set of elevations for this row of four houses which
directs attention upward and away from the
double-car garage doors at street level.
Diagonally across the intersection at 2900
Virginia Street are the **Virginia
Townhouses** (1983, Burdette Keeland &
Associates with Donald C. Reese), triangular in section with iron gates detailed after
the interlocking geometric figures of Josef
Albers. The ski-slope profiling does attract
one's attention, but the houses don't hold

their own at street level with the assurance
of the Kipling Townhouses.

2819 Ferndale Street   **N-9**
(1976) I. W. Coburn & Associates

The Chicago architect I. W. Coburn walled
off the street sides of this freestanding
house and organized rooms around two
patio gardens. Details are hard edged, but
the atmosphere is Mexican. The circles that
penetrate the chimney stacks are a signature
Coburn detail.

2905 Kipling Street   **N-10**
(1981) Val Glitsch

To cope with a sliver site at the end of a cul-
de-sac, Val Glitsch designed this tall, thin,
gable-roofed house as a clapboard-faced
superstructure set atop an exposed concrete
block substructure. The neighborhood,
with its eclectic mix of modern and florid
neo-Georgian row houses, is what Laura
Furman described in her novel *The
Shadow Line* as "shallow River Oaks:" not
in the mother community but near enough
to absorb some of its less conventional
spill-over population.

2709-2713 Ferndale Street   **N-11**
MacKie & Kamrath Building (1947)
MacKie & Kamrath

Fred MacKie and Karl Kamrath developed this office building complex; their studio was located at 2713. The small scale, the lovingly crafted organic materials, and the dynamic shaping of roof and wall planes, cut into with glass, still radiate their enthusiasm for the new.

2814 Virginia Street   **N-12**
Staub & Rather Building (1948)
Staub & Rather

Staub and Rather's associate, William C. Caldwell, designed a recessive contemporary style building to house their architecture studio. The angled, canopy-covered breezeway that leads from Virginia Street to the front door, with its big-scaled concrete *brise-soleil*, has more architectural presence than the building itself. Across the street, at **2809 Virginia Street**, is the trimly detailed wood pavilion constructed to house the architectural practice of William J. Anderson and Tom Wilson (1979, Anderson/Wilson).

2911-2913 Ferndale Street   **N-13**
(1976) Anderson/Wilson

A freestanding urban courtyard house that incorporates a retail shop; next door at 2915 and 2917 Ferndale are a pair of townhouses by the same architects.

3471 Westheimer Road   **N-14**
St. Luke's United Methodist Church (1951, 1954, 1957) Mark Lemmon

The Dallas architect Mark Lemmon specialized in Texan-sized Georgian style churches

for affluent Protestant congregations. St. Luke's is splendidly big.

3915 Essex Lane   **N-15**
Essex Houck Office Building (1962)
Burdette Keeland

Burdette Keeland had just completed graduate studies at Yale when he turned out this small, steel-framed building. A rectangle in plan, its stairs, elevators, and toilets were pulled outside the building envelope and housed in a collection of brick towers, in the manner of Louis I. Kahn and Paul Rudolph. The second story is cantilevered to one side above a driveway.

3830 Richmond Avenue   **N-16**
Houston Independent School District Central Administration Building (1969)
Neuhaus & Taylor

This monumental building, built of white cast-in-place concrete, was designed in the expressive style of the 1960s called (for obvious reasons) the New Brutalism. Tiers of office space step up in a pinwheel fashion, a quarter level at a time, wrapping around the four sides of a vast, central, skylit, air-conditioned court. The Board Room, the building's chief public space, is located in the basement, below the central court. Behind the administration building, at **3310 Timmons Lane**, is the ex-Houston

Teachers Credit Union Building of 1971 by McKittrick, Drennan, Richardson & Wallace, a less bombastic rendition of the Brutalist genre.

3600 block Cummins Lane   N-17
20 Greenway Plaza
Innova (1984) Cambridge Seven Associates and Lloyd Jones Brewer & Associates

Innova, a ten-story box sheathed in polished black Impala granite, was built to contain contract furniture manufacturers' showrooms. The stair-stepped openings on its north and south sides externalize the ingenious organizational scheme that Cambridge Seven's Charles Redmon devised for the building. Innova is fissured in two by a stepped-section escalator core that rises diagonally in two-story increments to a skylit exhibition and restaurant court at the top of the building. This provides for the admission of daylight into and views out from what otherwise is a windowless box. The architectural detailing, inside and out, is superlative.

Among the showrooms of individual interest are Sunarhauserman (Suite 660) by Frank O. Gehry & Associates and Brooks/Collier and Westinghouse Furniture Systems Division (Suite 706) by ISD and Peter D. Waldman & Christopher Genik. At the top of the building is Innova's own display, "Integration: A Journey Not A Destination" by 3D/International. Housed on the second level are the offices of the American Institute of Architects, the American Society of Interior Designers, and the Institute of Business Designers.

Innova, built by Century Development Corp. and the Mischer Corp., lies in Greenway Plaza, a 127-acre mixed use development carried out between 1967 and 1989 by Century Development Corp. Innova is located in Greenway's third tier, in what had been the Lamar-Weslayan subdivision. Century Development bought out the entire restricted subdivision in 1968 and an adjoining subdivision in 1969 in order to facilitate the westward expansion of Greenway Plaza.

3700 block Richmond Avenue   N-18
8-12 and 9-11 Greenway Plaza
(1982, 1978, 1979) Lloyd Jones Brewer & Associates

The reflective glass office buildings straddling Richmond Avenue (the rounded 15-story 8 and 12 and the slab-shaped 31-story 9 and 11) were also built as part of Greenway Plaza's third phase of develop-

ment. The uninflected, gridded surfaces of 9 (Coastal Tower) and 11 (Summit Tower) gleam like a pair of turquoise ice cubes; they are especially dramatic just before sunset. Sheathing buildings entirely in reflective glass quickly became a cliché in Houston. Consequently locals are always surprised when visiting foreign architects admire the visual effect this practice produces. Poised between 9 and 11 is "Archway" by Ben Woitena. The elegant skyways spanning Richmond are also by Lloyd Jones Brewer & Associates, as are the twin tower, 30-story Greenway Condominiums (1980, 1981) in the 3600 block of Timmons Lane. Century had a propensity for constructing buildings in pairs.

3500 block Richmond Avenue   N-19
1, 2, 3, and 5 Greenway Plaza
(1969, 1971, 1972, and 1973)
Lloyd, Morgan & Jones

Century's initial phase of development after it acquired the four-year-old, 41-acre Greenway office park in 1967 was this complex of buildings: the twin 11-story Eastern Airlines and Union Carbide buildings, followed by the 21-story Kellogg Building and the 31-story Conoco Tower. This entire phase incorporates a massive 3,500-car underground garage that represented the largest continuous concrete pour in Houston's construction history at the time of its erection. The garage encompasses The Underground, a subterranean retail concourse modelled, like 3 and 5, on the work of I. M. Pei. The Underground is connected to the second phase of Greenway's development, which included the **Stouffer's Hotel**

(1976, Lloyd Jones Associates) and the municipally-owned sports and entertainment arena, **The Summit** (1976, Kenneth Bentsen Associates, Lloyd, Jones Associates, consulting architects). Because of the expense involved with below-ground construction, Century developed the later phases of Greenway with conventional, above-grade parking structures. This actually makes for a more coherently organized site plan, given that Greenway Plaza is car-oriented and not a pedestrian environment. Across Richmond are two Century projects that predate its involvement with Greenway: the two-story **Dow Center** at 3636, an early Houston work of Caudill, Rowlett, Scott & Associates (1960), and the nine-story **3616 Richmond Building** (1966, Caudill Rowlett Scott). Both have been compromised by inappropriate alterations.

open-air courtyards. The building's formal image is indebted to Minoru Yamasaki's Northwestern Life Insurance Co. Building in Minneapolis; the veranda of stick-like columns supporting plaster vaults was intended to evoke historic colonnades while still remaining modern. It took Neuhaus & Taylor only four years (and four blocks) to go from this extreme of formalist attenuation to one of mass assertiveness in the HISD Central Administration Building.

3333 Richmond Avenue   N-20
Texas Instruments Houston Technical Laboratories [now Solvay America] (1957)
Ford, Colley & Tamminga

This was the first in an international series of manufacturing plants that San Antonio's best-known modernist architect, O'Neil Ford, and Corpus Christi's best-known modernist architect, Richard S. Colley, designed in collaboration for the Dallas-based Texas Instruments. The building is a low box, built above subterranean parking, faced with rough sawn panels of gray Georgia marble revetted to precast concrete back-up walls with exposed aluminum clips. Arthur and Marie Berger of Dallas, Texas's foremost modernist landscape architects, were responsible for the tree-shaded parking court, an amenity that should have been imitated much more widely in Houston. Unfortunately, the building has been badly mistreated. Ford and Colley's thin-slab porte-cochere has been replaced with a much clunkier model and numerous windows have been cut into the once-elegant curtain wall. Despite such abuse, the Houston Technical Laboratories retain the tense, thin-edged linearity and subtly proportioned surface modulations that made it such an assured statement of modern design when new.

3336 Richmond Avenue   N-21
Jefferson Chemical Co. Building (1965)
Neuhaus & Taylor

Prior to the development of Greenway Plaza, this was one of Century Development's largest office buildings, a four-story, glass-surfaced box, set atop a depressed parking garage, and organized around two

3102 Buffalo Speedway   N-22
Humble Research Center
[now Exxon Research Center] (1954)
MacKie & Kamrath

The Humble Oil & Refining Co. pioneered the transfer of technical support operations from the industrial East End and Ship Channel district, where such operations had been concentrated, to the west side of Houston, where its white-collar staff lived. As a result, Buffalo Speedway was transformed into one of the earliest suburban office corridors in Houston. MacKie & Kamrath's authorship is obvious in the horizontal organization of the elevations and the detailing of its brick and limestone facing. A third floor and a pair of wings were added to the building by MacKie & Kamrath in 1959.

3120 Buffalo Speedway   N-23
Humble Car Care Center
[now Research Exxon Car Center] (1970)
Kendrick/Cate Associates

The Humble Car Care Center was the most

elaborate in a series of buildings that Peter Papademetriou described as "prestige" service stations. These stations were exempted from standardized designs and often detailed to match some major building complex of the parent corporation, to which the station was adjacent. Kendrick/Cate repeated the red and white color scheme of MacKie & Kamrath's Humble Research Center, using exposed concrete—with cast-in-place graphics—in place of limestone to imbue the station and its canopies with the tough, grainy texture of the New Brutalism.

these, a pair of flat-roofed, courtyard offices, detailed with exposed glue-laminated wooden beams, and connected, in the best Los Angeles style, by a roofed central drive-through.

3323 Richmond Avenue   **N-26**
Phoenix Insurance Co. of Hartford
Building (1961) Neuhaus & Taylor

Gerald D. Hines and Century Development's Kenneth Schnitzer, between them, were chiefly responsible for Office Park, as the blocks of Richmond between Wakeforest and Buffalo Speedway were called. In reaction to the confused patterns of development in the Alabama corridor, they neatly lined up office buildings along Richmond. En route, typologies shifted from this classic Neuhaus & Taylor box-on-stilts-above-parking, built by Hines (the eyebrow overhangs are quintessential period pieces) to conventional multistory office blocks. Style was displayed exuberantly; every design mannerism from the first half of the 1960s is visible in these three blocks. A more sedate version of the Phoenix type, also by Neuhaus & Taylor for Hines, is the **Pontiac Motor Division Building** at 3121 Richmond (1961).

3121 Buffalo Speedway   **N-24**
Great Southern Life Insurance Co. Building
(1965) Skidmore, Owings & Merrill with
Wilson, Morris, Crain & Anderson

This clean-lined, ten-story corporate office building, set pavilion-like in a reflecting basin at the center of its flat, 16½-acre site, takes engineering determinism to perverse extremes. The long east and west fronts of the building are completely windowless above the lobby level; the walls serve as plenum ducts for the air-conditioning system. The end elevations are spanned by cast-in-place concrete edge beams, with the window glass deeply recessed. The building's public spaces, most of which are collected in a one-story pavilion set behind the office block, exhibit the antiseptic elegance so admired in the 1960s.

2990 Richmond Avenue   **N-27**
2990 Richmond Building (1966)
Neuhaus & Taylor

This five-story speculative office building, faced with curved masonry fins that peel back to reveal vertically aligned strip windows, was Hines's biggest building prior to the Galleria and One Shell Plaza. Harwood Taylor purposefully played off the adjoining 2900 Building (1964) and the 3000 Building (1964, Wilson, Morris, Crain & Anderson) in order to achieve a unified streetscape.

3230 Sul Ross Avenue   **N-25**
Macham Building (1959) Thompson
McCleary and Hamilton Brown

During the late 1950s the back streets off West Alabama Avenue were developed in a spontaneous—not to say haphazard—manner with small professional buildings, some built to house architects' studios. McCleary and Brown produced one of the best of

2627 Colquitt Street   N-28
The Zephyr (1985) Arquitectonica

Ever ready with a new slant on design,
Arquitectonica refaced this existing commercial building with parallelogram-shaped
windows framed with gold-spray-painted
aluminum, and writhing, flexible red drain-
pipes. Tenant spaces are occupied principally by galleries; Howard Barnstone designed
the serene interiors of the Davis-McClain
Gallery.

Post Oak

Post Oak was not transformed from countryside into the second city center of Houston overnight. But it gives the impression that change occurred with just such abruptness. Like the Louisiana and Smith street corridor downtown, Post Oak Boulevard exudes newness. Gleaming buildings, deflected into provocative shapes, are widely spaced on the flat prairie west of River Oaks, a plain artificially bounded on the east by Loop 610 and crisscrossed by major westbound thoroughfares: Richmond, Westheimer, San Felipe, and Woodway. Post Oak Boulevard is now what Main Street has historically been, the prime retail corridor of the city. It is anchored by the Galleria, an introverted, air-conditioned, pedestrian-scaled mixed-use complex. What one sees in Post Oak is downtown with all the big buildings pushed far apart in order to leave plenty of room for cars, both moving and parked.

Success, though, has brought to the district a recurrence of the very problem that occasioned the gradual disintegration of the downtown retail district—levels of traffic congestion that Houston motorists consider unacceptable. A far smaller percentage of the real estate in Post Oak is devoted to streets than is the case downtown, so that congestion here constitutes an even more serious problem. One suggestion for alleviation, not altogether facetious, has been to impose a grid of streets and blocks on the area. There has even emerged concern for the lack of pedestrian connections within the area (which force people to drive from place to place) and pedestrian amenities.

Post Oak now finds paradoxically that it has experienced that shift from periphery to center that River Oaks underwent. Houstonians who live within the confines of Loop 610 are apt to think of it as the suburban usurper of downtown Houston. But from the perspective of far Houston, downtown and Post Oak are the high density edges of the center city, roughly equivalent in Houston terms to downtown and midtown Manhattan, as the architect Cameron Armstrong has observed. Only in the Houston version, it's not Greenwich Village that lies in between but River Oaks.

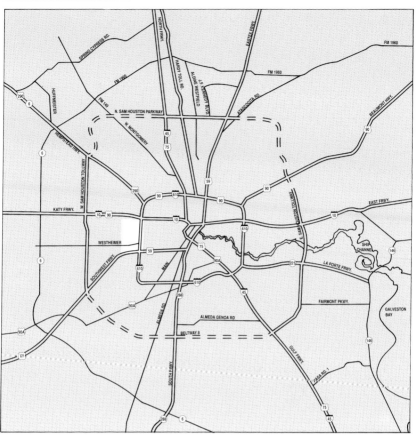

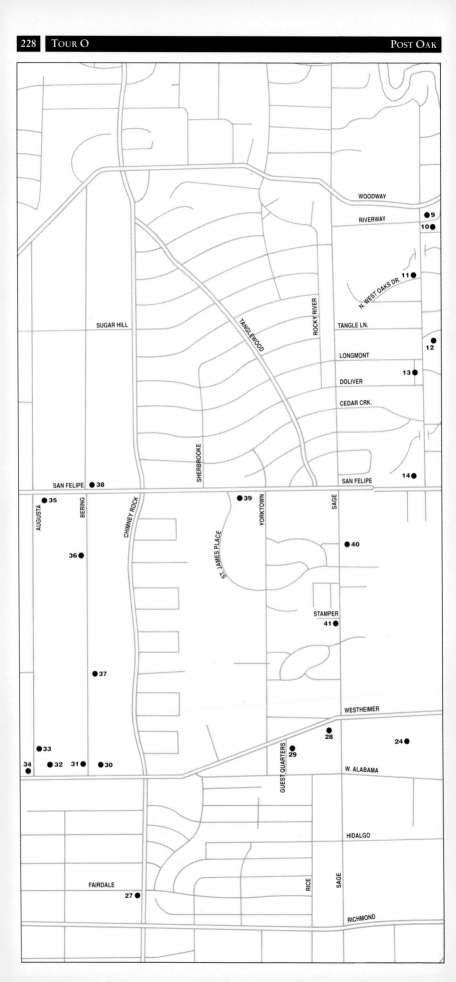

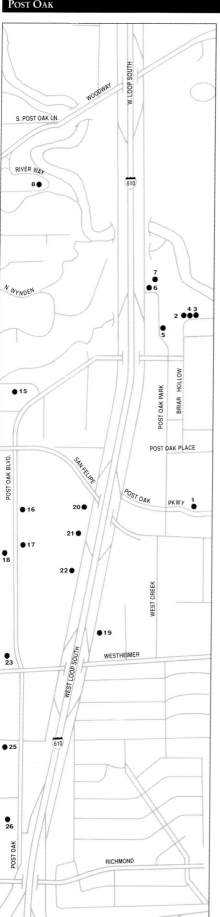

1. 5 Post Oak Park Drive
2. 54 Briar Hollow Lane
3. 63 Briar Hollow Lane
4. 65 Briar Hollow Lane
5. 1317 Post Oak Park Drive
6. 1177 West Loop South
7. 1111 West Loop South
8. 4 Riverway
9. 2 Riverway
10. 1 Riverway
11. 22 North West Oaks Drive
12. 11 North Wynden Drive
13. 5000 Longmont Drive
14. 5100 San Felipe Road
15. 1300-1400 Post Oak Boulevard
16. 1801 Post Oak Boulevard
17. 2001 Post Oak Boulevard
18. 1980-2000 Post Oak Boulevard
19. 2425 West Loop South
20. 1900 West Loop South
21. 2000 West Loop South
22. 2200 West Loop South
23. 5000 Westheimer Road
24. 5015 Westheimer Road
25. 2800 Post Oak Boulevard
26. 3000-3050 Post Oak Boulevard
27. 3100 Chimney Rock Street
28. 5333 Westheimer Road
29. 5353 Westheimer Road
30. 5718 Westheimer Road
31. 5800 Westheimer Road
32. 5830 Westheimer Road
33. 2603 Augusta Drive
34. 5858-5860 Westheimer Road
35. 5847 San Felipe Road
36. 1900 Bering Drive
37. 2333 Bering Drive
38. 5740 San Felipe Road
39. 5555 San Felipe Road
40. 1801 Sage Road
41. 5203 Stamper Way

ed on light steel columns to the desired height to form the roof of the house. The carport's brick end wall features a series of masonry arches along its base.

5 Post Oak Park Drive　　　　　O-1
Five Post Oak Park Building (1983)
Morris*Aubry Architects

The 28-story Five Post Oak Park is a sculpturally shaped office tower clad in travertine and bronze solar glass. Its flared base, stepped windows, and curved top betray the first stirrings of corporate postmodernism in Houston. Across the street at 1919 Briar Oaks Lane is the deluxe 12-story, 248-room **Remington on Post Oak Park Hotel** (now The Ritz-Carlton, 1982, Shepherd+Boyd), notable for its chic motor courts and upscale mod-trad decor. Next to the Remington, at 1811 Briar Oaks Lane, is **The Junior League of Houston Building** (1985, Morris*Aubry Architects), which does nothing to dispel the ethnic stereotype implied in the descriptive term Junior League Georgian.

65 Briar Hollow Lane　　　　　O-4
(1961) Bolton & Barnstone

This is one of Howard Barnstone's most sensational houses, a three-story pavilion apparently framed in steel, with walls that are entirely of glass, set far back on a site that falls away to Buffalo Bayou. The steel galleries that entirely surround what is actually a wood-framed house have been painted a peculiar mustard color and some of the glass panels are now opaque. But the crisp lines, sure proportions, and stunning transparency of the house remain quite captivating.

54 Briar Hollow Lane　　　　　O-2
(1960) Bolton & Barnstone

Surviving at the northern end of Briar Hollow Lane (for the time being) is an enclave of houses wedged between Buffalo Bayou on the north and the high-rise office and apartment buildings that consumed the rest of Briar Hollow in the 1970s and '80s. This beautifully modulated town house is solidly walled on its street side, but all glass at the back, where it sits high above the densely wooded bayou channel. Its urbane parking court and staged landscape plantings are by Fred Buxton.

63 Briar Hollow Lane　　　　　O-3
(1955) Ford, Colley & Tamminga

The San Antonio architect O'Neil Ford here exhibited the technical achievement that he participated in developing: the Youtz-Slick lift slab, a concrete slab poured on top of the foundation slab and then lift-

1317 Post Oak Park Drive　　　　O-5
Post Oak Park Townhouses (1966)
Charles Tapley Associates

Tapley, a landscape architect as well as an architect, grouped these row houses along narrow greenway corridors to preserve existing trees on the heavily wooded site. The developer insisted that house fronts be stylistically varied, but Tapley was able to design their rear elevations as handsomely composed planes of cedar, marked off by light-colored wood trim. This complex was one of the first increments of the 58-acre Post Oak Park, begun in Briar Hollow by Tenneco and the J. V. Dorfman Development Co. after the opening of the first segment of the West Loop South in the middle 1960s.

1177 West Loop South   O-6
U.S. Home Building [now 1177 West Loop
South Building] (1979)
Caudill Rowlett Scott

CRS's Paul Kennon was responsible for the
design of this doubly faced 18-story concrete-framed office building. Toward the
West Loop it presents a sleek silvery curve
that seems to respond to the dynamic
rhythm of passing traffic. The opposite site,
which faces Memorial Park, is jagged in
plan rather than curved, and clad in dark
bronze solar glass. The plan figure derives
from the work of the Finnish architect
Alvar Aalto; the flashy imagery is pure
Houston.

1111 West Loop South   O-7
Caudill Rowlett Scott Building (1969)
Caudill Rowlett Scott

William W. Caudill led the "design team" (a
CRS conceptual innovation) in producing
this unusual building to house the CRS
architectural practice. The one-story,
55,000-square-foot reinforced concrete
building lies beneath its parking lot, an
arrangement made possible by the site's
topographic slope down toward Buffalo
Bayou. Only the entry pavilion projects
above the roof-top parking court.

4 Riverway   O-8
Four Seasons Inn on the Park (1981)
S. I. Morris Associates

Morris's Guy Jackson configured this 11-
story, 383-room hotel in a crescent shape in
response to the curve of Buffalo Bayou
around the promontory on which the
building is set. Simply detailed externally,

the hotel contains sleekly finished public
spaces that are architectural in character,
and quite elegant. The SWA Group
installed the brightly colored wall trough
fountains in the swimming pool gardens,
borrowing from the Mexican architect Luis
Barragán. Unfortunately, the grounds go
under water when Buffalo Bayou over-
flows.

2 Riverway   O-9
IBM Building (1980) Caudill Rowlett Scott

IBM's regional headquarters office building,
a 17-story triangular shaped block with a
notched top, was conditioned in its design
by concerns for energy conservation. Its
longest side faces north, toward Woodway,
and its all-glass exteriors contain, ironically,
only narrow horizontal window bands at
each floor level. The windows were
designed to be opened, however.

1 Riverway   O-10
Allied Chemical Building (1978)
S. I. Morris Associates

John Hansen built the 25-story Allied
Chemical Building as the first increment of
Riverway, a 28-acre mixed-use complex that
he developed on what once were the polo
stable grounds of a family who lived in
Courtlandt Place. John Bertini and Guy
Jackson designed the stepped, faceted

tower, which is faced with alternating bands of granite aggregate precast concrete panels and bronze solar glass. Inasmuch as it is visible from the north curve of Post Oak Boulevard, Allied Chemical figures conspicuously on the Post Oak skyline, along with its companion, the 20-story **Internorth Building** (now 3 Riverway Building, 1980, S. I. Morris Associates). At **6 Riverway** is a one-story brick ranch house by Staub, Rather & Howze (1951). In unzoned Houston it should be no surprise to find a single-family house ensconced amid skyscrapers. The owners sold their estate to Hansen but retained occupancy of the house.

Bolton designed most of the houses on Longmont, including his own at 1. Hamilton Brown was responsible for 8 and 11 and Robert Sobel designed the house at 16.

22 North West Oaks Drive   O-11
(1939) H. A. Salisbury & T. G. McHale

When this trimly detailed American Georgian house was built, it was set in the country—the country estate subdivision of West Oaks, developed in 1938. West Oaks survives as an enclave of bucolic charm, even as the towers of Post Oak and speculative house builders close in on it.

11 North Wynden Drive   O-12
(1941) Donald Barthelme

In an adjacent section of West Oaks, Donald Barthelme built this simple, flat-roofed modern house for his family. The room perched up on the roof deck was Barthelme's studio. It was here that his children, among them the writers Donald, Frederick, and Steven, grew up.

5000 Longmont Drive   O-13
5000 Longmont (1962)
P. M. Bolton Associates

Preston M. Bolton developed and designed this community of courtyard houses aligned along a private street. The flat-roofed Miesian box, in which Bolton and his ex-partner Howard Barnstone specialized in the 1950s, was here faced with textured brick, high panelled wooden doors, and barred windows to give 5000 Longmont a slightly Mexican aspect.

5100 San Felipe Road   O-14
Four-Leaf Towers (1982) Cesar Pelli & Associates, Albert C. Martin & Associates, and Melton Henry Architects

Pelli's first project in Houston was to site and sheathe this pair of 40-story condominium apartment towers, built by the Milanese investors Lorenzo and Giorgio Borlenghi. Pelli designed the curtain wall as a complex grid of rose-, salmon-, and cream-colored spandrel glass, interspersed with solar glass windows to express the spatial organization of the 200 units within each tower. The choice of colors and the provision of faceted caps atop the penthouse levels were intended to give the project a domestic aspect. The towers figure prominently as spatial markers, thanks to their defined profiles and static relationship. Poised between them, atop the landscaped podium that conceals extensive underground parking, is Beverly Pepper's 50-foot tall "Polygenesis" (1981). The 10-acre site was landscaped by The SWA Group.

1300-1400 Post Oak Boulevard   O-15
Four Oaks Place (1983) Cesar Pelli & Associates and Melton Henry Architects

Pelli took advantage of the curve of Post Oak to station this group of towers—the 30-story Union Texas Petroleum Center in the middle, flanked by the 25-story Allied Bank Tower (now First Interstate) and the 25-story Weatherford Tower, and, off to the west, the 14-story Interfin Building—as an axial terminator. Pelli gave the three tallest buildings flat tops and horizontally banded curtain walls of intense blue spandrel glass and silver reflective vision glass to indicate

their open, loft-like, spatial arrangement. The parking structure, which is wrapped around the back of the towers, is surmounted by an arbor, beneath which pedestrians may pass between buildings. The Borlenghis' own Interfin Building is in transition between Four Oaks and Four-Leaf; it gets a cap and is colored brown. Just behind it, at **1515 South Post Oak Lane**, is Ma Maison, originally the country house of Dr. and Mrs. James Hill (1939, William Ward Watkin), which figured in *Baby Houston*, the novel written by Fanetta Wortham Hill's niece, June Arnold. It was saved and rehabilitated by Giorgio Borlenghi.

1801 Post Oak Boulevard   O-16
Post Oak Row (1972)
Skidmore, Owings & Merrill and Wilson, Morris, Crain & Anderson

Gerald D. Hines Interests built this strip center for intermediate use of property in Smith Office Park. The center is faced with a simple but nobly scaled portico composed of thick, wide-span steel beams and thin steel columns. Its modernist restraint contrasts tellingly with the **Saks Pavilion** across the street at 1800 Post Oak (1989, RTKL Associates), a retail mall in a phantasmagoric Palm Beach-Caribbean style that gushes postmodern luxe.

2001 Post Oak Boulevard   O-17
The Warwick Post Oak [now Doubletree Hotel at Post Oak] (1982) I. M. Pei & Partners and Richard Fitzgerald & Partners

James Ingo Freed, the Pei partner in charge of the design of the Warwick, treated precast concrete panels as the modern equivalents of dressed stone. The result is a provocative "rusticated" curtain wall screen behind which the hotel's balconies are inserted. The diagonal site planning of Post Oak Central across the street led to the configuration of the 14-story, 460-room hotel, a relationship better appreciated in diagram than in actuality. The great cascade of silver reflective glass that breaks through the front of the hotel contrasts strikingly with the shape and texture of the concrete curtain wall. Pei's office detailed the six-story lobby beneath the rolled glass vault and the hypostyle anteroom off the ballroom, to the left of the lobby.

1980-2000 Post Oak Boulevard   O-18
Post Oak Central (1973)
Johnson/Burgee Architects

Thanks to I. S. Brochstein, the custom woodwork manufacturer who owns this 17-acre site, Post Oak Central became Philip Johnson's first project for Gerald D. Hines Interests. The first building, the 24-story One Post Oak Central at 2000 Post Oak (1975, Johnson/Burgee and S. I. Morris Associates) established Johnson's theme: a sleekly banded charcoal and silver tower with faceted corners and two setback terraces. Two (1978, Johnson/Burgee and Richard Fitzgerald & Partners) was the same building, deflected 45° into a parallelogram. Three (1981, Johnson/Burgee and Fitzgerald) is the most contorted of all, a right triangle in plan, located at the apex of a triangular open space to which all three buildings conform. This exercise in geometric deformation was inspired by Johnson's engagement with Minimalist art of the 1960s and '70s, a fascination expressed simultaneously in his design of Pennzoil Place.

2425 West Loop South   O-19
One West Loop Plaza (1980) I. M. Pei & Partners and Richard Fitzgerald & Partners

The aluminum curtain wall system, scored into panels that depend for effect upon sure proportioning, is more impressive from a distance than close up. The 11-story building, developed by J. C. Helms, is U-shaped in plan and encloses a central atrium lit by north-facing clear glass carried on a vertical steel space frame. The building was to have been the first of several, which explains its orientation away from the freeway. James Ingo Freed was the Pei partner in charge of design.

1900 West Loop South　　　　**O-20**
3D/International Tower (1979)
3D/International

3D/I occupies as chief tenant the building that it designed for Hines Interests, a gleaming compilation of silver stainless steel spandrel and silver reflective glass, offset in plan to give it sculptural interest—and additional corner office spaces.

2000 West Loop South　　　　**O-21**
Control Data Corp. Building (1971)
Skidmore, Owings & Merrill and Wilson, Morris, Crain & Anderson

For this 22-story office slab, built by Hines Interests, SOM-Chicago's engineering partner, Fazlur R. Khan, devised the first instance of composite steel-concrete construction in the world. The light steel structural frame was erected, precast window units were slotted into its interstices, and these panels served as formwork for poured concrete that encased the steel, creating an economical structural system.

2200 West Loop South　　　　**O-22**
Stewart Title Building (1974)
Skidmore, Owings & Merrill and
S. I. Morris Associates

In the wake of Pennzoil Place, even the staid Chicago office of SOM shaped up, breaking out of the box (as Philip Johnson put it) with this ten-story, parallelogram-planned office building for Hines Interests. Stewart Title, Control Data, 3D/International, and the Warwick are located in the 41-acre Smith Office Park, Hines's first venture in the Post Oak area, developed with R. E. "Bob" Smith. At **2300 and 2400 West Loop South** are Hines's earliest projects in Smith Office Park, the five-story Litwin (1967) and six-story IMC (1966) buildings by Neuhaus & Taylor.

5000 Westheimer Road　　　　**O-23**
Sakowitz Brothers
[now Sakowitz Post Oak] (1959)
Eugene Werlin & C. H. Kiefner

Bernard Sakowitz astounded Houstonians by building so large a branch of his family's downtown specialty store at Westheimer and Post Oak, five miles from Main Street. His prescience paid off; after Sakowitz closed its downtown store in 1985, this became its flagship location. According to press releases of the period, the building was designed to look like a country club. Werlin & Kiefner seem to have interpreted this as a mandate for what is called "Hollywood Regency" in Los Angeles, the use of manneristically attenuated classical details applied to simple, symmetrical boxes, souped up with a few streamlined accessories.

5015 Westheimer Road　　　　**O-24**
Galleria (1969-1971) Hellmuth, Obata & Kassabaum and Neuhaus & Taylor

The Galleria is a Houston typological development of national, even international, consequence. It is a 45-acre, 3.9 million-square-foot mixed use development, a regional-sized shopping mall that concentrates in specialty retailing, to which are

attached two hotels, three multistory office buildings, and an astonishing 11,263 parking spaces. Gerald D. Hines, who built the Galleria, succinctly stated his ambition for it in 1969 when its first increments were opened: "A shopping center it is not. It will be a new downtown." Hines cited the Galleria Vittorio Emmanuele in Milan as the model for the Post Oak Galleria (although Rockefeller Center deserves some credit for suggesting the ice skating rink). But while the glass-vaulted passageways of Milan's Galleria are part of the street network of the central city, the Post Oak Galleria is an object in the landscape, connected to the outside world chiefly by automobiles. Its interior is a conditioned and controlled environment and its vision of public life is focused exclusively on consumption and diversion. Ultimately, it is a shopping center, not downtown.

The complex was built from east to west. The Houston branch of the Dallas specialty store, Neiman-Marcus, a free-standing building on Post Oak Boulevard, was the first segment to open (1969), followed by the 22-story Post Oak Tower (1969), the Galleria mall (1970), and the 20-story, 404-room Houston Oaks Hotel (now Westin Oaks, 1971). The 25-story ex-Transco Tower at 2700 Post Oak was completed in 1973. Galleria II, containing Lord & Taylor, the 12-story Galleria II Twin Towers, and the 23-story, 500-room Galleria Plaza Hotel (now Westin Galleria) opened in 1977. Marshall Field & Co., the only segment not designed by Hellmuth, Obata & Kassabaum, was completed in 1979. Galleria III, containing Macy's, opened in 1986. By that time the Galleria had led Post Oak in supplanting downtown as *the* retail center of Houston. It had more hotel rooms than downtown and the second highest concentration of office space in Houston.

Neiman-Marcus remains the most impressive work of architecture in the Galleria. Although the Post Oak store was satirized by Robert Venturi, Denise Scott Brown, and Steven Izenour in 1972 for its glib repackaging of the Brutalist architecture of the pioneer French modernist, Le Corbusier, the building is notable for its generous internal spaces, its use of natural light, and the quality of its interior design, carried out by Eleanor LeMaire & Associates just before Miss LeMaire's death. None of the other specialty stores in the Galleria approaches this level of quality, which must be ascribed in large part to the store's president, Stanley Marcus. Its prettied-up, smoothed-out Brutalism—the symmetrically stationed bustles on the second floor feature inset panels of onyx that are backlit at night—is a bit overwrought for a specialty store. Yet Neiman-Marcus does possess distinct facades and it is the only part of the Galleria that faces a public street with any show of confidence and style.

Massimo Vignelli's Helvetica graphics mark the public entrance to the three-level Galleria mall. (In proper suburban fashion, a significant number of those coming to the Galleria enter through the rear garages, off West Alabama.) Like the hotel and office towers, the mall avoids making any strong architectural commitment. The interiors are low-key, with dark carpeted floors and unobtrusive "street" furniture. The concept was to let the display windows and the central, skylit, 170-foot-long ice skating rink stand as the feature attractions. Galleria II (HOK and S. I. Morris Associates) is not impressive, despite the ten-story atrium that rises from the main concourse level up between the two office buildings. At Galleria III, HOK (and Richard Fitzgerald & Partners) totally abandoned its earlier aesthetic for neo-traditional imagery and tighter spaces. These are not unwelcome after the vacuousness of Galleria II. But they fail to impart a sense of urbanistic coherence to the complex. The exteriors of Galleria III, watered-down corporate postmodernism at its most tiresome, likewise seem to be starting over again rather than summarizing and concluding what has gone before.

Philip Johnson and John Burgee (with S. I. Morris Associates) designed Marshall Field & Co.'s curved planar limestone facade. This was to have been a screen for Claes Oldenburg's giant aluminum "Paintsplats (on a wall by P. J.)," free-form blobs of color that looked like they had come from giant paintbrushes flicked carelessly against the facade. As this proposal did not accord with Marshall Field's midwestern sense of style, the facade went up without the art. Even so, Marshall Field's liked the wall so much that they built one just like it at Hines's Galleria in Dallas.

The Galleria has become a surrogate for downtown in a city that no longer requires one of the old-fashioned sort. Its success made it the model for many mixed-use complexes, both in the U.S. and abroad, both in center cities and suburbs. Whether it will outlive the set of circumstances that brought it into being and survive to attain the historic distinction that will eventually accrue to it is a serious question. For in Houston, low margins of profitability inexorably lead to the disposal of non-performing resources. Not only does anything go here, everything goes.

2800 Post Oak Boulevard   O-25
Transco Tower (1983) Johnson/Burgee Architects and Morris*Aubry Architects

Although the Galleria is the anchor of the Post Oak district, its architectural symbol is the equivocal Transco Tower. At 64 stories, 901 feet in height, this is the third tallest building in Houston. Its isolated setting and tapered profile make it a landmark, one that has attracted a surprising degree of popular awareness and approbation.

building type associated with the rural Texas landscape, to which the beer garden behind the restaurant lends a convivial note of authenticity.

Johnson/Burgee modeled Transco on the setback Art Deco towers of the late 1920s but surfaced it entirely in reflective glass (applied, as John Burgee explained, as stone facing would have been in the '20s). It is the ghost image of a skyscraper from the city that Post Oak rejected, an ironic inversion that passively reflects its sub-urban environment. Crowning the tower is the Transco Beacon, a searchlight that rotates at night. Alongside the building is the 3-acre Transco Park, site of the **Transco Fountain** (1985, Johnson/Burgee Architects and Richard Fitzgerald & Partners), a stunning work of hydraulic engineering built by the Transco Companies and Hines Interests, the building's two principal tenants.

3000-3050 Post Oak Boulevard   O-26
The Lake on Post Oak Park
(1978, 1980, 1982) 3D/International

These three towers, built by Hines Interests and surfaced in bronze anodized aluminum and bronze solar glass, exhibit varied plan geometries. They are set in a pastorally landscaped park (Edward D. Stone, Jr., & Associates, landscape architects) containing an emergency storm run-off retention basin (a.k.a. the lake), a publicly mandated site feature.

3100 Chimney Rock Street   O-27
Cou-Cou's [now Fuddruckers] (1980)
Clovis Heimsath Associates

For the shape of this restaurant, Heimsath turned to a Texas-German building type, the conically roofed octagonal hall whose prototype is the Vereins-Kirche in the central Texas town of Fredericksburg. For its surfaces he resorted to turn-of-the-century industrial building materials: galvanized pressed metal shingles. The result could have been kitsch—but it's not. Instead Heimsath has provocatively reconstituted a

5333 Westheimer Road   O-28
Ranger Insurance Co. Building (1971)
Skidmore, Owings & Merrill and Wilson, Morris, Crain & Anderson

Hines Interests constructed this ten-story building as the first increment of Galleria West, a 15-acre office park adjacent to the Galleria. It is a classic Chicago frame building, its steel structural skeleton sheathed in bronze anodized aluminum and its interstices enclosed with flush set bronze solar glass. Next door, at 5251 Westheimer, is the less distinguished 11-story **Kaneb Building** (1976), also by SOM-Chicago for Hines, with its structural frame clad in travertine. At 2610-2670 Sage Road is **Galleria West**, a two-level retail building affixed to the front of a parking garage. Like Post Oak Row, its architecture consists of a wide-span armature of exposed steel structural members.

5353 Westheimer Road   O-29
Guest Quarters Galleria West (1982)
Skidmore, Owings & Merrill

Designed by the Houston office of SOM, the 26-story, 349-unit Guest Quarters hotel features the heavy-handed detailing that characterized its work. Rolled tops, fat circular moldings, and ribbed precast concrete spandrels are the decorative details on this offset tower, which is faced with brown Texas granite aggregate precast concrete. Where Guest Quarters excels is at ground level. The Westheimer frontage is planted with a tranquil glade of trees; entrance to the hotel is from a discreetly walled motor court at the back of the building. From Guest Quarters one can look across Westheimer to the extraordinarily long, nine-story **Bechtel Building** (1981) by the San Francisco office of Skidmore, Owings & Merrill at 5400 Westheimer Court. The site it occupies was part of a 110-acre tract where in 1958 R. E. "Bob" Smith and Judge Roy Hofheinz planned to build a giant shopping mall, Air-Conditioned City, a project that was in spirit a precursor to the Galleria.

Irving Phillips described this sculpturally convoluted building as incorporating something from every building along the Westheimer strip. It's hard to decide whether its straightforward, loft-like interior is a relief or a disappointment.

2603 Augusta Drive   O-33
Augusta Green Building (1984)
Morris*Aubry Architects

Houston's speculative office buildings of the late 1970s and early '80s display a range of solutions to the problem of "skinning" what is essentially the same building. Guy Jackson's response at the 16-story Augusta Green is assured and understated: alternating horizontal bands of polished and flame-finished Swedish red granite, set off by thin stainless steel strips that bracket the windows. The vertical notch marks the front door.

5718 Westheimer Road   O-30
One Westheimer Plaza [now MCO Plaza] (1982) Morris*Aubry Architects

A deftly inflected 22-story office tower, faced with alternating bands of travertine and bronze solar glass. Its elegant minimalism has been compromised by exhibition of the principal tenant's advertising logo.

5800 Westheimer Road   O-31
Memorial Lutheran Church (1965)
Todd Tackett Lacy

Gerald Tackett endowed this church with presence by capping it with a sharply profiled shingled roof culminating in a hooded skylight above the central worship space.

5830 Westheimer Road   O-32
J. Frank Jungman Branch, Houston Public Library (1974) W. Irving Phillips, Jr., & Robert W. Peterson

5858-5860 Westheimer Road   O-34
The Spectrum (1980 and 1981)
Urban Architecture

The sleek fascia of this up-scale strip shopping center incorporates back-lit graphics. It was such a refined detail for what is most often a down-and-dirty building type that copies proliferated instantly, a tribute to the ingenuity of Hossein Oskouie. His brash blue and silver eight-story office building behind the center, with its circular end bays, is a visual knockout.

5847 San Felipe Road   O-35
San Felipe Plaza (1984)
Skidmore, Owings & Merrill

This is the best building that Richard Keating produced during his tenure as head of the Houston office of SOM. Two of the firm's buildings downtown, First International and Allied, were conflated to obtain its semi-cylindrical, stepped profile. What is perhaps most impressive is the carefully detailed curtain wall of polished granite, in which light pink and gray granites are subtly combined. Built by the Farb Companies, the 45-story San Felipe Plaza presently marks the western boundary of the Post Oak district.

1900 Bering Drive   O-36
Emerson Unitarian Church (1974)
MacKie & Kamrath

For a Unitarian congregation, Kamrath turned to one of Frank Lloyd Wright's greatest works, Unity Temple in Oak Park, Illinois, of 1906. His tribute is so literal that it is a little startling to encounter. The church's exterior finish of stucco and wood stripping does not compare favorably with the original and internally its central space tends to leave the architecturally-aware a bit deflated. To the north is the church's community building, a vaulted roof pavilion supported on glue-laminated wood beams, an early Houston work of Caudill, Rowlett, Scott & Associates (1960).

2333 Bering Drive   O-37
The Park Regency Terrace Residences (1983) Venturi, Rauch & Scott Brown and McCleary Associates

A seldom-mentioned Venturi project, this is

a two-building, middle-income condominium apartment complex packing 80 units (and structured parking) onto a constricted 1½ acre L-shaped site. The Adamesque cutout at the entrance to the complex is the high point. What follows is a cautionary tale about the hazards that high design is apt to encounter in the speculative market.

5740 San Felipe Road   O-38
Seventh Church of Christ, Scientist (1958)
Langwith, Wilson, King & Associates

This church is a tribute to the enduring value of the Finnish-American architect Eliel Saarinen's unassertive but carefully shaped and finished buildings.

5555 San Felipe Road   O-39
Marathon Oil Tower (1983)
Pierce Goodwin Alexander

The diagonal orientation and vertically ribbed window bays of this 41-story corporate office tower, its deep-set openings, and the density and color of its flame-finished Carmen red granite exterior make the Marathon Oil Tower one of the best tall buildings in the San Felipe corridor. It is located in the 48-acre San Felipe Green office park, developed by Mark Lee & Associates.

1801 Sage Road   **O-40**
St. Michael The Archangel Catholic Church
(1966) Edward J. Schulte with Charles
Hightower

Philip Johnson proposed a design for this parish
complex in 1953, a brick, barrel-roofed Rund-
bogenstil church, in which the nave was contained beneath a series of free-standing vaults
like those in his New Canaan guest house. Had
it been built, it would have been—as Johnson
later exclaimed—"my first Romanesque design." It was rejected as too modern. What the
parish got instead was Cincinnati architect
Schulte's lavishly detailed quasi-modern church,
finished in brick, limestone, and gold-impreg-
nated stained glass. In acknowledgment of the
realities of suburban life, Schulte reoriented the
church so that its front door faces the back
parking lot rather than Sage Road.

5203 Stamper Way   **O-41**
(1955) Harwood Taylor

An exceptionally well-maintained modern
house designed in the spirit of the Los
Angeles architect Richard Neutra. The
wooden garage nearest the corner of
Stamper and Sage is a late, slightly intrusive,
but sympathetically detailed addition.

Tanglewood / Memorial / Spring Branch

At the end of the 1920s wealthy Houstonians discovered at their back door the dense pine forest that had captivated Frederick Law Olmsted in 1854, when he passed through it on his way to Houston. There a small number of families established weekend retreats where country pastimes—horseback riding, tennis, polo, and swimming—could be pursued. After the middle 1930s, year-round houses, usually on multiple-acre sites, began to be built along Buffalo Bayou near South and North Post Oak Lanes. A few isolated subdivisions followed in the late 1930s. Then, at the end of the 1940s, the tidal wave of suburban expansion that would engulf Houston's hinterlands in the succeeding decade broke over this large area. South of the bayou, the large subdivision of Tanglewood, which enticed the Houston Country Club into relocating there from its site in the East End in 1957, was the dominant development. North of the bayou, where the tree cover is denser and much more extensive, the entire area known as Memorial (after Memorial Park, the 1,500-acre forest park on its eastern edge) developed in a random series of small subdivisions tied to Houston by the winding Memorial Drive and Katy Road to the north.

Between Katy Road and Hempstead Highway, in an area known as Spring Branch, the forest thins out. Here, German place names indicate the one-time presence of German-owned dairy and truck farms, which supplied the markets of Houston in the 19th and early 20th centuries. The major streets, such as Long Point Road, exhibit the strip development characteristic of mid-century, with low commercial buildings pushed far back from the street to accommodate parked cars. Behind these thoroughfares, the restricted, if aging, subdivisions remain neat and tidy. But the aspect that confronts one along the major streets gives quite the opposite impression, especially where—as near the intersection of Long Point and Hempstead Highway—a commercial strip meets a highway-related industrial strip.

A reaction against the carelessness of postwar commercial development began after 1970. The freeway infrastructure superimposed on the surface street system, as represented by Loop 610 and the Northwest Freeway, displays a further stage in the explosion of scale and dispersal of buildings seen on Long Point Road. Yet new attitudes about the desirability of visual ordering, planning controls (privately administered, of course), and landscape improvements are evident as well. From the perspective of the freeway, however, these operate as elements of a code advertising a range of levels in the hierarchy of real estate developments, as much as they do phenomena to be experienced. In a half century, this section of Houston has progressed from countryside to an urban landscape that features the tree as symbolic artifact, an easily understood sign of country life.

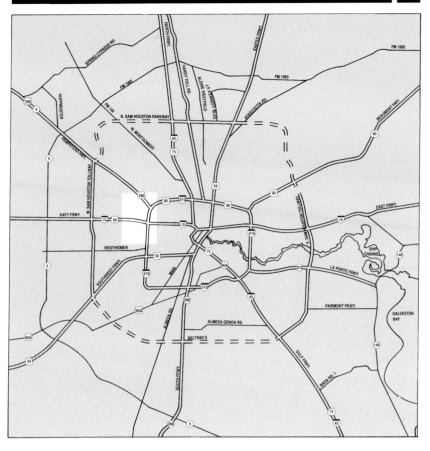

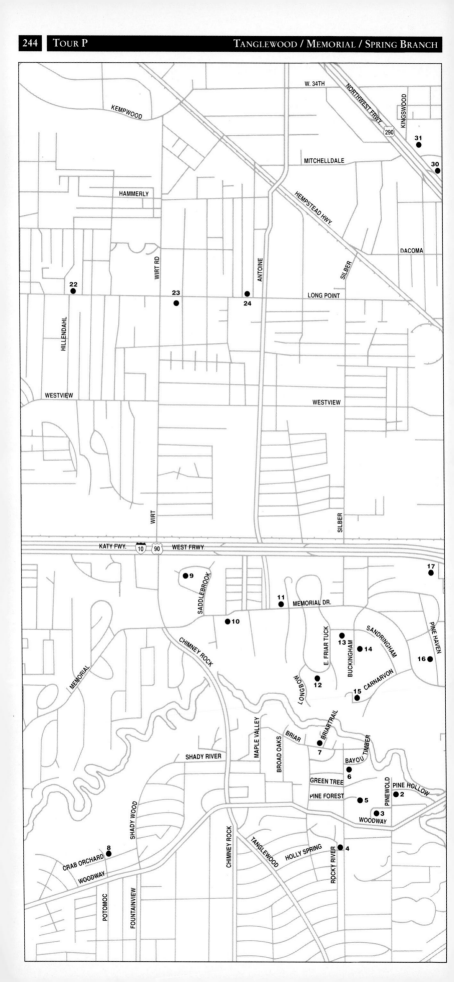

1. 4501 Woodway
2. 275 Pine Hollow Lane
3. 516 South Post Oak Lane, No. 10
4. 695 Rocky River Road
5. 7 Pine Forest Circle
6. 5135 Bayou Timber Lane
7. 2 Briar Trail
8. 6050 Crab Orchard Street
9. 33 Saddlebrook Street
10. 9845 Memorial Drive
11. 9704 Memorial Drive
12. 306 East Friar Tuck Lane
13. 9301 Sandringham Lane
14. 328 Buckingham Drive
15. 111 Carnarvon Drive
16. 431 Pinehaven Lane
17. 7401 Katy Freeway
18. 730 North Post Oak Road
19. 8550 Memorial Drive
20. 3535 West 12th Avenue
21. 7026 Old Katy Road
22. 8224 Long Point Road
23. 7803 Long Point Road
24. 7410 Long Point Road
25. 2020 Mangum Road
26. 4400, 4500, and 4550 Dacoma Road
27. 2550 North Loop West
28. 2600 North Loop West
29. 2900-2950 North Loop West
30. 10750 Northwest Freeway
31. 10810 Northwest Freeway

4501 Woodway   **P-1**
Houston Arboretum and Nature Center.
Aline McAshan Botanical Hall for Children
(1968) Neuhaus-Wingfield Associates

This concrete-framed pavilion is not one of
Hugo Neuhaus's most memorable buildings but it lends a note of urbanity to the
155-acre Arboretum. Exhibitions are set up
inside the building and one can also obtain
there instructions for a self-guided tour of
the grounds, which contain a number of
ecological settings characteristic of the
Houston region. The Houston Arboretum
and Nature Center is located in Memorial
Park. This forested, 1,500-acre tract was
acquired by Will C. Hogg's Varner Realty
Co., which sold it at cost and on very generous terms to the City of Houston in 1924
for use as a public park. Prior to Hogg's
acquisition of the site, it had been part of
Camp Logan, Houston's temporary World
War I training base, and the park is dedicated to the Houstonians who died in the war.
It is the largest park in the center of the city
and despite intensive use still preserves
much of its aboriginal character.

275 Pine Hollow Lane   **P-2**
(1956) Harwood Taylor

Harwood Taylor successfully domesticated
the strict architectural discipline of the
Miesian courtyard house in order to produce single-family houses that accommo-
dated their upper-middle-income occupants
without unduly diluting the architecture.
At the west end of this street lies **300
Pinewold Drive** (1933, John F. Staub—not
visible from the street), an evocation of a
colonial farm house that makes one feel as
though one had indeed been transported to
Connecticut.

516 South Post Oak Lane, No. 10   **P-3**
(1983) Anthony E. Frederick

Overshadowed by the huge bulk of **The
Decorative Center of Houston** at 5120
Woodway (1984, Morris*Aubry Architects)

is this slight, self-effacing, but elegant
townhouse.

695 Rocky River Road   **P-4**
(1955) Wilson, Morris, Crain & Anderson

Tanglewood, where this house is located,
was begun by William G. Farrington in
1948 as the postwar successor to River
Oaks, a status it never quite attained. This
was not because it lacked respectability.
Rather, Tanglewood lacks diversity and distinction. The full impact of the Eisenhower
era is visible here, matured and well maintained: big, low, one-story houses on large,
flat lots. One of the very few exceptions to
the prevailing stodginess is this flat-roofed
contemporary style house designed by
Ralph A. Anderson, Jr., with its eroded corner bay held firmly in place by the fascia's
ruling horizontal.

7 Pine Forest Circle   **P-5**
(1956) Joseph Krakower

This house is another Herb Greene production, as can be deduced from the way that
the heavy-lidded flat roof curves outward
in response to its setting at the end of a cul-
de-sac. One street to the north is Green
Tree Road, where a series of houses by
well-known architects are located: **5135
Green Tree** (1962, Staub, Rather &
Howze), **5027** (1968, Ford, Powell &
Carson), and **5008 and 5005** (1966,
Hamilton Brown). None are outstanding,
but the view from the end of the cul-de-sac
is. Green Tree is the power street in
Houston; this is George Bush territory.

5135 Bayou Timber Lane　　　**P-6**
(1969) Howard Barnstone & Eugene Aubry

In response to the clients' collection of American furniture, Barnstone and Aubry designed a house of many gables, fitted with bay windows and exquisitely finished with wood clapboards. The result is so lovely that it is disconcerting to find that the gables are merely picturesque volumetric protrusions above what is essentially a flat roof. The horizontally battened wood wall screening the motor court is quite striking. This house served as the prototype for most of Eugene Aubry's subsequent domestic production.

2 Briar Trail　　　**P-7**
(1961) Wilson, Morris, Crain & Anderson

Talbott Wilson designed this house for his family, a low, flat-roofed pavilion of glue-laminated post-and-beam construction surfaced on the street side with stucco-finished, redwood-framed panels and redwood screens. The overhanging roof slabs give the house a floating quality. At **1 Briar Trail** (which looks like a driveway but is a street) one can barely glimpse the ski-slope shed roof of an otherwise invisible, but huge, house by Frank Welch & Associates (1972). A block west, off Briar Drive, is Broad Oaks Circle, a cul-de-sac where **102 Broad Oaks** (1977, Frank Welch & Associates) and **202 Broad Oaks** (1971, Clovis Heimsath Associates) are totally occluded by foliage.

6050 Crab Orchard Street　　　**P-8**
(1966) A. Hays Town

This house, an adaptation of a one-story Greek revival cottage, is so subtle that one could drive by without noticing it. Yet the composition, the proportions, the pitch of the slate-covered roof, and the contrast between the stucco-surfaced front elevation and the brick side walls are rendered with

cool authority. Town, a Baton Rouge architect, is the last of the great eclectics.

33 Saddlebrook Street　　　**P-9**
(1955) Wilson, Morris, Crain & Anderson

Dean Emerson built this contemporary style house with planks of Styrofoam, sprayed on both sides with cement to enable it to carry the load of the roof. *Architectural Record* quipped that here the insulation had become the wall. The house is located in the subdivision of Saddlebrook, which was developed on a portion of the 300-acre Detering country estate, one of a series of weekend places built by wealthy Houstonians in the area during the 1930s. Construction of **The Park Laureate** at 10000 Memorial Drive (1986, House/Reh Associates) precipitated demolition of the Detering Lodge, designed by the New York architect Frank J. Forster. Still extant is the house of the Misses Detering at **10002 Memorial** (1958, Staub, Rather & Howze—not visible from the street), although its future is in doubt.

9845 Memorial Drive　　　**P-10**
St. Mary's Seminary (1954)
Maurice J. Sullivan-Charles F. Sullivan

Constructed on a 50-acre site in what was the country, this small complex of classroom and dormitory buildings, a chapel, and a refectory for the Roman Catholic diocesan seminary was Sullivan's last multi-building commission. He carried it out in the Lombard Romanesque style with which he had made his reputation three decades before at the Villa de Matel.

9704 Memorial Drive **P-11**
(1950)

Colonial New England was here transplanted to the woods of Memorial without concession to climate or landscape.

306 East Friar Tuck Lane **P-12**
(1971) Armon E. Mabry

Mabry went all the way on this, his last major work. It is a not-quite-symmetrically composed limestone-faced 17th-century French chateau; its construction contributed to the original client's financial undoing. The garden parterre that leads up to the house is flanked by exposed aggregate-paved driveways, an amusing commentary on the desire to combine authenticity and modern convenience.

9301 Sandringham Lane **P-13**
(1930) John F. Staub

Although altered, this tiny house still retains its original appearance. It was built as a Greek revival folly, a "gate house" for the weekend lodge of the W. T. Carter, Jr., family. In 1945 the Carter estate was redeveloped as the Sherwood Forest subdivision (hence the street names: Friar Tuck, Little John, Longbow). Staub's Carter Lodge is extant at 331 West Friar Tuck Lane (although it actually faces Longbow), but so disfigured by intemperate additions as to be unrecognizable. Down the mysteriously

crooked Longbow Lane is a notable collection of houses, but only one is visible from the street. These include **7 Longbow** (1969, Neuhaus-Wingfield Associates), **4 Longbow** (1976, W. Irving Phillips, Jr.), **3 Longbow** (1968, O'Neil Ford & Associates), and **2 Longbow** (1956, Wilson, Morris, Crain & Anderson).

328 Buckingham Drive **P-14**
(1954) Hermon Lloyd & W. B. Morgan

Hidden behind screen walls of pink Mexican brick, this linear modern house, planned and detailed in the manner of the Los Angeles architect Richard Neutra, conceals a curvilinear patio garden laid out by the San Francisco landscape architect Thomas D. Church. The flat, featureless front yard does not do justice to the house. At the end of the street, at **329 Buckingham**, is another modern house by Lloyd & Morgan (1958).

111 Carnarvon Drive **P-15**
(1960) Alden B. Dow

The Midland, Michigan, architect Alden B. Dow lived in Houston during the 1940s, when he planned the new town of Lake Jackson, 45 miles south of Houston, for the Dow Chemical Company. His only major building in Houston, however, is this large, flat house for a Dow corporate executive. It is organized around a courtyard, visible through the wood lattice screen. The thickness of the porte-cochere canopy suggests the scale of this house.

Across the street, and visible through the line of trees during the winter, is the side elevation of a house at **101 Carnarvon Drive**, a magnificent English Regency style country house (1939, John F. Staub). The owner's brother-in-law, William Stamps Farish, stabled his polo ponies on the tract of land now traversed by Carnarvon Drive, which was subdivided in 1941 to become the neighborhood of Bayou Woods. Along Carnarvon are Staub's last great house at **215 Carnarvon** (1962, now encrusted with fussy balustrades) and an elegant modern house by Harwood Taylor at **310 Carnarvon** (1956). Nearby is the last unsubdivided weekend estate in the area, the 100-acre Wiess stable tract (behind the white rail fence at Memorial and North Post Oak Lane). This contains the opulent stable and party house, a sort of private country club, by John F. Staub (1931—not visible from the street).

431 Pinehaven Lane   P-16
(1985) Compendium

Josiah R. Baker designed this ultra-postmodern house, faced with a base course of Mexican sandstone, panels of rose-colored stucco, and a roof of slate, subtly mixed in color. Square-sectioned windows and pyramidal roof shapes give it a picturesque aspect. Baker detailed interior fixtures and was responsible for furniture and fabric design as well. Herbert Pickworth was the landscape architect.

7401 Katy Freeway   P-17
First Baptist Church of Houston
(1976) S. I. Morris Associates

From the freeway, all that is visible is the educational wing, which is wrapped around the quarter-circular church, a 5,000-seat auditorium. The adjoining Christian Life Center, visible at the juncture of the Katy Freeway and Loop 610, is by Denny, Ray & Wines (1985).

730 North Post Oak Road   P-18
Antares Building (1969) Rapp Tackett Fash

Gerald Tackett explored the aesthetic possi-

bilities of precast concrete construction in this four-story office building. The canted sun-shade panels give a sense of depth to the elevations.

8550 Memorial Drive   P-19
Bayou Club (1940) John F. Staub

This small clubhouse—not visible from the street—represents Staub's adaptation of a Louisiana Creole plantation house. It looks very much at home in its forest clearing.

3535 West 12th Avenue   P-20
Big Three Industries Building
(1974) MacKie & Kamrath

This extraordinary corporate office building adapts the formal organizational principles of Frank Lloyd Wright's Unity Temple to the program of a multi-story office building. Both the building and the site details are solidly executed in cast-in-place concrete.

7026 Old Katy Road   P-21
Interior Resources Center
(1984, 1985) House/Reh Associates

Furniture and interior systems showrooms are housed here in a campus-like setting. Two and three-story buildings, connected by open-air corridors, are arranged around a shallow lake and—inevitably in Houston—a parking lot.

8224 Long Point Road   **P-22**
Spring Branch Savings & Loan Assoc.
Building (1956) Burdette Keeland and
Clyde Jackson

The Spring Branch area, located north of
Memorial, was developed during Houston's
great decade of suburban expansion, the
1950s. Long Point was a major commercial
strip and along it Burdette Keeland
designed this small, steel-framed, flat-
roofed Miesian pavilion. The shallow portico of the original pavilion has been filled in
to expand interior space and the building
has been joined by companions at 8210 and
8226. None is especially well maintained.

7803 Long Point Road   **P-23**
Long Point National Bank Building
(1957) MacKie & Kamrath

Battered planes of brick counter horizontally out-thrust canopies in this ex-bank
building, which represents an organic retort
to the "less-is-more" competition up the
street.

7410 Long Point Road   **P-24**
Long Point Clinic Building
(1957) Joseph Krakower

Herb Greene affixed delicate tubular projections to this little suburban clinic building. These are roofed with corrugated green
fiberglass, just the kind of tacky, modern
industrial material that Greene's mentor,
Bruce Goff, delighted in using.

2020 Mangum Road   **P-25**
James M. Delmar Field House
(1958) Milton McGinty

The thin-shell paraboloid roof canopy of
this gymnasium represents a comparatively
rare local use of a technology that was quite
popular in American architecture during
the late 1950s and early 1960s.

4400, 4500, and 4550 Dacoma Road   **P-26**
Humble Oil & Refining Co. Brookhollow
[now Exxon Brookhollow] (1971, 1972,
1975) Pierce Goodwin Flanagan

Sun control and the expression of cast-in-
place concrete construction were the architectural determinants of these three
corporate office buildings. They are located
in Brookhollow, a 170-acre mixed-use
development that was an early scene of
design-conscious office building in
Houston. It was the Humble Brookhollow
buildings that set the standard.

2550 North Loop West   **P-27**
2550 Brookhollow Building
(1975) Richard Fitzgerald & Partners

The Tenneco Building downtown served as
a model for this restrained, seven-story
office building, built by Russo Properties.

2600 North Loop West   **P-28**
Bridgestone One Building
(1976) Richard Fitzgerald & Partners

On the heels of Pennzoil Place, parallelo-
gram-plan buildings with unconventional
fenestration signalled the first step toward

more adventurous office building design taken by several Houston architectural offices. Here, Fitzgerald highlighted the folding back of the wall planes by dropping the sill levels of the window bands.

2900-2950 North Loop West   P-29
Brookhollow Central II and Brookhollow
Central III buildings
(1980 and 1982) 3D/International

The intersection of Loop 610 and the Northwest Freeway provided just the site for the play of oval geometries embodied in these two speculative office buildings, both constructed by P.I.C. Realty Co. The curtain walls of bronze solar glass and bronze anodized aluminum are souped up with red sill-level racing stripes.

10750 Northwest Freeway   P-30
Keystone Plaza
(1986) W. O. Neuhaus Associates

Neuhaus developed the design of this strip shopping center from the image of the false-fronted western frontier town, a relevant architectural analogy to the expedient real estate practices that transpire along freeway frontage roads in Texas. It is rendered here with wit and style. Behind the shopping center, at 2855 Mangum Road, is the unconventionally organized **Biehl Building**, a

five-story office building with integrated parking (1980, W. O. Neuhaus Associates).

10810 Northwest Freeway   P-31
Willis Flow Control Division of
Cameron Iron Works Building
(1980) Lockwood, Andrews & Newnam

The diagonally raked sectional cutaway of this small corporate office building gives it considerable presence in its freeway setting.

Mid
Westheimer /
Villages

Nowhere is the "anything goes" image that adheres to Houston more blatantly displayed than along the stretch of Westheimer Road between Chimney Rock Street and South Gessner Road. Middle-class subdivisions of the 1950s flank this strip, but they are hidden behind broad bands of commercial development that face Westheimer. Most of these date from the 1960s and early '70s, when Houston's suburbanizing ethos was at its least constrained. Not only do shopping centers, gas stations, and fast-food restaurants line up along Westheimer—each flashing signs or theme-styled inducements to passersby—but mega-garden apartment complexes compete for attention in a mixture of dimly recognizable "traditional" styles. The order of the strip is economic, rather than visual or experiential. The biggest-grossing land uses get the prime frontage.

Movement perpendicular to the strip entails passage through a descending hierarchy of economic generators before arriving at the restricted enclaves of single-family residences that the layers of development insulate. In some instances, developers have manipulated values by moving from the inside out, using inner layers of development to stimulate the attractiveness of the prime frontage for some purpose, such as a multistory office building, that might not be feasible otherwise. And one should not be surprised at encountering large tracts of undeveloped land, as in the 8000 blocks of Westheimer. This is merely a particularly dramatic example of the way in which Houston has grown by distension and subsequent infilling, rather than by a neat process of incremental extension.

Memorial Drive, between Chimney Rock and Gessner, is the antithesis of Westheimer Road. Between 1954 and 1956, the large agglomeration of subdivisions in what is now the center of Memorial obtained incorporation as six independent municipalities. The City of Houston acquiesced to this arrangement, but in 1957 annexed a strip surrounding all six towns. Zoning codes limit property use within the "villages," as they are collectively known, almost exclusively to single-family residences, often with minimum plot sizes of an acre or more. Schools and churches are the most visible exceptions to the single-family rule; commercial development is almost all concentrated along the Katy Freeway. As a result, Memorial Drive (which has been defiantly kept to a narrow road, flanked by open drainage ditches, which makes a series of right angle turns) is lined with expensive, if prosaic, houses. For despite economic affluence and dense vegetation, the Memorial villages are monotonous. The seemingly infinite repetition of the big, one-story house on the flat, wooded site becomes oppressive, the more so since almost all vestiges of Memorial's recent past as a rustic forest have been sacrificed for subdivision development.

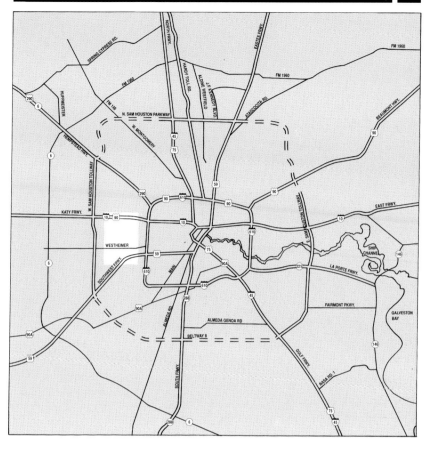

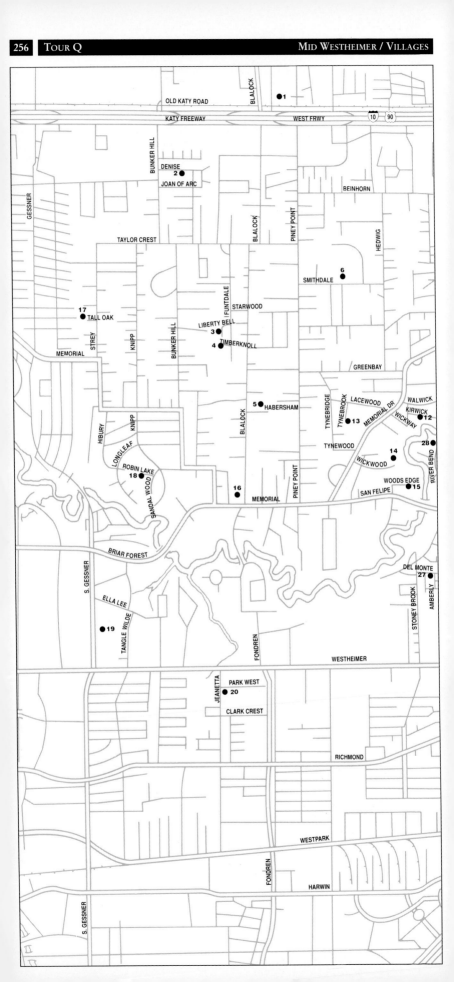

OLD KATY ROAD

BLALOCK

●1

KATY FREEWAY

WEST FRWY

10 90

BUNKER HILL

GESSNER

DENISE
2 ●

JOAN OF ARC

BEINHORN

PINEY POINT

BLALOCK

HEDWIG

TAYLOR CREST

SMITHDALE

6
●

STARWOOD

FUNTDALE

17
● TALL OAK

STREY

KNIPP

BUNKER HILL

LIBERTY BELL
3 ●

MEMORIAL

4 ● TIMBERKNOLL

GREENBAY

5 ● HABERSHAM

BLALOCK

TYNEBRIDGE

LACEWOOD

WALWICK

TYNEBROOK

MEMORIAL DR

KIRWICK

13
●

WICKWAY

12
●

HIBURY

KNIPP

LONGLEAF

TYNEWOOD

28
●

RIVER BEND

ROBIN LAKE

14
●

18 ●

SANDAL WOOD

WICKWOOD

WOODS EDGE

16
●

PINEY POINT

15
●

MEMORIAL

SAN FELIPE

BRIAR FOREST

DEL MONTE

27
●

S. GESSNER

ELLA LEE

AMBERLY

STONEY BROOK

TANGLE WILDE

19 ●

FONDREN

WESTHEIMER

JEANETTA

PARK WEST

20
●

CLARK CREST

RICHMOND

WESTPARK

FONDREN

S. GESSNER

HARWIN

1. 9430 Old Katy Road
2. 11730 Denise Street
3. 26 Liberty Bell Circle
4. 11715 Timberknoll Drive
5. 11510 Habersham
6. 11220 Smithdale Road
7. 203 Timberwilde
8. 108 Timberwilde
9. 414 Thamer Lane
10. 624 Shartle Circle
11. 10709 Memorial Drive
12. 10923 Kirwick Street
13. 323 Tynebrook Lane
14. 11010 Wickwood Drive
15. 9 Woods Edge Lane
16. 11612 Memorial Drive
17. 12020 Tall Oaks Road
18. 21 Robin Lake Lane
19. 2401 South Gessner Road
20. 8951 Park West Drive
21. 3838 Hillcroft Avenue
22. 3115-3121 Fountain View Street
23. 2929 Unity Drive
24. 2744 Briarhurst Drive
25. 2511 Nantucket Drive
26. 6126 Meadowlake Lane
27. 2110 Amberly Court
28. 1014 River Bend Street
29. 6400 Woodway

9430 Old Katy Road   **Q-1**
9430 Old Katy Road Building [now
Guardian Plans, Inc. Building] (1981)
House/Reh Associates

Stacked trays of office space, underscored
with white horizontal banding, endow this
four-story office building with a strong,
uncomplicated image.

11730 Denise Street   **Q-2**
St. Cecilia Catholic Church
(1978) Charles Tapley Associates

Built of brick bearing wall construction,
with structural masonry arches, the low,
square-planned church rises up into a low-
pitched pyramidal roof. Additions to the
parish complex are by Tapley Lunow
Architects (1989); the parish school was
designed by the Cincinnati architect
Edward J. Schulte (1958).

26 Liberty Bell Circle   **Q-3**
(1964) MacKie & Kamrath

With this house Kamrath embarked on an
exploration of Frank Lloyd Wright's early
work that was to mark his production of the
1970s. The model here is Wright's Isabel
Roberts House in River Forest, Illinois
(1908), with its story-and-a-half living room
thrust forward of the body of the house.

11715 Timberknoll Drive   **Q-4**
(1969) Caudill Rowlett Scott

Charles E. Lawrence of CRS designed this
triangular-plan house set beneath a high-
pitched roof. Its glazed perimeter is ringed

with a shallow moat. To the north, at **676
Flintdale Road**, is another CRS-designed
house, this the work of Thomas Bullock
(1964).

11510 Habersham   **Q-5**
(1941) J. T. Rather, Jr.

This was Rather's own house, originally set
on a small estate along Blalock Road. The
one- and two-story house was designed in a
non-doctrinaire modern style obviously
inspired by the mid-19th-century vernacular buildings of central Texas. Subdivision
of the property and unsympathetic alterations have compromised the house's
appearance.

11220 Smithdale Road   **Q-6**
(c. 1900)

The Smith ranch house complex—the main
house and several outbuildings—survives in
a large, flat meadow. Until the late 1930s
when suburban country houses began to be
built along what became Memorial Drive,
such rural homesteads were the only settlements in this dense pine forest. The Smith
House preserves, for now, an archetypal
Texas landscape setting: the one-story
wooden ranch house in a shady grove of
mature live oak trees, with its outbuildings
scattered about. Now hedged in with
ranchburger subdivisions, this complex
embodies a sense of the Memorial villages'
historic, presuburban character.

203 Timberwilde   **Q-7**
(1958) Thomas M. Price

Thomas M. Price, Galveston's foremost modernist architect, was responsible for this large one-story house. Masonry solar screens and a dynamically configured porte-cochere canopy give it a light, buoyant aspect.

108 Timberwilde   **Q-8**
(1967) Richard S. Colley

The Corpus Christi architect Richard S. Colley produced here one of his finest houses. Colley's aptitude for detailing materials and his precision at linear composition are displayed in the dun-colored brick wall surfaces and the thin projecting roof slab of this one-story house. The pyramid that rises above the center of the house shields an internal courtyard.

414 Thamer Lane   **Q-9**
(1969) MacKie & Kamrath

The composition and proportions, the handling of materials, and the telling decorative details visible in this house make one aware of how architecturally impoverished the Memorial villages are by comparison, and how architecturally rich they might have been. Hunterwood, the small subdivision where this house is located, is a case in point, despite the presence there of distinguished modern houses at **407 Thamer Circle** (1974, William T. Cannady, Anderson Todd and Raymond Brochstein), **443 Hunterwood** (1972, Charles Tapley Associates), **347 Hunters Trail** (1968, Ford, Powell & Carson), and a marvelously idiosyncratic house in the spirit of Bruce

Goff at **311 Hunters Trail** (1976) by Dr. Davey E. Lieb, an amateur architect. Ironically, Goff designed a house to be built at 414 Thamer Circle in 1971, but the clients opted for something more conventional instead.

624 Shartle Circle   **Q-10**
(1941) John F. Staub

Staub's partner, J. T. Rather, Jr., designed this Texas regional style country house on a large site that was subdivided in the 1960s into ranchburger estates. Its planar walls and tight, low-pitched roof recall the 19th-century Alsatian buildings of Castroville in central Texas. The lean-to gallery, infilled with big-scaled trellis work, introduces a shallow spatial layering characteristic of Rather's houses. Despite inappropriate alterations and the subtraction of an entire wing, this house radiates quiet superiority in the midst of numbing mediocrity.

10709 Memorial Drive   **Q-11**
Houston Racquet Club
(1969) MacKie & Kamrath

In addition to his architectural career, Karl Kamrath was a nationally-ranked tennis player and a founding member of the Houston Racquet Club. Thus the disappointing quality of the clubhouse comes as a surprise. The use of white brick robs the walls of the textural richness and density one expects of Kamrath. And the insensitive despoiling of the site to provide space for parked cars and tennis courts leaves the building unrelated to any natural feature. Down a driveway to the right of the clubhouse and past the tennis courts is the building that has occupied this site since it was a country estate, a compact two-story, dark brick house in the Texas regional style by J. T. Rather, Jr. (1941).

10923 Kirwick Street   **Q-12**
(1961) Caudill Rowlett Scott

William W. Caudill produced this house for his family. The tall shingled hood encloses a 36-foot high living room; the low, horizon-

tal eaves line denotes the 6-foot, 9-inch height of the adjoining dining room. As Caudill himself explained it: "My house says: 'I like contrast.'"

323 Tynebrook Lane **Q-13**
(1960) Bruce Goff with Joseph Krakower

This house by the Oklahoma (later Tyler, Texas) architect Bruce Goff is extraordinary. Subtly curved in plan in response to its location on a cul-de-sac, it carries the circular theme to a logical conclusion in the witty round windows that project (volumetrically, inside) above the thin, sloped roof membrane. Molded brick frames these windows; Herb Greene, a former student of Goff's, supervised construction. The two families who succeeded the original clients in residence were so devoted to the house that each had Goff carry out alterations and additions, the last set completed a year before his death in 1982.

11010 Wickwood Drive **Q-14**
(1963) MacKie & Kamrath

Over 300 feet in length, this is an organic mansion, built of river boulders from central Texas and enclosed with a low-pitched stepped roof surfaced with limestone pebbles and copper battens. Its 12,500-square-foot expanse is organized on a 30°-60° reflexive grid; angled wings project dramatically from a central spine into the bayou landscape. James Dalrymple of Dallas was the landscape architect. MacKie & Kamrath also designed the Wickwood subdivision

entry piers at Wickwood and Memorial (1963).

9 Woods Edge Lane **Q-15**
(1978) Robert E. Griffin

So wooded is this site that the house is difficult to see, even though it verges on the street. What is visible is a taut, stucco-surfaced elevation, containing a row of high-set clerestory windows. These underscore the linear organization of the house, but conceal its internal vistas and a parallel plane of glass through which the interior is opened to the forested landscape. Just up the street, at **13 Woods Edge**, is another reclusive modern house by W. O. Neuhaus Associates (1973).

11612 Memorial Drive **Q-16**
Memorial Drive Presbyterian Church
(1959, 1972) MacKie & Kamrath

Built of randomly coursed slabs of limestone, this large church complex is a striking sight. The soaring profile of the steel-framed roof of the church (1972) culminates at its apex in an unconventional carillon, suspended from the tip of the beam. The church, chapel, and educational building, planned around two internal courtyards, display exuberant organic decoration. Its leitmotif, the red square, was Frank Lloyd Wright's architectural insignia.

12020 Tall Oaks Road **Q-17**
(1954) Frank Lloyd Wright

This small concrete-block house (originally unpainted) is so perverse that it has engendered several sets of alteration intended to make it more liveable. The house is closed on the south (approach side) and opens to the north, which might be environmentally appropriate for a desert setting, but not for a hot, humid, coastal forest. Most of the interior space is concentrated in a long living room, equipped with banquette seating. As a result, the bedrooms are reduced to claustrophobic proportions and, because the house is planned on a 30°-60° reflexive grid, they are parallelograms. (Wright detailed parallelogram bunk beds and an organic TV antenna for the house, neither in place now.) Despite its quirkiness, Wright's hand is clearly evident: the prow-shaped master bedroom, for instance, induces an intense sensation of spatial projection, and the subtly battered profiling of the exterior walls rhythmically counters the horizontal extension of the redwood eaves. Given the copious tributes paid to Wright in the work of MacKie & Kamrath, it is disappointing that the master's one local building should be so willful and contrary.

21 Robin Lake Lane   Q-18
(1974) Howard Barnstone

This house is so self-effacing that it hides its true nature from the street. Barnstone reworked an existing house (the first independent work of Frank D. Welch, 1956), extensively altering the flat-roofed original and adding to it a series of glazed concourses that open out to a lush landscape garden. The sensational effect that results can just barely be experienced vicariously in a view through the front door, which is virtually the only feature that presents itself to the street. Next door, at **7 Robin Lake Lane** (1961), is a one- and two-story modern house surfaced with concrete, stone, wood, and masonry solar screens—and a spectacular sectional picture window that reveals an open-riser stair.

2401 South Gessner Road   Q-19
Esso Eastern of New Jersey Building [now Exxon Coal and Minerals Co.] (1971) Charles Tapley Associates and Robert Husmann & Associates

Tapley was involved in the initial planning of Friendswood Development Co.'s Woodlake, a mixed-use office, retail, and residential project, and he was able to carry forward some of his proposals for building responsibly in nature with the design of this three-part corporate office building. The buildings, glass pavilions shaded by their exposed concrete structural frames, are set atop a podium above underground parking.

The podium level can be approached from the garage below by way of a sunken central courtyard. Esso Eastern is an object in the landscape rather than an extension of it. But it seeks to work with, not in spite of, its surroundings. The Tapley office also designed the **Woodlake Recreation Center** (1971) at the northwest corner of Tanglewilde Avenue and Ella Lee Lane.

8951 Park West Drive   Q-20
Southwestern Bell Telephone Co. Area Accounting Center [now Southwestern Bell Telephone Co. Switch Center] (1978) Caudill Rowlett Scott

Tucked away on a back street adjacent to Piney Point, a small black community encircled by Houston's suburban growth, is this impressive corporate office building. A matte-finished aluminum panel wall system gives the center a taut, planar look, reinforced by flush-set glazing and shallow incisions that reveal the red-clad structural frame within. On the rear (southern) side, windows are recessed in wide bays to provide views of a tree-shaded lawn.

3838 Hillcroft Avenue   Q-21
Hillcroft Professional Building (1967) Jenkins Hoff Oberg Saxe

The programmatic components of this suburban office building are differentiated dramatically. The service core sits to one side of the office block, which is cantilevered far beyond the perimeter of the ground floor. Windows are spaced randomly, an effect enhanced by the rhythmic alternation of concrete fins. The vocabulary is that of the New Brutalism, which William R. Jenkins articulated frequently in the late 1960s.

3115-3121 Fountain View Street   Q-22
The Mesa: A Better Home and Living Center [now Fountainview Plaza] (1985) Arquitectonica

If Houston lay in an earthquake zone, one might well draw the conclusion that some seismic disaster had thrown this four-story retail and office building seriously out of whack. Rest assured: it's just Arquitectonica. The skewed columns and racked floor plates are all part of the fun, as is the ironically monumental stair facing Richmond Avenue and the sinuously parapeted access ramp on the building's back side. Turquoise and red accentuate the positive.

2929 Unity Drive   Q-23
Unity Church of Christianity (1975) Rapp Tackett Fash

Gerald Tackett broached the possibility of a pyramid at his Memorial Lutheran Church; here he went all the way, bestowing the age-old authority of this hieratic shape (surfaced in gleaming gold anodized aluminum) on a suburban New Age congregation. The palm trees in the parking lot appropriately nuance Unity's on-the-Nile aspirations and serve to remind that, as the critic John Pastier has observed, Houston and Cairo both lie on the 30th parallel of latitude.

2744 Briarhurst Drive   Q-24
Trafalgar Place Condominiums (1976) Jake Williams

Trafalgar West (1963), which occupies this block-long street, was one of the first of the garden apartment mega-complexes that began to be built in this part of Houston in the middle 1960s. The condominium building, a later addition, is a fantasy style production, as was common with this building type. It is, however, composed, detailed, and landscaped with sufficient conviction and consistency to make the imagery at

least mildly notable. This was rarely the case with the giant complexes.

2511 Nantucket Drive   Q-25
Todd Townhouses (1982) William T. Cannady & Associates and Anderson Todd

Following an amendment to the deed restrictions that permitted construction of up to four houses on one lot, this nondescript neighborhood, Westhaven, was almost entirely redeveloped for high density, high rent housing. The result is singularly dreary. It is amazing that so much building should add up to so little urbanity. One of the few exceptions to this state of affairs is this cluster of gray, stucco-surfaced row houses. Their clarity, simplicity, and unpretentiousness make them seem absolutely extraordinary on a street teeming with obnoxious bores.

6126 Meadowlake Lane   Q-26
(1957) William N. Floyd

Like most of the post-World War II subdivisions along the Westheimer corridor, Briar Grove is long in the north-south direction but relatively narrow in the east-west direction. It is unusual in being heavily wooded and in possessing a collection of modern houses, although these tend to be spaced widely among more conventional models. This nifty flat-roofed house features a device seen time and again on modern houses built in this part of Houston during the 1950s: the porte-cochere in place of the front porch. Here it is combined with wall panels of thin Roman brick, lit by thin horizontal clerestory windows slotted between exposed glue-laminated wooden beams. Across the street at **6131 Meadowlake Lane** is a worthy companion by Hugh E. Gragg (1956). Two other modern houses are located at **2003 Briarmead Drive** (1959, Larson & Wingfield) and **6243 Olympia Drive** (1955, Harwood Taylor).

2110 Amberly Court   **Q-27**
(1988) C/A Architects

A thin gabled section, taut wall planes, and brilliantly striped surfaces make this row house by Ralph A. Anderson, Jr., stand out from its prosaic surroundings.

1014 River Bend Street   **Q-28**
(1963) Neuhaus & Taylor

Here the Miesian modern house of the 1950s has begun to metamorphose into a New Formalist pavilion. River Bend contains a number of architect-designed houses that display the disparate trends of the 1950s and early '60s: **1000 River Bend** (1957, Staub, Rather & Howze), **1001 River Bend** (1959, Cowell & Neuhaus), **1106 River Bend** (1955, Bruce Wallace), **7623 River Point Drive** (1958, Bolton & Barnstone), and **1010 Riverglyn Drive** (1967, Golemon & Rolfe).

6400 Woodway   **Q-29**
Second Baptist Church of Houston
(1986) Calhoun, Tungate, Jackson & Dill

When the sociologist of religion, William Martin, described Second Baptist Church as a "superchurch," he did not exaggerate. The

congregation's $25 million, 6,000-seat church, built adjacent to its existing neo-Georgian style complex (1961, Wirtz, Calhoun, Tungate & Jackson), defies simple characterization. It is inert externally yet phantasmagoric inside, where the vast octagonal worship space is decorated with oddly-spaced, quasi-classical pilasters, window walls of stained glass, and the steel dome that rides ambiguously above the outside of the container. The earlier church, though not outstanding, is legible architecturally; its supersuccessor is not. It is a blunt, ambivalent object rising awkwardly alongside a big parking lot, an archetype of the self-sufficient, enclosed, suburban environmental package that acknowledges no connections to or responsibility for the outside world.

Bellaire / Westbury / Sharpstown

Southwest Houston contains a succession of examples of the American suburb as it has evolved during the 20th century. Bellaire, an independent city since 1918, was started as a planned community, an early 20th-century version of Houston Heights, connected to the center of Houston by a long extension of the Main Street streetcar line. Like the Heights, this neighborhood of moderate-income residences was laid out with a central boulevard divided by a wide median, Bellaire Boulevard, as its chief civic feature. Also tied to Main Street and Bellaire Boulevard were the subdivisions developed along Brays and Willow Waterhole bayous in a patchwork array in the 1950s and '60s. Located on the treeless prairie, these were the ultimate middle-class white neighborhoods of southwest Houston. The most extensive of Houston's bayou parkways, along Brays Bayou, is an impressive civic achievement for the 1950s, a decade in which public-spirited planning in Houston was simply disregarded. Its existence is a tribute to Ralph Ellifrit, then director of the city's Department of City Planning, who compelled developers to donate property along the bayou for this parkway as a condition for approval of their plats.

Sharpstown, north of the bayou parkway, is a textbook example of community planning of the 1950s. It is joined to the center of Houston, nine miles distant, by the Southwest Freeway; Sharpstown's developer, Frank W. Sharp, coordinated the donation of a long stretch of right-of-way to ensure that the freeway be built through the middle of Sharpstown. Wide arterial thoroughfares divide neighborhoods, which are focused on schools, parks, and churches. There is a commercial center around the shopping mall, ringed with secondary retail, offices and apartments, a university campus, a large hospital, a medical professional center, office parks, an industrial sector, and a large public golf course. Sharpstown has all the components of a small city, but none of the characteristics—not even the compensatory urban gesture of a grand boulevard like Bellaire's, although Bellaire Boulevard is also Sharpstown's main street.

During the 1960s, Houston's middle-class Jewish community relocated upstream along the Brays Bayou Parkway to constitute the most visible ethnic presence within southwest Houston. It is now here that Houston's increasing racial and ethnic diversity is becoming evident as middle-class Hispanic and Asian families settle in these neighborhoods. The transformation of entire shopping strips along arterial streets into Chinese or Indian business enclaves exemplifies the quiet but radical change in images of middle-class normality that is occurring. The corner of Bellaire and Hillcroft, in the odd, mixed, residential and light industrial corridor between Bellaire and Sharpstown, is where an early Fiesta Mart store is located. This Houston grocery chain has been built by responding to the emerging demographic trends visible in southwest Houston, stocking an unusually wide array of international products in recognition of the fact that for increasing numbers of Houstonians these are not exotic specialties, just the necessities of everyday life.

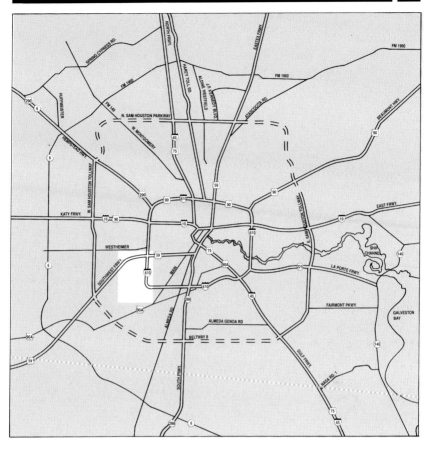

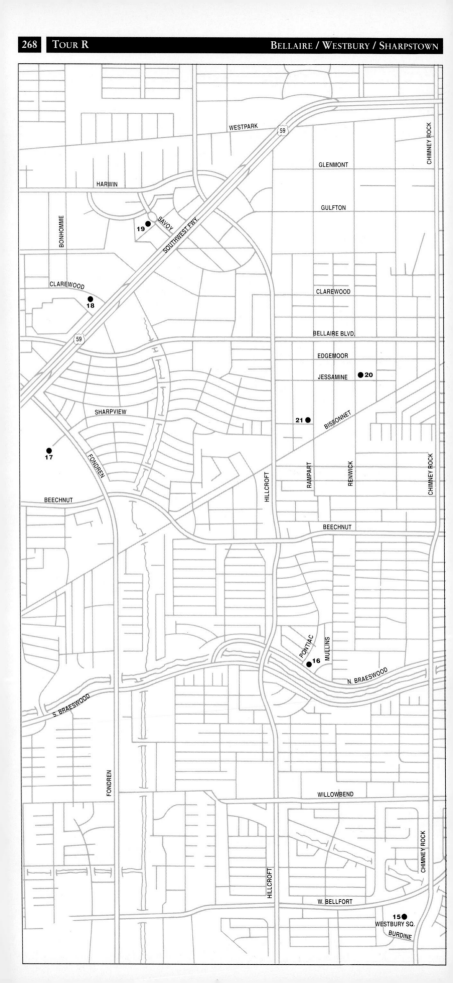

1. 4747 Southwest Freeway
2. 4800 Fournace Place
3. 6500 West Loop South
4. 4600 Bellaire Boulevard
5. 5301-A Bissonnet Avenue
6. 4900 Jackwood Street
7. 5146 Jackwood Street
8. 9602 Moonlight Street
9. 5043 Glenmeadow Drive
10. 10002 Willowgrove Drive
11. 10211 Willowgrove Drive
12. 10920 Willowisp Street
13. 4910 Willowbend Boulevard
14. 5515 Gasmer Street
15. 5300 block West Bellfort Boulevard
16. 5600 North Braeswood Boulevard
17. 7502 Fondren Road
18. 7255 Clarewood Street
19. 6161 Savoy
20. 7101 Renwick Street
21. 7336 Rampart Street

4747 Southwest Freeway   **R-1**
Houston Post Building (1970)
Wilson, Morris, Crain & Anderson

The office building and production plant of
the *Houston Post* appears to be a modern
castle. However, as is frequently the case
with American buildings designed in the
New Brutalist mode, it is a rectangular box
around which concrete silos have been picturesquely arrayed. The windowless chamfered turrets contain stairs, toilets,
air-conditioning equipment, and photo-
copying machines. The designer, Ralph A.
Anderson, Jr., here devised one of the first
examples of "freeway" architecture in
Houston: a building that projects a formal
image which is strong yet simple enough to
be apprehended from a speeding car.

4800 Fournace Place   **R-2**
Texaco Office Building
(1977) S. I. Morris Associates

This 10-story office building, designed by
Winton F. Scott, is V-shaped in plan to
maximize its north-south exposure. For
energy conservation purposes, its horizontal window bands also have a V-profile
which permits the admission of daylight
while screening out direct solar penetration.
As a result of its symmetrical composition
and repetitive window pattern, the building
presents a hieratic aspect that is rather overwhelming, especially when seen from
Fournace, where the central service core
abuts the street.

6500 West Loop South   **R-3**
Prudential Insurance Co. Building
(1977) S. I. Morris Associates

Eugene Aubry shaped the Prudential's ex-
regional corporate headquarters building
with great flair. Its grid of buff-colored,
precast concrete fins and lintels is broken to
induce shifts in scale that identify the front
entrance and emphasize the ends of the
three-block, 665-foot long building. The
fins facing the freeway are angled in plan to
ward off the east sun. Red porcelain racing
stripe headers above each window give the

building a special lilt; these running bands
of color enliven Prudential and put it in
tune with the flow of traffic on the West
Loop.

The loop passes here through the suburban city of Bellaire, whose "skyline" is
dominated by the work of the Morris
office. Across the freeway from Prudential
are **6565 and 6575 West Loop South** (1978
and 1980), both for McCord Development
Co. Farther south are the **Sperry Univac
Building** at 6700 West Loop South (1974),
the **Scientific Design Building** at 6750
(1977), the **San Jacinto Savings Building** at
6800 (1981), and, on Bellaire Boulevard, the
4710 Bellaire Building (1975) and the
Crown Central Petroleum Building at
4747 (1981), all built by John Hansen.

4600 Bellaire Boulevard   **R-4**
Faith American Lutheran Church (1959,
1963) Travis Broesche & Associates

During the late 1950s and early 1960s,
Broesche's firm produced a number of
buildings inspired by the architecture of
Frank Lloyd Wright. This church is the
finest work from that period. Bellaire
Boulevard, where it is located, is the central
thoroughfare in the town plan laid out in
1909 by the Kansas City landscape architect
Sid J. Hare. Hare also produced a community tree-planting plan to conceal the fact
that Bellaire sat in the midst of an open
prairie, four miles southwest of Houston.
The live oak trees within the generous
medians have done their work. These were
planted by the nurseryman Edward Teas,
whom the developer of Bellaire, W. W.
Baldwin, persuaded to settle in the new
community. Teas Nursery Co. still operates
from its original location at 4400 Bellaire
Boulevard.

5301-A Bissonnet Avenue   **R-5**
Southwestern Savings Association Building
(1960) Fleming Associates

The landscape architect C. C. Fleming produced this boomerang-shaped pavilion,
faced with canted panes of glass and a

dropped horizontal grill to shield it from the sun.

circular, steel-framed pavilion, capped with a folded plate roof, which is only part of a much larger contemporary style house.

4900 Jackwood Street   **R-6**
St. Thomas Episcopal Church
(1972) Harvin C. Moore

In the long continuum of Lombard Romanesque style churches in Houston, St. Thomas represents the last of the line. Its traditional look is somewhat at variance with the rest of the parish group, which is designed in a 1950s contemporary style.

5146 Jackwood Street   **R-7**
1955 Parade of Homes House
(1955) Burdette Keeland

These blocks of Meyerland, once characterized by Larry McMurtry as the dullest subdivision in Houston, were built out with 30 houses constructed for the Houston Home Builders Association's Parade of Homes in 1955. W. K. King broke ranks with the contemporary style ranch houses and allowed Keeland to produce this flat-roofed, steel-framed, Miesian courtyard house, furnished by the Knoll Planning Unit. It was so much more expensive to build than the other houses that King withheld the sales price. Yet despite flouting suburban conformity, the house is intact and well maintained. It is U-shaped in plan, organized around a small courtyard entered through the side-facing front door.

9602 Moonlight Street   **R-8**
(1964) Robert Cohen

This is a quite extraordinary production, a

5043 Glenmeadow Drive   **R-9**
(1961) Howard Barnstone & Partners

An oddly-shaped site on a cul-de-sac occasioned the design of this courtyard house, an implicit rebuke to the surrounding Meyerland ranchburgers. Barnstone emphasized privacy by walling out the environs and focusing internal spaces on a series of enclosed gardens. The hipped roof and clerestory windows identify the living-dining-kitchen pavilion. Because Barnstone so carefully modulated the house's exterior surfaces, they do not appear blank or dull. The other houses on the cul-de-sac took note. That at **5035 Glenmeadow** is by Israel Stein (1962); that at **5039** is a scream.

10002 Willowgrove Drive   **R-10**
(1960) William R. Jenkins

The architect's own house, a series of framed pavilions cranked in plan in response to its corner site.

10211 Willowgrove Drive   **R-11**
(1957) William R. Jenkins

Reflecting the popularity in Houston of a "Palladian" interpretation of modern architecture in the 1950s, this flat-roofed, steel-framed house is organized around an axis that proceeds from the vaulted carport-portico, through an open plan living area, across a rear patio, and culminates in a sun

deck on the bank of Willow Waterhole Bayou.

he left the office of Ludwig Mies van der Rohe. This pair of small, steel-framed buildings is precisely organized and carefully detailed, in the best Miesian tradition. Unfortunately, their exposed steel framing has been painted brown.

10920 Willowisp Street   **R-12**
(1956) William R. Jenkins

Jenkins was responsible for most of the houses in this little enclave of modernity, a cul-de-sac at the end of Willowisp, around which Willow Waterhole Bayou curves. This house emphasizes the thinness and linearity that advanced technology (incarnate in the exposed wood beams and slender steel columns) made possible. Jenkins also designed **10910** (1958) and **10911** (1956), where he and his family briefly lived.

5300 block West Bellfort Boulevard R-15
Westbury Square
(1960) William F. Wortham, Jr.

Ira Berne, developer of the Westbury subdivision, launched Westbury Square as an alternative to the conventional suburban shopping center. Centered on a circular plaza from which irregular pedestrian alleyways radiate, it is densely built. Berne filled the complex with specialty shops rather than chain stores, which made it attractive to a market beyond the surrounding subdivisions. Above many of the shops, adjacent to the plaza, and along both West Bellfort and Chimney Rock, Berne located apartments and townhouses to reinforce the urban character of the square. Unfortunately, the opening of the Galleria in 1970 precipitated a decline from which Westbury Square never recovered. Its kitsch Main Street-cum-Mediterranean village styling, shoddy design standards, lack of visibility from surrounding streets, and confusing layout have frustrated attempts at revival.

4910 Willowbend Boulevard   **R-13**
Willowbend Medical and Dental Clinic
(1961) Wilson, Morris, Crain & Anderson

This pair of professional buildings, organized around internal courtyards and joined by a multilane drive-through, projects the "good design" ethos with which enlightened architects attempted to reform the expanding periphery of the city in the 1950s. The Willowbend Clinic, like the nearby Jenkins houses, is exceptional rather than typical in its milieu. But it demonstrates that, for a time at least, architecture was pursued as a serious response to middle-class life in the suburbs.

5515 Gasmer Street   **R-14**
Shell Pipe Line Co. Buildings (1961)
Cowell & Neuhaus, David Haid, Associate

The Chicago architect David Haid worked briefly with Hugo V. Neuhaus, Jr., just after

5600 North Braeswood Boulevard   R-16
Congregation Beth Israel Temple
(1967) Irving R. Klein & Associates

The New Formalism was the term coined to describe such buildings as Temple Beth

Israel, home of the oldest Jewish congregation in Texas. The peripheral colonnade which rises to a ceiling of plaster vaults, capped with a flat-lidded roof, has a vaguely classical look, although its immediate antecedents were contemporary: in particular, the work of the Michigan architect Minoru Yamasaki. The expressive wing of the Modern Movement is given its due with the drum-like bay that protrudes from one side of the building. New Formalism tried to annex the dignity of classical architecture; it aspired to make the new pretty and refined. At Beth Israel this works to some extent, because of the building's size and its siting on a large flat lawn around which the boulevard curves. Nonetheless, the temple is at best a period piece. Across Brays Bayou and slightly downstream is the **Jewish Community Center** at 5601 South Braeswood Boulevard (1969), also by the Klein office.

7502 Fondren Road   **R-17**
Houston Baptist University.
Academic and Student Center Building (1963) Hermon Lloyd & W. B. Morgan and Milton McGinty

Houston Baptist University occupies a 200-acre campus in Sharpstown, Houston's ultimate 1950s suburban real estate development. Begun in 1954, Sharpstown surpassed Levittown to become the largest subdivision in the U.S. Frank W. Sharp, the developer, sold this site to the newly-chartered school in 1958.

The Academic and Student Center Building is a local reaction (amusing for doctrinal as well as architectural reasons) to Philip Johnson's campus for the University of St. Thomas. The low, two-story building, configured around a large central courtyard, is faced with brick and glass, inset in an exposed structural frame, here of concrete rather than steel. As at St. Thomas, the scale is almost domestic, so that the building feels more like a high school than a university. What HBU lacks is the precision of Johnson's Miesian details, the clarity of his proportions, and the ambition to be noble rather than merely nice.

The approach drive from Fondren Road is a suburban landscape classic, a divided boulevard spatially modulated by tall, slender, aluminum light standards. The campus entrance is by Langwith Wilson King Associates (1987). Lloyd, Morgan & Jones designed the Edward Durell Stone-like **Atwood School of Theology** (1964). Behind the Academic and Student Center Building is a plaza containing a screen of free-standing columns salvaged from the

demolished Galveston County Courthouse in Galveston (1899, Messer, Sanguinet & Messer) and beyond this lie the **Mabee Teaching Center** and the **Cullen Science Center** buildings (1978, Golemon & Rolfe Associates). Southwest of these lies Houston's Baptist hospital, **Memorial Hospital** (1976, S. I. Morris Associates).

7255 Clarewood Street   **R-18**
Spa Building (1970)

Peter Papademetriou has likened this four-story building, its curtain wall recessed deeply behind a reticulated grid of square bays, to the Casa del Fascio by Giuseppe Terragni, one of the landmarks of European modern architecture of the 1930s. The Italian original faced the piazza of Como; the Houston homage, its reinforced concrete structural frame now painted an ignominious brown, lies near the heart of "downtown" Sharpstown, a loose cluster of multi-story apartment buildings and low-rise office buildings ringing **Sharpstown Center** (1961, Sidney H. Morris & Associates, reconstructed 1980, Nikita Zukov), the first air-conditioned shopping mall in Houston. Sharpstown is singularly bereft of distinctive architecture. Thus, this no doubt unintentional tribute to a classic of the Modern Movement must suffice as a local monument.

6161 Savoy   **R-19**
Texas Bank & Trust Tower
(1974) Lloyd Jones Associates

Regency Square, developed by Marvin E. Leggett & Associates, is one of a series of office parks along Harwin Drive, on Sharpstown's northern frontier. The formless layout of most of these developments and the bland architecture bespeak the rather low expectations that attended commercial development in Houston's suburbs through the 1960s. Regency Square represents the beginnings of the great reversal in design apathy. Lloyd Jones Associates' 12-story precast concrete-faced block and its twin, the **Colonial Savings Tower** at 6200 (1978), are unassertive but sufficiently considered in their design, detailing, and the spatial relationship they establish between them to attract notice. The faceted and reflective **Cowperwood Regency Building** at 6001 (1978) and the green **Texaco Oil Co. Computer Services Building** at 6464 (1980), both developed and designed by the New York architects Morse & Harvey, play off the solemnity of the Lloyd Jones buildings.

7101 Renwick Street   **R-20**
Kirby Building Systems Building (1975)
S. I. Morris Associates

Attached to what was the production plant of a pre-engineered metal buildings manufacturer, this two-story front office building is a disingenuously simple design of light steel framing infilled with solar glass window panes. The glass is deeply recessed along the Renwick frontage, providing space for ample plantings that perceptually dissolve easy distinctions between what is outside and what is not.

7336 Rampart Street   **R-21**
Houston Fine Art Press Building
(1987) Carlos Jiménez

Built to house the studio of an art printing establishment, this building occupies a long but very narrow lot in a mixed neighborhood of warehouses, light industry, and garden apartments between Sharpstown and Bellaire. Jiménez took advantage of the site constraints, extruding a gable-roofed bay, containing exhibition and office spaces, into a rear production area that spans the width of the lot. By cleverly manipulating the section, Jiménez opened a north-facing monitor in the roof to light the production area. The elementary geometries, intense pink stucco finish, and austere high-walled motor court of the Fine Art Press interact with the shaded strip of lawn alongside the front bay and the blue sky to produce an arresting and quite poignant image, "a little outpost of the faith beside its barbaric neighbors," as Wilhelm Hahn has written.

Peripheral Tours

New Houston, the latest phase in the ring cycle of Houston's concentric outward growth, is anchored by four planned communities: Clear Lake City on the southeast (now part of the City of Houston), Kingwood on the northeast, The Woodlands on the north, and First Colony on the southwest. Connected to downtown Houston by radial freeways, these communities represent a new vision of exurban life, one not dependent on access to the center—neither downtown nor the retail center at Post Oak—as a matter of necessity. Because these communities lie at a distance from the center and because they are surrounded by sufficient concentrations of middle-class population, they can support retail services commensurate with those of Post Oak, as well as attract employment centers, especially the outposts (sometimes even the headquarters) of major corporations, which choose to locate in the far suburbs because that is where their employees prefer to live. The completion of new freeway loops—the Sam Houston Parkway and, eventually, the Grand Parkway—will facilitate circumnavigation of the four quadrants of new Houston. No longer will drivers be required to pass through downtown, now understood not merely as the central business district but all the area within Loop 610.

Encompassed within the realms of new Houston are a number of existing communities whose identities are likely to remain intact. Along Houston's eastern frontier lie a series of towns, among them Pasadena, the second largest city in the county and the twelfth largest in the state. The paradisiacal associations of its California-inspired name notwithstanding, Pasadena is an industrial city on the south bank of the Houston Ship Channel, a 50-mile-long canal that the U. S. Army Corps of Engineers excavated between 1902 and 1914 to bring ocean-going vessels from the Gulf of Mexico through Galveston Bay and up Buffalo Bayou. The Ship Channel is the agent that transformed the fields of eastern Harris County into the densest concentration of petrochemical industries in Texas. Along with its neighbors on both sides of the channel, Pasadena is home to the largest concentration of white working-class families in the Houston area. Pasadena is also where Gilley's Club, the country-and-western music dance hall featured in "Urban Cowboy", was located. Pasadena emulated Houston's example in 1960 by annexing a huge portion of east Harris County, into which it is now expanding, casting off its older (post-World War II) sections with abandon.

Near Pasadena and its neighbor, Galena Park, rises the San Jacinto Monument, an astonishing sight in the midst of the ship channel's refinery row. On the east rim of the county, where Buffalo Bayou empties into Galveston Bay, is the old resort community of Bay Ridge, the most venerable in a series of resorts along the bayshore that turn inland to follow the curvature of Clear Lake, metamorphosing into new Houston suburbia along the way. Clear Lake City, the oldest of the four planned communities, was developed here in conjunction with the Johnson Space Center, an event

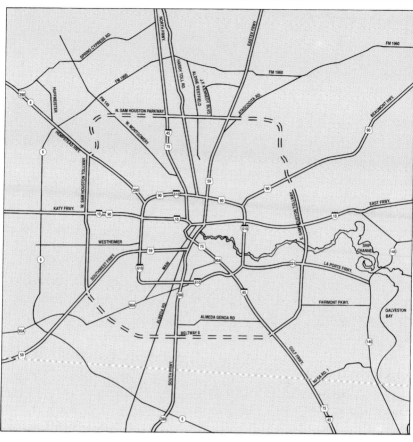

that caused Houston to style itself as Space City in the 1960s. West of Clear Lake, the rural towns of Friendswood and Pearland have been swept up and transformed by Houston's suburban growth, as have Humble, northeast of Houston Intercontinental Airport, and a string of tiny rural settlements along the western rim of Houston, which now survive largely as place names. Southwest of Houston, Sugar Land, an important agricultural-industrial center, has emerged from its long role as a company town to pursue annexation Houston-style. Like a serpent devouring much larger prey, it has consumed Sugar Creek and is presently digesting First Colony.

Outer Houston now gives the term Space City renewed currency. For it is the apparent limitlessness and elasticity of space that characterizes one's experience of the "city" that this vast territory comprehends. Yet even at the edges of new Houston, one finds traces of an older Texas, sometimes picturesque, more often tough, stubborn, and down at the heels, whether it be an ex-oil camp, a black rural enclave, or a slow-going crossroads settlement in no hurry to change, even though Houston is at the door.

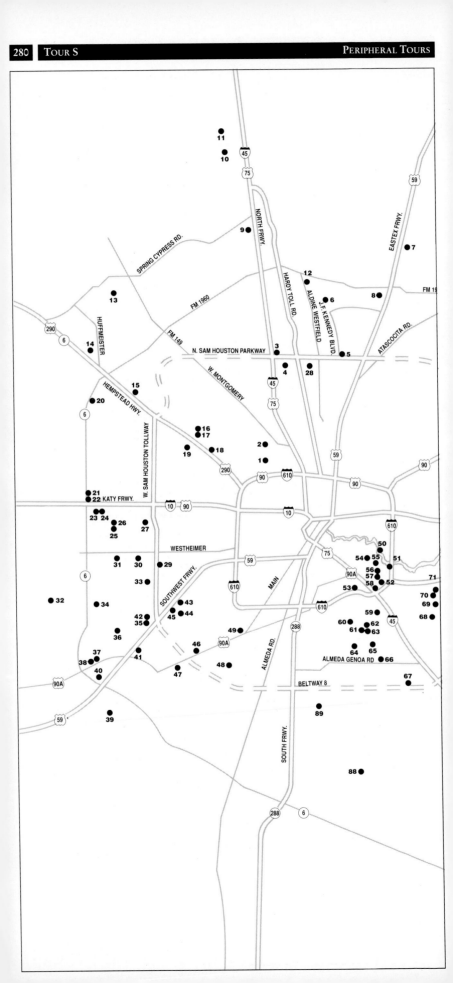

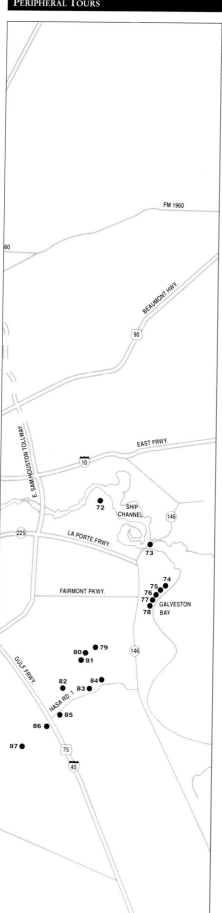

1. 3604 Brinkman Road
2. 865 Paul Quinn Street
3. 12400 Greenspoint Drive
4. 400 North Sam Houston Parkway East
5. 3663 North Sam Houston Parkway East
6. 2800 North Terminal Road
7. 810 Kingwood Drive
8. 19300 block Hightower Road
9. 20201 North Freeway
10. 2120 Buckthorne Place
11. 2455 Woodloch Forest Drive
12. 3320 Farm-to-Market Road 1960 West
13. 15415 North Eldridge Parkway
14. 11507 Huffmeister Road
15. 8350 Jones Road
16. 7000 Hollister Road
17. 6700 Hollister Road
18. 6200 Pinemont Street
19. 13103 Northwest Freeway
20. 7934 North Highway 6
21. 1212 North Highway 6
22. 1010 North Highway 6
23. 501 Westlake Park Boulevard
24. 13401 Katy Freeway
25. 600 North Dairy Ashford Road
26. 200 North Dairy Ashford Road
27. 311 Electra Drive
28. 1300 West Sam Houston Tollway South
29. 10375 Richmond Avenue
30. 2811 Hayes Road
31. 12401 Westheimer Road
32. 6511 Clodine Road
33. 10200 Bellaire Boulevard
34. 13700 Beechnut Street
35. 10455 South Kirkwood Drive
36. 12635 West Bellfort Avenue
37. 806 Lakeview Drive
38. 198 Kempner Street
39. 4400 Palm Royale Boulevard
40. 1250 Shoreline Drive
41. 12201 Southwest Freeway
42. 9800 Centre Parkway
43. 8181 Southwest Freeway
44. 8341 Bissonnet Avenue
45. 9506 South Gessner Road
46. 14410 Minetta Street
47. 955 Highway 90A
48. 13925 South Post Oak Road
49. 11530 Main Street
50. 8400 block Clinton Drive
51. East Loop and Houston Ship Channel
52. 7903 South Loop East
53. 144 Winkler Drive
54. 7228 Canal Street
55. Navigation Boulevard East and Harrisburg Boulevard
56. 801 Broadway
57. 915 Broadway
58. 2500 Broadway
59. 4101 Broadway
60. 6711 Bellfort Street
61. 7370 Sims Drive
62. 6410 North Haywood Drive
63. 6720 South Haywood Drive
64. 7155 South Santa Fe Drive
65. 8401 Travelaire Road
66. 8030 Braniff Street
67. 10765 Kingspoint Road
68. 2305 Redwin Drive
69. 1001 East Southmore Avenue
70. South Tatar Street and East Harris Avenue
71. 821 South Main Street
72. 3800 Park Road 1836
73. State Highway 146 and Houston Ship Channel
74. 311 Bay Ridge Road
75. 431 Bay Ridge Road
76. 515 Bay Ridge Road
77. 1520 Roscoe Avenue
78. 816 Park Avenue
79. 8600 Bay Area Boulevard
80. 3700 Bay Area Boulevard
81. 2700 Bay Area Boulevard
82. 1055 Bay Area Boulevard
83. 2101 NASA Road 1
84. 3303 NASA Road 1
85. 18101 Walnut Street
86. Gulf Freeway and Farm-to-Market Road 518
87. 304 East Viejo Road
88. 17130 McLean Road
89. 15107 Cullen Boulevard

3604 Brinkman Road   **S-1**
St. Rose of Lima Parish Hall and School
(1948) Donald Barthelme & Associates

This exquisite parish school and hall (the latter originally served as a temporary church) was the project that brought Barthelme to national attention. Built adjacent to the subdivision of Garden Oaks, it is a diminutively scaled complex of shaped pieces: the rectangular classroom wing—blind on the west (parking lot) side but open to the east (playground) side—with its monopitch roof and clerestory, and the parish hall, which is splayed in plan and section, yet so subtly as to hardly call attention to its folded wall plane and sloped roof. The precision of the detailing—the crisp, thin-shell canopies to either end of the school wing, the brick wall cross, and the beaten copper entrance doors—causes these buildings to resonate with an intensity that their small size would not lead one to anticipate. As Henry-Russell Hitchcock noted in 1959: "With the simplest of means and a wholly secular vocabulary of design, Barthelme has created a serene devotional atmosphere..." Alas, the parish did not turn to Barthelme when it built a permanent church (1960, George Fasullo). And the addition of the Parish Activity Center (1987, John Martin) to the west side of the parish hall, although well intended architecturally, parodies rather than complements the original. Brown paint is much in evidence, muddying the original multi-hued color scheme. The reclining red terra cotta figure of St. Rose of Lima (1950) is nowhere to be seen. Modeled by Joseph Bulone, a sculptor then connected with the Cranbrook Academy, it was fiercely denounced for its modernity and alleged irreverence at the time of its installation.

865 Paul Quinn Street   **S-2**
Highland Heights Elementary School
(1959) Donald Barthelme & Associates

Highland Heights School, located near Houston Acres Homes Estates, a predominantly black, subsistence-garden subdivi-

sion, was Barthelme's last major building in Houston. Its folded plate roof structure was very unconventional by the formulaic public school design standards prevalent in Houston in the 1950s. Free-standing screen walls give the building a recessive aspect.

12400 Greenspoint Drive   **S-3**
Wyndham Hotel Greenspoint
(1984) Morris*Aubry Architects

The gabled parapets and banded brick wall surfaces of this 15-story hotel are more impressive at a distance than on close inspection, where the perceptible thinness of what is, after all, a curtain wall clashes with its architectural conception as a masonry bearing wall. The Wyndham Hotel is located in Greenspoint, a 220-acre mixed-use development begun by Exxon's Friendswood Development Co. in 1976 near the intersection of North Sam Houston Parkway and the North Freeway and in proximity to Houston Intercontinental Airport. Buildings in Greenspoint are spaced out between parking garages, although a retail strip connects the hotel and several of the buildings along Greenspoint Drive. **Six Greenspoint** (1987, Pierce Goodwin Alexander) at 12450 Greenspoint Drive exhibits deft planar massing and the contrast of two shades of granite aggregate precast concrete panels. The **PetroLewis Tower** (1983, Sikes Jennings Kelly), 16945 Northchase Drive, just behind the Wyndham, is at 23 stories the tallest building in Greenspoint. The eight-story **One Greenspoint Plaza** at 16855 Northchase Drive and the 16-story **Two Greenspoint Plaza** at 16825 Northchase Drive (1978, 1980, S. I. Morris Associates) display Eugene Aubry's predilection for designing buildings in series, exploring here the random cantilevering of shallow window bays to fragment the boxy shapes of the buildings and provide multiple corner office spaces.

400 North Sam Houston Pkwy. East   **S-4**
First City Bank-North Belt Building
(1983) Gwathmey, Siegel & Associates and
Urban Architecture

The New York architects Gwathmey Siegel produced a series of speculative office buildings along North Sam Houston Parkway—the two-story **Internorth Energy Building** at 256, the three-story **Damson Oil Building** at 260, and the four-story **Northpoint Building** at 262 (1978, 1978, 1979), all for Ronald Bouchier—that culminated in this 12-story building for Treptow, Murphree & Co. Like the shorter buildings, First City is organized programmatically.

Circulation and services are differentiated from the trays of office space by being collected into a tower on the west side of the building. The arrangement of windows varies from side to side according to solar orientation. Whereas Charles Gwathmey faced the earlier buildings with precast concrete, he sheathed the First City Building in an all-glass curtain wall, horizontally banded with iridescent pearl and ivory spandrel glass and reflective window glass that is wrapped expressively around the building's curved northeast corner. Farther east on Sam Houston Parkway, which began to emerge as a major office corridor in the mid-1970s, are two large corporate complexes, **NL Industries North Belt Complex** at 3000 (1979, 1981, Pierce Goodwin Alexander) and **Hydril Technology Center** at 3300 (1980, Albert C. Martin & Associates).

3663 North Sam Houston Pkwy. East   S-5
Gateway I Building
(1982) Richard Fitzgerald & Partners

This six-story, brick-surfaced speculative office building asserts its presence by virtue of its knife-edged angled corners and a shift from the scale of the structural grid (expressed in the horizontal bands of flush-glazed windows) to the big-scaled, deep-set notches at either end of the building, a feat that the Fitzgerald office duplicated with the eight-story **Gateway II** (1984), around the corner at 15333 Drummet Boulevard.

2800 North Terminal Road   S-6
Houston Intercontinental Airport
(1969) Golemon & Rolfe and
George Pierce-Abel B. Pierce,
Control Tower (1969) I. M. Pei & Partners

Houston Intercontinental Airport (IAH) was the second airport in the U.S. to be designed especially for jet traffic and the first to employ an arrangement of linked unit terminals. IAH, as Reyner Banham acknowledged, "is recognized as a conceptual breakthrough, where movement patterns were finally allowed to dominate the whole design concept." The airport com-

plex reduces neatly to a flow diagram that operates both laterally and vertically to minimize the distance travellers must walk within a terminal or between terminals. To that end, not only do cars and public transportation pick up and deliver at each unit terminal, but cars can, for a not inconsiderable fee, be parked directly in each terminal. There is also a subterranean people-mover tram that shuttles between terminals (one of the more problematic features of the operation, as it turned out). The architectural design is a slick rendition of the New Brutalism. Externally, the design articulates the spatial organization of the terminals. These have no real facades, but since one never has the opportunity to contemplate the buildings as isolated objects, it doesn't really matter. Generous dimensions, muted colors, and variations in texture and lighting have allowed the interiors of the two original terminals, A and B, to age gracefully. (Expropriation of public spaces to accommodate retail expansion is another matter.)

The weakest point in the site organization is, as William T. Cannady noted soon after completion, the right-angle turn that incoming cars must negotiate around the seven-story, flying saucer-shaped **Airport Hotel** (now Houston Airport Marriott, 1971, William B. Tabler & Associates; Annex, 1981, Golemon & Rolfe Associates), which breaks the continuity of movement and induces uncertainty about which direction to take. The master plan called for the addition of new terminals to the east of the hotel, duplicating A and B. Instead of orderly phased growth, however, plans for expansion were shelved due to political considerations, and then revived when Terminal C (1982, Golemon & Rolfe Associates and Pierce Goodwin Alexander) was built especially for Continental Airlines. Its much larger size reflected the specific requirements of the prime tenant, but it adhered in concept to the master plan. This is not true of the International Terminal (1990, Harry Golemon Architects and Pierce Goodwin Alexander Linville). Golemon's Mario Bolullo produced a handsome and spirited building with the public presence that Terminals A, B, and C lack. But the ease with which the architects who devised the original master plan rejected the logic and discipline of that plan is troubling. In Houston, even a public body dealing with one of the most important public buildings in the city seems unable to make long-term commitments to environmental order and clarity.

The 6,000-acre site of what originally was known as Jetero airport is 21 miles north of downtown, a significant distance when property acquisition began in 1960. IAH lies midway between two radials, the North Freeway and the Eastex Freeway, and is now served by a third, the Hardy Toll Road, all of which are connected by the Sam Houston Parkway ring road. This conjunction of air and auto routes made the airport a major node for real estate development of the Houston variety: commercial strips along the freeways backed by a patchwork of residential subdivisions. This patchwork does not closely tail the commercial corridors but is instead dispersed on a scale more regional than local and now spills northward into Montgomery County.

810 Kingwood Drive S-7
Kingwood Information and Sales Office Building (1986) 3D/International

Stationed at the entrance to Kingwood, a 13,000-acre planned community developed on the north bank of the San Jacinto River just outside the town of Humble, by Friendswood Development Co. and the King Ranch, Inc., is this complex of airy pavilions surrounded by shallow pools of water. The design pays tribute to Kingwood's first sales pavilion, designed by Charles Tapley Associates in 1971, which served the development of Kingwood's first subdivision, Trailwood Village (north and south of the main drag, Kingwood Drive, between Trailwood Village and Woodland Hills). Tapley advised on the design of a linear greenway system threaded through the center of Trailwood Village as a nature preserve; his firm also designed a pool and bath house in the 2100 block of Running Springs that no longer exists. As 3D/I's sales pavilion attests, Kingwood's original ecological look has been superseded by more conventional images of affluent, suburban domesticity. The pair of office buildings at **1801 Kingwood Drive** (1976, Charles Tapley Associates) and the **Kingwood Fire Department Station #1** at 1863 Kingwood Drive (1975) still relay something of the initial civic style. Otherwise, Kingwood has a reassuringly normal look that is perhaps its most ingratiating feature.

19300 block Hightower Road S-8
Three H Services Center (1975) John Zemanek with Alexander McNab and Charles Keith Associates

This community center is located in Bordersville, a low-income, black neighborhood that has existed here, on the edge of Humble, since the late 1920s. Zemanek's building group is of wood post-and-lintel construction, surfaced with cement asbestos panels,

stock aluminum window sash, and corrugated composite sheet roofing. The feeling is Japanese, but tough and gritty rather than delicate or precious. Isolated in a clearing in the midst of an East Texas piney woods landscape, the Three H Services Center, which was built to compensate residents for the neighborhood's lack of public services, now backs up to the thriving commercial corridor along the Eastex Freeway.

20201 North Freeway S-9
Goodyear Airship Operations Administration Building (1969) Caudill Rowlett Scott

William T. Cannady designed this structure for CRS, a modest waiting room for passengers riding the Goodyear Blimp (with support spaces attached) and a terrace for public viewing of the blimp's arrivals and departures. Rather than producing an insignificant building—the program required no more and the competition is an adjacent freeway, the large, flat landing field, and a huge hangar for the blimp (1970, Neuhaus & Taylor)—Cannady buried the building within a grass berm, propped a 30-foot-high triangulated glass wedge above the public entrance, and converted the roof into a 500-foot-long promenade. This minimal, anti-architectural strategy is quite effective spatially. It allows viewers on the terrace promenade to experience the exhilarating panoramic sweep of flat landscape spread out before them while keeping an eye on the stream of traffic reflected in the glazed wedge. Glass, mullions, hand rails, slate floor paving inside, and the asphalt terrace paving are all black.

2120 Buckthorne Place S-10
The Woodlands Information Center (1975) Bennie M. González

Two clusters of wedge-shaped buildings, splayed in section, confront each other across a wood-deck-floored courtyard with dramatic gestures. González, a Scottsdale, Arizona architect, conceived the tensely configured cluster in response to the tall,

thin loblolly pine trees that cover much of The Woodlands. The Woodlands was envisioned by its developer, Houston oilman George P. Mitchell, as an antidote to suburban sprawl. It is a 17,000-acre new town, 28 miles north of downtown Houston, opened in 1975—the only one of 13 such communities developed under the U.S. Department of Housing and Urban Development's Title VII new towns program not to have failed economically. Its success is due in part to the fact that The Woodlands was developed according to conventional suburban real estate practices. Aside from the eerie screens of pine trees that oppressively mask all signs of human occupation in Grogan's Mill, the first of a network of "village" subdivisions to be developed, The Woodlands is not essentially different from the other new towns on Houston's periphery. Mitchell paid special attention to environmental factors in the initial planning. The Philadelphia landscape architects Wallace, McHarg, Robert & Todd planned its extensive system of flood control waterways and forest preserves. Architecture was not as high a priority and the result is a lack of distinction in public, commercial, and residential construction. The obsessive woodsiness of Grogan's Mill has been relaxed in Panther Creek and Cochran's Crossing, newer villages west of Lake Woodlands on the Woodlands Parkway, and Research Forest, the office park district along Research Forest Drive, west of the north end of Grogan's Mill Road. But as the scabrous strip along the North Freeway at the very gates of The Woodlands indicates, there is no escape. High-minded private munificence is simply no match for the freewheeling real estate dynamics of a city without planning controls.

2455 Woodloch Forest Drive   S-11
The Woodlands Water Resources Building (1985) Taft Architects

Predictably obscured by a screen of trees, this little building is the architectural highlight of The Woodlands. Its portico typologically identifies it as a public building,

for it is as close as The Woodlands comes to having a city hall. (Because The Woodlands lies within Houston's Extra-Territorial Jurisdiction, it cannot seek incorporation as a city or be annexed by another municipality. However, Houston is under no obligation to exercise its prerogative to annex. Until it does so, the developer remains in control.) The building contains the administrative offices of the eight Municipal Utility Districts that serve the presently developed parts of The Woodlands. Developers finance the installation of water and sewer services in unincorporated areas in Texas by creating Municipal Utility Districts to sell construction bonds, which tax the new property owners within the service area to pay off the bonds. Taxpayers do elect the governing boards of MUDs. Therefore, this building houses the only institution of local governance in The Woodlands.

Taft combined brick, split-faced concrete block, and panels of scored stucco with keen attentiveness to the affective properties of color and texture. The dark green anodized aluminum mullions contrast piquantly with the gold-green vegetation and the brown-green water in the drainage ditch, whose diagonal alignment prompted the building's stepped plan, visible on the south side. The interior is arranged around a double-volume civic hall. By resorting to architecture rather than to pseudo-environmental camouflage, Taft has made a building that engages its setting far more profoundly than do other buildings in The Woodlands. The ingenuity, intelligence, and articulateness of their work give this little building big presence.

3320 Farm-to-Market Road   S-12
1960 West
Northwoods Presbyterian Church (1983) Charles Tapley Associates

FM Road 1960 merges with State Highway 6 to loop from Humble, on the northeast, around through Sugar Land on the southwest, at a distance of about 18 miles from the center of Houston. In the late 1970s it became the axial ring of Houston's most recent phase of concentric expansion. As the main street of northwest Harris County (only a small segment presently lies within Houston's city limits), FM 1960 has attracted the usual mad array of shopping centers, public institutions, mid-rise office buildings, and convenience stops. In the midst of this very evidently non-master-planned setting, the Northwoods Presbyterian Church, designed by Charles Tapley and Gerald Moorhead, introduces a welcome note of calm. Its rust-colored stucco walls, steeply-pitched copper roof, greenish-gray pine-shingled gables, and rotated square windows, cleverly filled with diagonal arrays of gray, bronze, and gold reflective solar glass instead of stained glass, are quietly but intensely colorful. The effect is serene and unsentimental; the interior is spacious and austere.

15415 North Eldridge Parkway **S-13**
St. Mary's Episcopal Church
(1988) Gregory Harper Associates
with Gerald Moorhead

The parish house and temporary church of this suburban parish consist of a relaxed collision of shapes and low-budget materials.

11507 Huffmeister Road **S-14**
Christ The Redeemer Catholic Community
(1983) Charles Tapley Associates

The burdens imposed upon institutions attempting to keep pace with Houston's constant expansion are evident in this extensive, but low-budget, parish complex. From the street, and across a parking lot, the stucco screen wall provides a forceful identifying image. Behind it is the low-set church (the diocese now imposes a height limit in order to control operating expenses), which inside is a fine example of liturgically-ordered architectural design. Tapley's designer, Gerald Moorhead, combined spatial expansiveness with a sense of personal intimacy and exhibited a sure control of natural light.

8350 Jones Road **S-15**
Foundry United Methodist Church
(1982) Clovis Heimsath Associates

This is a provocative building complex. The educational wing is faceted in plan and rotates out of one side of the church, in an arrangement reminiscent of the work of Alvar Aalto. But the relationship between the two components is awkward and undeveloped; the church itself is merely a box. The cartoon-like billboard images attached to the faceted bays of the educational wing were sketched by Heimsath and executed in ceramic tile by the artist Pat Johnson. They

cleverly consecrate locally visible means of communication and display. Yet the images are not quite bold enough to be seen clearly from Jones Road, across the parking lot that is in front of, rather than behind, the church. The building doesn't quite live up to the ideas that informed it.

7000 Hollister Road **S-16**
Reed Rock Bit Drilling Technology Center
[now 7000 Hollister Building] (1985)
White Budd Van Ness Partnership

This sleekly-skinned complex of low-rise buildings, buoyed by projecting cylindrical circulation stacks, is situated in Northwest Crossing, a 245-acre mixed-use development begun by Joe A. McDermott and Northwest Hollister Corporation in 1975. It projects the vision of suburban neatness, order, and control for which the term "planned" has become the coded expression in Houston real estate parlance. The gleaming hermeticism of the Technology Center encapsulates this ethos architecturally.

6700 Hollister Road **S-17**
Northwest Corporate Park (1982)
Morris*Aubry Architects

Like most of the widely-spaced buildings in Northwest Crossing, this is a speculatively-built office building. Its bifurcated facade of granite aggregate precast concrete panels and dark green reflective glass gives it a tense but cool image that holds its own in this open landscape.

6200 Pinemont Street   **S-18**
J. Everett Collier Branch, Houston
Public Library (1985) MRW Architects

Rotational geometry is combined with the
recollection of rural vernacular buildings to
animate this small branch library. The careful articulation of the supporting structure,
infilled with glass clerestories and dark tile
wall facing, reinforces its presence tectoni-
cally and materially. The interior does not
measure up to the exterior, however.

13103 Northwest Freeway   **S-19**
Cameron Ironworks World Headquarters
Building (1978) 3D/International

The client's role as a major local industrial
enterprise specializing in the production of
steel components for oilfield and petrochemical equipment is symbolized in the
wide-span, white-painted, steel-framed
construction of its seven-story office building. The approach is reductivist rather than
Miesian, however; the building looks
monotonous because no variation in scale is
introduced. The one instance of counter-
point is dissonant: the free-standing brick-
faced shafts at the back of the building, in
which circulation is clustered, detract from
the simplicity of the building by introducing inconsistent sculptural elements.

7934 North Highway 6   **S-20**
St. John's Lutheran Church [now Heritage
Presbyterian Church] (1916)

The tall, thin steeple of this wood frame
country church is a distinctive landmark on
the prairie. The Heritage Presbyterian congregation saved the building and moved it
to this site with the assistance of Friendswood Development Co., whose extensive

Copperfield residential community lies
across Highway 6.

1212 North Highway 6   **S-21**
Addicks United Methodist Church (1915)

Like the ex-St. John's, this Methodist country church that served the rural community
of Addicks, a vernacular wooden box with
a staged front tower and steeple and pointed arch openings, is characteristic of a
church type that was once a fixture in the
Southern landscape. Also like St. John's, it
now faces the new world of West Houston:
Park Ten, a 550-acre office and industrial
park begun in 1970 by Wolff, Morgan &
Co. Park Ten established the Katy Freeway
as the axis of the Energy Corridor, a
favorite site for the suburban office and
research installations of major energy corporations since the late 1970s.

1010 North Highway 6   **S-22**
Fat Frank's Grub and Saloon
[now Cattleguard Restaurant & Bar]
(1985) Taft Architects

With their customary wit and prowess, Taft
Architects have deconstructed the western-
themed fast-food restaurant. The details,
color, and craftsmanship are exceptional for
this type of building.

501 Westlake Park Boulevard   **S-23**
The Amoco Center
(1983) Skidmore, Owings & Merrill

This dark gridded, 28-story tower, infilled with light green solar glass, is the tallest building in the Energy Corridor. In addition to a lower unit, it is joined by the 17-story **Westlake Park Two Building** (1982) and the 19-story **Westlake Park Three Building** (1983) at 500 and 550 Westlake Park Boulevard. All were designed by the Houston office of SOM for Gerald D. Hines Interests. Next door to Westlake Park, at 13501 Katy Freeway, is the **Exxon Chemicals Americas Headquarters** complex (1980, Pierce Goodwin Alexander), which is barely visible from the street. Just beyond Westlake Park's back door, at 15375 Memorial Drive, is the very visible **ARCO Oil & Gas District Offices** complex (1986, CRS Sirrine).

13401 Katy Freeway   **S-24**
United Carbon Co. Research Laboratory
Building (1962) **Demolished in 1991**
Skidmore, Owings & Merrill

Planning for this research complex not only predated the Energy Corridor by 20 years but predated construction of the Katy Freeway as well. The ex-United Carbon lab consists of a low, attenuated, white-painted steel and glass pavilion, backed by a high, windowless, brick-faced box. Produced by the New York office of SOM, these sit in dazzling contrast to their forested environs. The complex survived an attempt to redevelop the property in 1983, which would have entailed demolition of the SOM buildings for replacement by a series of towers designed by Arquitectonica. Just around the corner, at 801 North Eldridge Parkway, is the **McDermott Engineering Office Complex** (1981, Jack Reber), with its pyramidal incline of prestressed, precast con-

crete sun baffles. Also on North Eldridge, but on the north side of the Katy Freeway, is the outspread, brightly reflective **Hyatt Regency West Houston** (13102 Katy Freeway, 1984, LAN).

600 North Dairy Ashford Road   **S-25**
Conoco Building (1985) Kevin Roche,
John Dinkeloo & Associates

The Connecticut architect Kevin Roche cites the Kellum-Noble House in Sam Houston Park as inspiring the sun-defying architectural treatment of this 3-story, 16-building corporate headquarters complex. It is located on a 62-acre site that backs up to the huge Addicks Reservoir, a flood retention basin encircled by high, grass-lined dikes. Roche's wide-spread, aluminum-framed, fiberglass awnings are Conoco's most identifiable element. They extend so far forward of the buildings that they acquire a strong, gestural quality, especially on faceted end bays. The awnings are joined by a network of second-story pedestrian bridges that encircle the buildings and shade first-floor windows. Because almost all offices have outdoor exposure, controlling the admission of sunlight was critical. The bridges also traverse an artificial lagoon, into which the complex is set.

Conoco is organized on a circulation diagram that integrates pedestrian and vehicular movement. It has no real front door (the public enters at the middle of the complex from a ground-level parking garage) but doesn't require one since public access is carefully guarded. Conoco represents a high level of technical skill in designing the optimal corporate office environment. But its inevitable repetitiveness, its self-effacement, and its insulation give the complex a slightly oppressive sense of bureaucratic control that undermines the ingenuities and amenities of the architecture.

200 North Dairy Ashford Road   **S-26**
Shell Woodcreek Exploration and
Production Offices Building
(1980) Caudill Rowlett Scott

Next door to Conoco, CRS addressed similar issues in planning this corporate complex for the Shell Oil Co., a four-story, seven-building group in which almost all offices obtain natural light and views out. The precast concrete elevations were designed to filter and diffuse daylight into the interior; the triangular-shaped bays each contain an internal courtyard, maximizing views to the out-of-doors without unduly expanding the building's perimeter or its internal circulation.

As one traverses the Katy Freeway eastward from Shell, one passes on the north twin parallelogram-planned buildings, set back far from the freeway at 12141 and 12121 Wickchester Lane, **One and Six Woodbranch Energy Plaza** (1983, Gunnar Birkerts & Associates and Morris*Aubry Architects), the first increments of a never-completed ten building complex. At the southeast corner of Katy Freeway and West Sam Houston Tollway North is **Town and Country Mall** (1983, Charles Kober Associates), a three-level, 1.5-million-square-foot regional shopping mall in which Richard Haas's 70-foot-long mural "Houston" (1982), above the mall entrance to J. C. Penney Co., was painted out in order to expand an upper-level food court. To the east of the mall, at 10505 Town and Country Way, is the **Town and Country Station, U.S. Post Office** (1978, Clovis Heimsath Associates), outfitted with a roof full of solar collectors.

oper Ronald Bouchier. Inset balconies facing south toward Briar Forest, a complex connection between the parking deck and vertical circulation inside, and the subtle, stepped bays of the front elevation, facing the tollway, break away from conventional design formulas without becoming mannered or arbitrary. South of Briar Forest Drive lies the 83-acre CityWest Place, with its one major building, the 25-story **ParkWest Tower** at 2500 CityWest Boulevard and Westheimer Road (1983, Sikes Jennings Kelly).

10375 Richmond Avenue   **S-29**
Enserch Tower (1982)
Lloyd Jones Brewer & Associates

Sam Houston Tollway splits in two the 1,347-acre Westchase complex, a mixed-use development begun in 1975 by Westchase Co. and Tenneco Realty on what was then the western edge of Houston. The broad, flat tract is now dotted with gleaming mid-rise office buildings, condominium apartment complexes, two large hotels, and a big, clumsily picturesque shopping center, **Carillon West** (1976, Charles Lanclos) at 10001 Westheimer Road. Westchase illustrates the standards for ambitious commercial real estate developments that came to prevail in Houston in the mid-1970s: strict development and building controls exercised through deed restrictions, comprehensive improvements and landscaping, and provision for mixed, rather than single, use. The most visually striking of the buildings along Richmond, the principal office corridor in Westchase, is the 21-story Enserch Tower, a compilation of gray solar glass and flashing stainless steel stripes that Lloyd Jones Brewer's designer, Robert Fillpot, sent over the top with a giant, rolled soffit. Enserch's high profile, reflective finishes, and flamboyant composition are attributes

311 Electra Drive   **S-27**
(1958) William N. Floyd

This low contemporary house, once occupied by the architect William W. Caudill and his family, is in the subdivision of Memorial Bend. Apart from the fact that street names are derived from the titles of operas (Butterfly, Tosca, Traviata, Figaro), the remarkable thing about Memorial Bend is that many of its houses were designed by the architect William N. Floyd, one of the investors in the subdivision's development. Floyd's crisp, undemonstrative modern style gives Memorial Bend an inherent quality lacking in the surrounding neighborhoods of west Memorial.

1300 West Sam Houston   **S-28**
Tollway South
Amax Petroleum Building (1980)
Gwathmey, Siegel & Associates

Charles Gwathmey displayed considerable ingenuity in manipulating the program for a low-rise speculative office building when he designed this four-story structure for devel-

shared by other office buildings along Richmond and Wilcrest. In their neatly manicured, controlled environment, these buildings collectively present an image of an exurban Brave New World. As time passes, the luster of newness will fade and the growth of the live oak trees will change the character of Westchase. For the time being, however, its precision and brittle perfection make it seem just a bit surreal, especially in contrast to the Westheimer strip at its front door.

2811 Hayes Road   S-30
Chevron Geosciences Building
(1983) Caudill Rowlett Scott

The design of this corporate office and research complex reflects specific programmatic requirements, so that it differs considerably from the surrounding speculative office buildings. An angular plan geometry reconciles the office slab with a large rear block. The two are connected with a high, glazed circulation spine directly accessible from a porte-cochère inserted beneath the office slab with much structural ado. A facing of horizontal bands of precast concrete in different finishes introduces color, texture—and relief—into the land of reflective glass.

12401 Westheimer Road   S-31
Superior Oil Co. Geophysical
Research Laboratory Building (1967)
Todd Tackett Lacy

This ex-research laboratory is a steel and glass pavilion configured around an interior courtyard. Paradoxically, given its all-glass perimeter, the building's laboratories were encased in windowless cubicles. Superior's awesome flatness, underscored by the depth of its Cor-ten steel fascia (all services were collected into this "attic" zone to permit maximum flexibility), bespoke its prairie setting, which remained rural until the mid-1970s. Even into the 1980s, cattle still grazed on Superior's broad grounds, allowing the research building to figure as a

precise, elegant, unobtrusive foil to its rustic landscape setting.

6511 Clodine Road   S-32
Clodine Country Store

The country store in Clodine (pronounced Claw'-dean) is the real thing, not a gentrified ersatz. It sits here, seemingly innocent of its vulnerability, just beyond the advance line of suburban invasion that has already engulfed Addicks, Piney Point, and Alief. Clodine Road (FM Road 1464) goes south for ten miles to Main Street (Highway 90A) through the lush, rural countryside of Fort Bend County. The subdivisions are almost in sight, however.

10200 Bellaire Boulevard   S-33
Brown & Root Southwest Houston Office
Building (1980) S. I. Morris Associates

Brown & Root, Houston's largest engineering and heavy construction company, selected as a site for this expansive, three-story office building a large tract along the Sam Houston Tollway, almost midway between Katy Freeway and the Southwest Freeway, 13 miles southwest of its headquarters near downtown Houston. Accessibility by white-collar employees sent Brown & Root, as it has so many other large corporate employers in Houston, to a new kind of exurban settlement where the concept of center has been superseded by the desire for individual, personal connection, with the landscape rearranged accordingly. That the tollway was not completed until eight years after the Brown & Root Building opened merely served to confirm the corporation's prescience. By the time they are finally built, public infrastructure improvements in Houston have already generated the sorts of uses that they were projected to serve.

Eugene Aubry provided for Brown & Root a low-rise building configured in plan like a bow tie, with cylindrical service and circulation stacks lined up along its north and south faces. The central arced opening indicates the location of a skylit, vertical spine that cuts through the center of the building. As an image Brown & Root is compelling, especially because of the way its light-colored, horizontal mass seems to ride the undulating berms installed by Charles Tapley Associates, the landscape architects. At close range, though, the building is monotonous, due to its flatness and lack of color and detail.

and buff brick to give the small building visual impact. Its shallow, concave south front, which peaks at the center, seems to be informed spatially by the panoramic vista that it faces across the treeless coastal plain. This face, behind the building's street front, will bound one side of a garden atrium if Tapley's master plan is carried out as designed.

13700 Beechnut Street   S-34
Fame City (1986)
Pierce Goodwin Alexander

As Bruce C. Webb observed, "The last chapter of the history of fun in America would deal with the desleazing of places of amusement, neutralizing their unsavory reputations by giving them the fresh look of a shopping mall." What makes Fame City so titillating and sinister is not its rather too obvious entrance portal but its prophetic content. Fame City is America as mall. Not just the building type of the shopping mall, but its politics of diversion and control are encapsulated in this entertainment emporium.

10455 South Kirkwood Drive   S-35
Robert D. Cummings Elementary
School (1984) MRW Architects

This handsomely detailed elementary school, faced with ribbed concrete block and bright blue banding, was designed to use daylight rather than shut it out. Thus the monitors, which MRW pulled out at intervals and expressed as volumetric extrusions in order to articulate the spatial organization of the building.

12635 West Bellfort Avenue   S-36
St. Thomas Aquinas Catholic Church
(1982) Charles Tapley Associates

This parish hall and office complex, the first increment of an eventual parish center, impresses itself as a strong figural and spatial presence in the landscape. Until not too long ago, its ten-acre site was a cotton field. Tapley and his associate, Gerald Moorhead, used boldly scaled alternating bands of red

806 Lakeview Drive   S-37
Casa de Mañana
(1928) William Ward Watkin

W. T. Eldridge, for whom this house was built, was a cofounder of the Imperial Sugar Co., a subsidiary of Sugarland Industries, which wholly owned the town of Sugar Land. Eldridge built the only large house in his company town, a true country house, although it now sits in the midst of suburbia. Watkin's stucco-faced, tile-roofed Mediterranean style design is an expanded version of his Cohen House on the campus of Rice University.

198 Kempner Street   S-38
Imperial Sugar Co. Char Filter House
(1926) Dwight P. Robinson & Co.

Sugar was first grown in the fertile Brazos River lowlands of Fort Bend County in the 1820s and producing sugar plantations had been established along Oyster Creek by the time of the Texas Revolution in 1836. From the 1890s through the 1910s, Sugar Land (the name dates from the 1850s) was the center of the Texas "sugar bowl," its fields worked by convict labor contracted from the State of Texas. In 1908 the largest producer was bought out by W. T. Eldridge and the Galveston investor I. H. Kempner, who formed Sugarland Industries and began the Imperial Sugar Co. In the 1920s the Char Filter House was built to refine West Indian sugar, after cane had ceased to be grown locally. The town of Sugar Land was developed on company property to the north of the refinery and it was not until the late 1940s that Sugarland Industries began to sell real estate to residents of the town. Since the late 1950s, Sugarland Industries has sold its former fields for transformation into the bedroom suburbs of Houston, including the 1,000-acre Sugar Creek and First Colony.

4400 Palm Royale Boulevard   **S-39**
Sweetwater Country Club (1983) MLTW/Turnbull Associates, Charles Moore, and Richard Fitzgerald & Partners

The crown jewel of First Colony is Charles Moore and William Turnbull's country clubhouse, a pyramidally-roofed, brick-faced mass sculpturally eroded by (what else?) the driveway entrance to the building. Set up on an artificial mound, the clubhouse is a relaxed, expansive, and benign presence. But it is not distinguished architecturally, externally or internally. It seems more like a building in the style of Charles Moore than one by Moore himself. First Colony, where it is located, is a 9,300-acre planned community developed by Sugarland Properties, a joint venture of Gerald D. Hines Interests and the Royal Dutch Shell Pension Fund.

1250 Shoreline Drive   **S-40**
One SugarLand Park Building (1982) Johnson/Burgee Architects and Richard Fitzgerald & Partners

Only one of a projected cluster of three-story speculative office buildings designed for a site on Oyster Creek in the office park district of First Colony has been built by Hines Interests. It is even less momentous architecturally than the Sweetwater

Country Club. Johnson claimed the Feilner House in Berlin by the 19th-century Prussian architect Karl Friedrich Schinkel as his historic source for the banded facades of buff and red brick. Quite visible to the west is the **Fluor Daniel Houston Operations Center** on its own little island at 1 Fluor Drive (1984, Welton Becket & Associates). While Johnson/Burgee sought to make One SugarLand Park, in Burgee's word, "warm," the Becket office aimed for, and achieved, the opposite climatic effect with its huge four-building complex, which ascends in height from one to seven floors, like an array of silver icebergs.

12201 Southwest Freeway   **S-41**
Texas Instruments Building (1968) Ford, Powell & Carson and Richard S. Colley

Although Ford and Colley initiated their 25-year-long sequence of production plants for Texas Instruments with the Houston Technical Laboratories on Richmond Avenue, it was with their Semiconductor Plant for the company in the Dallas suburb of Richardson that they established the architectural vocabulary that Colley reproduced in many of the subsequent plants. The characteristic attributes visible here are the use of gray Georgia marble panels (revetted with exposed clips) and pink Mexican brick as facing materials on the south, facing the freeway, and the expression of the servicing stacks, alternating with panels of bronze solar glass, on the side facing Airport Boulevard, all capped by a flat-lidded concrete roof. Colley's tectonic assembly of materials and straightforward ordering of elements give this large manufacturing plant the quiet refinement of a corporate office building.

9800 Centre Parkway   **S-42**
Centre One Building (1983) Skidmore, Owings & Merrill

The Farb Companies developed the 72-acre Centre, planned by Craig Hartman of the Houston office of SOM. Hartman designed the one office building constructed there, the 11-story Centre One. Faced with white precast concrete panels, the building is subdivided vertically into three planes by shallow vertical incisions. Scored planes and delicately modulated surfaces distinguish the **Retail Centre**, a two-block long strip shopping center at Centre Parkway and Bissonnet, also designed by Hartman. Until heavy-handed leasing agents eager to boost rentals tarted up its originally pristine exteriors, the Retail Centre, with its parking lot full of Washingtonia palm trees, was an oasis of architectural sanity along the raucous Bissonnet corridor.

8181 Southwest Freeway   S-43
KPRC Channel Two Studio
(1972) Wilson, Morris, Crain & Anderson

Eugene Aubry adroitly organized this television studio in three distinct elements: a studio block to the left, a long, faceted office wing to the right, and the triangular transmitting tower out front. The double-height, top-lit, glazed spine, a recurring feature in Aubry's work in the 1970s, is KPRC's unifying element.

8341 Bissonnet Avenue   S-44
Emanu El Memorial Park, Kagan-Rudy Chapel (1983) Clovis Heimsath Associates

This hexagonal, domically-roofed, open-air pavilion, built of reinforced concrete, is one of Clovis Heimsath's best buildings. It embodies a feeling of silence, repose, and gentle loss that is quite moving, yet subtle. Heimsath incorporated Jewish religious symbols and architectural details in the design; Maryann Heimsath was responsible for the stained glass panels in the dome.

9506 South Gessner Road   S-45
Church of the Epiphany
(1973) Clovis Heimsath Associates

Heimsath's interest in geometrical manipulation led to the complex shapes generated by rotating the ridge beam of this church so that it spans the square-planned nave on the diagonal. The roof was treated as a warped plane, folded around the diagonally canted wheel window that is oriented northeast, on the axis of Bissonnet Avenue. The result is visually striking. But Epiphany's brick, stone, and shingled surfaces, which totally conceal its acrobatic framing, are architectural non sequiturs.

14410 Minetta Street   S-46
(1934) F. McM. Sawyer

Roy B. Nichols, then postmaster of Houston, developed this subdivision, Main Street Gardens, 12 miles outside Houston on the Main Street highway. Nichols had Sawyer design for him this diminutive, picturesque Mediterranean style house, which is built of reinforced concrete.

955 Highway 90A   S-47
Tang City Plaza (1985) BSL & Associates

This "Chinese" style shopping center, designed by BSL's Robert Liu, is a cross cultural solecism along the wide open spaces of the Main Street highway. It was intended as a center for Asian retail businesses.

13925 South Post Oak Road   **S-48**
Fire Station #59 (1968) Todd Tackett Lacy

The precision of Anderson Todd's Miesian
detail was brought to bear with authority
on this suburban steel, brick, and glass fire
station. Street widening has brought Post
Oak Road right up to the building's front
apron. Just north of the station, at 13855
South Post Oak Road, is Hugo V. Neuhaus,
Jr.'s ex-**Madison Southern National Bank
Building** (1970), which is also a steel-
framed, brick-faced pavilion.

11530 Main Street   **S-49**
Brochsteins Inc. Building (1940, 1947)
I. S. Brochstein with Lenard Gabert

When I. S. Brochstein designed this building for his custom wood-working plant,
South Main Street was the undisputed axis
of Houston. With its civic attributes—the
streamlined central pylon and ceremonial
reflecting basin—Brochsteins still defers to
Main Street's honorific status.

8400 block Clinton Drive   **S-50**
Houston Public Elevator
[now Public Grain Elevator] (1926)

The immense network of clustered grain
storage bins, conveyor houses, and loading
chutes makes the Public Elevator the dominating presence on the Long Reach of the
Houston Ship Channel. The cluster of bins
behind the tallest cluster and the entire row
perpendicular to the tallest cluster are additions to the original. The complex can also
been seen, across the water, from the east
end of Harbor Drive, east of 75th Street.

East Loop and   **S-51**
Houston Ship Channel
Sidney Sherman Bridge (1972) A. C. Kyser,
Texas Highway Department, designer

The Ship Channel bridge, carrying Loop
610 across Buffalo Bayou, was the longest
strut-girder bridge in the U. S. at the time
of its completion. Two steel strut girder
structures, one on each bank, carry ten
lanes of traffic across the channel. The
bridge is 1,230 feet long and rises 135 feet
above the water. Visible from the bridge on
a clear day is one of the most exhilarating
prospects of Houston. The downtown skyline falls into alignment perspectively with
the Greenway Plaza and Post Oak skylines,
giving the impression of a single file of tall
structures expanding Manhattan-like across
the coastal prairie. Directly abutting the
bridge on the south bank (downstream)
side is the **Houston Mill & Elevator Co.**
grain mill and elevators (1922, Burrell
Engineering & Construction Co.).

7903 South Loop East   **S-52**
YMCA East End Branch Building
[now Cossaboom Branch]
(1955) Milton McGinty

One of a series of neighborhood YMCAs
that the McGinty office designed in the
mid-1950s, this four-story building consists
of a slab, programmatically organized to
display horizontal window bands, a vertical
service and circulation tower, and the
exposed fire stair that projects off one end
of the building as an architectural exclama-
tion mark. Nearby, at the intersection of the
South Loop and the Gulf Freeway, lies the
greatly-altered **Gulfgate Shopping City**
(1956, John Graham Co. and Irving R.
Klein & Associates). Gulfgate was Houston's first regional shopping mall and it was
built by Theodore Berenson and Allied
Stores Corp. at Houston's first freeway
interchange.

144 Winkler Drive   **S-53**
Freeway Baptist Church (1972)

Proclamation of the word is what this little church is all about.

7228 Canal Street　　　　　　**S-54**
Canal Street Health Center
(1952) Robert C. Smallwood, MacKie & Kamrath, consulting architects

Abandoned by the City of Houston, this ex-neighborhood health center is a compact, scrupulously detailed example of organic architecture, a bit of Usonia transposed to the East End.

Navigation Boulevard East and　　**S-55**
Harrisburg Boulevard
Magnolia Compress & Warehouse Co. Building (1914)

Built along the cotton docks of the ship channel's Long Reach by the Weld-Neville Cotton Co., this formidable warehouse exposes its thick, cast-in-place concrete frame, the rectangular interstices of which are filled with brick panels punctured by the smallest of windows. The Magnolia warehouse is one of the oldest structures associated with the Houston Ship Channel, which was dedicated on 10 November 1914. Just south of the Magnolia warehouse, Harrisburg Boulevard bridges Brays Bayou at the point where it empties into Buffalo Bayou. The street name changes to Broadway and one enters the oldest town in Harris County, the Mexican *ayuntamiento* of Harrisburg, founded in 1826 by John R. Harris, a member of Stephen F. Austin's original Old 300 colony of Anglo-American settlers, the man for whom Harris

County is named, and the great-grandfather of the architect Birdsall P. Briscoe.

801 Broadway　　　　　　　**S-56**
John R. Harris Elementary School
(1971) Clovis Heimsath Associates

This addition to an existing building consists of the antigravitational projection of deep, brick-faced soffits above the classroom windows. Architecturally, it is the only bright spot along Broadway. No trace of Harrisburg's comparatively ancient past has been allowed to remain and what is left, principally business buildings of the 1930s and '40s, is falling into total decay. At the east end of East Magnolia Street is Glendale Cemetery, in which the plots of such pioneer families as Harris, Briscoe, Milby, Tod, and Allen are located.

915 Broadway　　　　　　　**S-57**
Hill Top Village Apartments (c. 1943)

Built during World War II by W. D. Woodruff on the site of his lumber yard, this complex of rental units is humorously organized into stepped, gabled house fronts, which may explain the derivation of the name.

2500 Broadway　　　　　　　**S-58**
James W. Deady Junior High School
(1928) Louis A. Glover

The Glover family was involved in real estate development in this section of Harrisburg, which perhaps accounts for the fact that Glover designed both **Charles H. Milby Senior High School** (1601

Broadway) and Deady Junior High. Deady displays resplendent terra cotta decoration, a type of ornament popular in the 1920s but comparatively rare in Houston. Glover also was responsible for the tile-faced modern wing added to the school in 1950.

4101 Broadway   **S-59**
Park Place Baptist Church (1961)
Ben F. Greenwood with E. Gene Hines

A contemporary rendition of the pointed style, executed at large scale.

6711 Bellfort Street   **S-60**
Bellfort Square Office Building
(1966) Arthur D. Steinberg

This is one of the zaniest buildings in Houston. As if the warped penthouse weren't enough, the building is faced with green aggregate precast concrete panels and gold anodized aluminum mullions.

7370 Sims Drive   **S-61**
(1937) H. A. Salisbury & T. G. McHale

Salisbury and McHale brought their best River Oaks manner to the subdivision of Garden Villas in this precisely composed and detailed American colonial farmhouse. To the left of the main house is a smaller version, the guest house.

6410 North Haywood Drive   **S-62**
(1950)

This is a fine example of the Riverside Terrace contemporary look: low slung, with low-pitched roofs, clerestory strip windows, and a dramatically glazed bay juxtaposed with the obligatory chimney pylon.

6720 South Haywood Drive   **S-63**
Garden Villas Park Recreation Building
(1959) William R. Jenkins

The big scale of the steel-framed basketball court canopy makes for an impressive open-air space. The adjoining recreation building, based on a nine-square, neo-Palladian grid (a bit stretched in the middle), is a very mannered interpretation of the architecture of Mies van der Rohe. The urbane style and suburban scale of the recreation building fit perfectly into the ambiance of Garden Villas, laid out in 1925 by the architect Edward Wilkinson for the developer W. T. Carter, Jr. Wilkinson devised a radial street plan focused on the site that came to be filled with the **Garden Villas Elementary School** (7185 Santa Fe Drive, 1932, Stayton Nunn and Edward Wilkinson). Belying the incipient monumentality of the town plan was Garden Villas' self-proclaimed image as a garden community, where families of modest means could supplement their incomes with produce raised in their own back yards. Because of plentiful open land nearby, Garden Villas still seems very much on the edge of Houston. It is a characteristic Texan place—uncurbed streets lined with pecan trees, rambling wooden houses with multiple additions, open yards, just the sort of neighborhood for people who probably prefer not to live in neighborhoods. Garden Villas lets them have it both ways. A historical note: In 1926 Garden Villas advertised one of Wilkinson's one-story houses as a "ranch-type house," the first known use of that term in Houston.

7155 South Santa Fe Drive   S-64
Emsco Derrick & Equipment Co. Building
[now LTV Energy Products Co.]
(1942) Fooshee & Cheek

The Dallas architects Fooshee & Cheek
designed this restrained, very dignified suburban office building, faced with a smooth
skin of limestone and glass block window
panels. It has been respectfully maintained
despite subsequent additions (1959,
Golemon & Rolfe).

8401 Travelaire Road   S-65
Houston Municipal Airport Terminal
and Hangar (1940) Joseph Finger

In 1937 W. T. Carter, Jr., sold an airfield that
he and his family had operated for 11 years
to the City of Houston, which completed
this passenger terminal and hangar complex
three years later with assistance from the
Public Works Administration. Finger's
pyramidally-massed sky-city gateway is a
modernistic delight, as is the architec-
turally-coordinated hangar to the south. In
1988 the City's Department of Aviation
demolished a series of crude additions to
the terminal and had Barry Moore Architects rehabilitate the exterior; the hangar
remains in need of attention. This terminal
was superseded by a new terminal (now
William P. Hobby Airport), built on the
north side of the field, at the head of
Broadway, in 1954 (Wyatt C. Hedrick).

8030 Braniff Street   S-66
Houston Firemen's Training Academy
[now Houston Fire Department Training
Academy] (1967) Jenkins Hoff Oberg Saxe

The training academy comprises a campus
of widely-scattered, tough-looking, brick-
faced buildings framed with thick, cast-in-
place concrete members. The Drill Tower
and the smoke-blackened Fire Building

stand out. *Progressive Architecture* pronounced it "a landscape that may look
straight out of the TV series Star Trek."

10765 Kingspoint Road   S-67
Best Products Co. Showroom,
Indeterminate Facade (1975) SITE

What more unlikely place to come across
one of the most published images of architecture of the 1970s than here, a back street
across from Almeda Mall? The *Indeterminate Facade*, one of 11 showrooms that
the New York sculptor James Wines and his
collaborators artfully manipulated for Best
Products Co., is an attempt to subvert the
banality of the American suburban landscape. Wines is amused by the often contra-
dictory, frequently apocalyptic interpretations that this simulation of disaster has
evoked. Meanwhile, the showroom per-
forms its daily task of dispensing wares,
unperturbed by the ersatz catastrophe that
has befallen it.

2305 Redwin Drive   S-68
(1958) Brooks & Brooks

Tucked into an otherwise unexceptional
neighborhood along Vince's Bayou in
Pasadena is this neatly detailed '50s modern
house. Its front elevation consists of planes
of wood and brick relieved by volumetric
intrusions and projections, and a raised
band of clerestory windows.

1001 East Southmore Avenue   S-69
First Pasadena State Bank Building
[now Bank One Pasadena]
(1962) MacKie & Kamrath with Lloyd
Borget and Doughtie & Porterfield

Pasadena's only skyscraper is this distinctive 12-story tower, a glass-curtained shaft that appears to project forward from a brick-faced spine containing the stairs, elevators, and toilets. The sculptural shaping of offset volumes and masses is quite effective, although its impact is undercut by the building's crude detailing, an unexpected fault for MacKie & Kamrath. The lobby and banking hall interiors are particularly garish. Even so, the First Pasadena State Bank Building is remarkable. In a decade in which the design of American tall buildings was especially conformist, it stands out as a spirited alternative, developed on principles derived from the work of Frank Lloyd Wright.

South Tatar Street   S-70
and East Harris Avenue
Pasadena Town Square (1982)
Caudill Rowlett Scott

About 1960 the center of Pasadena shifted from the compact (and now deserted) downtown at North Main Street and the La Porte Freeway to the corner of Southmore and Tatar, 1½-miles to the southeast. It is now in the process of sliding a further 2¾-miles south to the Fairmount Parkway corridor, a process that construction of this small shopping mall by Federated Stores Realty was intended to arrest. Pasadena Town Square was designed to function as the city center that Pasadena literally left behind. The public space is generously dimensioned, well-lit, and furnished with numerous amenities. Still, it is an insulated environment rather than a downtown. It turns inward rather than outward and does

not attempt to make connections to any of the public buildings around it. Pasadena Town Square sums up Pasadena's post-downtown predicament. It has no public face, projects no public image, and thus cannot function as the representative center that it was intended to be.

824 South Main Street   S-71
St. Pius V Catholic Church
(1959) T. G. McHale

After the First Pasadena State Bank Building, St. Pius V is Pasadena's outstanding public building. McHale's blocky tower, a late rendition of the Bertram Goodhue style of planar setback composition, is an emphatic spatial marker in this flat, predominantly domestic, go-as-you-please landscape. Cantoned piers of rough-faced limestone bracket inset screens filled with anagrammatic Christian ornament. Contrasting with the monumental bulk of the tower are the attenuated copper flèche and the thin, stepped nave.

3800 Park Road 1836   S-72
San Jacinto Battleground State Park
San Jacinto Monument
(1938) Alfred C. Finn

In the midst of the petrochemical corridor along the Houston Ship Channel stands the San Jacinto Monument, a reinforced concrete obelisk, 570 feet tall, faced with Texas shell limestone and capped by a three-dimensional version of the Lone Star. The obelisk was erected by the State of Texas with assistance from the Public Works Administration. It commemorates the Battle of San Jacinto, 21 April 1836, when a small force of Anglo-Texians led by Sam Houston surprised and routed the Mexican army, which had camped on this plain opposite the confluence of the San Jacinto River and Buffalo Bayou, and captured its

leader, the Mexican president Antonio
López de Santa Ana. Santa Ana was forced
to concede the independence of Texas from
Mexico and 21 April has ever since been
celebrated in Texas as San Jacinto Day. The
State of Texas commenced site acquisition
at the battlefield in 1883 but not until 1909
did the legislature designate the site as a
state park. Preparation for the centennial of
Texas independence in 1936 led Jesse H.
Jones, then chairman of the federal government's Reconstruction Finance Corp., to
propose construction of this monument in
1935. Jones's perennial architect, Alfred C.
Finn, got the job and tradition has it that
Jones sketched the obelisk, with its 3-D
star, that Finn's office obligingly produced.

High, raised terraces surround the base of
the monument, which contains the San
Jacinto Museum of History and an elevator
that carries sightseers to an observation
deck at the top of the shaft. The relief carving at the base of the shaft, the modeling of
the bronze entrance doors, and the crowning star are the work of William M. McVey.
At the water end of the principal axis is the
U.S.S. Texas, a 1914 vintage battleship
involved in World Wars I and II. It was
restored in 1990. At the channel end of Park
Road 1836 one can take the Lynchburg
Ferry across the Houston Ship Channel to
Crosby-Lynchburg Road, which leads to
the East Freeway (I-10).

In its heroic scale, radical symmetry and
frontality, and isolation, the San Jacinto
Monument is the only work of architecture
that stands up to the intimidating, imper-
sonal engineering operations that dominate
the landscape of production along the Ship
Channel. Its elementary geometry is
extended laterally across the prairie by the
1,750-foot-long reflecting basin, which
stretches out in front of the monument. The
ritual character of this approach sequence
was undermined in 1985, however, when
the Texas Parks and Wildlife Dept. demolished the flanking driveways in order to use
the basin as a flood retention pond. Thus
one now approaches the monument from
its side flank rather than frontally.

There is something unsettling about the
San Jacinto Monument. Its hieratic character, and the ceremonial conception of public
life that this implies, are so disconnected
from the landscape in which it stands and
the Texas tourist families who are its chief
votaries that the monument seems meant
for some other place, some other culture,
and to have ended up here by mistake. It
bespeaks epic deeds and heroic stature,
attributes that here have manifestly passed
from people to objects of processing and
production.

State Highway 146   S-73
and Houston Ship Channel
Fred Hartman Bridge (1992) District 12,
State Dept. of Highways and Public
Transportation, designer

The Hartman Bridge spans the Ship
Channel to connect La Porte and Baytown.
Two roadways are carried 178 feet above
the channel on cables suspended from two
pairs of reinforced concrete "double-dia-

monds," one pair to each side of the channel. The diamond-shaped towers are 440
feet high; the bridge itself is 1,250 feet long.

311 Bay Ridge Road   S-74
(1928) John F. Staub

Bay Ridge, a high promontory at the rim of
Galveston Bay just south of Morgan's Point,
where Buffalo Bayou merges with the bay,
is a place to which well-to-do Houstonians
began to retreat in the 1890s. The constant
breeze blowing off the water provided the
only antidote to the steaminess of coastal
summers before the introduction of air-conditioning. Staub's bay house for a Houston
family was more elaborate than most of the
simple cottages along Bay Ridge Road, but
he acknowledged the local carpenters' vernacular with its 2-over-2 windows. Major
rooms look out across the wooded downhill
slope toward the water.

431 Bay Ridge Road   S-75
(1928) Joseph Finger

This pink stucco-surfaced, tile-roofed
Mediterranean house is indicative of the
suburbanization that Bay Ridge began to
undergo in the late 1920s. Like earlier houses, however, it is entirely open on the bay
side behind a screened loggia with full-
width sleeping porch above. The original
clients, Mr. and Mrs. W. H. Irvin, maintained their own zoo across the street at
430, one of the sights of Bay Ridge in the
1930s.

515 Bay Ridge Road   S-76
(1928) Alfred C. Finn

When Ross S. Sterling decided to leave his house in Rossmoyne and live year-round at the bay, he had Finn's designer, Robert C. Smallwood, produce this Newport-sized, limestone-faced, neo-Georgian country house, patterned rather closely on the work of the New York architect Charles A. Platt (especially the imposing semicircular Ionic portico on the water side). The expansive grounds are bare of trees, so that the huge house is clearly silhouetted against the water and the sky. The balustraded roof terrace provides a splendid prospect point for viewing the immensely tall ships that traverse the Ship Channel, which lies just beyond the Bay Ridge beach. Across the street at 514 are the garage and servants' quarters. Further south on Bay Ridge Road, although not always clearly visible from the street, are a house by Birdsall P. Briscoe (615), a delightful Victorian cottage built by an original member-family of the Bay Ridge Park Association (811), and a house by Sanguinet & Staats (835).

1520 Roscoe Avenue   S-77
(1927) Sally Winn Reynaud

Mrs. Reynaud designed this shingled cottage, a bundle of tense shapes with a marvelously improvised air, for her own family.

816 Park Avenue   S-78
Kirwin Memorial Chapel [now St. Mary's Catholic Church] (1927) Maurice J. Sullivan

This brick-faced, tile-roofed Lombard

Romanesque style church was built as the chapel of St. Mary's Seminary, which was located here until it was moved to Sullivan's new campus in Houston in 1954. Prior to 1901 when the Diocese of Galveston acquired the property, it had been the site of the Sylvan Beach Hotel, a Victorian resort hotel on the bayshore, around which the town of La Porte was laid out by the La Porte Improvement Co. in the 1890s.

8600 Bay Area Boulevard   S-79
Armand Bayou Nature Center, Interpretive Building (1977) Pierce Goodwin Alexander

The Interpretive Building is reached by a raised wooden boardwalk that traverses a small portion of the low-lying, marshy landscape characteristic of parts of the bay area. The one-story building, raised on piers and surrounded by a veranda, pays homage to the Gulf coast cottage type, although literalism is avoided. The Natural Plant Greenhouse is by W. O. Neuhaus Associates (1983). This 1,800-acre park is being selectively restored to its aboriginal prairie condition with the removal of later tree growth and its replacement with prairie grasses.

3700 Bay Area Boulevard   S-80
IBM Federal Systems Division Regional Office Building (1986) CRS Sirrine

This is an authoritative building. Its crescent-shaped, six-story mass spatially defines the broad curve of Bay Area Boulevard. Its centered composition and restrained coloration—gray granite base course, pink granite walls, reflective glass punched windows, and blue metal trim—give it a strong but subtle presence. Here a postmodern vocabulary has been intelligently articulated not just to project a corporate image but to discharge a civic responsibility. The IBM Building creates a sense of place by addressing its site in a spatially positive, architecturally urbane manner. The channel gardens on the concave side of the building were laid out by the San Francisco landscape architects Peter Schwartz and Martha Walker.

2700 Bay Area Boulevard   S-81
University of Houston Clear Lake Campus Bayou Building (1976) S. I. Morris Associates, Golemon & Rolfe, and Pitts, Phelps & White

John Bertini and Guy Jackson of S. I. Morris Associates conceived this laterally expansive, three-story, aluminum and glass-faced building as a machine in the garden, a precise, technologized object that contrasts maximally with its wooded surroundings. Across Horsepen Bayou, to the south, are the **Arbor Building**, the first building on the campus, of concrete tilt-wall construction (1971, Van Ness & Mower), and the **Developmental Arts Building** (1979, S. I. Morris Associates), the campus's athletic center. The latter was designed as an experiment in energy conservation techniques. Faced with porcelain-enameled insulated metal panels, it was equipped with roof-mounted, flat-plate solar collectors intended to fuel the heating, air-conditioning, and the heating of water for the building.

1055 Bay Area Boulevard   S-82
First State Bank Building [now First City Bank of Clear Lake] (1966) Welton Becket & Associates

This concrete and glass pavilion, designed for the Humble Oil & Refining Co. and the Del E. Webb Corp., developers of Clear Lake City, dates from the community's inception. Clear Lake City was planned in 1962 on 10,000 acres excerpted from the ex-West ranch, which Humble had acquired in 1938. It is a classic version of the American suburban dream, 1960s-Southwestern style. Single-family houses dominate. The entire community is built around a golf course, laid out to function as a system of greenway "fingers." Commercial buildings are segre-

gated along major thoroughfares and multi-family housing is located to serve as a buffer. It doesn't look all that much different from the rest of Houston, except for its compulsive tidiness. The isolated, clean-lined, structurally expressive pavilion was the preferred public building type; the Becket office's bank is a case study example. Nearby, at 16511 Diana Lane, is the **Community Recreation Center** (1964, Caudill Rowlett Scott). Subsequent additions have diluted the clarity of its original organizational scheme, but not its architectural blandness, which is all too typical of Clear Lake City as a whole.

2101 NASA Road 1   S-83
National Aeronautics and Space Administration Manned Spacecraft Center [now the Lyndon B. Johnson Space Center] (1964) Brown & Root with Manned Spacecraft Center Architects (Brooks & Barr, MacKie & Kamrath, Harvin C. Moore, and Wirtz, Calhoun, Tungate & Jackson), Charles Luckman Associates, planning and design consultants.

Constructed between 1962 and 1964, the initial buildings of the Manned Spacecraft Center illustrate the trivialization that the Modern movement underwent in the 1960s at the hands of architects in the employ of the American power elite. The Luckman office and Lyndon B. Johnson's favored builder and architects, Brown & Root and Brooks & Barr of Austin, imposed their version of modernist order on this flat 1,600-acre site. Visually weightless, free-standing buildings, faced with white precast concrete and dark solar glass, are widely dispersed in a sea of green turf. Numerous parking lots and an extensive street grid were pragmatic insertions. On oppressively humid days the trek from air-conditioned building to air-conditioned building can be wilting: the landscaping provides visual relief only. A new Visitor Center, planned by Walt Disney Imagineering and scheduled for completion in 1991, is supposed to compensate for the presently bleak experience that visitors to the space center's exhibition building are likely to have.

3303 NASA Road 1   S-84
[now Lunar & Planetary Institute Building] (1930) Joseph Finger

NASA Road 1 is the nightmarish antithesis of Clear Lake City and the other "planned" communities that it skirts, Nassau Bay, Taylor Lake Village, and El Lago: a chaotic strip along the north shore of Clear Lake where all the action is, and all the traffic

too. Its foremost architectural sight is this sprawling, Mediterranean style country house, built by the lumberman, oilman, and banker J. M. West on the 35,000-acre ranch that he assembled in the 1920s midway between Houston and Galveston. Like the Sterling House at Bay Ridge, the West House was larger and much more pretentious than the houses that Houstonians had built previously on Clear Lake. The exterior detailing of the stucco-surfaced, tile-roofed, U-shaped villa is superlative, especially the cast concrete classical decoration. Most of the reception rooms were restored in 1968 by Brown & Root when the house, which had been unoccupied and vandalized, was adapted for use as a research and conference center. Unfortunately, the most distinctive space, the magnificent Art Deco playroom that occupied the angled wing, has lost its specially-designed furniture and fountain. Only the zigzag marble floor paving and a Cubistic relief panel above the fireplace remain. Mason C. Coney laid out the gardens. A swimming pool and classical bathhouse pavilion survive at the rear of the house as does a small formal garden on axis with the angled wing. (The house and grounds are not open to the public.)

18101 Walnut Street   **S-85**
Webster Elementary School [now Margaret S. McWhirter Primary School] (1955) George Pierce-Abel B. Pierce

Located in what was, until the 1960s, a country town on the railroad line between Houston and Galveston, this elementary school bespeaks the impact of Donald Barthelme's modern public school buildings in Brazoria County (especially his West Columbia Elementary School of 1951) on the Houston architectural profession. The elementary school was *the* modernist building type in Texas during the 1950s and the most inventive examples tended to be built in small towns, outside the conservative big city school districts. The Pierce firm's designer, Edwin J. Goodwin, Jr., here clustered classrooms in groups of four beneath

a broad, sheltering roof plate; the gymnasium is programmatically shaped with the aid of glue-laminated wooden arches. Goodwin was indebted to Barthelme for his use of tile wall hangings and pierced masonry solar screens. The school is well maintained and has been expanded in the original style. Across the street, at 18100 Walnut Street, is **Webster High School** (now Webster Intermediate School, 1939, R. G. Schneider), a fine modernistic design that has not fared quite so well.

Gulf Freeway and   **S-86**
Farm-to-Market Road 518
NASA Value Center (1989)
Hermes Reed Hindman

Hermes Reed Hindman's designer, Mark Boucher, added considerable zip to the strip with this exuberant shopping center, anchored by a Fiesta Mart store. The flying bow string trusses, curved parapets, and perforated fascias bring wit, style, and an appropriately big scale to a high visibility location.

304 East Viejo Road   **S-87**
(1962) Cowell & Neuhaus,
David Haid, Associate

In the best Texas rural tradition, this ex-ranch house sits ensconced in a grove of mature live oak trees. But that is its only concession to tradition. Otherwise, this is one of the most rigorous, and beautiful, examples of architecture in the Houston area inspired by the precepts of Ludwig Mies van der Rohe. The house is a glass-enclosed pavilion, sandwiched between pine-timber framed floor and roof plates and elevated three feet above grade on four pairs of pine columns. It is a symmetrical, yet more rustic, version of Mies's Farnsworth House outside Chicago. In the town of Friendswood, farther west along Farm-to-Market Road 518, is another startlingly modern house, a classic courtyard house in the Mies-Philip Johnson manner, at **150 Providence Drive** (1959, Bolton & Barnstone). It is, however, invisible from the street.

17130 McLean Road   **S-88**
Sri Meenakchi Temple (1984)

This north Indian, *nāgara*-type temple, reproduced at reduced scale, is a poignant reminder that the inhabitants of the bed-room subdivisions pushing relentlessly across the fertile agricultural lands of Brazoria County have come to Houston from all over the world. Here, at the edge of the suburban new world, a Hindu commu-nity has recreated, at least externally, a memory of the old world, a stucco-faced temple built by craftsman brought from India for the purpose.

15107 Cullen Boulevard   **S-89**
Christia V. Adair Park
Christia V. Adair Mural
(1984) John Biggers, painter

Located in a small pavilion at the east end of the park entrance road is a concave panel on which Biggers painted a series of lay-ered, architecturally resonant images drawn from the life and work of Christia Adair, a Houston civil rights activist.

Acknowledgments

The American Institute of Architects, Houston Chapter, expresses its thanks to the many individuals and organizations that made preparation and publication of this guidebook possible. The donors who generously underwrote production of the book: The Anchorage Foundation of Texas and its president, Anne S. Bohnn, for making possible the research for and writing of this book; Gerald Moorhead for the generous donation of his service as photographer; The members of the chapter's Guidebook Committee, Allen G. Weymouth, Karol Kreymer, Barry Moore, and Gerald Moorhead; The members of the Board of the Houston Architecture Foundation, Ray B. Bailey, William W. Hall, Macey Reasoner, John W. Focke, Martha Murphree, Joanne Adams, John Breeding, Peter Brown, Stephen Cook, Eileen Crowley, Robert Eury, Roger Galatas, Mitchell Jeffrey, Cathy Mincberg, and Logic Tobola, II, for underwriting the production; The members of the AIA, Houston Chapter Executive Committee, John W. Focke, Frank S. Kelly, Daniel B. Barnum, Thomas E. Giannini, Thomas H. Stovall, David G. Puckett, D. Kirk Hamilton, Kathy Heard, Logic Tobola II, William W. Hall, Jr., and the Chapter staff, Martha Murphree, executive director, Tammy Betancourt, assistant to the director, and Debby Clemensen, secretary. The staff of Herring Design, which designed and produced the book: Jerry Herring, Steve Freeman, Ellen McCormick, William Soo, Frank Evans. MacInterfaces for the loan of a computer. To The Museum of Fine Arts for supplementary photography of Bayou Bend, (built 1927, garden facade, Museum of Fine Arts, Houston, Gift of Miss Ima Hogg). To Paul Hester, Joe Aker, Rick Gardner and Graham B. Luhn, for supplementary photography. To Gilbert Retouching for the cover photo composite. To Peter C. Papademetriou, Drexel Turner, Barrie Scardino, Jeffrey Karl Ochsner, and Gerald Moorhead who carefully laid the groundwork for preparation of this book. Houston Public Library, the chief repository of historical data on Houston, and most especially its Houston Metropolitan Research Center, Louis J. Marchiafava, archivist, Thomas H. Kreneck, first assistant archivist, Michael E. Wilson, architectural archivist, Nancy Hadley, assistant archivist, and its Texas and Local History Department, Doris Glasser, manager, Will Howard, assistant manager, Donna Dixon, Douglas Weiskopf, Ellen Hanlon, librarians. Associated General Contractors of America, Houston Chapter, Pat Kiley, executive director, and Jeri Haynes, DiverseWorks, Caroline Huber and Michael Peranteau, co-directors. Harris County Heritage Society, Jane Ellen Cable, executive director, and Betty Chapman. City of Houston and its Municipal Art Commission, Carol Neuberger, director, its Department of Parks and Recreation, Donald G. Olson, director, its Cultural Arts Council, Mary Anne Piacentini, executive director, and its Archeological and Historical Commission, Kelly Thompson Frater, chair. Greater Houston Preservation Alliance, Margie C. Elliott, executive director. Orange Show Foundation, Susanne Demchak, executive director. Rice University: the Woodson Research Center, Nancy Boothe, director, and Brown Art and Architecture Library, Jet M. Prendeville, librarian, of the Fondren Library, and the School of Architecture, Paul Kennon, dean, Alan Balfour, associate dean, and O. Jack Mitchell, former dean. Texas Historical Commission and its National Register Department, James Wright Steely, director, Peter Flagg Maxson, John Ferguson, and Kenneth A. Breisch, former staff members. University of Houston: the Architecture Library, Margaret Culbertson, librarian, and Lynn Sterba, assistant librarian, and the College of Architecture, Peter J. Wood, dean, and Jean Krchnak, director of the media center. The University of Texas at Austin and its Architectural Drawings Collection, Lila Stillson, librarian. Surpik Angelini, Cameron Armstrong, Eugene Aubry, Joel Warren Barna, Howard Barnstone, Donald Barthelme, Ellen Beasley, V. Nia Dorian Becnel, Mrs. E. A. Blackburn, Natalie de Blois, Selden W. Bobbitt, Minnette B. Boesel, Dr. and Mrs. Jules H. Bohnn, Deborah V. Brauer, Mrs. Birdsall P. Briscoe, I. S. Brochstein, Raymond D. Brochstein, Steve Brooks, Glenda Callaway, William T. Cannady, Chris Carson, Susan Chadwick, Frances F. Chamberlain, Barbara Cochran, Joseph P. Colaco, Rudolph Colby, Mack H. Colley, Mimi Crossley, Dana Cuff, George Cunningham, Leslie Barry and Patrick R. Davidson, Mike Davis, Herman Dyal, Jr., Joanne Edmundson, Edwin A. Eubanks, Richard Fitzgerald, Patricia Sins and Anthony E. Frederick, Mr. and Mrs. John H. Freeman, Jr., Larry Paul Fuller, Laura Furman, Christopher Genik, Mary Carolyn Hollers George, Diane Y. Ghirardo, Elizabeth S. Glassman, Elizabeth P. Griffin, The Hon. and Mrs. John Grimes, Barbara Goldstein, Lee Govatos, Jay C. Henry, Olive S. Hershey, Lynn Bensel and Mark A. Hewitt, Dr. and Mrs. Frank Hill, Alan Hirschfield, Mrs. Henry W. Hoagland, Ann Holmes, Mrs. Thomas W. Houghton, Gladys House, Katherine S. Howe, Richard Ingersoll, George O. Jackson, Jr., Terrell James, William R. Jenkins, Carlos Jiménez, Lenwood E. Johnson, Mrs. Douglas Johnston, John Kaliski, Karl Kamrath, Mr. and Mrs. Burdette Keeland, Susan B. Keeton, Karl Laurence Kilian, Barry Klein, Nat W. Krahl, Mrs. Efrem Kurtz, Truett Latimer, Pamela Lewis, Charles Walker Ligon, Rafael Longoria, Richard Longstreth, Phillip Lopate, Graham B. Luhn, Clark L. Martinson, Elizabeth McBride, Roger Moore, Robert Morris, Mr. and Mrs. Peter Morris, Mr. and Mrs. S. I. Morris, Jr., Hugo V. Neuhaus, Jr., W. O. Neuhaus III, Mr. and Mrs. Stayton Nunn, Jan O'Brien, Gladys Barrow Odekerken, Spencer Parsons, John Pastier, Mrs. Oliver Pennington, W. Irving Phillips, Jr., Thomas M. Price, Neil Printz, Janet F. Rice, Judith Richards, Robert C. Richter, Jr., Lorraine P. Roberts, Dr. and Mrs. Willard B. Robinson, Evelyn F. Rosenthal, Peter G. Rowe, Andrew John Rudnick, Danny Samuels, Paul W. Schieffer, Jacqueline André and W. Richard Schmeal, Yolita L. Schmidt, Winton F. Scott, Jon Schwartz, Frank C. Smith, Jr., Douglas Sprunt, John F. Staub, Susan Bogar and Robert A. Stem, William F. Stern, James Susman, Simone W. Swan, Taft Architects, Charles Tapley, Anderson Todd, Bart Truxillo, Michael Underhill, Esther de Vecsey, Janet Wagner, Peter D. Waldman, The Rev. Jeffrey H. Walker, Sally S. Walsh, Bruce C. Webb, Frank D. Welch, Eugene Werlin, Evelyn Weymouth, Elizabeth Wells White, Kathleen S. Wild, Lorraine Wild, Ann Quin Wilson, Susan and Gordon Wittenberg, The Rev. John D. Worrell, The Rev. Charles M. Wyatt-Brown, R. Scott Ziegler, Barrie Zimmelman. AIA gratefully acknowledges the generosity and assistance of NPL and especially Odin Clay in the preparation of the photographic materials.

Index